Media, Technology and Education in a Post-Truth Society

Digital Activism and Society: Politics, Economy and Culture in Network Communication

The *Digital Activism and Society: Politics, Economy and Culture in Network Communication* series focuses on the political use of digital everyday-networked media by corporations, governments, international organizations (Digital Politics), as well as civil society actors, NGOs, activists, social movements and dissidents (Digital Activism) attempting to recruit, organise and fund their operations, through information communication technologies.

The series publishes books on theories and empirical case studies of digital politics and activism in the specific context of communication networks. Topics covered by the series include, but are not limited to:

- the different theoretical and analytical approaches of political communication in digital networks;
- studies of socio-political media movements and activism (and 'hacktivism');
- transformations of older topics such as inequality, gender, class, power, identity and group belonging;
- strengths and vulnerabilities of social networks.

Series Editor

Dr Athina Karatzogianni

About the Series Editor

Dr Athina Karatzogianni is an Associate Professor at the University of Leicester, UK. Her research focuses on the intersections between digital media theory and political economy, in order to study the use of digital technologies by new sociopolitical formations.

Published Books in this Series

Digital Materialism: Origins, Philosophies, Prospects by Baruch Gottlieb

Nirbhaya, New Media and Digital Gender Activism by Adrija Dey

Digital Life on Instagram: New Social Communication of Photography by Elisa Serafinelli

Internet Oligopoly: The Corporate Takeover of Our Digital World by Nikos Smyrnaios

Digital Activism and Cyberconflicts in Nigeria: Occupy Nigeria, Boko Haram and MEND by Shola A. Olabode

Platform Economics: Rhetoric and Reality in the "Sharing Economy" by Cristiano Codagnone

Communication as Gesture: Media(tion), Meaning, & Movement by Michael Schandorf

Forthcoming Titles

Chinese Social Media: Face, Sociality, and Civility by Shuhan Chen and Peter Lunt

Media, Technology and Education in a Post-Truth Society: From Fake News, Datafication and Mass Surveillance to the Death of Trust

EDITED BY

ALEX GRECH

The 3CL Foundation and the University of Malta, Malta

emerald
PUBLISHING

United Kingdom – North America – Japan – India – Malaysia – China

Emerald Publishing Limited
Howard House, Wagon Lane, Bingley BD16 1WA, UK

First edition 2021

Reprints and permissions service
Contact: permissions@emeraldinsight.com

British Library Cataloguing in Publication Data
A catalogue record for this book is available from the British Library

ISBN: 978-1-80043-907-8 (Print)
ISBN: 978-1-80043-906-1 (Online)
ISBN: 978-1-80043-908-5 (Epub)

Printed and bound by CPI Group (UK) Ltd, Croydon, CR0 4YY

For Liz and Jacob, who keep me sane in troubled times. Soon, we will find our way back to some hilltop town with a trattoria and a well-thumbed menu with no translation.

Contents

About the Contributors

Bryan Alexander is an internationally known Futurist, Researcher, Writer, Speaker, Consultant, and Teacher, working in the field of how technology transforms education. He is currently a Senior Scholar at Georgetown University and teaches graduate seminars in their Learning, Design and Technology program.

Abeer Al-Najjar is an Associate Professor of Media and Journalism Studies at the American University of Sharjah. She has published two books and several articles and chapters on media, gender and religion; media framing of political conflict and war; and journalistic ethics and practices.

Walter Fernando Balser is an Instructor in Organizational Leadership at the University of Denver and the University of South Florida. His scholarship focuses on applying leadership orientations and processes more aligned with rapid decentralization of knowledge in society. He is also the Founder of the Open Partnership Education Network.

Devraj Basu is a Senior Lecturer in Finance at Strathclyde Business School. He has researched equity markets, commodity markets, alternative investments, and fintech and data analytics as applied to markets, including projects on precision timing into blockchain clearing and on analyzing markets using topological data analysis.

Ruben Brave, Co-founder of Make Media Great Again, is a Dutch Internet Pioneer, Media Professional, and Technology, Media, and Telecom Entrepreneur with a focus on social entrepreneurship. Since 2004, he is the Founder of academic business incubator Entelligence.nl for funding and guidance regarding startups in media, automation, health, and lifelong learning.

Michael Bugeja, a distinguished Professor of Journalism and Communication at Iowa State University of Science and Technology, and is the author of *Interpersonal Divide in the Age of the Machine* (Oxford Univ. Press, 2018) and *Living Media Ethics* (Routledge/Taylor & Francis, 2019).

Steve Diasio is a Clinical Professor of Entrepreneurship and Innovation at the University of South Florida. Steve's contributions include extending the open innovation paradigm through his investigation with IBM Innovation Jams. Steve argues that open innovation is relevant beyond products/services and through technology can support decision-making.

John Domingue, KMi Director at the Open University, has published over 280 refereed articles. John's current work focuses on how a combination of block-chain and Linked Data technologies can be used to process personal data in a decentralized trusted manner and its application in the educational domain.

Hossein Derakhshan is a Visiting Fellow at London School of Economics and Political Sciences. As a pioneer of blogging, podcasts, and tech journalism in Iran, he spent six years in prison there over his writings and activism since 2008. His research has been focused on mass personalization, platforms, information disorder, and journalism.

Joshua Ellul is a Senior Lecturer in the Department of Computer Sciences at the University of Malta and Director of the Centre for Distributed Ledger Technologies and Chairperson of the Malta Digital Innovation Authority.

Massimiliano Fusari is an Academic Scholar and results-driven Digital Strategist in the Analysis and Production of Visual Storytelling. Alongside his academic teaching at the University of Westminster (UK), Massimiliano delivers bespoke training for UN agencies, governments, and third-sector institutions. Currently developing the mobile app MIA – *The Meta-Image* – to enhance specific hands-on competencies on visual storytelling formats.

Murdoch Gabbay has spent 20 years teaching the Mathematical Foundations of Computing and, most recently, Blockchain. He has written extensively on subjects including abstract algebra, the design of high-performance programming languages, and blockchain technologies and smart contracts.

Alex Grech is a Strategist and Change Consultant. He is the Executive Director of the 3CL Foundation and teaches new media at the University of Malta.

Daniel Hughes is a Computational Phenomenologist who has spent most of his life building companies.

Taylor Kendal is an Educator, Writer, Designer, and Chief Program Officer at Learning Economy. His work with the US Department of Education, US Chamber of Commerce Foundation, and Library of Congress has led to a complex love affair with legacy institutions, innovation, design, and (de)centralized networks.

Phillip D. Long is a Senior Scholar at Georgetown University's Center for New Designs in Learning and Scholarship, a Special Advisor to the CIO & Faculty Affiliate at ASU, and Community Manager for the T3 Innovation Network's LER Pilot Initiative. Former Academic Technology Strategists at MIT. His works focus on distributed ledgers, digital credentials, and systems offering individual agency.

Ġorġ Mallia is an Associate Professor and Head of the Department of Media and Communications, University of Malta. He researches primarily in the areas of instructional technology, transfer of learning, new media impacts, personal communications, and graphic narrative and storytelling.

Soudeh Oladi is a Lecturer and Researcher at that Ontario Institute for Studies in Education, University of Toronto. Her scholarship focuses on equity, decolonizing education, as well as spirituality in education.

Gordon J. Pace is a Professor of Computer Science at the University of Malta. His research focuses on means to ensure that computer systems work as expected, particularly in FinTech and RegTech. Recently, he has worked on frameworks and tools to improve dependability of blockchain systems.

Harry Anthony Patrinos is the Practice Manager for the Europe and Central Asia regions of the World Bank's education practice. He specializes in the economic benefits of schooling, quality of education, school-based management, and public-private partnerships. He has many publications (more than 50 journal articles) in academic and policy literature.

Emma Pauncefort is a Learning Science Practitioner with a background in literacy criticism and cultural history. Through the work of her UK-based education consultancy, Dilectae, and its headline initiative The Critical Literacy Project™, her vision is to empower learners with connected and critical lifelong learning toolkits.

John P. Portelli is a Professor at the University of Toronto where he teaches in the Departments of Social Justice Education, Leadership, and Higher and Adult Education. He is also a Policy Advisor at the Ministry for Education and Employment, Malta, and the Chair of the Board of 3CL.

Toni Sant is the Director of the Digital Curation Lab at MediaCityUK with the University of Salford's School of Arts and Media and also a Founding Member of the Wikimedia Foundation-affiliated user group Wikimedia Community Malta. In 2020, he became the first Malta-based Wikipedian in Residence.

Natalie Smolenski is an Anthropologist and Political Theorist who writes about Contemporary Transformations in Governance and Political Economy. She examines how structures of human subjectivity contribute to the constitution of knowledge that holds.

Allan Third is a Research Fellow at the Open University, working on the exchange of meaning and trust in decentralized platforms, with a strong focus on Healthcare, Education, and Internet of Things applications and a particular interest in Linked Data and blockchain technologies for social justice.

Anna Topolska is a Historian of Eastern Europe focused on visual studies and a Polish-English translator of texts in the humanities. She is currently working on her first book *Memory and Visuality. Representations of the Second World War in Poznań, Poland in the* 20th *and* 21st *Centuries.*

Lina Zuluaga is a Teaching Fellow at the Data Wise Harvard's project and leads the initiative Rebuilding Human Capital Post-Covid at Georgetown University. In 2018, the US Department of Education recognized her TalentoLab's standard methodology for cities and universities as one of the top 25 global innovations reshaping the connection between employment and education by using data analytics and blockchain certifications.

Acknowledgments

To the following people, thank you!

All the authors in the collection, for their patience and grace.

Speakers and delegates at the "Understanding the Post-Truth Conference," particularly those who traveled to a small island in October 2019 on a whim, remain in touch in the belief that the pandemic is another reason for repurposing education, media, and technology for the public good.

Courtnie Bonett, for working her way through checklists galore, formatting and getting this book across the finishing line.

Athina Karatzogianni, for telling me to get this book done. And those Facebook updates!

Evarist Bartolo, for quietly supporting The 3CL Foundation from its inception.

John Portelli and Joe Cauchi, for conversations and their knowledge of the fine art of quiet subversion.

Kirk Perris, for reading the first proposal for the book and making very valuable suggestions.

Dan Hughes, for introducing me to the blockchain, and Natalie Smolenski, for deconstructing self-sovereign identity like nobody else can.

The good people at Emerald.

Chapter 1

Introduction to Media, Technology and Education in a Post-Truth Society

Introduction

Alex Grech

Abstract

This collection of essays has its roots in a collective desire to understand the workings of the post-truth society, and how education, media and technology may contribute to mitigating its worst excesses. This chapter introduces the origins of the book project.

Keywords: Media; education; technology; post-truth; polymath; sociology; social networks

> *post-truth.* Adjective. Relating to or denoting circumstances in which objective facts are less influential in shaping public opinion than appeals to emotion and personal belief.

> *society.* Noun. A large group of people in a defined territory, who live together in an organised way, and share a common culture.

> "No, facts is precisely what there is not, only interpretations."
> Friedrich Nietzsche (1967). The Will to Power. Section 481.

> "I think we are living through a frightening and deeply uncertain time, and though there are dementing and cynical voices out there, which are being emboldened and amplified by social media – that loony engine of outrage – they do not represent the voices of the many, or the good."
> Nick Cave (2020). The Red Hand Files. Issue #122 October 2020.

Media, Technology and Education in a Post-Truth Society, 1–8
Copyright © 2021 by Emerald Publishing Limited
All rights of reproduction in any form reserved
doi:10.1108/978-1-80043-906-120211001

Origins

The genesis of this book is on record, in a whimsical video in June 2019[1] and the filmed proceedings of a two-day international conference on the island of Malta in October 2019,[2] convened with media scholars, blockchain experts, film-makers, philosophers, anthropologists, politicians, public prosecutors, data lawyers, bankers, activists, journalists, rock star technology editors and teenage students. The conference was activist by design. Assemble a bunch of brilliant thinkers and doers, get them to spar around the esoteric subject of the post-truth society in a historic building in Valletta and develop a collective manifesto to combat post-truths. By the end of the two days, the plan was to set up an interdisciplinary global network and reconvene in a different geographical context early in 2020 and explore pilot projects for collaboration.

The pandemic shelved many big ideas and plans. When the world closes down, the premise is that the failings of the post-truth society are swept away in the collective, urgent need to secure factual information, survive, adjust to a new age of social distancing and prepare for probable, impending economic collapse. Instead, with the pandemic in its first or second wave,[3] this collection surfaces with contributions from some of the original cohort in far-flung places, and others who reached out after the conference. Perhaps a book is an unexpected but necessary deviation from the intended pathway but nonetheless a more permanent and resilient outcome in the age of the often temporary, fleeting and forgotten outputs in digital format.

From the moment that 'post-truth' became Oxford Dictionary's Word of the Year of 2016,[4] the term has been derided by academia. In reviewing a book on the subject, Hardoš (2019, p. 311) writes about a 'vague, but very popular concept in our discourse... a distinct phenomenon that may be a moral panic, a conceptual muddle of lies, propaganda, and bullshit (in the Frankfurtian sense), or merely a discursive shortcut for numerous disquieting social, political, and technological developments'. In opposition to this view, the point of departure for this collection is an interest in deconstruction, disconnects and possible solutions to the 'manifestations' of an ongoing, palpable information crisis through an interdisciplinary lens.

By manifestations, I mean the association of the post-truth society with a raft of social ills: the decline and fall of reason; the disruption of the public square; the spread of false and/or misleading information and fake news; culture wars; the rise of subjectivity; co-opting of language; filter bubbles, silos and tribes; attention economy deficits; trolls; echo chambers, polarisation and hyper-partisanship; conversion of popularity into legitimacy; manipulation by 'populist' leaders and nationalist governments and contempt for outsiders and fringe actors; algorithmic control; big data and personal data capture; targeted messaging and native advertising.

These terms have become part of the vernacular, with the blame for their proliferation frequently attributed to the affordances of social media platforms. Naim (2019) writes of the paradox of trust, where the crisis of confidence in government, politicians, journalists, scientists and experts ('let alone bankers business executives or the Vatican') is countered by 'trust in anonymous messages on Facebook, Twitter and WhatsApp'. This view echoes a much-critiqued treatise in 2014 by Tom Nichols in *The Federalist* followed by a book in 2017 in which he associated the death of expertise with a Google-fuelled, Wikipedia-based, blog-sodden collapse of any division between professionals and laymen, students and teachers, knowers and wonderers – in other words, between those of any achievement in an area and those with none at all.

That is quite a departure from the early literature on social media, when the technology was celebrated for its potential for innovation and positive change within the social world, a tool for the democratisation of information and political mobilisation through the wealth of networks (Benkler, 2006); the emergence of horizontally engaged smart mobs (Rheingold, 2002); cultural production (Jenkins, 2006); produsage (Bruns, 2007); a revitalised public sphere (Shirky, 2011) – or at the very least, a private sphere (Papacharissi, 2010). Castells (2009), a primary promotor of the network society, believed that mass self-communication would empower connected citizens to a personalised soapbox without the permission of information gatekeepers such as publishing houses and powerful intermediaries.

This optimism slowly dissolved into weariness and suspicion of online discourse and business practices on social media platforms. Social media platforms are increasingly associated with defective online mobilisation (Tufekci, 2017), the applications of big data science (O'Neil, 2017; Schneier, 2015), surveillance capitalism (Fuchs, 2017; Zuboff, 2015), black-boxed algorithms (Pasquale, 2015) and a veritable Pandora's box of social ills and the erosion of truth. Writing about the death of truth, Kakutani (2018, p. 88) observes: 'The Internet doesn't just reflect reality anymore; it shapes it'. This has much to do with the permeability of social media and the willingness of platform owners to harvest user data to be made available for targeted marketing purposes to those who can pay, irrespective of who their identity or motives.

Those in power, whom we trust within democratic systems of political representation, or those whom we do not know – from Russian trolls to the Cambridge Analytica of this world – have long invested in new media to disseminate misinformation and undertake targeted mass surveillance of citizens, without risk of impunity. We edge towards a world where reality has become a matter of personal opinion – as opposed to a compendium of informed knowledge – even if we hesitate to call this a compendium of 'facts'. We are losing a sense of shared reality and the ability to communicate across social, partisan and sectarian lines. Baudrillard (2010) might associate this as a 'moment' of stupidity – since he claims stupidity is one of the attributes of power, the accursed share of the social (including stupidity) which would take us back to the 'power figures' of primitive societies, and explain why most limited, unimaginative individuals stay in power the longest' of primitive societies.

The blame game also extends to old media – to its permeability to lies, to its need to remain relevant to a digital audience and compete with social media, sell advertising and still appear to be 'politically correct'. For instance, LBC gave Nigel Farage access to prime-time radio slots under the guise of providing a platform for alternative voices, irrespective of whether these were the voices of lies and racism. On 7th June 2020, James Bennet, a senior editor at *The New York Times*, was forced to resign amid a furious backlash over the newspaper's publication of a controversial and unfiltered comment piece penned by a Republican senator, Tom Cotton, a junior senator for Arkansas and a fierce ally of Donald Trump.[5]

In practice, the new media ecosystem has long incorporated old media in its hub, with commentary and repurposing of 'news' not restricted to the online media platform of the news media collateral, but now extending to the personal broadcast systems available on Facebook, Twitter, WhatsApp, blogs and podcasts – to name a few. In the open bazaar of ideas, opinions and chaos, far from the wisdom of the crowd, big data and the algorithms provide an outlet for the post-truth society's worst excesses. For Couldry and Hepp (2017), the social world is a communicative construction, manifested by 'mutual transformations of the media and the social world' (p. 3) where communicative actions, practices, forms and patterns of action contribute to the construction of the social. Media and communication shape the social, and that digital media, digital communication and digital data introduce a new kind of interdependence, where the interdependence comes to depend on the media; media, in fact, becomes constitutive of the social. The dominance of few social media companies as unelected, unaccountable referees of the public sphere makes the problem of regulating attention in an age of information glut challenging, at best (Tufekci, 2020).

In response to this chaotic environment, this collection is based on the following foundation premises:

- *The post-truth problem is real.* It is not an imaginary issue, but a palpable ongoing crisis that is undermining the foundations of society and is getting worse. Yuval Harari (2019) devotes one of his *21 Lessons for the 21st Century* to the subject; the common good, trust, responsibility, ethics and civic engagement are under attack from the actions of unknown third parties. It may not be possible to have consensus on the attributes of 'truth'; but truth *does* matter. The political and socio-cultural landscape we inhabit today is permeable to truth decay, through a regime of misinformation pumped out in industrial volume by trolls and from the mouth and Twitter feeds of populist leaders (Kakutani, 2018). The term 'truth' remains a loaded and contentious term, but the post-truth lexicon of 'fake news', 'fake science' and 'alternative facts' is part of the vernacular.
- *The post-truth problem is nuanced and needs a critical approach.* As an example of contradictions, my own work as a strategist and change agent has regularly traversed technology, new media platforms, education and public policy. The concern is that actors in these specific areas have been contributing to the worst excess of the post-truth society, as much as others in the same areas seemingly operating as forces to provided solutions for the common good. Education systems based on acquiring and transferring knowledge suddenly appear remarkably disconnected from false narratives (Fisher Thornton, 2010), the operations of the networked public sphere and those who seek profit from user-generated content.
- *Unbiased and current knowledge is needed to inform workable solutions that resist the excesses of the post-truth society.* The most powerful antidote to the post-truth society is to have engaged and well-informed citizens who resist and counter the agendas of those who thrive from the erosion of trust. There is a

need for an informed response from those whose actions may provide future leadership and make a difference.

Structure of This Book

The authors in this volume offer very different perspectives on the post-truth society and to the possible solutions for its manifestations. When they were invited to contribute to the book, the editorial signposting was limited to the title of the collection and links to the video footage of the original conference. The end product reflects the interdisciplinary backgrounds of the authors and frequently divergent, even conflicting world views.

The collection is grouped in three interconnected sections, around the topics of education, media and emerging technologies. Some contributions sit more comfortably in the academic tradition than others: in the post-truth world where everything gets hybridised, this is a sign of the times. What the contributions have in common are that they are the product of people with inquisitive minds and an activist bent, questioning the adequacy of the tools of their trade against the ongoing wave of misinformation. There is an undercurrent of a need for social justice and human dignity in many of the essays. There are also tensions between those who believe that the way to solve trust issues is to build solutions on decentralised technologies and those who prescribe an investment in digital literacies and new models for education.[6] Even among those who see decentralisation as an opportunity to kick-start web 3.0 and reboot the aspirations of disillusioned generation, there is no consensus that the blockchain can fix the age of untruths and disinformation in a hurry.

The contributions do not need to be read in sequence. The intention is to hopefully encourage readers to 'join the dots' between subject areas and ideas or proposed solutions to a common problem.

Beyond This Book

The search for facts-based truths has taken a surreal turn in the age of the pandemic. Every claim for the logic of wearing a mask and social distancing is countered by arguments from anti-vaxxers and those concerned about mental health, personal freedoms, herd immunity and the fragile economy. There are fears that nation states will seize the opportunity to invest in 'under the skin surveillance technologies' (Harari, 2020) and more populist policies while citizens are forced into lockdown. As countries begin their COVID-19 vaccination campaigns, geopolitical considerations and conspiratorial thinking are intermingled in controversies regarding the efficacy of particular vaccines.[7] A surge in anti-Asian violence has accompanied the spread of the pandemic.[8] Dr Anthony Fauci, the US Director of the National Institute of Allergy and Infectious Diseases (NIAID), believes that we are going through a time that is 'disturbingly anti-science in certain segments of our society'.[9]

Work on this book started in the midst of the Trump presidency. As I write, we are a few months into the term of his successor, a man widely heralded as the anti-Trump. Yet the intervening period has confirmed that any hope of a return to normality, however conceived, is fanciful. Trump and his associates spent the majority of his final weeks in office attempting to delegitimise the electoral results and riling up his supporters with the mantra 'stop the steal'. On January 6th, 2021, thousands stormed the U.S. Capitol building, an insurgence reminiscent of the armed takeover of democratic institutions (Runciman, 2018). For a while, the Q-Shaman and other followers of social media-fuelled conspiracy theories played out their roles on the Senate floor. Facebook, Twitter and a raft of other social media companies subsequently removed Trump from their platforms,[10] sparking concerns of censorship and the power concentrated in the hands of a handful of tech billionaires.[11] Congressional Democrats continue to lobby the White House about the need to reform Section 230 of the US Communications Decency Act of 1996, which protects tech companies from liability over content posted by users on their platforms while also enabling the same firms to continue to shape political discourse. The Department of Justice in the US is pursuing its long-awaited antitrust lawsuit against Google.

Will Big Tech eventually be held accountable for harmful or untruthful misinformation that spreads on their platforms? Can new media models coded for the public good, finally liberated from native advertising, ever be feasible? The doubts that linger about the media ecosystem that propelled Trump to office and sustained him whilst there look set only to grow, and not only in the United States. *The Epoch Times*, the Falun Gong-backed newspaper, uses Facebook pages to create right-wing misinformation and fuel an anti-China agenda (Roose, 2020). Feel-good videos and viral clickbait sell subscriptions and drive traffic back to its partisan news coverage - a global-scale misinformation machine that repeatedly pushes fringe narratives into the mainstream. US-style commercial broadcast media looks set to expand into the UK market with the creation of GB News, a channel that its chairman Andrew Neil claims will address a perceived gap in the market for "the vast number of British people who feel underserved and unheard by their media".[12] It is to feature segments with names such as "woke watch". Schools in many countries remain open, while universities worldwide hang on to the hegemony of their business models by forcing young people move around countries to student accommodation, only for them to be incarcerated and taught online. False narratives remain the order of the day (Fisher Thornton, 2020).

And yet, there is push back. In Europe, data governance reforms and regulation continue to be mooted regularly to address the social ills generated by the technology industry and facilitate the development of alternative solutions in member states. *The Great Hack* and *The Social Dilemma* are streaming on Netflix. The *DeepTrust Alliance*, a multi-industry organisation using a network approach to create standards to combat digital fakes (Harrison, 2020), believes it is still possible to instil trust across the entire internet through robust partnerships between social media giants and large and small innovators capable of fixing the problem.[13] Morozov's *The Syllabus*[14] combines algorithmic filtering, categorisation and systematic human curation across six languages to combat falsehoods and salvage the most thoughtful intellectual output from the ever-mounting great pile of information. Last-ditch effort to change the narrative in the run up to elections is also countered by the return of the media gatekeepers after a considerable absence, although news continues to rely on storytelling, emotions and feelings.[15]

The world of untruths, fake news and erosion of trust in media, technology, education and governance continues to morph, on the waves of the pandemic, populism and social distancing. The need to resist and question and plan for a better future remains, despite the fear of what tomorrow brings.

Notes

1. See https://www.youtube.com/watch?v=iUDjbOflA50&t=44s&ab_channel=CommonwealthCentreforConnectedLearning
2. See https://connectedlearning.edu.mt/videos-post-truth-conference/
3. There is little consensus on this issue; see https://www.hopkinsmedicine.org/health/conditions-and-diseases/coronavirus/first-and-second-waves-of-coronavirus
4. See https://languages.oup.com/word-of-the-year/2016/
5. Titled 'Send in the Troops', it called for the president to invoke the Insurrection Act of 1807 and use US military forces against citizens to quell unrest sparked by the death of George Floyd. In the days following its publication on 3 June, numerous current and former *Times* journalists criticised the decision to run it and the newspaper added a note to the essay on 5 June conceding it 'fell short of our standards and should not have been published'.
6. As a background to the 'Think vs Build' approach to solving the post-truth problem, watch the panel discussion on technology, conflicts and self-sovereignty at https://connectedlearning.edu.mt/aiovg_videos/panel-2-technology-conflicts-self-sovereignty-qa/
7. https://www.theguardian.com/commentisfree/2021/mar/19/eu-astrazeneca-vaccine-stance-spain-europe-covid
8. https://www.today.com/news/anti-asian-violence-history-anti-asian-racism-us-t210645
9. https://www.ecowatch.com/trump-fauci-coronavirus-science-health-2648404107.html?rebelltitem=4#rebelltitem4
10. https://www.axios.com/platforms-social-media-ban-restrict-trump-d9e44f3c-8366-4ba9-a8a1-7f3114f920f1.html
11. https://www.msn.com/en-us/news/politics/bernie-sanders-thinks-donald-trump-s-removal-from-twitter-was-a-mistake/ar-BB1eSZ9i
12. https://www.itv.com/news/2020-09-25/andrew-neil-announces-24-hour-gb-news-channel-to-rival-bbc-and-sky
13. https://www.deeptrustalliance.org/blog/e88cxlgv3b8wmtgk587ui3dteu9vlv
14. https://www.the-syllabus.com/
15. https://www.nytimes.com/2020/10/25/business/media/hunter-biden-wall-street-journal-trump.html

References

Baudrillard, J. (2010). *Carnival and cannibal, ventriloquous evil.* London, New York, NY, Calcutta: Seagull Books.

Benkler, Y. (2006). *The wealth of networks: How social production transforms markets and freedom.* New Haven, CT: Yale University Press.

Bruns, A. (2007). Produsage: Towards a broader framework for user-led content creation. In *Creativity and cognition: Proceedings of the 6th ACM SIGCHI conference on creativity & cognition*, Washington, DC. 13–15 June 2007.

Castells, M. (2009). *Communication power*. Oxford, NY: Oxford University Press.

Cave, N. (2020). *In this time of illness, cynicism and cruelty, do you receive many mean or vile messages? How do you cope with that kind of negative energy?* Retrieved from https://www.theredhandfiles.com/cope-with-negative-energy/

Couldry, N., & Hepp, A. (2017). *The mediated construction of reality*. Cambridge: Polity Press.

Fisher Thornton, L. (2020). *Truth and misinformation: How to spot false narratives (Part 1)*. Retrieved from https://leadingincontext.com/2020/02/26/truth-and-misinformation-how-to-spot-false-narratives-part-1/

Fuchs, C. (2017). *Social Media. A critical introduction*. London: Sage.

Harari, Y. (2019). *21 lessons for the 21st century*. London: Vintage.

Harari, Y. (2020). *The world after coronavirus*. Retrieved from https://www.ft.com/content/19d90308-6858-11ea-a3c9-1fe6fedcca75

Hardoš, P. (2019). Lee McIntyre: Post-truth. *Organon F, 26*(2), 311–316.doi:10.31577/orgf.2019.26210

Harrison, A. (2020). *Defining the problems of deepfakes and disinformation*. New York, NY: DeepTrust Alliance.

Jenkins, H. (2006). *Convergence culture: Where old and new media collide*. New York, NY: NYU.

Kakutani, M. (2018). *The death of truth*. London: William Collins.

Naim, M. (2019). *Who do you trust? We don't believe the government or the experts, but we do believe anonymous social media posts*. Retrieved from https://english.-elpais.com/elpais/2019/02/28/inenglish/1551342251_361360.html

Nichols, T. (2014). *The death of expertise*. Retrieved from https://thefederalist.com/2014/01/17/the-death-of-expertise/

Nietzsche, F. (1967). *The will to power*. Trans. W. Kaufmann and R. J. Hollingdale. New York, NY: Random House, Section 481.

O'Neill, C. (2017). *Weapons of Math Destruction. How big data increases inequality and threatens democracy*. London: Penguin Books.

Papacharissi, Z. (2010). *A private sphere: Democracy in a digital age*. Malden, MA: Polity Press.

Pasquale, F. (2015). *The black box society: The secret algorithms that control money and information*. Cambridge, MA: Harvard University Press.

Rheingold, H. (2002). *Smart mobs: The next social revolution*. Cambridge, MA: Basic.

Roose, K. (2020). *How the epoch times created a giant influence machine*. Retrieved from https://www.nytimes.com/2020/10/24/technology/epoch-times-influence-falun-gong.html

Runciman, D. (2018). *How democracy ends*. London: Profile Books.

Shirky, C. (2011). The political power of social media. Technology, the public sphere and political change. *Foreign Affairs, 90*(1), 28–41.

Tufekci, Z. (2020). Retrieved from https://zeynep.substack.com/p/the-problem-with-all-the-tech-hearings

Zuboff, S. (2015). Big other: Surveillance capitalism and the prospects of an information civilization. *Journal of Information Technology, 30*, 75–89.

Part 1
Repurposing Education for the Post-truth Society

Chapter 2

Post-truth Society: Toward a Dialogical Understanding of Truth

John P. Portelli and Soudeh Oladi

Abstract

The post-truth moment comes at a time of deference for epistemic authority, which has serious implications for democracy. If democracy implies an epistemology, attempting to live a democratic way of life implies a theory about the nature of knowledge among other theoretical aspects (e.g. political and ethical). At the time of 'fluid modernity', the post-truth politics of renouncing truth damages the foundations of democracy, for how could we proceed with a democratic way of life without truth as a common denominator for deliberation? While a defining feature of the post-truth era is its intrinsic relativism, Gellner (2013) warns this could lead to 'cognitive nihilism'. Thus, it is imperative to (i) find our way back to reasonableness (based on both reason and emotions) based on a Freirean dialogic middle ground, instead of renouncing truth (that is any notion of truth), and (ii) critically discuss possibilities for various approaches to truth-seeking. While it is important to question the foundation and reasonableness of truth, two crucial issues arise: which theory of knowledge and whose theory of knowledge should be accepted as the epistemological basis of truth? Moreover, this chapter will argue that a more plausible notion of truth is neither one that is based on intrinsic objectivity nor intrinsic relativism, but one that is based on the relationship between objectivity and subjectivity; that is a relational (nor relative) and dialectic understanding of truth which does not rule out the existence of facts but questions the political constructs of facts. The final section of the chapter focuses on the application of the understanding of truth as a relational dialogical epistemology. While arguing for a dialogical theory of truth, the chapter also problematizes the predominant view of evidence-based research and policy and offers an in-depth discussion of how our understanding of the relational dialogical notion of truth can be utilized in the analysis of cases involving pro-active discrimination and affirmative action.

Media, Technology and Education in a Post-Truth Society, 11–28
doi:10.1108/978-1-80043-906-120211002

Keywords: Theory of truth; relational and dialectic understanding of truth; epistemology; affirmative action; democracy and truth; Freirean perspective

The post-truth moment comes at a time of submissiveness for epistemic authority, which has important implications for democracy. At the time of 'fluid modernity' (Koro-Ljungberg, Carlson, & Montana, 2019), the post-truth politics of renouncing 'truth' damages the foundations of democracy. While a defining feature of the post-truth era is its intrinsic relativism, Gellner (2013) warns this could lead to 'cognitive nihilism'. Hence, it is essential to find our way back to reasonableness, based on both reason and feelings, and find a Freirean dialogic inter-relational ground, instead of renouncing truth (that is any notion of truth), and critically discuss possibilities for various approaches to truth-seeking. This chapter argues that a more plausible notion of truth is neither one that is based on intrinsic objectivity nor intrinsic relativism, but one that is rooted in the relationship between objectivity and subjectivity; that is a relational and dialectic understanding of truth which does not rule out the existence of facts but questions the political construct of facts. The final section of the chapter focuses on the application of our understanding of truth as a relational dialogical epistemology. As we develop our theory of truth, we also problematize the predominant view of evidence-based research and policy and discuss how our understanding of the relational dialogical notion of truth can be utilized in the analysis of cases involving pro-active discrimination and affirmative action.

Theories of Truth: A Brief History

The post-truth moment comes at a time of deference for epistemic authority, which has serious implications for democracy. If democracy implies an epistemology, attempting to live a democratic way of life implies a theory about the nature of knowledge among other theoretical aspects (e.g. political and ethical). At the time of 'fluid modernity' (Koro-Ljungberg et al., 2019), the post-truth politics of renouncing truth damages the foundations of democracy and makes it difficult to proceed with a democratic way of life without some understanding of truth as a common denominator. In this context, it is important to revisit different epistemological understandings and interpretations of truth. Blackburn (2005) outlines the intellectual ancestry of different theories of truth including correspondence, coherence, social constructivist, pragmatist and deflationist:

> The absolutist descends from Plato through almost all religious philosophers, through Descartes to G. E. Moore ... The relativist temperament descends from the Greek sophists such as Gorgias and Protagoras, through Hobbes to Darwin ... to Nietzsche and William James, and in our own generation to writers such as Michel Foucault or Richard Rorty (Blackburn, 2005, p. xix)

Rooted in the philosophical contributions of Socrates, Plato and Aristotle, correspondence theory of truth identifies a direct relationship between thoughts or language and objects and emphasizes that true beliefs and statements correspond to the objective reality, which is assumed to be given and there for us to discover. Plato's famous dialogue about language and naming, *Cratylus*, addresses this issue in detail (Petković, 2018). The discussions in this Platonic dialogue centre on whether truth or correctness of the names which are assigned to different things is a matter of general agreement or the nature of the things which are named. Plato's inclination to truth claims and disdain for the sophists, whom he classifies as relativist manipulators, is evident as he questions a simple premise: if everyone has their own truth, how can wisdom and folly be distinguishable? Specifically, 'if what appears to each man is true to him, one man cannot in reality be wiser than another' (Plato n.d., 386c). A similar logic that repudiates multiple contradictory 'truths' is present in Descartes' *Discourse on Method* where the second rule of method asserts: if there are two persons with different judgement on the same thing, at least one is wrong (Descartes & Cress, 1998).

The coherence theory avoids the problems associated with correspondence theory by ruling out radical scepticism (Walker, 2018). For Nietzsche, as a relativist, truth 'does not necessarily denote the antithesis of error, but in the most fundamental cases only the posture of various errors in relation to one another' (Nietzsche, 1967, Book III, 536). In a review of Rescher's *The Coherence Theory of Truth* (1973), Ford (1974) maintains that while coherence presupposes logical consistency, it cannot provide the meaning of truth but it can be the arbiter of factual claims. Rooted in the rationalist, system-building framework of metaphysical supporters of coherence such as Leibniz and Spinoza, it is claimed that a statement that is true or false either coheres or fails to cohere with a system of other statements. Such a statement is a

> ...member of a system whose elements are related to each other by ties of logical implication as the elements in a system of pure mathematics are related ... [thus] a statement cannot properly be called true unless it fits into the one comprehensive account of the universe or reality (White, 2006, p. 308).

Rescher (1973) posits that the coherence approach needs to be reexamined to give us a way out of our epistemological struggles with truth. Such reexamination has led to the assertion that the weakest link of a pure coherence theory is that it fails to incorporate 'a proper sense of the way in which actual systems of belief are sustained by persons with perceptual experience, impinged upon by their environment' (Blackburn, 2005, p. 88). Another criticism levelled against coherence theory is that 'if it holds all truth to consist in coherence, it is untenable: there must be some truths that do not, truths about what people believe. This causes problems for traditional coherence theories' (Walker, 2018, p. 2019). In other words, it ends up in the same conundrum as relativism. In order to justify itself as a tenable position, it has to make reference to something that lies outside of the position itself.

While Rorty's (1998) position on truth is a considered a deflationary one, Foucault's 'regimes of truth' as well as the assertion that truth is either a part of, or embedded within, a power structure led the way for a post-modern and relativist understanding of truth. Foucault argues that truth does not embody an essential, transcendental, neutralized form. From a Foucauldian perspective, 'truth(s) emerges through an amalgamation of various historical practices and discourse, and it is propped up by various forms of power/knowledge' (Koro-Ljungberg et al., 2019, p. 588). Badiou (2009) goes as far as calling Foucault's approach suitable for the nihilistic age of democratic materialism. In Badiou's (2009) view, Foucault's history of the regimes of truth has one major flaw: '[it] could only describe the regimes themselves while bracketing off the question of their truth' (as cited in Prozorov, 2019, p. 19).

The question of truth has been directly approached by philosophers throughout history. Italian Christian philosopher Thomas Aquinas believes that 'Truth is the agreement between intellect and object (*adæquatio rei et intellectus*)' (as cited in Künne & Kunne, 2003, p. 102). According to Künne and Kunne (2003), the definition of truth offered by Aquinas can be traced back to the Persian philosopher-scientist Ibn Sina (Avicenna) who lived in the early eleventh century. In early Islamic philosophy, Avicenna defined truth in his work *Kitab Al-Shifa, The Book of Healing*, as: 'What corresponds in the mind to what is outside it'. Avicenna's definition of truth, De Haan (2018) points out, is that '[t]ruth is also said of the veridical belief in the existence [of something]' (p. 38). According to De Haan (2018):

> Avicenna distinguishes between 'true' (*haqq*) and 'veridical' (*s ādiq*) statements. The 'true' is primarily identified with the way reality grounds beliefs, whereas the 'veridical' refers to the way statements and beliefs depend upon reality as a truthmaker. This is why, for Avicenna, the primary sense of truth is not epistemological, but metaphysical, since the locus of truth is first found in things. It is the truth of things that is the foundation for veridical cognition. (pp. 28–29)

Once Avicenna defined the 'true' and 'veridical' senses of truth, he made a case for an understanding of truth in an in-between space where intellect and being collide.

A similar desire for defining truth in an in-between space can be seen in constructivist conceptions of truth. The roots of social constructivist theory of truth can be found in the Vicoan principle of *verum ipsum factum* – that 'truth itself is constructed' (Berlant et al., n.d.). The constructivist theory argues that truth, much like knowledge, is constructed by social processes and is rooted in historical and cultural contexts. Hegel and Marx were among thinkers who supported this constructivist notion of truth.

Traces of constructivist inclination can also be found in the American pragmatic theory of truth and supported by philosophers like James, Dewey and Peirce. According to Misak (2018), pragmatism originated in Cambridge, Massachusetts, in the 1860 in *The Metaphysical Club* where these three philosophers

(James, Dewey, Peirce) crossed paths as members of a short-lived reading group (p. 283). In the pragmatic discourse, the importance of putting one's concepts into practice is echoed in Dewey's linking of truth to inquiry (Misak, 2018) and James' (1909) assertion that 'the "true" is only the expedient in our way of thinking, just as the "right" is only the expedient in our way of behaving' (p. 29). According to Misak (2018), Dewey tried to bring the external world into his pragmatism when he claimed that, '[w]hen we experience something we act upon it, we do something with it; then we suffer and undergo the consequences' (as cited in Misak, 2018, p. 294). The pragmatic form of constructivism has been criticized on the ground that ultimately it rests on some form of act utilitarianism, which, in turn, relies on a relativistic epistemology (Peters, 1975).

The Brazilian critical pedagogue, Paulo Freire's perception of truth can be outlined along the lines of social constructivist thinkers such as Dewey. Freire (2000) proposes praxis as 'reflection and action upon the world in order to transform it (p. 51)'. According to Freire, 'Only human beings *are* praxis – the praxis which, as the reflection and action which truly transform reality, is the source of knowledge and creation…Through their continuing praxis, men and women simultaneously create history and become historical-social beings' (Freire, 2000, p. 101).

From a Freirean perspective, truth is something to be made by human beings with the aim of improving upon life at both the individual and collective level. While Freire's epistemology is social constructivist in nature, in the sense that knowledge is basically understood to be created by human beings rather than given, his position is very different from Dewey's pragmatism. Freire dissociated himself from utilitarianism and other forms of relativism. For Freire, knowledge arises out of the dialectic between the subject (the agent) and the object (the world).

Truth and Truthfulness

In an essay on education and freedom, Bertrand Russel makes a distinction between 'truth' and 'truthfulness'. Truth, Russel (1966) maintains, is for the gods while truthfulness is for human beings to struggle with. Let us imagine this within the context of an educational setting. A teacher asks what is the best way to get everyone in class to pay attention and follow the rules. One response is 'bring a shotgun to class and shoot anyone who disobeys'. The only way one can assert that this is a disproportionate and inadequate response is if there is some connection to the notion of truthfulness. Once we establish that a notion of truthfulness is imperative in decoding different situations, the question becomes 'what is the notion of truthfulness?'

If truthfulness is not involved in a democratic way of life, then can we really proceed with a *democratic* way of life? Truthfulness within a democratic way of life requires that we question its reasonableness and foundation. A democratic way of life requires every now and then that we challenge the notion of truthfulness that we may be working within a certain democratic community. One such challenge can be found in the words of Nobel Prize laureate Harold Pinter who stated:

> There are no hard distinctions between what is real and what is unreal, not between what is true and what is false. A thing is not necessarily either true or false; it can be both true and false. I believe that these assertions still make sense and do still apply to the exploration of reality through art. So as a writer I stand by them but as a citizen I cannot. As a citizen I must ask: What is true? What is false? (as cited in Mendietta, 2017, p. 8)

It is exactly fundamental questions such as 'what is true?' or 'what is false?' that have encouraged intellectuals to further deconstruct the understanding of truth and truthfulness. In *Truth and Truthfulness*, Williams (2002) asserts, 'the concept of truth itself – that is to say, the quite basic role that truth plays in relation to language, meaning, and belief – is not culturally various, but always and everywhere the same' (p. 61). According to Williams (2002), it is every individual's decision to choose truth as the correspondence of words and things or abandon it. If a person chooses truth, they are truthful which means the individual has chosen truthfulness. Williams (2002) contends that 'a passion for truthfulness may initiate a process of critique that debunks the supposedly "objective" claims in some field – history, say – exposing them as nothing of ideology or hidden social forces' (p. 3).

If all sides agree that there has to be some element of truth in operation – the question, to phrase it in Rorty's terms would be: Is truth arising within our framework or does truth arise outside of our framework? Rorty (1982) argues, in a pragmatist way, that it would arise within our own framework. However, if we are serious about democracy, are we morally allowed to escape giving some form of an answer to the question of the relationship between democracy, truth and truthfulness? Mendieta (2017) distinguishes between democratic truthfulness (i.e. truth as a relation to others) and ethical truthfulness (i.e. truth as a relation to ourselves). According to Mendieta:

> Neither [democratic truthfulness and ethical truthfulness] can subsist without the other; each potentiates the other. A democracy that does not care about truth, is a democracy that does not care about either the character of its citizens or its legitimacy – and thus we may as well trade it for despotisms, oligarchies, and timocracies, to use the catalogue of bad forms of society Plato catalogued in his *Republic*. (2017, n.p.)

Democracy and Truth

To gain a more vivid picture of how democracy and truth are interrelated, it is imperative to look at the agonistic versus epistemic divide more closely. Dalaqua (2019) resurrects an important question about whether democracy, as an agonistic claim, is rooted in the realm of passionate conflicts or reasonable consensus. Dalaqua uses 'epistemic democracy' to denote any theory that places value on democratic deliberation because, in his own words, 'it can further knowledge and truth' (p. 588). The search for 'the correct answer' in political deliberations by democratic theorists has, according to him, essentially destroyed the 'constitutive role of passions and conflict' in the realm of politics (Miguel, 2014, p. 281). It is important to distinguish between 'right' and 'correct' before proceeding to the next section. Right and correct are not the same in that the right answer indicates that a value aspect is included other than facts, while correct indicates it is a matter of facts. Since the 'correct' outcome is independent of and prior to political discussion, citizens are not free to decide which course of action they will take. Instead, they are obliged to acquiesce willy-nilly to the 'true' answer that their supposedly impartial and reason-driven deliberation reveals. This line of thinking easily justifies the substitution of democracy (the rule of the many) for epistocracy (the rule of the wise). After all, 'if the intention is to find the correct answers, a group of technocrats would certainly fare better than the ignorant many'. (Miguel, 2014, p. 281, as cited in; Dalaqua, 2019).

The overemphasis on reason and sidelining of passions and affects is a problem that needs to be addressed, according to Mouffe (2000), who also argues that 'by conflating democracy with a passionless deliberation that aims at "truth", epistemic theorists deprive people from the liberty to challenge political decisions' (p. 65). As stated by Mouffe, the negation of passions also leads to the negation of the dimension of antagonism that is inherent in human relations (2000, p. 101). For Mouffe, democracy should aim for agonism and not antagonism. The latter means that opposing or differing positions conceive of each other as enemies that need to be destroyed; the former implies indeed difference in views, even very strong differences, but the aim is never to eradicate or annihilate the other side.

There has been no shortage of critique on epistemic democracy, especially in relation to how making the value of democracy dependent on knowledge and truth can potentially mean that democracy will resist conflict, dissent and multiple political positions (Dalaqua, 2017). James (1909), for instance, believes that truth is constantly in 'battle' and that 'the greatest enemy of any one of our truths may be the rest of our truths' (Lecture II, What Pragmatism Means). Dalaqua (2017) highlights the need to distinguish between lower-case truth and capital 'T' Truth. The distinction allows for a discussion around whether foundationalist[1] perceptions of truth are as polarizing as anti-foundationalists[2] claim. In this space, Haack (2019) argues that:

> While there is only one truth, i.e., one phenomenon of being true, and one unambiguous truth-concept, there are many and various truths, i.e., many and various true propositions, beliefs, claims, etc., about the many different things, stuff, kinds, laws, events, etc., in the world. (Haack, 2019, p. 260)

The question for anti-foundationalists like Rorty would be the following: If democracy has no foundations of any sort, then how can it be distinguished from other forms of power relations? Arguing that democracy requires some foundation does not commit one to believing that that foundation has to be on an absolutist and foundationalist basis. In other words, if one believes that democracy has to have a basis, the basis could be from inside or outside. Another important question that arises is whether we need inclusivism or equity as the basis of democracy? Ultimately, the issue at hand is not how democracy is represented as an object which exists in and of itself. We conceived of democracy, and we constructed it. The question is what construct is democracy? And can this construct of democracy survive without some justifiable notion of truth?

The Post-truth Era

Any discussion of post-truth requires us to address a number of important questions. Some of these questions include whether by post-truth, we mean a denial of truth (any notion of truth) or a denial of certain notions of truth. Is a belief in the emergence of a post-truth era in line with the view that we are ready to discard truth? Does reference to post-truth mean that the notion and existence of facts in and of themselves can be denied? Additionally, are facts considered a social construct, and if so, does it make sense to refer to something as 'a fact'? While the Oxford Dictionary (2016) defines post-truth as 'relating to or denoting circumstances in which objective facts are less influential in shaping public opinion than appeals to emotion and personal belief', unpacking how 'objective facts' are identified is of paramount importance.

A defining feature of the post-truth society is the existence of epistemic ambiguity. While it may seem unavoidable to create the binary post-truth society/ truth society, Han (2018) warns against such dichotomy. The problem, Han (2018) asserts, is that it is not possible to identify a specific period of time in history that can be categorized as a truth society. Bowell (2017) highlights another problem with the term post-truth, in that the use of *post* implies that the concept of truth is outdated and can even be dismissed. The apparent casting aside of truth is seen by some as giving up on democracy, for as Jasanoff and Simmet point out, 'how could people possibly reason together if they could not agree on a common factual basis for deliberation?' (2017, p. 752). A problem that lies at the heart of such an assertion is whether truths and facts are identical. For instance, one may admit that facts exist, but this fact is not necessarily identical to claiming to have the truth.

The path forward is one fraught with uncertainty yet filled with measured hope, as highlighted by Jasanoff and Simmet (2017) who propose,

> a pathway *back* to reason as an alternative to 'witless, sightless' rejections of truth. The act of diagnosis, a prerequisite for knowing how to proceed, requires us to fully embrace the discussion of values and purposes as integral to the project of making epistemic truth. (p. 756).

Modernist intellectuals like Gellner (2008) have warned about the consequences of rejecting truth in the postmodern context, fearing that it could lead to cognitive nihilism (p. 88). Kalpokas et al. (2019) paint a rosier picture by maintaining that post-truth does not necessarily mean discarding truth and embracing lies, but define post-truth as the blurring of distinction between the two extremes of the pendulum (p. 2). British philosopher Julian Baggini (2017) is quick to point out that we should avoid bleak prognoses such as the one offered by Gellner. Thus, instead of cynic and defeatist prognoses in relation to our inability to distinguish between truth and lies (p. 7–8), we should avoid advancing relativism which in turn reinforces the post-truth discourse (Kalpokas, Kalpokas & Finotello, 2019, p. 2).

In *A Short History of Truth: Consolations for a Post-Truth World* (2017), Baggini introduces a rubric of 10 rules to help navigate what he terms the dangers of the post-truth era:

- 'Spiritual "truths" should not compete with secular ones but should be seen as belonging to a different species.
- We should think for ourselves, not by ourselves.
- We should be sceptical not cynical.
- Reason demands modesty not certainty.
- To become smarter, we must understand the ways we are dumb.
- Truths need to be created as well as found.
- Alternative perspectives should be sought not as alternative truths but as enrichers of truth.
- Power doesn't speak the truth; truth must speak to power.
- For a better morality we need better knowledge.
- Truth needs to be understood holistically'. (p. 107)

Hope, Dialogue and Post-truth: A Freirean Perspective

While a defining feature of the post-truth era is its intrinsic relativism, Gellner (2013) warns this could lead to 'cognitive nihilism'. Thus, it is imperative to find a way forward that safeguards some justifiable understanding of truth and, hence, democracy itself. Our thesis is based on a way forward that relies on reasonableness that accounts for the equally important role of both reasons and emotions, rather than a position that privileges either of them, that is a position that neither, on the one hand, subsumes emotions as a cognitive quality nor, on the other hand, completely disregards the role of reason. Our position is grounded in the Freirean dialogic in-between space, instead of renouncing truth (that is any notion of truth), and critically discuss possibilities for various approaches to truth-seeking. Here, an important point to consider is the distinction between subjectivity, objectivity and intersubjectivity. Freire is among intellectuals who write about intersubjectivity as a way to go beyond the whole dispute between the subjectivity or objectivity mentality.

Freire's (1998) position that unfinishedness is an essential part of the human experience is in line with the connection John Stuart Mill makes between truth and democratic deliberation which 'is not final but open, not a finished product but a continuing adventure' (as cited in Garforth, 1980, p. 179). In the space afforded by the Freirean unfinishedness, 'hope is a natural, possible, and necessary impetus' (Freire, 1998, p. 69). In *Pedagogy of Freedom*, Freire (1998) points out how:

> ...passing through the world is not predetermined, pre-established. That my destiny is not a given but something that needs to be constructed and for which I must assume responsibility. I like being human because I am involved with others in making history out of possibility, not simply resigned to fatalistic stagnation. (Freire, 1998, p. 54)

Freire's notion of radical democracy makes way for the 'dialogical man' who engages in 'the united reflection and action' that is aimed at transforming and humanizing the world (Freire, 2000, p. 89).

An issue that needs to be addressed here is whether we can argue that knowledge is always political. While some have argued in favour of this position, there are those who claim that knowledge cannot always be political. That is the challenge, in some way, that Freire poses to us. Freire's notion of dialectic, both in terms of reality and knowledge, is not a matter of subjectivity or objectivity, but it is always an in-between. In his seminal book *Pedagogy of the Oppressed* (1970), Freire noted:

> ...the radical is never a subjectivist; for him the subjective aspect exists only in relation to the objective aspect (the concrete reality which is the object of his analysis). Subjectivity and objectivity thus join in a dialectical unity producing knowledge in solidarity with action, and vice versa. (p. 22)

This quote is the most explicit and direct quote in Freire's corpus through which he outlines his ontological and epistemological foundation of his dialectical philosophy. The radical, that is the person who goes to the root of an issue or problem and who steers away from mainstream slogans, is neither merely a subjectivist nor an objectivist. For Freire, both our human reality and epistemology are not a matter of either/or. To be real and to know in their fullest and most noble way entails the tensions and the back and forth between the subjective and objective conditions. Reality is neither a matter of being within nor outside of a human being; reality is in the joining of the two aspects. And the same holds for knowledge. For Freire, this ontological and epistemological declaration which he argues for throughout his works is at the same time a manifestation of his political position that denies the contradictory notion of neutrality based on a liberal understanding of impartiality and de-contextuality.

In *Truth and Politics* (2006), Hannah Arendt focuses on the struggle between politics and truth. Specifically, Arendt states: 'Politicians have never been regarded as particularly honest whereas "truth-seekers" have always been an endangered species' (2006, p. 227). For Freire, the radical is the 'truth-seeker'; but truth-seeking is neither a purely psychological nor a purely objectified event. The truth arises out of the struggle and the dialectic between the subject and the object; the struggle for the truth for Freire is in itself a political process, one that has to avoid oppressive conditions. Hence, for Freire, truth is not merely a matter of facts (although he does not deny the notion of facts); it is also a matter of moral values and beliefs. For Freire, oppressive conditions are simply inexcusable and immoral.

Another issue worthy of consideration in our discussion about truth is the nature of evidence. Here, the question that needs to be asked is what counts as evidence? Within the liberal tradition, going back to Mill in the nineteenth century, rationality, as a procedural given, is considered sufficient for justice to prevail. One of the major critiques of liberalism is overlooking the fact that rationality as an epistemology is itself involved in power relationships. Therefore, rationality is not a neutral and purely descriptive procedure, but it is in itself an exhibition of certain power relationships.

The emphasis on an evidence-based discourse works with a very narrow notion of evidence, namely empirical evidence of a certain (western/liberal) kind. While evidence, rooted the Latin word *videre* [to see] – implies that we do not see simply in empirical ways, but we see in many different ways. To reduce evidence only to one way of seeing (the correspondence between the object and what the subject sees) is to create a form of epistemological or cognitive imperialism and colonialism based exclusively on a purely logical positivist perspective. For educational philosopher Heesoon Bai (Bai, Morgan, Scott, & Cohen, 2016), the element of spirituality, as well as elements of contemplation and empathy need to be part of the discussion on evidence. Excluding the realm of spirituality in the discussion on evidence results in limiting seeing [*videre*] to only one form.

As stated by Schindler (2020), there is a lack of balance 'between the subjective and the objective, between the self and the world, between agent and structure' (p. 19). Drawing on Freire's work, Farrell, Ángel, and Maciel Vahl (2017) propose accepting and acknowledging our uncertainties and incompleteness and advancing more dialogical spaces. In response to how the 'murky middle ground' between truth and falsehood inherent in the post-truth ethos (Rider, 2017) can be challenged, Farrell et al. (2017) underline the three themes:

> [A first theme is] 'truth imposed' that is the fallacy of a single truth that authoritarian regimes, authoritarian families and authoritarian teachers want to impose. A second theme is the 'ignored truth' that is apparent in the post-truth era. It is the contempt or ignorance of facts that leads us to an authentic understanding of our context. A third theme is 'truth co-constructed' or dialogued which is seeking truths collectively and with broad participation; it is the Freirean Utopian ideal. It is the recognition of the plurality of voices that can be included to arrive at an authentic and shared understanding of our context. (Farrell et al., 2017, p. 84)

Freire argues that to speak truthfully, there must be 'coherence between what we say and do' (Freire & Ara, 1998, p. 51) and that 'true is to be found in the "becoming" of dialogue' (Freire & Faundez, 1989, p. 32). Dialogue, Freire (2000) believes, cannot exist without hope which is an ontological requirement for human beings. Hope, in turn, is rooted in human being's incompleteness, 'from which they move out in constant search – a search which can be carried out only in communion with others' (Freire, 1998, p. 91). In *Letters to Cristina: Reflection on My Life and Work*, Freire (2016) does warn that in alienated societies human beings 'oscillate between ingenious optimism and hopelessness' (p. 10). To fill the gap between ingenious optimism and hopelessness, dialogue, as an act of creation, is proposed as a remedy (Freire, 2000, p. 89). Moreover, dialogue cannot exist, in the absence of faith, humility, hope, critical thinking and profound love for the world and for people (Freire, 2000). Thus, dialogue becomes a key element that can overcome the lack of balance between the subjective and the objective in our search for truth. The Freirean philosophy reiterates the connections human beings have with history, power and social constructs. Schindler (2020) echoes these sentiments by stating that true knowledge is never 'purely' objective nor 'merely' subjective, but always from what emerges between the tensions and the dialectic between both at the same time (p. 2).

Dialogic Understanding of Truth: An Ontario Scenario

The final section of the essay focuses on the application of our understanding of truth as a relational dialogical epistemology. We also problematize the predominant view of evidence-based research and policy, and explore how our understanding of the relational dialogical notion of truth can be utilized in the analysis of a case involving pro-active discrimination and affirmative action. Here, the Freirean dialogic space that engenders an inter-subjectivist approach to truth-seeking becomes particularly important in situations where liberal perceptions of truth are emphasized – that is, understandings of truth that completely rely on 'evidence-based research' which is deemed to be tautological with purely and exclusively empirical data; no other forms of data are acceptable in such an understanding. Jasanoff and Simmet (2017) problematize the liberal perception of truth, stating that,

> ...for conservative critics of the global economic and political order, it was not truth per se that needed to be challenged. Instead, their quarrel was with particular truths that liberals and experts accept as self-evident (p. 752).

Ultimately, the issue of evidence is revisited within the intricate relationship between theory and practice and the very nature of the relationship we envisage between the two.

One case study that will be analyzed in this context is the application for the establishment of the Africentric Alternative Schools (AASs) in Toronto and the controversies surrounding it. In 2008, the Toronto District School Board (TDSB) approved a proposal to open an ethno-centric school to address the needs of increasingly marginalized black students. The establishment of the school was justified within the choice policy ethos of the province and TDSB (Gulson & Webb, 2012). While alternative schooling has been part of the Toronto educational fabric for years, the idea of Afrocentric schools met with a different form of resistance (James, 2011). The Afrocentric schools, which are open to all students of any ethnic background, are based on the holistic epistemology and spiritual-philosophical and educational beliefs arising from the communal Indigenous way of life in the African continent.

Then Premier of Ontario, Dalton McGuinty (2003–2013), expressed disappointment over TDSB's decision to approve the opening of an Afrocentric school and explicitly stated that the proposal will neither be supported nor funded by the Liberal Ontario government. The rationale behind such an assertion was partly rooted in identity politics and the belief that Afrocentric schooling and curricula is a form of exclusive education as opposed to inclusive education. This is while, a different argument brought to the fore by Dei (1995), distinguished between segregation by force and segregation by choice. The Premier emphasized that there was no evidence that such a school was in the interest of black or other students. Hence, he concluded, that on the basis of evidence-based research, there is no justification for the establishment of the school. The problem with this mode of reasoning is that it exclusively relies on the narrow liberal understanding of evidence as noted earlier. It does not allow for any other form of justification based on moral or philosophical grounds. Moreover, the liberal stance as expressed by the Premier does not realize that unless the school board was allowed to open such a school, there would never be any evidence in Toronto of the purely empirical kind for such a school. And hence the establishment of such a school would be doomed to never happen. The Premier following the popular understanding of 'evidence-based research' fell into the fallacy that holds that facts speak for themselves; that is, facts have value irrespective of the relationship they have with a value system. Moreover ironically, he failed to realize that his so-called 'evidence-based' position was, in fact, a very loaded value position in itself! Finally, it is worth noting that there has been a lot of evidence showing that the current public school system in Toronto has been failing black students – a fact that it seems was not given sufficient attention by the media (Gulson & Webb, 2013; James, Turner, George, & Tecle, 2017; Johnson, 2013; Laflamme-Lagoke & Negura, 2014) notwithstanding the clear statement made by the TDSB:

> The Africentric Alternative School began operating in September 2009 in response to an initial community request for such a school in June 2007 to address a high dropout rate and achievement gap affecting students of African descent. In January 2008, a report titled Improving Success for Black Students was presented to the Board of Trustees with a number of recommendations. Ultimately, the Board approved a recommendation to establish the Africentric Alternative School to open in September 2009 at Sheppard Public School. (TDSB, 2015).

The majority of the opposition to Africentric schooling in Toronto invoked a colour-blind ideology that focused on Canada's multicultural heritage. The media played a critical role in perpetuating the view that Africentric schooling is not inclusive and, in fact, seeks to segregate students across race lines. According to Wallace (2009):

> ...all three major Toronto dailies condemned the proposal. The *Toronto Star* argued the 'idea smacks of segregation, which is contrary to the values of the school system and Canadian society as a whole', while the *Globe and Mail* ran a column that called black-focused schools 'as insulting as they are ridiculous'. Even more vehement in its criticism, the *National Post* said the 'concept of special schools for black students is one of those terrible ideas that refuses to die'. (as cited in Gulson & Webb, 2017, p. 8)

As stated by Gulson and Webb (2012), Africentric schools were considered 'un-Canadian', all the while denying the history of black slaves in Canada and converting 'the assertion of political power and the need to address systemic historical disadvantage into a threat to national identity' (p. 705). The counter-argument to ethno-centric schools being 'un-Canadian' centred on the need to problematize the deficit mentality associated with black students and the necessity to remedy the ongoing failure of Toronto public schools to educate black learners (Gulson & Webb, 2016). Gulson and Webb (2016) point to the language adopted by TDSB regarding the establishment of AASs by maintaining that the statement seems to have been created in a vacuum as if 'there is no history prior to 2007' (p. 155) without a reference to the saliency of race and racism in Canada. The official TDSB statement is as follows:

> Such a Liberal outlook reflects a vision of equity that can afford to ignore race and in its place take up the issue of choice (Johnson, 2013). The Liberal pragmatism advances a particular understanding of truth, not by entirely eliminating equity concerns but rather by embedding them within choice and accountability frameworks. (Forsey, Davies, & Walford, 2008, p. 15)

There is another form of evidence that challenges the Liberal Agenda, where, for instance, in the TDSB, black students are twice as likely as white students to be labelled as having non-identified special education needs while also being disproportionately placed in streams that do not lead to tertiary education (James et al., 2017, pp. 30–34). Additional evidence in support of Afrocentric schools came with a 'focus on presenting Africans as subjects rather than objects' (Laflamme-Lagoke & Negura, 2014, p. 101). Mazama (2001) follows a Freirean paradigm when stating that liberation is the ultimate goal of Africentric education which leads to generating knowledge that is liberating and empowering. A TDSB trustee who voted for AASs maintained,

> It was all about how do you meet the needs of the students and their families? And it wasn't that an Africentric school was the answer. It was that there wasn't one answer (Gulson & Webb, 2013, p. 177).

When there is no single truth, it is imperative to engage in a dialogic discourse to ensure if various dimensions of an issue are explored and afforded equal voice. The traditional relationships that expect theory to dish out quick fix solutions that will work always and everywhere irrespective of context eliminates any possibility of self-determination, autonomy and agency. The need for an intersubjective perspective and to avoid apocalyptic diagnoses that are fatalist in nature is becoming increasingly clear.

Conclusion

This chapter has argued that a more plausible notion of truth is neither one that is based on intrinsic objectivity nor intrinsic relativism, but one that is based on the relationship between objectivity and subjectivity; that is a relational (not relative) and dialectic understanding of truth which does not rule out the existence of facts but questions the political constructs of facts. While it is important to resuscitate the moribund discussion around the foundation and reasonableness of truth, an issue that arises is which theory of knowledge and whose theory of knowledge should be accepted as the epistemological basis of truth. Here, epistemology is no longer simply a matter of knowledge, but it becomes a matter of power relationships. Knowledge becomes political and not something neutral that exists in and of itself irrespective of context.

Notes

1. Foundationalists believe that all knowledge or justified belief rest ultimately on a foundation of non-inferential knowledge or justified belief. Fumerton, Richard. "Foundationalist theories of epistemic justification" (2010).
2. Anti-foundationalism rose after moral theory and practice were regulated by rationally justified objectives and impersonal standards of rationality which led to the disappearance of the necessary social and conceptual preconditions for the knowledge of those standards and, thus, of moral truths. Trifiró, Fabrizio. "Macintyre's Tensions: between anti-liberal foundationalism and anti-foundationalist liberalism" (2006), p. 130.

References

Arendt, H. (2006). Truth and politics. *Between past and future* (pp. 223–259). New York, NY: Penguin.

Badiou, A. (2009). *Logics of worlds*. London: Continuum.

Baggini, J. (2017). *A short history of truth: Consolations for a post-truth world*. London: Quercus Publishing.

Bai, H., Morgan, P., Scott, C., & Cohen, A. (2016). Prolegomena to a spiritual research paradigm. In J. Lin, R. L. Oxford, & T. E. Culham (Eds.), *Toward a spiritual research paradigm: Exploring new ways of knowing, researching and being* (pp. 77–96). Charlotte, NC: IAP.

Berlant, L., Butler, J., McClary, S., Mulvey, L., Adorno, T., Marcuse, H., … Althusser, L. From Wikipedia, the free encyclopedia.

Blackburn, S. (2005). *Truth: A guide*. Oxford: Oxford University Press.

Bowell, T. (2017). Response to the editorial 'Education in a post-truth world'. *Educational Philosophy and Theory, 49*(6), 582–585.

Dalaqua, G. H. (2017). Democracy and truth: A contingent defense of epistemic democracy. *Critical Review, 29*(1), 49–71.

Dalaqua, G. H. (2019). Democracy as compromise: An alternative to the agonistic vs. epistemic divide. *Kriterion: Revista de Filosofia, 60*(144), 587–607.

De Haan, D. D. (2018). Avicenna's healing and the metaphysics of truth. *Journal of the History of Philosophy, 56*(1), 17–44.

Dei, G. J. S. (1995). Examining the case for "African-centred" schools in Ontario. *McGill Journal of Education/Revue des sciences de l'éducation de McGill, 30*(002).

Descartes, R., & Cress, D. A. (1998). *Discourse on method*. Indianapolis, IN: Hackett Publishing.

Farrell, B., Ángel, N., & Maciel Vahl, M. (2017). Hope and Utopia in post-truth times: A Freirean approach. *Revista Brasileira de Alfabetização, 1*(6), 81–97.

Ford, L. S. (1974). A review of Nicholas Rescher, the coherence theory of truth. *Philosophy and Phenomenological Research, 35*(1), 118–120.

Forsey, M., Davies, S., & Walford, G. (Eds.). (2008). *The globalisation of school choice?* Oxford: Symposium Books Ltd.

Freire, P. (1998). *Pedagogy of freedom: Ethics, democracy, and civic courage*. Lanham, MD: Rowman & Littlefield Publishers, Inc.

Freire, P. (2000). *Pedagogy of the oppressed* (30th anniversary ed.). New York, NY: Bloomsbury.

Freire, P. (2016). *Letters to Cristina*. Milton: Routledge.

Freire, P., & Ara, A. M. (1998). *Pedagogy of the heart*. New York, NY: Bloomsbury Publishing USA.

Freire, P., & Faundez, A. (1989). *Learning to question: A pedagogy of liberation*. New York, NY: Continuum.

Garforth, F. W. (1980). *Educative democracy: John Stuart Mill on education in society*. Oxford: Oxford University Press.

Gellner, E. (2008). *Nations and nationalism* (2nd ed.). Ithaca, NY: Cornell University Press.

Gellner, E. (2013). *Postmodernism, reason and religion*. Routledge.

Gulson, K. N., & Webb, P. T. (2012). Education policy racialisations: Afrocentric schools, Islamic schools, and the new enunciations of equity. *Journal of Education Policy, 27*(6), 697–709.

Gulson, K. N., & Webb, P. T. (2013). "A raw, emotional thing" School choice, commodification and the racialised branding of Afrocentricity in Toronto, Canada. *Education Inquiry, 4*(1), 167–187.

Gulson, K. N., & Webb, P. T. (2016). Not just another alternative school: Policy problematization, neoliberalism, and racial biopolitics. *Educational Policy, 30*(1), 153–170.

Gulson, K. N., & Webb, P. T. (2017). *Education policy and racial biopolitics*. Bristol: Policy Press.

Haack, S. (2019). Post "post-truth": Are we there yet? *Theoria, 85*(4), 258–275.

Han, D. (2018). From postmodernity to a post-truth society? *Journal of Comparative Studies/Komparatovistikas Almanahs*, 11.

James, W. (1909). *Pragmatism and four essays from the meaning of truth*. New York, NY: World Publishing Company.

James, W. (1949). *Pragmatism: A new name for some old ways of thinking*. Harlow: Longmans Green & Co.

James, C. E. (2011). Multicultural education in a color-blind society. *Intercultural and multicultural education: Enhancing global interconnectedness*, *39*, 191–210.

James, C. E., & Turner, T. (2017). *Towards race equity in education: The schooling of Black students in the Greater Toronto Area*. Toronto, ON: York University.

James, C. E., Turner, T., George, R., & Tecle, S. (2017). *Towards race equity in education: The schooling of black students in the Greater Toronto Area*. Toronto, Ontario, Canada: York University. Retrieved from https://edu.yorku.ca/files/2017/04/Towards-Race-Equity-in-Education-April-2017.pdf

Jasanoff, S., & Simmet, H. R. (2017). No funeral bells: Public reason in a 'post-truth'age. *Social Studies of Science*, *47*(5), 751–770.

Johnson, L. (2013). Segregation or "thinking black"? Community activism and the development of black-focused schools in Toronto and London, 1968-2008. *Teachers College Record*, *115*, 1–25.

Kalpokas, I., Kalpokas, I., & Finotello (2019). *A political theory of post-truth*. London; New York, NY: Palgrave Macmillan.

Koro-Ljungberg, M., Carlson, D. L., & Montana, A. (2019). Productive forces of post-truth (s)? *Qualitative Inquiry*, *25*(6), 583–590.

Künne, W., & Kunne, W. (2003). *Conceptions of truth*. Oxford: Oxford University Press.

Laflamme-Lagoke, M., & Negura, L. (2014). Social representations of the Africentric school as portrayed through the Toronto newspapers. *Canadian Journal of Counselling and Psychotherapy*, *48*(2).

Mazama, A. (2001). The Afrocentric paradigm. *Journal of Black Studies*, *13*(4), 387–405.

Mendieta, E. (2017). Rorty and post-post-truth. *Los Angeles Review of Books*, *22*(07), 2017.

Miguel, L. F. (2014). *Democracia e representação: territórios em disputa*. São Paulo: Editora Unesp.

Misak, C. (2018). The pragmatist theory of truth. In M. Glanzber (Ed.), *The oxford handbook of truth* (pp. 283–308). Oxford: Oxford University Press.

Mouffe, C. (2000). *The democratic paradox*. New York, NY: verso.

Nietzsche, F. W. (1967). *The will to power (Book III)*. New York, NY: Vintage.

Oxford Dictionaries. (2016). Word of the year. Retrieved from https://en.oxforddictionaries.com/word-of-the-year/word-of-the-year-2016

Peters, R. S. (Ed.). (1975). *Nature and conduct* (Vol. 8). London: Macmillan International Higher Education.

Petković, K. (2018). Ideology and truth: The return of the old couple in the post-truth era. *Političke perspektive*, *8*(3), 7–39.

Plato. (n.d.). [cca 360 BC[1]]. Cratylus (trans. Benjamin Jowett). Retrieved from http://classics.mit.edu/Plato/cratylus.html. Accessed on February 24, 2019.

Prozorov, S. (2019). Why is there truth? Foucault in the age of post-truth politics. *Constellations: An International Journal of Critical and Democratic Theory*, *26*(1), 18–30.

Rescher, N. (1973). The coherence theory of truth.

Rider, S. (2017). Response to the editorial 'Education in a post-truth world'. *Educational Philosophy and Theory*, *49*(6), 582–585.

Rorty, R. (1982). *Consequences of pragmatism: Essays, 1972–1980*. Minneapolis, MN: U of Minnesota Press.

Rorty, R. (1998). *Truth and progress*. Cambridge: Cambridge University Press.

Russell, B. (1966). *Philosophical essays*. New York, NY: Simon & Schuster.

Schindler, S. (2020). The task of critique in the times of post-truth. *Review of International Studies*, *46*(3), 376–394.

Toronto District School Board. (2015). Africentric alternative school: Together we build, succeed and lead. Retrieved from http://www.tdsb.on.ca/FindYour/details.aspx?schno=3949&displayModule=DetailsofaSchool

Walker, R. C. (2018). The coherence theory of truth. In *The Oxford handbook of truth* (pp. 219). Oxford: Oxford University Press.

Wallace, A. (2009). *The test. This Magazine*. Retrieved from https://cdn.dal.ca/content/dam/dalhousie/pdf/faculty/jrj-chair/The%20test_Africcentric%20Schools_This%20Magazine_2009.pdf

White, A. R. (2006). Coherence theory of truth. In D. M. Borchert (Ed.), *Encyclopedia of philosophy* (2nd ed., Vol. 2, pp. 308–313). Detroit, MI: Macmillan Reference USA. Gale eBooks. Retrieved from https://link-galecom.myaccess.library.utoronto.ca/apps/doc/CX3446800385/GVRL?u=utoronto_main&sid=GVRL&xid=22c11acf

Williams, B. A. O. (2002). *Truth & truthfulness: An essay in genealogy*. Princeton, NJ: Princeton University Press.

Chapter 3

Macroauthorities and Microliteracies: The New Terrain of Information Politics

Bryan Alexander

Abstract

A continuum model helps us understand contemporary information politics. One end describes authority-centric approaches, including governments and digital corporations, while the other focuses on teaching individual skills and the understanding needed to grapple productively with the digital information ecosystem. The extremes represent opposed views of human agency, current information enterprises, and the nature of media. We apply this continuum to two examples, QAnon and COVID-19. Two instances attempt to connect the model's two poles. We conclude with a forecast of the continuum's viability and then project its application forward in education.

Keywords: Macroauthorities; microliteracies; information politics; media; QAnon; COVID-19

> Things are in the saddle,
> And ride mankind.
> –Ralph Waldo Emerson, *Ode, Inscribed to William H. Channing* (1846)

The modern era has seen the politics of information concerned with the proper structure of authority. The history of this is fairly well researched. Librarians, publishers, governments, and churches negotiated and fought to expand or delimit the extent to which authorities – including themselves – could shape access to information. Licensing, censorship, copyright, endorsement, professional training, custom, soft power campaigns, and the publication of content became tools in this contest. The rise of the networked digital technologies during the last third of the twentieth century saw authorities lose some ground as certain information control systems weakened or collapsed, while individual rights to information access and use expanded and supported by libraries, lawyers, demotic practice, and various

Media, Technology and Education in a Post-Truth Society, 29–37
Copyright © 2021 by Emerald Publishing Limited
All rights of reproduction in any form reserved
doi:10.1108/978-1-80043-906-120211003

instances of a libertarian ethos. The twenty-first century saw authority reasserted through a series of strategies and practices, including China's "Great Firewall," police forces using social media to track people, large corporations hosting content platforms with business models based on data-mining users, and organized campaigns of digital abuse tied to offline violence and political organizations. The politics of information are now transformed, located on a grand continuum of action and analysis anchored on the one end by macroscale authorities and on the other by appeals to individuals. As a result, contemporary discussions of information politics often turn on questions of large-scale authority.

In the following discussion, we will develop this continuum by articulating its foundational principles, and then trace its instantiation through a range of examples, concluding with gestures towards forecasting and education.

The appeal to large-scale authority draws on several causes, of which an emergent model of information as political actor looms largest. In 2020, we are increasingly anxious about populations dividing into dangerously opposed or actively warring factions based on their reliance on, and production of, separate sources of trusted information. This differs in many ways from the mass propaganda methods of a century past, in that the authorities are not so much producers of content as conduits for information, platforms upon which discussions can be held. They have a subtler power than that wielded by Goebbels or Mao. Information gatekeepers do their jobs too well, in a sense, not only straining out distrusted content but using that process to build another gate against a population. In this model, we prefer to exist within segmented echo chambers rather than living within unified societies sharing common authorities. Such schisms breed political instability and unrest. We can find examples of this in the United States and some European nations.

A related model focuses not on division but on a dark form of unity. Here, authoritarian politicians and states seek to organize information ecosystems into politically supportive mechanisms. This model has much in common with the preceding, since it is often predicated on dividing a domestic population into a good majority being abused by a villainous minority. Instances include: India, where Modi's government opposes a Hindu majority to a Muslim minority; Myanmar, with a government encouraging popular action against the Rohingya population; China, against the Falun Gong movement. China's government may have additional access to this political model concerning Uighurs.

Many responses to these perceived threats mirror them by taking the form of mobilizing authorities against individual actors and their information uses. Activists call for greater governmental regulation of for-profit digital enterprises to encourage them to actively monitor expressions they host, blocking some contents and creators (Mozilla Foundation, n.d.).

Critics of the Silicon Valley content business model (free plus data mining) urge users to return to directly and financially supporting media, especially in its traditional forms. Conservative attacks on news media have elicited additional calls to ally with what we just recently called legacy media. In this politics, artificial intelligence appears as another authority to be appealed to, or as a powerful tool authorities can use to reorganize information at a macroscale (Thompson, 2020).

Individual agency plays at best a subordinate role in this view. Instead information overrides a person's autonomy, rendering them passive, programming them. This understanding appears in political language when we hear constructions of videos radicalizing a person into jihad or families torn asunder by competing news organizations.

> [A] coordinated campaign… "used thousands of inauthentic assets to boost President Juan Orlando Hernandez of Honduras on a massive scale to mislead the Honduran people…"

> In the three years I've spent at Facebook, I've found multiple blatant attempts by foreign national governments to abuse our platform on vast scales to mislead their own citizenry…. (Silverman, Mac, & Dixit, 2020)

Here, individuals appear as not well educated. This does not refer to formal educational achievement, but to a given person's ability to be able to avoid manipulation by Facebook or the Partido Demokratiko Pilipino–Lakas ng Bayan. This politics cannot afford to trust individuals, since they are too often prey for these macroactors.

Therefore, individual choice and responsibility falls away as authoritative (and sometimes authoritarian) information becomes a causal force on its own. In this politics, we seek to defend individuals by trying to inflect the behavior of massive organizations in a way that echoes older pleas to royalty or divinity.

At the same time, we also see an opposing politics, one based on the individual. This draws on generations of civil liberties or libertarian thinking, which sought to maximize individual flourishing and potential. Corporate, state, or ecclesiastic power were often enemies, as they sought control and conformity. Gatekeepers were to be distrusted and bypassed or defanged. Common threads run from the twentieth century's major censorship trials over literature to the New Left's rejection of party discipline and Leninism, from John Perry Barlow's "A Declaration of the Independence of Cyberspace" (Barlow, 1996, February 8) to WikiLeaks and bitcoin.

The information literacy movement is another example of this politics, insofar as it teaches individual users or patrons or consumers (the terms are contested) how to seek, identify, and use information for their own purposes and through their own choices. It draws on decades of media literacy, which sought to empower media consumers to understand marketing and manipulation, but updates that field for the internet age. For example, the American Library Association describes this literacy in precisely individual terms:

> [I]nformation literacy is a set of abilities requiring individuals to "recognize when information is needed and have the ability to locate, evaluate, and use effectively the needed information." To be

information literate, then, one needs skills not only in research but in critical thinking. (American Library Association, 2020)

These are skills we need when gatekeepers have fallen away or become no longer trustworthy. In their stead, consumer and producer must learn the information on how to operate independently.

Similarly, the Association of College and Research Libraries' most recent and well developed information literacy document contains many descriptions of how that curriculum can empower individuals in their information activities. Their set of "dispositions" under the "Research as Inquiry" rubric concerns "asking increasingly complex or new questions whose answers in turn develop additional questions or lines of inquiry in any field." It addresses not groups or institutions, but:

Learners who are developing their information literate abilities.

- *Consider research as open-ended exploration and engagement with information;*
- *Appreciate that a question may appear to be simple but still disruptive and important to research;*
- *Value intellectual curiosity in developing questions and learning new investigative methods;*
- *Maintain an open mind and a critical stance;*
- *Value persistence, adaptability, and flexibility, and recognize that ambiguity can benefit the research process;*
- *Seek multiple perspectives during information gathering and assessment;*
- *Seek appropriate help when needed;*
- *Follow ethical and legal guidelines in gathering and using information;*
- *Demonstrate intellectual humility (i.e., recognize their own intellectual or experiential limitations).*[1]

This is an approach to information politics focused on individual minds moving through information spaces. It is diametrically opposed to the politics previously mentioned, which are predicated on large-scale authorities as the most important determinants of information.

We can find other cases of this politics, even without involving libraries or information literacy. Publisher (and, therefore, information gatekeeper and authority by definition!) Tim O'Reilly (2016) describes his process of determining if a given internet meme is truthful or not. The method involves Googling, checking with multiple sources, evaluating authorities, careful readings – in short, the learned behavior of an empowered individual.

Thus elaborated, we can understand and anticipate the interaction of these political extremes. The authority-oriented side sees fake news and organized disinformation as tools to successfully mobilize populations, while the individual side argues that its pedagogy and curriculum teach those groups to apprehend and see through manipulation. The gatekeeper end of the spectrum seeks to influence and improve authorities as they conduct information through the world, while the antigatekeeper end addresses itself to the people directly. Gatekeepers argue for the professional skills of their authorities, seeing them as finely honed, frequently tested, and better at navigating and shaping the modern information environment than the understanding a typical person may possess. Antigatekeepers point to the long record of information authorities failing to do their jobs well either through accident or willful collusion with less salubrious authorities. The progate side relies on curated information systems, such as the iTunes Store or expert-generated playlists. The proindividual tendency wants to share the most current knowledge about how to make the most of a wild media landscape.

There is a kind of democracy to the individual-oriented side of our spectrum, although not one necessarily bound to particular parties. There is an assumption of authority's rightful place in our attentions in the minds of their opponents, but that does not automatically make its partisans authoritarian. If we play this proposed spectrum against the classic left-right continuum, we can find pro- and antigatekeeper sides to both. For example, some contemporary liberals can call for governments to compel digital companies to control (i.e., monitor and censor) user content, while other progressives deem apparently trustworthy media enterprises to be handmaidens to imperialism and tyranny. As Chris Hedges (2016) puts it:

> The media landscape in America is dominated by "fake news." It has been for decades. This fake news does not emanate from the Kremlin. It is a multibillion-dollar-a-year industry that is skillfully designed and managed by public relations agencies, publicists and communications departments on behalf of individuals, government and corporations to manipulate public opinion. This propaganda industry stages pseudo-events to shape our perception of reality…
>
> Journalists long ago gave up trying to describe an objective world or give a voice to ordinary men and women. They became conditioned to cater to corporate demands.[2]

Indeed, the information politics spectrum we develop cuts across other political understandings. We can use the QAnon phenomenon as an example. Critics view it as a kind of mental infection, an information force that seizes minds, turning them into viral spreaders and perpetuating its sinister growth. People are prey in this view, corrupted, and controlled. There are also appeals to authority within the Q movement/worldview, starting with admiration for its titular if still unmasked interlocutor, powerful and knowledgeable. Q adherents also celebrate the leader of the world's most powerful nation, seeing him in a struggle with dark forces that are also large-scale authorities. In a sense we can see the Q world as a narrative about competing authorities, presidents battling intelligence agencies.

Yet this view blinds us to the atomized, even anarchic nature of the Q enterprise. It lacks any formal leader, since Q offers no pretense to rule or organization, and especially as content putatively published by Q himself has been swamped by fan creation. It may celebrate Donald Trump, but has to hope for his acknowledgment and symbolic support, rather than his deliberate leadership. There is no central authority for the movement, no Q HeadQuarters (QHQ). Instead, Q activists insist that interested people do their own research and come to their own conclusions. Obviously, they hope that such independent work will lead them to the movement, but such practice is a world removed from classic propaganda or even Google ad marketing.[3]

The coronavirus pandemic offers another example of this continuum in play. As of this writing, COVID-19 continues to wrack the world with upwards of 30 million infections and one million people dead.[4] The politics of information are very much in play. In terms of our continuum, many call for greater adherence to authorities in a dangerous time. Some call out a perceived flood of misleading or actively damaging information as an "infodemic."

> Fake news, misinformation, and conspiracy theories have become prevalent in the age of social media and have skyrocketed since the beginning of the COVID-19 pandemic. This situation is extremely concerning because it undermines trust in health institutions and programmes...

The logical call for action is to improve gatekeeping, both at the levels of institutions and individual thought:

> Immediate, coordinated action is needed from the global political, corporate, and scientific community to maintain the integrity and credibility of professional expertise and rebuild public trust. (The Lancet, 2020)

At the same time, we have seen a similar flood of information and tools aimed at individuals. The World Health Organization, Johns Hopkins University, and the Centers for Disease Control and Prevention have published reports, dashboards, updates, infographics, and advisories for public benefit. Elsevier and Wiley have made certain medical research available for free. The *Financial Times* and *The Chronicle of Higher Education* have similarly dropped paywalls for their COVID-19 coverage. This is an opposing strategy to that *The Lancet* calls for, an empowerment of individuals rather than a buttressing of institutions. To be sure, such sharing of open content can also be good for the sharers' reputations, constituting a kind of marketing, but to describe it solely as such would be to miss the very different information politics involved.

We can find cases where the two ends of our continuum bend towards each other. On a basic sense, both are connected, of course, in that large-scale organizations are made of people, a la Thomas Hobbes' sovereign or *Soylent Green*, and that individuals make choices to work in groups, which can scale up to massive levels. In a deeper sense, we can see attempts to bridge these opposites. For example, the early Obama administration called for a national information literacy celebration. The founding document sounds at times like it occupies the individualist end of our continuum, one very friendly to Barlow or Assange:

> We now live in a world where anyone can publish an opinion or perspective, whether true or not, and have that opinion amplified within the information marketplace. At the same time, Americans have unprecedented access to the diverse and independent sources of information, as well as institutions such as libraries and universities, that can help separate truth from fiction and signal from noise...

> The ability to seek, find, and decipher information can be applied to countless life decisions, whether financial, medical, educational, or technical.

Yet, this call is not solely for individual benefit. These empowered people then combine into a nation:

> An informed and educated citizenry is essential to the functioning of our modern democratic society, and I encourage educational and community institutions across the country to help Americans find and evaluate the information they seek, in all its forms.

In a sense, or at least in this case, information literacy produces large-scale interaction from the bottom up, rather than by seeking to protect persons by mobilizing macroorganizations from the top (Obama, 2009).

Journalist Jesse Walker offers another way of connecting both ends of our continuum. He argues in the libertarian vein that individuals have more power to discern truth within the information torrent than the authority-inclined side allows. Yet, he also sees some of these macroplatforms as flawed or even dangerous. Walker does not see this as a contradiction. Instead, individuals have new powers to navigate the new information landscape:

> The bad news is that Facebook is filled with bullshit. The good news is that we now have amped-up, networked bullshit detectors. No discussion of "fake news" will get anywhere unless it takes both of those facts into account...

> This may be the first time in human history when a whispering campaign can come with footnotes. Rumors are undeniably resilient, but they are far easier to trace, track, and debunk now than they were when Franklin Roosevelt or Al Smith was running for president. (Walker, 2016)

Walker may be pointing to a new synthesis here, where the two opposed ends of the emerging information politics spectrum connect. At the least, there is a description available, if not a prescription, allowing us to see and think through individuals moving thoughtfully through a fraught environment.

If this authority-versus-individual continuum model has any descriptive power for the information environment of our time, we should be able to deploy it in the service of forecasting. Looking ahead to the next decade, the continuum tells us to expect both polar extremes in operation, as well as their occasionally dialectical interaction. There will be more calls to establish, celebrate, protect, and reform large-scale authorities as they shape and interact with information, which we can view as an extension of progatekeeping thought. Such politics will evolve with political and technological developments. For instance, as virtual and extended reality content production ramps up, it is likely we will see competing publishers appear, along with aggregators and censors, both independent as well as located within larger authoritative organizations. The calls for authority should also experience uneven success. They do, after all, address a heterogenous set of macrolevel institutions. We have already seen examples of such unevenness in American attitudes towards information and content "control," which sees that nation's residents more favorably disposed towards businesses performing that function than the federal government (Mitchell, Grieco, & Sumida, 2018). At the same time, information literacy will likely extend to address virtual reality/extended reality (VR/XR), teaching individuals how to seek, identify, and use content in that medium. There will be a politics of evading or resisting these new, virtual world authorities.

We should also expect to see this continuum continue to play out in the education space. Information literacy's individual emphasis is already established, especially in libraries. Its opposite is also present in the forms of teaching students to respect authorities or to dread certain macroprojects: Wikipedia, *Fox News*, the Murdoch empire, advertising in general, etc. Do educators see students as capable of being practical, even wise navigators of the 21st century's information environment? Or does schooling seek to protect students from a terrifying space that threatens to warp minds into deplorable attitudes and behaviors? In the information politics of education, we can perceive a microcosm of a broader, global struggle.

Notes

1. "Framework for Information Literacy for Higher Education," Association of College and Research Libraries, filed by the ACRL Board on February 2, 2015, adopted by the ACRL Board, January 11, 2016, http://www.ala.org/acrl/standards/ilframework.
2. The classic account is Edward S. Herman and Noam Chomsky, *Manufacturing Consent: The Political Economy of the Mass Media*, New York, NY: Pantheon Books: 1988.
3. NB: Please do not interpret this discussion to see the author as supporting Q.
4. See https://coronavirus.jhu.edu/.

References

American Library Association. (2020). Information literacy. Retrieved from https://literacy.ala.org/information-literacy/

Barlow, J. P. (1996, February 8). *A declaration of the independence of cyberspace*. San Francisco, CA: Electronic Frontier Foundation. Retrieved from https://www.eff.org/cyberspace-independence

Hedges, C. (2016). 'Fake news' in America: Homegrown, and far from new. Retrieved from https://www.truthdig.com/articles/fake-news-in-america-homegrown-and-far-from-new/

Mitchell, A., Grieco, E., & Sumida, N. (2018). Americans favor protecting information freedoms over government steps to restrict false news online. Retrieved from https://www.journalism.org/2018/04/19/americans-favor-protecting-information-freedoms-over-government-steps-to-restrict-false-news-online/

Mozilla Foundation. (n.d.). Facebook: Stop group recommendations. Retrieved from https://foundation.mozilla.org/en/campaigns/facebook-stop-group-recommendations/

Obama, B. (2009). National information literacy, 2009, by the president of the United States of America. Retrieved from https://web.archive.org/web/20121021192357/http://www.whitehouse.gov/assets/documents/2009literacy_prc_rel.pdf

O'Reilly, T. (2016). How I detect fake news - Tim O'reilly. Retrieved from https://medium.com/@timoreilly/how-i-detect-fake-news-ebe455d9d4a7#.ddf5w6sgd

Silverman, C., Mac, R., & Dixit, P. (2020). Whistleblower says Facebook ignored global political manipulation. Retrieved from https://www.buzzfeednews.com/article/craigsilverman/facebook-ignore-political-manipulation-whistleblower-memo

The Lancet. (2020). The COVID-19 infodemic. *The Lancet Infectious Diseases, 20*(8), 875. doi:10.1016/s1473-3099(20)30565-x

Thompson, C. (2020). YouTube's plot to silence conspiracy theories. Retrieved from https://www.wired.com/story/youtube-algorithm-silence-conspiracy-theories/

Walker, J. (2016). "Fake news" is easier to trace and debunk than ever before. Retrieved from https://reason.com/2016/11/22/fake-news-is-easier-to-trace-and-debunk/

Chapter 4

The Learning Challenge in the Twenty-first Century*

Harry Anthony Patrinos

Abstract

Truth matters; and the norms associated with a democratic society, such as the common good, responsibility, ethics, and civic engagement, are under attack with the emergence of the post-truth society. There are concerns worldwide that public education is failing us on pushing back on disinformation. Schools are not seen as developing skills that permit students to adequately differentiate truth from nontruths. In this context, the education system also faces some unprecedented challenges. The quality of education in most of the world is low, and only slowly improving. Also, future workers are concerned with automation's threat – or perceived threat – to jobs. In most countries, education systems are not providing workers with the skills necessary to compete in today's job markets. The growing mismatch between demand and supply of skills holds back economic growth and undermines opportunity. At the same time, the financial returns to schooling are high in most countries, and growing skill premiums are evident in much of the world. Schooling remains a good economic and social investment, and there are record numbers of children in school today. The skills that matter in the coming technological revolution are likely the same as what is needed in a media environment of disinformation. More and better education, and noncognitive skills, will not only prepare students for the future world of work; they will also prepare them to navigate the increasingly complex post-truth society.

---

*This is an updated version of a paper by the same name, published by the author in April 2020 as a World Bank Policy Research Working Paper No. 9214, Available at SSRN: https://ssrn.com/abstract=3575178. The essay is also based on the author's remarks at the Understanding the Post-truth Society Conference in Valletta, Malta, 11 October 2019. The author thanks participants at the conference for comments, as well as Alex Grech, Simon Thacker, and Gustavo Arcia. The views expressed here are those of the author and should not be attributed to the World Bank Group.

Media, Technology and Education in a Post-Truth Society, 39–53
doi:10.1108/978-1-80043-906-120211004

They will be able to detect fake news – or deliberate disinformation spread through news or online media. It will also allow young people to gain trust. In other words, better education is democratizing, to the extent that it promotes truth, values, and civic engagement.

Keywords: post-truth; education 4.0; automation; learning; skills; noncognitive skills

Truth matters; and the norms associated with a democratic society, such as the common good, responsibility, ethics, and civic engagement, are under attack with the emergence of the post-truth society. There are concerns worldwide that public education is failing us on pushing back on disinformation. Schools are not seen as developing skills that permit students to adequately differentiate truth from nontruths.

The education system also faces some unprecedented challenges. The quality of education in most of the world is low, and only slowly improving. Also, future workers are concerned with automation's threat – or perceived threat – to jobs. In most countries, education systems are not providing workers with the skills necessary to compete in today's job markets. The growing mismatch between demand and supply of skills holds back economic growth and undermines opportunity.

The skills that matter in the coming technological revolution are likely the same as what is needed in a media environment of disinformation. More and better education, and noncognitive skills, will not only prepare students for the future world of work; they will also prepare them to navigate the increasingly complex post-truth society. They will be able to detect fake news – or deliberate disinformation spread through news or online media. It will also allow young people to gain trust. In other words, better education is democratizing, to the extent that it promotes truth, values, and civic engagement.

The Challenge

The twentieth century, and especially the last half, was an education revolution. There are more people in school today than ever before. We will soon reach convergence on years of schooling in the coming decades. In nearly all countries, though to varying degrees, educational progress has lagged for groups that are disadvantaged due to low income, gender, disability or ethnic, and/or linguistic affiliation. In 1950, the average level of schooling was 6 years in advanced countries; it is more than 10 years today. It was less than 2 years in Africa in 1950; it is more than 5 years today. East Asia went from 2 to 7 years between 1950 and 2010: this is a more than 200% increase. Globally, in 1900 the average level of education was less than 2 years of schooling; it was still only 2 years by 1950; but it increased to more than 7 years by 2000 and it is projected to reach 10 years by 2050. This is a more than fivefold increase in a century and a half (Barro & Lee, 2013).

There are many benefits to investing in education. They include social benefits. They also include economic or financial benefits. One very concrete and comparable, as well as measurable, benefit is the wage impact. That is, as one completes more years of schooling or earns a degree or certificate, their earnings increase relative to what they would have been without that investment. And since we forego earnings in order to study, then one can say we are investing in ourselves. As we know, an investment can result in a financial rate of return (just like investing in anything else, such as the stock market, bonds, housing, and so on). In fact, it is estimated that every year of schooling raises earnings by 9% a year over a lifetime (Psacharopoulos & Patrinos, 2018). A university degree has a rate of return of 15%. These are truly high returns and they have remained high over time. They are high during periods of economic growth as wages rise. They are high during periods of financial distress when foregone earnings are lower.

Despite the revolution in access to school there is still an enrollment problem. According to UNESCO there are more than 290 million children and youth out of school for the school year ending in 2020.[1] In 2018, UNESCO had estimated that the then total of 260 million included 59 million children of primary school age, 62 million of lower secondary school age, and 138 million of upper secondary age.[2]

Even more importantly, there are another 260 million children in school but who cannot read (UNESCO). This is particularly worrying. Also, according to UNESCO, 1 in 4 young people in developing countries are unable to read. The World Bank recently released its learning poverty estimates.[3] Learning poverty means being unable to read and understand a simple text by age 10. It is estimated that more than half of the world's 10-year-olds are in learning poverty. The Bank has also estimated the gaps in learning outcomes between countries and regions of the world as part of its Human Capital Project. The harmonized learning outcomes show the gap between highest performers in the world (in East Asia, Europe, and North America) and the lowest performers (mostly low-income countries) to be 2 to 3 standard deviations (Patrinos & Angrist, 2018). While these are technical terms, they mean that almost the entirety of low-income countries' education outcomes are eliminated once the quality of learning is considered. In other words, there is not much learning taking place in low-income developing countries (Angrist, Djankov, Goldberg, & Patrinos, 2019). The situation is only slightly better in middle-income countries.

The types of skills being demanded are changing. There is more demand now for analytic and nonroutine skills, and less demand for manual skills. In other words, the skills demanded are more complex. This puts a premium on learning (Autor, Levy, & Murnane, 2003; Autor & Price, 2013). It is also found that the labor market is increasingly rewarding social skills; that is, jobs requiring high levels of social interaction. Employment and wage growth were particularly strong for jobs requiring high levels of both math skill and social skills. This is because in a world where machines will undertake more of the routine skills, there will be a premium for social skills which reduce coordination costs and allow workers to work together more efficiently (Deming, 2017). Higher social skills lead to higher wages because they reduce the cost of trading tasks with other workers, allowing one to specialize in their most productive tasks and trade output with others. Thus, there is a premium to team-based work and teamwork, all made easier with social skills.

This is a reversal from what occurred during most of the twentieth century. As countries built their education systems and the population received more schooling, the economic benefits were realized. These included national economic growth and private returns to schooling. The increases in schooling levels also promoted equity as wage gaps declined. This occurred when the increase of educated workers was higher than the demand for them. This had the effect of boosting income for most people and lowering inequality. An influential summary of the state of the art concluded that "higher average levels of schooling exert an equalizing effect on income distribution" (Psacharopoulos, 1977; Psacharopoulos & Marin, 1976; Winegarden, 1979). The Nobel Prize–winning economist Jan Tinbergen (1974) argued that skill-biased technological progress – with its consequences for income inequality – necessitates an important role for education in mediating the demand for higher order skills.

However, since about 1980, it is argued that educational supply is no longer meeting educational demand. Since much of the disconnect is because of skill-biased technological change, then this has been referred to as the race between education and technology (Tinbergen, 1974; Goldin & Katz, 2009). Education no longer seems to have the mediating effects. If there is no change in the supply of education – its quality, that is – then the net effect could be a rise in inequality. Those with lower levels of education and especially lower quality of schooling will be at a distinct disadvantage.

The Automation Challenge

In 2017, the Japanese insurance company, Fukoku Mutual Life Insurance, replaced 34 human insurance claim workers with IBM Watson Explorer (McCurry, 2017). The artificial intelligence (AI) will scan hospital records and other documents to determine insurance payouts, factoring injuries, patient medical histories, and procedures administered. Automation of these research and data gathering tasks will help the remaining human workers process the final payout faster. Fukoku Mutual will spend $1.7 million to install the AI system, and $128,000 per year for maintenance. The company saves roughly $1.1 million per year on employee salaries by using the IBM software, meaning it hopes to see a return on the investment in less than two years. Watson AI is expected to improve productivity by 30%.

Though an isolated case, it is not expected to be the last. What is also interesting is that it is highly educated, white collar, workers that are being targeted. The immediate cost savings are also reason to believe we will see more of this in the years to come.

As already mentioned, technological change heralds a renewed race between the supply and demand for schooling, or between education and technology. The ability of workers to compete is handicapped by the poor performance of education systems in most developing countries (Barro & Lee, 2015). The returns to schooling are high in most developing countries, and growing skill premiums are evident in much of the world (Montenegro & Patrinos, 2014). In high-performing economies, such as those in East Asia, we may have reached the limits of the industrial model and what once worked for developed countries may not work for developing countries. Automation implies deskilling in many aspects and a need for new skills for many (Bentaouet Kattan, Macdonald, & Patrinos, 2018).

The coming automation – robots, machines, and AI – will become increasingly relevant. More and more jobs will become targets. Therefore, the risk or perceived risk that your job is likely to be automated will increase.

That is not to say that all AI is negative. There are proponents who say that increased automation and AI will solve many of our problems. The collective intelligence of humanity will increase, and we will live longer, healthier, and more satisfying lives (Kurzweil, 2005). In a 1930 essay, the economist John Maynard Keynes (1932) argued that automation will lead us to a life of leisure because of increases in productivity and a 15-hour work week.

The technological singularity (also, simply, "the singularity") is the hypothesis that the invention of artificial superintelligence will abruptly trigger runaway technological growth, resulting in unfathomable changes to human civilization. According to this hypothesis, an upgradable intelligent agent (such as a computer running software-based artificial general intelligence) would enter a "runaway reaction" of self-improvement cycles, with each new and more intelligent generation appearing more and more rapidly, causing an intelligence explosion and resulting in a powerful superintelligence that would, qualitatively, far surpass all human intelligence. Vernor Vinge (1993), who coined the term *technological singularity*, argued that this would signal the end of the human era. More recently, Stephen Hawking (2016) warned about AI.

Whatever the likely long-term effects, there is still the concern about jobs. While the threat may be perceived or overblown, it is nevertheless true that automation implies deskilling in many aspects and a need for new skills for many, especially for workers in developing countries. The ability of both current and future workers to compete is handicapped by the poor performance of education systems in most developing countries (Acemoglu & Restrepo, 2018; Bentaouet Kattan et al., 2018). Whether automation means the elimination of jobs – or according to more optimistic economists – the creation of new jobs, recent technological developments imply large disruption to the labor market (Frey & Osborne, 2017).

It is estimated that a large number of occupations in East Asia are prone to automation, having a 50% or higher probability of being automated (Bentaouet Kattan et al., 2018). With this estimate of the probability of being in an "automation-safe occupation" we can also see other characteristics of being "safe." There are occupations that are more likely to be impacted upon by automation, namely those based on repetitive and routine tasks. Other tasks are complemented by automation, meaning that the worker becomes more productive.

Who is less likely to be negatively affected by automation? It turns out that education has an important role to play. Those with more education are less likely to be in jobs that are easy to automate. Skills also matter. Those with higher scores on cognitive achievement tests are also more likely to be immune to jobs that might be automated. In fact, the higher the cognitive score, the safer the worker is.

There is a high value-added in this regard with postsecondary education. That is, those workers with higher-order cognitive skills and in possession of a postsecondary education have the lowest probability of being in an automation-prone occupation.

One implication for education systems is to put everyone through university. However, this would be extremely costly. A more affordable option would be to improve the cognitive skills of those with basic and secondary education. But that could be expensive, too, and it would also require fundamental changes to the education system and further investment into what works to improve learning outcomes.

One thing we need less of is vocational studies. It turns out that school-based, preemployment, publicly provided vocational education deemphasizes cognitive skills. Those are precisely the skills that are needed to improve one's chances of obtaining a good job that is less likely prone to automation. Those in vocational secondary have substantially lower cognitive skills according to an analysis using PISA data (Bentaouet Kattan et al., 2018).

Also of importance are so-called noncognitive skills, or socioemotional skills, which include the "Big 5" personality traits of extraversion, conscientiousness, openness to experience, emotional stability, and agreeableness (Heckman, 2011). There is evidence that noncognitive skills – particularly openness to experience – are positively associated with being in a nonautomation-prone occupation (Bentaouet Kattan et al., 2018). Also, vocational education programs tend to emphasize technical skills over cognitive *and* noncognitive skills, placing such graduates at a further disadvantage. Frey and Osborne (2017) and Brynjolfsson and McAfee (2014) find that noncognitive skills such as creativity, social intelligence, and advanced perception will be humans' comparative advantage over machines given current technological trends.

Implications for Education Systems

Education systems are faced with the double challenge of improving the quality of education to make it relevant to the labor market given the automation challenge and giving students the ability to navigate the post-truth society. As daunting as that challenge might be, it turns out that the solution to both problems is more and better education. The challenge, however, is that this is expensive and difficult. At the same time, governments have to increase educational attainment, improve cognitive skills, and teach noncognitive skills. These are expensive and difficult tasks, and the evidence base on how to improve noncognitive skills is limited.

The labor market returns to schooling are high and this alone justifies expanding access to education. For compulsory schooling, the guidance is clear. It is the government's responsibility to finance schooling. At the higher education and postcompulsory levels, the onus is not on government to fully provide and finance it, but certainly to put in place the conditions for increasing access to quality opportunities. This is an area where financial innovations make sense. There are options for governments, such as using the evidence from labor market returns to education to implement financial innovations – and use future earnings to finance higher education (Bentaouet Kattan et al., 2018). High returns suggest it makes sense to expand higher education – but in an equitable and sustainable manner.

In terms of increasing cognitive skills, the task is difficult, and developing countries lag far behind. Yet, we know how to do it. Education systems that do well prepare children early on, reform continuously, and use information for improvement. There is a need to focus on basic skills, early development, and to measure and improve early reading. High-performing East Asian countries offer some useful lessons (World Bank, 2018). These include: (1) aligning institutions to ensure basic conditions for learning in place in all schools; (2) concentrating effective, equity-minded public spending on basic education, including the channeling of public resources to schools and districts that are falling behind; (3) ensuring children are ready to learn in school; (4) selecting and supporting teachers throughout their careers to allow them to focus on the classroom, starting with raising the selectiveness of who becomes a teacher; and (5) assessing students to diagnose issues and inform instruction.

However, since automation implies deskilling and a need for new skills then many current workers would need opportunities to learn. It is important to give opportunities to workers to invest in relevant skills for the labor market that make them benefit from, and remain immune to, automation.

While there is some emerging evidence on how to improve social skills for creativity (Sanchez Puerta, Valerio, & Gutierrez Bernal, 2016), the psychology literature shows little consensus on how to define or teach it (Beghetto & Kaufman, 2014). There are few empirical studies on how to improve it (Grigorenko, Jarvin, Tan, & Sternberg, 2008). However, new methods of measuring creativity in terms of divergent thinking have been developed (Plucker & Makel, 2010) opening the way for more empirical work. Nevertheless, countries need to figure out how to invest in relevant skills (see Fig. 4.1). These include: problem-solving skills to think critically and analyze; learning to learn skills in order to acquire new knowledge throughout a lifetime; communication skills including reading and writing;

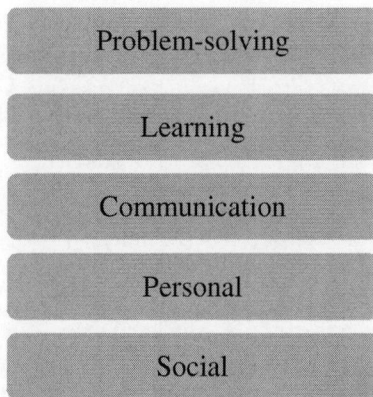

Problem-solving

Learning

Communication

Personal

Social

Fig. 4.1.   The Skills That Matter. *Source:* Patrinos (2016).

personal skills for self-management, making sound judgments and managing risks – extremely relevant in the post-truth age where people need to be able to tell fact from fiction; and social skills for collaboration, teamwork, management, leadership, and conflict resolution (Patrinos, 2016).

More and better education, and noncognitive skills, will not only prepare students for the future world of work but also prepare them to navigate the increasingly complex post-truth society. They will be able to detect fake news – deliberate disinformation spread through news or online media. It will also allow young people to gain trust. The ability to make sense of information from multiple sources is a challenge. It is particularly difficult to distinguish between useful information and mistruths from online sources. A study found that many young people are not able to evaluate information that flows through social media channels (Wineburg, McGrew, Breakstone, & Ortega, 2016). The ability to identify reliable information is a global competence that the OECD has developed a framework for. It requires people to triangulate information by seeking confirmation from multiple sources and be able to evaluate the validity of news and information. PISA 2018 results show that students in East Asia are better at distinguishing a fact from an opinion than other high-performing countries. This is from the reading test in PISA 2018 that includes an assessment of the ability to tell whether a source is credible (Schleicher, 2019). In PISA terms, the ability to differentiate between fact and opinion is at level five or above on PISA's six levels of reading proficiency. On average across all countries, 7% of 15-year-olds achieve a level five, and just 1.3% get up to level six. For Singapore, the percentage of top performers is triple that of the OECD average; that is, 26% of students achieved a level five or above, with 7.3% reaching level six (Civinini, 2019). In other words, better education is democratizing, to the extent that it promotes truth, values, and civic engagement. At the same time, globalization and automation mean it is now more important than ever that schools focus on developing student's creativity (Beard, 2018).

COVID-19 presents a challenge. The spreading of false or inaccurate information – mis- or disinformation – is a serious threat to public health during the pandemic (Laato, Islam, Islam, & Whelan, 2020). The spreading of such misinformation could result in the lack of adherence to recommended public health measures, or engagement in nonrecommended behaviors. The World Health Organization (WHO) Response Strategy specifically identifies tackling the COVID-19 "infodemic" as a research priority. The two most widely viewed cable news shows in the United States are Hannity and Tucker Carlson Tonight, both on Fox News. While Carlson warned his viewers about the threat posed by COVID-19 since early February 2020, Hannity dismissed the risks then changed his position by late February. A new study shows that Hannity's viewers changed behavior in response to COVID-19 later than other Fox News viewers, while Carlson's viewers changed behavior earlier (Bursztyn, Rao, Roth, & Yanagizawa-Drott, 2020). In fact, FOX news viewership is causally associated with decreased practice of social distancing during the early stages of the COVID-19 pandemic. Simonov, Sacher, Dubé, and Biswas (2020) show that a 1% point increase in cable viewership reduces the propensity to stay at home by 8.9% points compared to the prepandemic average. This is one case of misinformation driving health behavior during a pandemic.

There are others. In Brazil, when the president publicly dismissed the risks associated with COVID-19, the social distancing measures of citizens in progovernment localities declined compared to those places in which support is weaker (Ajzenman, Cavalcanti, & Da Mata, 2020).

Education plays a role. In fact, a lack of education seems to be associated with the wrong ideas about the pandemic. In a Pew Research Center poll that asks Americans if COVID-19 was made in a laboratory, nearly 3 in 10 people do believe it (Schaeffer, 2020). However, those who are more educated are less likely to believe in this conspiracy. In Jordan, belief in conspiracy related to COVID-19 is associated with a lower educational level (Sallam et al., 2020). One obvious solution is to raise education levels; that will take time. Another solution is to train people specifically about health risks.

In fact, the health literacy component of a large-scale adult literacy program in South Africa yielded measurable outcomes and proved that the intervention had enabled adults to better understand health messages (Lopes & McKay, 2020). However, it is important that beneficiaries of such information have at least a basic level of literacy and numeracy skills to enable them to receive and act on vital information during a pandemic or disaster (Lopes & McKay, 2020). Thus, it is important that efforts to reduce the impact of disinformation build on lifelong learning systems.

Literacy and numeracy are important, fundamental building blocks. But computers are going to be far better than humans at processing these forms of explicit knowledge. This means that it is important to also build the skills that AI cannot emulate. Such noncognitive, socioemotional skills are also the types of skills that will serve young people well as they deal with disinformation and build trust in society. Empathy, agreeableness, and openness will serve them very well. Since machines will be better at routine, codifiable tasks according to a set of rules; then people need to become better at open-ended tasks that require flexibility, creativity, and judgment. These include skills to promote social interaction.

Education 4.0?

We have all heard of Industry 4.0 or the Fourth Industrial Revolution, popularized by the World Economic Forum.[4] It's useful to contrast that to what is happening in education. If Education 1.0 is the traditional schoolhouse, with a teacher and students, then we might think of 2.0 as the education system with collaboration, more use of technology, and the teacher as facilitator. Education 3.0 might be the world of connected learning, personalized instruction, and open access. Then Education 4.0 is a system of lifelong learning driven by autonomy and purpose; that is, just in time learning, ubiquitous, and available to all (Vander Ark, 2017).

While there is already evidence that lifelong learning raises productivity and earnings (Desjardins, 2016; Dorsett, Lui, & Weale, 2010), it will become more critical to our lives, community, and society in the future, post-truth society. It contributes towards making people well rounded and to be able to leverage knowledge (Drucker, 1992).

Therefore, economic necessity and the need to disentangle truth from nontruth has become a necessity, making lifelong learning imperative (World Bank, 2003). In today's labor market, people need to learn how to learn, to relearn, unlearn, and learn again (Patrinos, 2020). There are also significant health benefits. Research suggests the importance of implementing lifelong learning and early cognitive training to prevent a mental decline in older adults, and early interventions in the adult age can serve as a preventive tool to promote brain rewiring and neuroplasticity so that learning would improve. It could also impact the decline of Alzheimer's disease, isolation, and depression in older adults (Hertzog, Kramer, Wilson, & Lindenberger, 2008). Further, there is evidence that different types of dementia cause different types of damage to the brain and at different rates for different people (Ray & Davidson, 2014), and lifetime intellectual enrichment appears to delay the onset of cognitive impairment and dementia (Vemuri et al., 2014). For example, a study looking at people genetically predisposed to Alzheimer's disease (Vemuri et al. 2014) showed that lifelong intellectual activities help to delay the onset of this type of dementia.

Going forward, we will be able to use AI to produce individualized learning. It might be too expensive to do that now, but in the future costs could be much lower, thus making it possible to use it on a wide scale.

In the meantime, promoting more and better education – to produce critical thinkers – will be expensive. For basic education, we need to become more efficient. For postsecondary education, we need to use innovative financing, especially to promote lifelong learning. This means new sources of financing, including income-contingent loan programs, and individualized learning accounts (Chapman, 2006; Findeisen & Sachs, 2016; Oosterbeek & Patrinos, 2009; Palacios, 2003). Essentially, income contingency means using future earnings to pay for today's education. One only starts paying back once they reach a certain income level. This is a system introduced in Australia in 1986 which has spread to many more countries today. It could also be used for lifelong learning. Financing university, postsecondary and lifelong learning is key for equity, sustainability, quality, and efficiency.

Summing up, the priorities for countries to invest in their people in order to make them compete in the twenty-first-century world of work and be able to navigate the post-truth society are as follows:

(1) *Focus on basic skills first* – this means a sound foundation of solid reading skills. This is what top performers did/do very well, including European leaders such as Estonia and Finland and East Asian stars such as Japan, Korea, and Singapore.

(2) Raise the productivity of schooling – this means raising the value-added of teaching/learning. High performers and the most improved countries (in terms of internationally comparable student achievement scores) do this very well. For example, in Vietnam, primary school children learn about twice as much

as comparable students in other developing, middle-income countries such as Peru (Singh, 2019).

(3) Teach relevant skills – namely, problem-solving, learning to learn, communications, personal management, and social skills (see Fig. 4.1 above; Patrinos, 2016).

(4) Avoid early specialization – since the jobs of the future are unknown and people will change jobs more frequently, then it is difficult to predict what precise job skills one will need. Education systems that select students early into vocational streams are not likely to be able to prepare people for the world of work of the future. Early selection into vocational studies is associated with lower academic scores, lower lifetime earnings, and more likely to put people at risk of automation. This is primarily because such programs deemphasize the cognitive skills that one needs for the world of work – and most likely needed for navigating the post-truth reality.

(5) Finance higher education – including using evidence from labor market returns to education to implement financial innovations such as using future earnings to finance higher education (Patrinos, 2016). These programs would allow more students to receive a higher education and make it more financially sustainable for the country. It also means creating a "new" source of education finance – namely, future earnings paid back based on income contingency – which promotes sustainability, effectiveness, equity, and fairness. It would also allow for higher levels of education, which means more protection from automation and better ability to navigate the post-truth society.

What Should Future Research Focus on?

We still need to learn more about *how to* raise the productivity of schooling. While it is recognized that high-performing systems manage to teach their students more in each period, it is still not clear how this is done, other than having good teachers, well-managed classrooms, and prepared students. All of these are investments. But we need more evidence on which elements exactly work to improve the quality of education. There are good techniques for imparting reading skills quickly in the early primary years, but less is known about how to accelerate learning in the secondary school years. This is especially a challenge for disadvantaged populations.

It is imperative that we impart relevant skills. The investment in relevant skills includes: problem-solving skills to think critically and analyze; learning to learn skills in order to acquire new knowledge throughout a lifetime; communication skills including reading and writing; personal skills for self-management, making sound judgments, and managing risks; and social skills for collaboration, teamwork, management, leadership, and conflict resolution. The question, however, is how to do it and how to do it cost-effectively. As well as how to incorporate these skills into the existing school curriculum.

While the digital age gives us new problems such as the post-truth phenomenon, it also imparts new opportunities. To improve learning outcomes and combat fake news we need to use technology effectively. The questions are: How to promote the good use of technology for improving learning? How to use technology to enhance learning outcomes and teach youth how to think critically? and How to complement the teaching–learning experience?

Finally, since we need to expand education, including higher education, then we need to improve the current methods of financing education. Beyond the compulsory level, it is worthwhile to explore new and innovative finance programs such as income contingent loan payments or income share agreements. These might also be used for lifelong learning. These programs work best in advanced economies with robust taxation systems (for repayment).

Notes

1. See https://en.unesco.org/news/290-million-students-out-school-due-covid-19-unesco-releases-first-global-numbers-and-mobilizes.
2. See http://uis.unesco.org/en/topic/out-school-children-and-youth.
3. See https://www.worldbank.org/en/topic/education/brief/learning-poverty.
4. Industry 1.0 refers to the first industrial revolution. Industry 2.0 is the second industrial revolution (1870–1914). The third industrial revolution occurred in the late twentieth century, also known as the digital revolution. Industry 4.0 is the next stage, comprising the link between cyber and human systems.

References

Acemoglu, D., & Restrepo, P. (2018). The race between man and machine: Implications of technology for growth, factor shares, and employment. *American Economic Review, 108*(6), 1488–1542.

Ajzenman, N., Cavalcanti, T., & Da Mata, D. (2020). More than words: Leaders' speech and risky behavior during a pandemic. Available at SSRN 3582908.

Angrist, N., Djankov, S., Goldberg, P. K., & Patrinos, H. A. (2019). *Measuring human capital*. World Bank Policy Research Working Paper No. 8742. World Bank Group, Washington, DC.

Autor, D. H., Levy, F., & Murnane, R. J. (2003). The skill content of recent technological change: An empirical exploration. *The Quarterly Journal of Economics, 118*(4), 1279–1333.

Autor, D. H., & Price, B. (2013). *The changing task composition of the US labor market: An update of Autor, Levy, and Murnane (2003)*. MIT Working Paper, Massachusetts Institute of Technology, June.

Barro, R., & Lee, J. W. (2013). A new data set of educational attainment in the world, 1950-2010. *Journal of Development Economics, 104*, 184–198.

Barro, R., & Lee, J. W. (2015). *Education matters: Global schooling Gains from the 19th to the 21st century*. New York, NY: Oxford University Press.

Beard, A. (2018). *Natural born learners: Our incredible capacity to learn and how we can harness it*. Paris: Hachette UK.

Beghetto, R. A., & Kaufman, J. C. (2014). Classroom contexts for creativity. *High Ability Studies, 25*(1), 53–69.

Bentaouet Kattan, R., Macdonald, K. A. D., & Patrinos, H. A. (2018). *Automation and labor market outcomes: The pivotal role of high-quality education.* World Bank Policy Research Working Paper No. 8474. World Bank Group, Washington, DC.

Brynjolfsson, E., & McAfee, A. (2014). *The second machine age: Work, progress, and prosperity in a time of brilliant technologies.* New York, NY; London: W.W. Norton & Company.

Bursztyn, L., Rao, A., Roth, C., & Yanagizawa-Drott, D. (2020). Misinformation during a pandemic. Working Paper (2020-44). University of Chicago, Becker Friedman Institute for Economics, Chicago, IL.

Chapman, B. (2006). Income contingent loans for higher education: International reforms. *Handbook of the Economics of Education, 2,* 1435–1503.

Civinini, C. (2019). Students in East Asia are better at distinguishing a fact from an opinion than UK students, the latest programme for international student assessment results show. Web Blog Post. *Times Educational Supplement.* Retrieved from https://www.tes.com/news/chinese-students-better-spotting-fake-news-pisa

Deming, D. J. (2017). The growing importance of social skills in the labor market. *The Quarterly Journal of Economics, 132*(4), 1593–1640.

Desjardins, R. (2016). Employment and the labour market. In T. Schuller, K. Rubenson, & S. Brink (Eds.), *Third global report on adult learning and education.* Hamburg: UNESCO Institute of Lifelong Learning (UIL).

Dorsett, R., Lui, S., & Weale, M. (2010). *Economic benefits of lifelong learning.* National Institute of Economic and Social Research, NIESR Discussion Papers.

Drucker, P. (1992). *The age of discontinuity.* New York, NY: Routledge.

Findeisen, S., & Sachs, D. (2016). Education and optimal dynamic taxation: The role of income-contingent student loans. *Journal of Public Economics, 138,* 1–21.

Frey, C. B., & Osborne, M. A. (2017). The future of employment: How susceptible are jobs to computerisation?. *Technological Forecasting and Social Change, 114,* 254–280.

Goldin, C. D., & Katz, L. F. (2009). *The race between education and technology.* Cambridge, MA; London: Harvard University Press.

Grigorenko, E. L., Jarvin, L., Tan, M., & Sternberg, R. J. (2008). Something new in the garden: Assessing creativity in academic domains. *Psychology Science Quarterly, 50,* 295–307.

Hawking, S. (2016). This is the most dangerous time for our planet. *The Guardian.* Retrieved from https://www.theguardian.com/commentisfree/2016/dec/01/stephen-hawking-dangerous-time-planet-inequality

Heckman, J. J. (2011). *Integrating personality psychology into economics.* National Bureau of Economic Research Working Paper No. 17378.

Hertzog, C., Kramer, A. F., Wilson, R. S., & Lindenberger, U. (2008). Enrichment effects on adult cognitive development: Can the functional capacity of older adults Be preserved and enhanced? *Psychological Science in the Public Interest, 9*(1), 1–65.

Keynes, J. M. (1932). Economic possibilities for our grandchildren (1930). In J. M. Keynes (Ed.), *Essays in persuasion* (pp. 358–373). New York, NY: Harcourt, Brace.

Kurzweil, R. (2005). *The singularity is near: When humans transcend biology.* New York, NY: Viking.

Laato, S., Islam, A. N., Islam, M. N., & Whelan, E. (2020). What drives unverified information sharing and cyberchondria during the COVID-19 pandemic? *European Journal of Information Systems, 29,* 1–18.

Lopes, H., & McKay, V. (2020). Adult learning and education as a tool to contain pandemics: The COVID-19 experience. *International Review of Education*, 66, 575–602. doi:10.1007/s11159-020-09843-0

McCurry, J. (2017). Japanese company replaces office workers with artificial intelligence. *The Guardian*. Retrieved from https://www.theguardian.com/technology/2017/jan/05/japanese-company-replaces-office-workers-artificial-intelligence-ai-fukoku-mutual-life-insurance

Montenegro, C. E., & Patrinos, H. A. (2014). *Comparable estimates of returns to schooling around the world*. World Bank Policy Research Working Paper No. 7020. World Bank Group, Washington, DC.

Oosterbeek, H., & Patrinos, H. A. (2009). Financing lifelong learning. *Empirical research in vocational education and training*, 1(1), 19–37.

Palacios, M. (2003). *Options for financing lifelong learning*. World Bank Policy Research Working Paper No. 2994.

Patrinos, H. A. (2016). The skills that matter in the race between education and technology. Prepared for the 2016 Brookings Institution Blum Roundtable.

Patrinos, H. A. (2020). Lifelong learning. Web blog post. Education for Development. World Bank.

Patrinos, H. A., & Angrist, N. (2018). *Global dataset on education quality: A review and update (2000–2017)*. World Bank Policy Research Working Paper No. 8592. World Bank, Washington DC.

Plucker, J. A., & Makel, M. C. (2010). Assessment of creativity. In J. C. Kaufman & R. J. Sternberg, (Eds.), *The Cambridge handbook of creativity*. Cambridge: Cambridge University Press.

Psacharopoulos, G. (1977). Unequal access to education and income distribution. *De Economist*, 125, 383–392.

Psacharopoulos, G., & Marin, A. (1976). Schooling and income distribution. *The Review of Economics and Statistics*, 58, 332–337.

Psacharopoulos, G., & Patrinos, H. A. (2018). Returns to investment in education: A decennial review of the global literature. *Education Economics*, 26(5), 445–458.

Ray, S., & Davidson, S. (2014). Dementia and cognitive decline: A review of the evidence. *Age UK*, 27, 10–12.

Sallam, M., Dababseh, D., Yaseen, A., Al-Haidar, A., Taim, D., Eid, H., ... Mahafzah, A. (2020). COVID-19 misinformation: Mere harmless delusions or much more? A knowledge and attitude cross-sectional study among the general public residing in Jordan. medRxiv.

Sanchez Puerta, M. L., Valerio, A., & Gutierrez Bernal, M. (2016). *Taking stock of programs to develop socioemotional skills: A systematic review of program evidence*. Washington, DC: The World Bank.

Schaeffer, K. (2020). Nearly three-in-ten Americans believe COVID-19 was made in a lab. *Pew Research Center Factank Blog*. Retrieved from https://pewrsr.ch/2XlJqAa

Schleicher, A. (2019). *PISA 2018: Insights and interpretations*. Paris: OECD.

Simonov, A., Sacher, S. K., Dubé, J. P. H., & Biswas, S. (2020). *The persuasive effect of fox news: Non-compliance with social distancing during the covid-19 pandemic* (No. w27237). Cambridge, MA: National Bureau of Economic Research.

Singh, A. (2019). Learning more with every year: School year productivity and international learning divergence. *Journal of the European Economic*, 18(4), 1770–1813. doi:10.1093/jeea/jvz033

Tinbergen, J. (1974). Substitution of graduate by other labour. *Kyklos, 27*(2), 217–226.

Vander Ark, T. (2017). Growing talent for the 4th industrial revolution. Web blog post. Getting Smart.

Vemuri, P., Lesnick, R. B., Przybelwski, S., Machulda, M., Knopman, D., Mielke, M., & Jack, C. (2014). Association of lifetime intellectual enrichment with cognitive decline in the older population. *JAMA Neurology, 71*, 1017–1024.

Vinge, V. (1993). The coming technological singularity: How to survive in the post-human era. (Department of Mathematical Sciences, San Diego State University).

Wineburg, S., McGrew, S., Breakstone, J., & Ortega, T. (2016). Evaluating information: The cornerstone of civic online reasoning. Stanford Digital Repository.

Winegarden, C. R. (1979). Schooling and income distribution: Evidence from international data. *Economica, 46*(181), 83–87.

World Bank. (2003). *Lifelong learning in the global knowledge economy.* Washington, DC: World Bank.

World Bank. (2018). *Growing smarter: Learning and equitable development in East Asia pacific.* Washington, DC: World Bank.

Chapter 5

The Pretruth Era in MENA, News Ecology, and Critical News Literacy

Abeer Al-Najjar

Abstract

The MENA (Middle East and North Africa) region is in a critical moment in its information and news ecology, exhibiting signs of pretruth and posttruth syndromes. Between the "pretruth" and "posttruth" there is a gap that circumvented "truth." The state of information in the MENA region brings back the dystopian Orwellian notion of the "Ministry of Truth." A poetic term in anticipation of this moment of the crisis of truth. Sharing the latter with the rest of the world, the pretruth moment is engraved in the region's history of precarious political and religious authoritarian control and manipulation of information and news and low press freedom. In the region, truth is told, hidden, distorted, and manufactured by a blend of humans and bots, where both artificial intelligence and social humans are involved in this process of multipolarized disinformation operations with multifarious sponsors, actors, and beneficiaries that have distinct and often clashing agendas and interests. To understand the ecology of truth, facts, news, and information in the Middle East, studies ought to be situated within the ecosystem of information and media technologies in the globalized national and transnational societies of the region and consider both the role of the regionally oriented neoauthoritarian regimes and that of interested rising and established global powers. Central to this ecosystem is the dynamic interaction among three actors: communication technologies (the focus here is on the Internet); media, public, and activists' use of these technologies to mobilize, inform, and present alternative narratives, and to resist or confirm state narratives; and the authoritarian political regimes and their containment strategies for legacy media (particularly television) and the Internet.

Keywords: MENA; posttruth; Arab journalism; news and information ecology; critical news literacy; political control

Media, Technology and Education in a Post-Truth Society, 55–72

Copyright © 2021 by Emerald Publishing Limited

All rights of reproduction in any form reserved

doi:10.1108/978-1-80043-906-120211005

Posttruth in the Middle East: Critical Questions

The Arab region and the wider Middle East and North Africa, with their many failed states, authoritarian regimes, "dysfunctional politics," and fragile and exclusive economies (Boukhars, 2014), have moved from the scarcity of information to abundance; from a few state-led media enterprises to a plethora of politically and ideologically motivated news and information organizations and networks. The semi-complete censorship of the twentieth century has been made obsolete by the arrival of the Internet and its affordances and impact on news and information ecologies. There is no other point in modern history that symbolizes the loss of control over media spaces in the Middle East as the Arab Spring 2011, in which activists and revolutionaries destabilized long-standing authoritarian regimes that previously enjoyed decades-long grips on media and communication. The last decade shows that the Middle East is an important informational space with a highly connected technological environment. There are around 423 million Arabic speakers around the world (World Population, 2020), and Arabic is spoken in 22 states. As of the end of March 2020, Internet penetration in the Middle East and North Africa (MENA) reached over 70%, above the world average of 58% (Internet World Stats, 2020).

Since 2011, counterrevolutionary political and military actors, authoritarian regimes, and dictators adopted every technology possible to recenter themselves in this fast-evolving media space, employing electronic armies, computational propaganda, active cyber warfare, cyber securitization strategies, trolls, bots, and artificial intelligence. Truth, facts, and legitimacy have never been more contested within meta-narratives of pan-Islamism, global jihad, the war on terror, and national identities.

In addition to globally shared trajectories relevant to twenty-first-century media ecologies, the short-lived rise of the individual, and the erosion of public trust, democracy, liberal values, personal privacy, and human rights, the Middle East is passing through important geographical, political, and military trajectories that make it more challenging to address the "posttruth era." On the one hand, some countries went through regime transformations as in the case of Egypt and Tunisia in 2011, and Sudan and Algeria in 2019. On the other hand, Yemen, Libya, Syria, Lebanon, and Iraq have or had faced disintegrated and destabilized geographies and regimes, visible in the proliferation of competing armies, governments, parliaments, parties, and political actors, in addition to foreign troops, mercenaries, and regional and global interventions and interests.

Central to any attempt to grasp the current standing of truth and fact in the region is the need to pay attention to the reemergence of media ecology as an interdisciplinary notion connecting individuals, groups, and regimes with technologies within their political, social, and cultural environments (Postman, 2000). The word ecology implies "the study of environments; their structure, content and impact on people" (Postman, 1970, pp. 160–161). Neil Postman's seminal work on media ecology suggests two fundamental questions in understanding the environment surrounding the use of any media or its ecology. "To what extent does a medium contribute to the uses and development of rational thought" and "meaningful information"? And "to what extent does a medium contribute to the development of democratic process"? (Postman, 2000, p. 13). Assuming the Internet is the medium of the twenty-first century, in which even mainstream media make sure to platformize their content and offer streamlined, convergent, and personalized services online, then in our search for the status of truth we need to focus on the Internet and the opportunities and risks it offers different actors to leverage their legitimacy and power.

To understand the ecology of truth, facts, news, and information in the Middle East, studies ought to be situated within the ecosystem of information and media technologies in the globalized national and transnational societies of the region and consider both the role of the regionally oriented neoauthoritarian regimes and that of interested wising and established global powers. Central to this ecosystem is the dynamic interaction among three actors: communication technologies (the focus here is on the Internet); media, public, and activists' use of these technologies to mobilize, inform, and present alternative narratives, and to resist or confirm state narratives; and the authoritarian political regimes and their containment strategies for legacy media (particularly television) and the Internet. These three forces are the two central players in media ecology, "human beings," and "technologies" (Stephens, 2014).

How can we discuss truth-seeking and fact-finding in the rapidly evolving media ecology in the Middle East? How has the shift from the one-to-many model of communication to the many-to-many model within the Middle East changed the approaches used by media organizations, individuals, and powerful actors including governments? How are the Arab regimes, whether authoritarian or semi-authoritarian, in addition to other actors (political and military) changing their strategies for controlling the *many*, by employing media organizations, global brand news and name affiliations, expansions of media projects, in addition to using violence, imprisonment, repression, trolls, propagandists, and financial incentives?

Truth, Posttruth, and the Current News and Information Ecology

Google Scholar reports more than 17,000 results for "posttruth" since 2016 (search conducted July 4, 2020). Notions of posttruth, fake news, and deepfakes are increasingly common terms in the literature on media, journalism, democracy, political communication, and public opinion. Misinformation, disinformation, "fake news, rumour bombs, and lying" or the "subclasses of deceptive communication" (Harsin, 2018, p. 7) are a few other forms of manipulation threatening citizens' rights, particularly the right to be informed. Katherine Connor Martin, head of Oxford's US dictionaries division, defined "posttruth" as "relating to or denoting circumstances in which objective facts are less influential in shaping public opinion than appeals to emotion and personal belief" (Kroet, 2017). McIntyre (2018, p. 9) suggested that a posttruth nontruth teller could be a "deceiver, indifferent, cynical or delusional". Zarzalejos (2017, p. 11) understood posttruth more dramatically to indicate the "supremacy of emotional speeches." It is perceived as the antithesis of the democratic values of an informed citizenry, transparency, and accountability (Eberwein, Fengler, & Karmasin, 2019; Penders, 2018). The language of "fake" or "alternative news" and "hoaxes" all fall under the "semantic umbrella of posttruth," whereas the critical assessment of news and information sources and "fact-checking would be the antidote against the word" posttruth (Zarzalejos, 2017, p. 11). This is in addition to a good understanding of media and information sources and the ability to differentiate facts from falsehoods and opinions.

Connecting truth to knowledge, Harsin (2018) formulated three levels of issues associated with posttruth. He illustrates that

> ...the public problems for which PT is shorthand are epistemic (false knowledge, competing truth claims); fiduciary (distrust of society-wide authoritative truth-tellers, trust in micro truth-tellers); and ethico moral (conscious disregard for factual evidence – bullshitting – or intentional, strategic falsehoods/lying—dishonesty), the latter of which is often bracketed or abstracted into institutional logics of political strategy. (Harsin, 2018, p. 5)

At the heart of the current dystopian critique of the status of truth in the recent media ecology, which is framed as the lack or loss of truth, is the impact it has on public opinion (Llorente, 2017; Zarzalejos, 2017). In the posttruth era

> ...personal beliefs – which for many are irrefutable – have gained strength in the face of logic and facts, and have become established as assumptions shared by society, causing bewilderment in public opinion. (Llorente, 2017, p. 9)

This is problematic for the democratic values of an informed citizenry, responsibility, and accountability since "facts themselves take second place, while 'how' a story is told takes precedence over 'what'" (Llorente, 2017, p. 9) the story is. The dystopia is darker when we learn that about the "growing evidence that social media platforms support campaigns of political misinformation on a global scale" (Woolley & Howard, 2017, p. 7), despite announcing and claiming otherwise. In this era, truth is not only buried in the information overload, hidden from the public, spun, manipulated, and contested but worse, "*it* [the truth] is being challenged as a mechanism for asserting political dominance" (McIntyre, 2018, p. xiv).

Governmental, organizational, and political attempts to manipulate public opinion and deceiving the public are not new. Yet, in this media and information ecology, the magnitude of attempts, the multitude of parties involved, and the potential for widespread and immediate reach have made the situation loom as a dystopian novel. In 2004, Ralph Keyes warned that what he then called the "posttruth era" presents itself not only on our behavior but also on our acceptance and justification of deception and lying. He observed that historically

...Even though there have always been liars, lies have been told with hesitation, a dash of anxiety, a bit of guilt, a little shame, some sheepishness. Now, clever people that we are, we have come up with rationales for tampering with truth so we can dissemble guilt-free. (Keyes, 2004, pp. 13–14)

In his book *When Presidents Lie*, Eric Alterman (2004, p. 305) argues that regardless of our awareness of its existence

...the presidency now [as of president George W. Bush] operated in a 'post-truth' political environment. American presidents could no longer depend on the press – its powers and responsibilities enshrined in the First Amendment – to keep them honest. (Alterman, 2004, p. 305)

An important addition along the same line of presidential behavior were Donald Trump's constant attacks on the press and public trust in the press as a democratic institution, and his use of Twitter to prevent any mediation, fact-checks, or contextualization of his political speech. Trump's discourse on Twitter reached a much larger target audience than any other medium could provide him, 80 million followers, enabled by an organization (Twitter) that saw no interest in his abuse of the platform, rather an opportunity for growth.

The notion of fake news in particular was utilized at the start of President Trump's term to attack American journalism as a trusted public organization in which American citizens seek credible information. That same journalism had helped the president to circulate the term by following their journalistic values of focusing on people with power. Trust in journalism in the United States was undermined long before Trump, particularly during George W. Bush's presidency when American officials' statements were largely uninvestigated prior to the invasion of Iraq (2003). "Media's greatest failure in modern times" is when

...major news organizations aided and abetted the Bush administration's march to war on what turned out to be faulty premises. All too often, skepticism was checked at the door, and the shaky claims of top officials and unnamed sources were trumpeted as fact. (Kurtz, 2013, para. 3–4)

As with the term fake news, the posttruth era describes a unique and fast-changing moment of media ecology that complicates any discussion and renders conceptualizations, articulations, applications, and solutions transient and elusive. Posttruth was largely conceptualized from a Western-centric perspective and driven by threats to Western democracies in the aftermath of the 2016 presidential elections in the United States and the EU referendum in the United Kingdom, with their accompanying or preceding revelation of news and information on misinformation campaigns (Llorente, 2017). As with other associated terms, fake news is a "term of American origin" (Harsin, 2018, p. 9) and much of the literature on posttruth originates from the United States (Kavanagh & Rich, 2018). In many countries of the Global South, and particularly in the Middle East, political and social truth was scarce even before the posttruth era.

Truth, Posttruth, and the Contemporary News and Information Ecology in MENA

MENA has witnessed a combination of foreign, regional, and national actors introducing news media and information titles and sources and employing a variety of information manipulation strategies and tactics. Although many of these tools and strategies belong to what is known as the posttruth era, others go back to long-standing pretruth information and news manipulation practices. In the postcolonial Arab states (1950s–1990s) governments used news media and journalists for self- and policy promotion, as mouthpieces and filters. In the Middle East, censorship was dominant (Amin, 2002), freedom of the press remained low compared to the rest of the world even till 2020, and access to information in most Arab states was limited.[1]

Freedom House listed seven Middle Eastern countries as "the least freed region in the world" (Freedom House, 2019). Of the 180 countries examined in 2019, the "bottom 10 percent" in freedom of the press were countries from the Middle East (Scher, 2019). In a study of access to information in four Arab countries, Jordan, Morocco, Lebanon, and Tunisia, Almadhoun concluded that even countries with regulations acknowledging the public right to information "a culture of secrecy prevails over that of openness" (2015, p. 37). Similarly, in Iran, implementation of the Publication and Free Access to Information Act 2009 has been "very slow" and the Act itself includes "problematic provisions that undermine its effectiveness and make it weaker than international standards" (Article 19, 2017, p. 2). Although Turkey enacted its Law on Right to Information in 2004, Kocaoglu (2013) argues that important measures still need to be taken so the law can be effective. Adakli (2017) asserts that the right to information as well as the freedom of the press in Turkey has been undermined and hindered in the past few years. Israel continues to persecute Palestinian journalists and media organizations using "incitement of violence" as an excuse (Palestine Centre for Development and Media Freedoms, 2019). Palestinian digital rights, including access to information, their right to privacy, and even to access the Internet, have been regularly violated by the Israeli occupation's complete control over ICT infrastructure in the West Bank and Gaza Strip (AbuShanab, 2018).

The MENA region shares a few features of the posttruth era due to Internet penetration, high national, regional, and global interconnectivity and cross-connectivity, and the similarities in the media ecologies which share platform technological infrastructures and the use of disinformation, misinformation, propaganda, and other forms of deception and manipulation including trolls, bots, and electronic armies. Yet, most of MENA is still in a "pretruth" society when one considers access to information, freedom of the press, and the independence of news media.

The Arab Spring took many regimes by surprise. The reach, utility, and impact that social media afforded protestors in countries such as Egypt, Tunisia, and Syria was fundamental to the post–Arab Spring strategies and the emergence of authoritarian regimes and counterrevolutionary actors.

> …Given the powerful capability of the latter [social media], people using Twitter (particularly in countries with strict media censorship laws) have the potential to promote social change through this social medium. (Chaudhry, 2014, p. 943)

Daud (2014, p. 221) argued that social media "stimulated democratization," facilitated "cyber-dissent," expanded "social inclusion," and was the "catalyst" for the Arab Spring. "Twitter's power to mobilize citizens and demand social change worries other authoritarian governments who feel their reign also may be at risk of an uprising from their people" (Chaudhry, 2014, p. 944). Arab regimes realized that the new media ecology represented by social media and high levels of Internet penetration has destabilized the "knowledge" and information arrangements in the region and that complete utilization of and monopoly over the media is close to impossible using traditional censorship, repression, and violence strategies. Sismondo (2017, p. 3) warns that "If the post-truth era starts by blowing up current knowledge structures, then it isn't very likely to be democratization, and in fact most likely leads to authoritarianism." Hence, counterrevolutionary regimes and actors started changing their censorship and information control mechanisms, overloading the formerly scarce information sphere in MENA with overloads of information, news sources, and content, and flooding their national and regional infospheres with bots, trolls, and rumors. In doing so, authoritarian regimes turned "social media platforms [into] conduits for manipulative disinformation campaigns" (Woolley & Howard, 2017, p. 5).

This counter use of social media intensified since the Gulf Crisis in Summer 2017 between Qatar and "the Quartet" (Saudi Arabia, UAE, Bahrain, and Egypt) (Kinninmont, 2019). The crisis itself was a result of fake news, as the Quartet declared it would sever diplomatic ties with Qatar over statements released by Qatar News Agency quoting Emir Tamim. On the same day, Qatar announced that the website of the news agency was hacked and the statements were not true. The Quartet countries, and Saudi Arabia in particular, have also for a long time been asking Qatar to close down or silence *Al Jazeera* over its critical news and programming (Kinninmont, 2019; Roberts, 2017). In Saudi Arabia "news media are state-owned or controlled, limiting the range of perspectives they carry" (Hubbard, 2019, para. 4). The same rule applies to Saudi media abroad, whether in Dubai, London, or elsewhere. Al Jazeera seemed for years the only Arabic-speaking broadcaster – with considerable viewers and ratings – beyond the Kingdom's space for information manipulation.

Many regimes moved from censors and propagandists to spammers, advocates, rumor disseminators, and trolls. The Internet and social media changed from being instruments of freedom (Christensen, 2011; Whitten-Woodring, 2009) in the wake of the Arab Spring and earlier, to instruments of deception and authoritarianism in the subsequent decade.

> ...Social media has become co-opted by many authoritarian regimes. In 26 countries, computational propaganda is being used as a tool of information control in three distinct ways: to suppress fundamental human rights, discredit political opponents, and drown out dissenting opinions. (Bradshaw & Howard, 2019, p. i)

Discussing fake news on the COVID-19 pandemic in the Arab countries, Oraib Rantawi argues that "social media can't be controlled with the tools we know, even though they violate the sovereignty of states and shape public opinion" (Abumarya, 2020, para. 12–13). Hence, moves were taken by Egypt, Saudi Arabia, Morocco, and the Palestinian Authority to control fake news. The countries went "so far as to detain purveyors of false information about the number of COVID-19 infections" (Abumarya, 2020, para. 12–13). The pandemic was viewed by many of the regimes as a "national security" threat. Rintawi claims that with the pandemic "now there is an additional border that cannot be secured using traditional methods" (Abumarya, 2020, para. 14). Fake news also was argued to affect "political stability" in many of the Arab countries (Rampersad & Althiyabi, 2020, p. 1). Even before the spread of news and information about fake news in the Middle East, Twitter accounts associated with Middle Eastern governments including Saudi Arabia, Egypt, the UAE, Turkey, and Iran were suspended by the Twitter transparency project (Twitter Blog, 2020). In August 2018, Twitter suspended and "released [the details of] 770 accounts with potential Iranian origins" (Elswah, Howard, & Narayanan, 2019). According to Twitter, these "accounts [were] engaging in coordinated behavior which appeared to originate in Iran" (Harvey & Yoel, 2018, para. 6). Efforts and networks to manipulate public opinion in the Middle East have also been commissioned by Russia, China, and the United States, in addition to regional actors including Israel.

Jared Kushner, the son-in-law of former US President Donald Trump, commissioned a large-scale data mining operation. His announced objective was to classify the Arab news channels and sources according to their popularity and their attitude toward US policies in the region and to develop a strategy to reach Arab communities and market US policies, particularly the "deal of the century" (Wilner, 2019) known as "the steal of the century." In 2004, the United States launched *Alhurra* (The Free), an Arabic-language TV station, and *Radio Sawa* (Together) to "win the hearts and minds of the Arabs." The launch followed the American invasion of Iraq in 2003. For the US administration, existing transnational Arab media, such as *Al Arabiya* and *Al Jazeera*, were too critical of its policies and actions, especially during its invasion of Iraq in 2003.

Similarly, Russia, an old Cold War ally of Arab nationalist regimes, is infamous in the Arab region for backing Bashar al-Assad's regime in Syria and defending the atrocities he committed against his people (Cosentino, 2020). Russia has a regional ally in this mission, Iran. Both countries have assisted Assad's regime militarily and informationally. They both have Arabic-speaking news media (the Arabic speaking *Russia Today*; the Iranian *Al Alam* [The World], the pro-Iranians channels *Al Mayadeen* and *Al-Manar*, and the newspaper *Al Akhbar*). These channels have magnified and mainstreamed Bashar's messages and added to the chaotic news and information landscape. Stanford Internet Observatory examined the Russian involvement in Libya and suggested that Russian "actors [associated with the Russian President Vladimir Putin] are taking a Cold-War-era strategy of supporting local media outlets and updating it for the digital age" and that "it is clear that Russian actors are exerting influence via traditional as well as social media channels" (Grossman, DiResta, & Kheradpir, 2020, para. 1–2). In addition, Iran, Turkey, and Israel seem to be involved in Arab countries' wars, policies, and information spheres to serve their agendas. In June 2020, Assistant Secretary General of the Arab League Hossam Zaki warned that "The Turkish interference in Libya, Syria, Iraq and its use of foreign fighters and terrorists to Libya is rejected and condemned by the Arab world" (Al Arabiya, 2020, para. 3–5). Adjudicating the truthfulness of news and information in the current media ecology is becoming challenging, not only on the Internet but also for mainstream media in MENA.

It is increasingly becoming challenging to ascertain "authenticity in the Arab media ecosystem" (Grossman, DiResta et al., 2020, para. 3). Therefore, "It's not just fake news we need to be wary of, but fake journalists" (Rownsley, 2020, para. 8), commentators, and analysts. "Post-truth functions and it is reproduced also because its condition is strategically exploited by State actors and foreign policy initiatives" (Cosentino, 2020, p. 87). In September 2019,

> Twitter disabled accounts from users in several Middle Eastern countries and suspended the account of disgraced official Saud al-Qahtani for violating rules on platform manipulation. Previously one of Prince Mohammed's closest aides, the Saudi official was at the center of efforts to intimidate critics and dominate online conversations. He controlled hundreds of automated accounts with millions of followers and his presence on social media earned him the nickname "Mr. Hashtag". (Jones, 2019, para. 7)

Two months later, in December, Twitter suspended more than 88,000 "state-backed" accounts that were identified as "fake and spammy" (Twitter Safety, 2020). This was Twitter's "largest-ever state-tied takedown" (Grossman, Khadija, DiResta, Kheradpir, & Miller, 2020). The accounts were involved in a disinformation campaign "manipulation" connected to Saudi Arabia (Holmes, 2019). A Twitter investigation found that these accounts were "amplifying messages favourable to Saudi authorities, mainly through inauthentic engagement tactics such as aggressive liking, retweeting and replying" (Twitter Safety, 2020). They were connected to Smaat, a Saudi marketing company that handles many governmental accounts in the country (Holmes, 2019).

It is no surprise that Saudi Arabia is focused on controlling Twitter, as the social network is the "town square" of Saudi Arabia. The country has "one of the world's largest Twitterspheres" (Hubbard, 2019, para. 6). Since the country

> ...has not banned the site, [...] it has taken extensive measures to shape the information that appears there and to silence or drown out dissidents who use it to post critical views. (Hubbard, 2019, para. 2)

In July 2020, *The Daily Beast* uncovered a network of 19 fake personalities who have been writing to news media as commentators and analysts for a year. The politically directed network of fake commentators in support of the United Arab Emirates published articles in "conservative North American outlets like Human Events and The Post Millennial"; in Asian media, like the *South China Morning Post*; and Israeli and Middle Eastern publications, including *The Jerusalem Post* and Al Arabiya (Rownsley, 2020, para. 9).

The Truth in Transnational Arab Journalism: Counterbalancing News Sources and Competing Truths

Veteran Arab journalist Jihad Khazen argued that Arab regimes cannot control satellite television, their strength being that they are "crossing boundaries and evading censors" (1999, p. 90). For decades, many Arab regimes attempted to tackle the criticism they face in Al Jazeera by pressuring the channel, closing its offices, persecuting its journalists, and placing pressure on its patron, Qatar. Al Jazeera changed the ecology of information, news, and opinion in the Arab region as it was the first 24/7 news channel in Arabic that is beyond direct sponsorship, although within the control of its patron and its regional and global expansionist strategies.

Transnational news in the Middle East at large and particularly within the Arab countries have been growing since regimes were not able to silence or neutralize Al Jazeera. Many regimes also learned of the privileges that the channel grants the small state of Qatar both regionally and globally. Al Arabiya was commissioned by the Saudi government in 2003 to "counterbalance" the effect of Al Jazeera, and many other channels have subsequently emerged (Interview with AlRashid. 2015). Particularly since 2012, a year after the Arab Spring, several channels have been established, maximizing the offers and news affordances of citizens in the region, particularly the Arabic-speaking public. State interests and sensibilities were at the heart of this growth of news outlets, as every channel minds the image, policies, and ambitions of its sponsoring and hosting states, and counters the news provided by other channels, mainly Al Jazeera. Although Al Jazeera and Al Arabiya showed consistent coverage of the US invasion of Iraq in 2003, leading to the emergence of the US-sponsored Alhurra, the channels' reporting diverged on several other stories, including the Palestinian-Israeli conflict (Al-Najjar, 2020). The Arab Spring was an important episode in Arab news and information control and manipulation.

In addition to the use of the press and TV news stations which grew in number and reach, other instruments of regaining power over the infosphere have emerged in the post Arab Spring years. The Syrian regime created the Syrian Electronic Army (SEA), a hacktivist arm of "cyber worriers" (Al-Rawi, 2014) to fix its image and spread its version of the revolution (Warren & Leitch, 2016). ISIS emerged with its slick propaganda and terrorizing machine in 2014. Many counterrevolutionary Arab regimes targeted activists and protestors physically and morally, rallying a bouquet of new regulations, surveillance mechanisms and spying technologies, smear campaigns and campaigners, and troops and bands of promotional pro-pagandists to spread misinformation, ignorance, false news, and defamatory speech against protestors, in addition to the hypersecuritization of the national image, "symbols" – meaning political leaders – and communication. One of the key tropes was the *a'amil* (foreign agent) accusation, another was of moral decay, using the term *shawaz* (deviant in English). Cosentino (2020) studies the defamatory disin-formation campaign against "White Helmets," a volunteer-based search and rescue organization that worked within Syria and Turkey (Cosentino, 2020; Cosentino & Alikasifoglu, 2019) oppositional to Asad's regime. The group faced a Russian-backed Syrian regime defamatory campaign linking the group to al-Qaeda and its global terror network (Solon, 2017). Harsin calls the strategy used in this social media campaign "rumor bombs," for "bombing the field of attention" regardless of their believability, as these rumors, although old in political propaganda, are new in their "clear effect on public culture". Rumor bombs are "professionally oper-ationalized in popular political struggles" (2018, pp. 8–9).

Propagandists include experts divided into two extremes on major stories. In Egypt, for instance, there are those in support of the Muslim Brotherhood who consider its president, ousted in 2013, as the first legitimate leader and the underdog. On the other side, there are those claiming that the coup of 2013 was a new revo-lution and that the Muslim Brotherhood is a terrorist organization full of traitors implementing the foreign propaganda of the global Muslim Brotherhood, Qatar, and Turkey. In Syria, Assad's regime claimed that he was not facing public unrest or a revolution but terrorist Islamist organizations, a narrative that took greater prominence as ISIS emerged in Syria and Iraq. The narrative turned later to include, in his words, a "universal conspiracy against his regime and the resistance bloc," referring to the conflict with Israel and the Russian-backed bloc of Syria, Iran, and the Lebanese Hezbollah. These competing narratives battled on TV screens and mainstream newspapers and eventually moved to Twitter, Facebook, and other social media platforms. Facebook, in particular, "remains the dominant platform for cyber troop activity" in computational propaganda (Bradshaw & Howard, 2019, p. 2). Both perspectives had some resonance with segments of the Arab population, playing along both chronic and pressing as well as national and regional grievances.

In countries with greater stability, like Jordan and Morocco, cyber polariza-tion became more visible with the appearance of certain groups of cyber defenders of the regime with hypernationalist loyalist speech, *al-Saheeja* in Jordan and *al-Ayasha* in Morocco. These groups helped to create and circulate hypernationalist patriotic messages, and troll and defame members and leaders of the opposition, activists, and critics of the regimes. An important analogy used by these groups, emphasized on TV screens in countries beyond their own, warns that protests and opposition should stop to avoid becoming another Syria. Countries with greater wealth used international public relations agencies in the United States and Europe, and bought global news brands to franchise and advocate their messages and propaganda, including Sky News, Bloomberg, the Huffington Post and *The Independent*. The latter regimes also invested heavily in surveillance systems and spyware infrastructure. The contestation between at least two narratives was happening at national levels on TV screens, newspapers, and social media simultaneously, maximizing the reach and priming of one of these narratives over the other. Largely, the journalistic practices of major news organizations in selecting, framing, and interviewing failed to provide any balance or contain elements of more than one frame or narrative of the same story. For example, although Al Jazeera regularly interviewed "experts with opposing views," the selection of these experts, the questions asked, and the anchors' interventions rarely helped to provide balance or fairness to the story.

In this post-Arab spring media ecology, narratives and counternarratives often work synchronously and travel seamlessly across screens, platforms, and media outlets. Information, misinformation, and disinformation can begin in mainstream media and travel to social media, and vice versa. Grossman, Khadija et al. (2020) study of the Twitter and Facebook disinformation networks promoting Military General Khalifa Haftar in Libya made it to the mainstream media outlets. On the other hand, many journalists in Egypt and Syria took the news from their own or opposing channels and spread them on social media. The study on Libya pinpoints the use of mainstream media to legitimize illegitimate social media activities. Grossman, Khadija et al. (2020) coined the term "hashtag laundering" for this activity. Hashtag laundering means "attempting to legitimize manufactured social media trends by covering them in media – indicates that this operation extended from social into broadcast channels." The authors note that

> ...many media outlets published stories about hashtags [...], with the intent of making them seem like significant, organic social happenings. In one example, a publication wrote up an article implying that Libyans were so against Turkey that an anti-Turkey hashtag was trending. This laundering happened on numerous occasions, despite the fact that the hashtags did not actually go viral. (Grossman, Khadija et al., 2020, p. 4)

News that feeds into one narrative, as explained above, suited the interests of global actors including Russia and China. Increasingly Russia is invested not only militarily in MENA but also in its news and information. "The most powerful forms of computational propaganda involve both algorithmic distribution and human curation – bots and trolls working together" (Woolley & Howard, 2017, p. 5). Similarly, almost "45 percent of Twitter activity in Russia is managed by highly automated accounts" (Woolley & Howard, 2017, p. 4). With Chinese and Israeli activities in misinformation still under the radar of study in the region, Russia emerged as an important player in the news, information, and disinformation sphere in the MENA with shifting tactics and alliances.

Truth Decay, Distrust, and Critical Media Literacy

This global moment of posttruth, "truth decay" (Kavanagh & Rich, 2018; Huguet, Kavanagh, Baker, & Bluementhal, 2019) connects to many national and regional nodes of pretruth, posttruth, or truth chasms in MENA. Asghar (2012, p. 295) asserts that truth is the "first casualty of [the] battle between texts and contexts" particularly when false news is "contextualized by facts" (Harsin, 2018, p. 9). In MENA, truth is told, hidden, distorted, and manufactured by a combination of humans and bots, where both artificial intelligence and humans are involved in this process of multipolarized, disinformation operations with multifarious sponsors, actors, and beneficiaries that have distinct and often clashing agendas and interests. These operations involve "the use of algorithms, automation, and human curation to purposefully distribute misleading information over social media networks" (Woolley & Howard, 2017, p. 3). "The rise of Truth Decay has been brought on, at least in part, by an increasingly complex and saturated information ecosystem" (Huguet et al., 2019, p. ix). This led to developing new forms of technology; human interactions where, again, actors and states with more resources can use an assortment of technologies, individuals, and strategies to guide not only the information (false or truthful) that a citizen can find but also to control and even engineer or manufacture what s/he cannot find. Previous studies identified two important practices in the context of MENA, "rumor bombs" (Harsin, 2018) and "hashtag laundering" (Grossman, Khadija et al., 2020, p. 4). The latter strategies indicate the two tendencies, the first to occupy public attention regardless of the believability of the lie/fact and the second is mainstreaming inauthentic content and disguising it through moving it from social media to traditional news media organization.

In the face of operating systems and networks of disinformation and truth submerging, the public and citizens are left with sophisticated and plausibly diverse sets of sources of information, news, and opinions, which when compared to powerful well-funded operations seem primitive. Approaches to addressing this phase of media ecology and the posttruth era that is largely marked by the dissemination, and mainstreaming of lies include

> ...techno-curation such as AI filtering of PT claims/stories; human fact checking, especially rooted in journalism; strategic human responses to cognitive bias; more rigorous self-regulations by social media providers; and media literacy initiatives. (Harsin, 2018, p. 20)

Kavanagh and Rich (2018) recommend researching the nature, aspects, drivers, and prospects of "truth decay" as a way to determine which strategies and approaches are suitable to tackle the issue.

Four decades ago, Neil Postman argued for replacing teaching English with media ecology. The purpose of education, he asserted, is to equip the individual with a "survival value" (Postman, 1970, p. 160). This would involve teaching students and perhaps citizens "how to evaluate... an article, a web page, a website or a news story for currency, reliability, accuracy, and purpose or point of view" (Frederiksen, 2017, p. 104). Media literacy, although introduced with other sets of responses, is present in much of the literature on facing fake news, political manipulation, and posttruth. Another common response is reforming journalism as an institute fundamental to democracies to reclaim public trust. Media literacy is a "foundational concept for understanding the future of journalism" as it affects the way audiences (users) decode news text and how they "evaluate the political 'bias' of a journalistic work" (Peters, 2013, p. 172). Hence, media literacy affects public trust in journalism, and hence, its public reception and use.

Although many educational programs in media literacy have been taught at schools and universities, researchers find that individual citizens are vulnerable to misinformation, disinformation, and other nefarious practices in the posttruth era. Hence, identifying and exploring the knowledge, skills, and competencies necessary to enable citizens to navigate through this information ecology, without being vulnerable to political manipulation, is fundamental to any international, regional, or national response strategy. Postman (2010) argues that media literacy is a "never complete" process. Media literacy is best approached as an important component of public life and all relevant media should be considered for introducing it. Vulnerability to cyber lies, computational propaganda, and campaigns of disinformation is not limited to young people at school and universities, as it poses as a lifelong necessity with potentials of flexibility, adaptability, and sustainability. Part of this crosscutting educational exercises should be addressed by good journalism, as it appears to be a cross-age lifelong process necessitated by the fast-changing media ecologies. As Woolley and Howard (2017) point out, actors sponsoring computational disinformation campaigns are aware of negative news publicity their activity provokes, hence they keep adapting their strategies to minimize researchers' and platforms' ability to detect them.

In MENA, news literacy is even more urgent for numerous reasons: the lack of media literacy in schools and universities in many countries, the decline of the human development in education that was achieved in the Arab world during the first decade of the twenty-first century (Arab Human Development Report, 2016), and the scarcity of information on media use and trends beyond marketing purposes, in addition to the intensified hyper securitized and manic nationalized disinformation campaigns with a mixture of actors. Research on media literacy in the region is new and has appeared only in the past decade (Al-Najjar, 2019, 2020; Grizzle, 2016; Melki, 2013, 2015; Saleh, 2009).

Hence, any discussion of media literacy program or curriculum design should be informed by the streams of constant and change in media ecology and factored in its design. It should also consider the methods for delivery focusing on access and reach to its content, to guarantee its inclusivity. The way media literacy is conceptualized is centered around three main functions: to be able to produce, access, and interpret media messages. The literacy that is necessary for posttruth media ecologies ought to have specific foundational features, including its coverage of an array of constant and changing media features and its central focus on critical selection, assessment, and use of messages, sources, and contexts.

Note

1. See https://freedomhouse.org/report/freedom-and-media/2019/media-freedom-downward-spiral.

References

Abumarya, D. (2020). Fake news threatening many nations. *The Media Line*. Retrieved from https://themedialine.org/by-region/fake-news-threatening-many-nations/

AbuShanab, A. (2018). Connection interrupted: Israel's control of the Palestinian ICT infrastructure and its impact on digital rights. Association for Progressive Communication. Retrieved from https://www.apc.org/en/pubs/connection-interrupted-israel%E2%80%99s-control-palestinian-ict-infrastructure-and-its-impact-digital

Adakli, G. (2017). Access to public information in Erdoğan's Turkey. *Osservatorio Balcani e Caucaso Transeuropa*. Retrieved from https://www.balcanicaucaso.org/eng/Areas/Turkey/Access-to-public-information-in-Erdogan-s-Turkey-178001

Al Arabiya. (2020). Turkey. Copying Iran's interference in Arab affairs': Arab League official. *Al Arabiya English*. Retrieved from https://english.alarabiya.net/en/News/middle-east/2020/06/16/-Turkey-copying-Iran-s-interference-in-Arab-affairs-Arab-League-official

Al-Najjar, A. (2019). Abolish censorship and adopt critical media literacy: A proactive approach to media and youth in the Middle East. *Journal of Media Literacy Education*, *11*(3), 73–84.

Al-Najjar, A. (2020). *Public media accountability: Media journalism, engaged publics and critical media literacy in the MENA*. LSE Middle East Centre Paper Series (35). LSE Middle East Centre.

Almadhoun, S. (2015). Access to information in the Middle East and North Africa region. Retrieved from https://www.transparency.org/files/content/activity/2012_RDAAIMNA_ATIMNARegion_EN.pdf

Al-Rawi, A. K. (2014). Cyber warriors in the middle east: The case of the Syrian electronic army. *Public Relations Review*, *40*(3), 420–428.

Alterman, E. (2004). *When presidents lie: A history of official deception and its consequences*. New York, NY: Penguin.

Amin, H. (2002). Freedom as a value in Arab media: Perceptions and attitudes among journalists. *Political Communication*, *19*(2), 125–135.

Article 19. (2017). *Iran: Review of the publication and free access to information Act 2009*. Article 19. Free World Center, London. Retrieved from https://www.refworld.org/pdfid/59cccc574.pdf

Asghar, J. (2012). The postmodernist relativization of truth: A critique. *Islamic Studies*, *51*(3), 295–312.

Boukhars, A. (2014). North Africa: Back to the future. Carnegie Endowment for International Peace. Retrieved from https://carnegieendowment.org/2014/01/10/north-africa-back-to-future-pub-54145

Bradshaw, S., & Howard, P. N. (2019). Social media and democracy in crisis. In S. Bradshaw & P. N. Howard (Eds.), *Society and the internet: How networks of information and communication are changing our lives* (pp. 212–227). Oxford: Oxford University Press.

Chaudhry, I. (2014). Arab revolutions: Breaking fear|# hashtags for change: Can Twitter generate social progress in Saudi Arabia. *International Journal of Communication, 8*, 19.

Christensen, C. (2011). Discourses of technology and liberation: State aid to net activists in an era of "Twitter Revolutions". *The Communication Review, 14*(3), 233–253.

Cosentino, G. (2020). *Social media and the post-truth world order: The global dynamics of disinformation.* Cham: Palgrave Macmillan.

Cosentino, G., & Alikasifoglu, B. (2019). Post-truth politics in the Middle East: The case studies of Syria and Turkey. *Artnodes, 2019*(24), 91–100.

Daud, A. (2014). The role of "cyber-dissent" in stimulating democratization in the MENA region and empowering youth voices. In R. Raddawi (Ed.), *Intercultural communication with Arabs* (pp. 221–236). Singapore: Springer.

Day, I., Lazzarini, P., de Caen, S., AlHendawi, A., Khuri, F. R., Chaaban, J., ... Session, S. (2016). *The Arab human development report 2016 youth and the prospects for human development in a changing reality.* New York, NY: The United Nations Development Program.

Eberwein, T., Fengler, S., & Karmasin, M. (Eds.). (2019). *Media accountability in the era of post-truth politics: European challenges and perspectives.* New York, NY: Routledge.

Elswah, M., Howard, P. N., & Narayanan, V. (2019). Iranian digital interference in the Arab world. Data Memo. Project on Computational Propaganda, Oxford, United Kingdom, 1850–1867.

Frederiksen, L. (2017). Fake news. *Public Services Quarterly, 13*(2), 103–107.

Freedom House. (2019). *Freedom in the world 2019.* Freedom House. Retrieved from https://freedomhouse.org/sites/default/files/Feb2019_FH_FITW_2019_Report_ForWeb-compressed.pdf

Grizzle, A. (2016). Preliminary comparative analysis of media and information literacy in the MENA region. In *Opportunities for media and information literacy in the Middle East and North Africa* (pp. 21). Gothenburg: Nordicom.

Grossman, S., DiResta, R., & Kheradpir, T. (2020). Blurring the lines of media authenticity: Prigozhin-linked group funding Libyan broadcast media. Stanford Internet Observatory. Retrieved from https://cyber.fsi.stanford.edu/io/news/libya-prigozhin

Grossman, S., Khadija, H., DiResta, R., Kheradpir, T., & Miller, C. (2020). Blame it on Iran, Qatar, and Turkey: An analysis of a Twitter and Facebook operation linked to Egypt, the UAE, and Saudi Arabia. Stanford Internet Observatory. Retrieved from https://fsi-live.s3.us-west-1.amazonaws.com/s3fs-public/20200402_blame_it_on_iran_qatar_and_turkey_v2_0.pdf

Harsin, J. (2018). Post-truth and critical communication studies. In *Oxford research encyclopedia of communication* (pp. 1–33). Oxford: Oxford University Press.

Harvey, D., & Yoel, R. (2018). An update on our elections integrity work. *Twitter Blog.* Retrieved from https://blog.twitter.com/en_us/topics/company/2018/an-update-on-our-elections-integrity-work.html

Holmes, A. (2019). Twitter just suspended over 88,000 accounts tied to a Saudi disinformation campaign. *Business Insider.* Retrieved from https://www.businessinsider.com/twitter-removed-accounts-saudi-arabia-disinformation-campaign-2019-12

Hubbard, B. (2019, November 7). *Why spy on Twitter? For Saudi Arabia, It's the town square.* The New York Times. Retrieved from https://www.nytimes.com/2019/11/07/world/middleeast/saudi-arabia-twitter-arrests.html

Huguet, A., Kavanagh, J., Baker, G., & Blumenthal, M. S. (2019). *Exploring media literacy education as a tool for mitigating truth decay.* Santa Monica, CA: RAND Corporation.

Internet World Stats. (2020). Internet usage in the Middle East: Middle East internet usage and population statistics. Retrieved from https://www.internetworldstats.com/stats5.htm

Jones, R. (2019). In Saudi Arabia, Twitter has become a tool to crack down on Dissent: The Saudi government's attempts to control Twitter have mirrored a broader crackdown on dissent in the kingdom. *The Wall Street Journal.* Retrieved from https://www.wsj.com/articles/in-saudi-arabia-twitter-has-become-a-tool-to-crack-down-on-dissent-11573126932

Kavanagh, J., & Rich, M. D. (2018). *Truth decay.* Santa Monica, CA: RAND Corporation.

Keyes, R. (2004). *The post-truth era: Dishonesty and deception in contemporary life.* New York, NY: Macmillan.

Khazen, J. (1999). Censorship and state control of the press in the Arab world. *Harvard International Journal of Press/Politics, 4*(3), 87–92.

Kinninmont, J. (2019). *The Gulf divided: The impact of the Qatar crisis.* London: The Royal Institute of International Affairs, Chatham House.

Kocaoglu, B. U. (2013). Right to information in Turkey in the scope of accountability. *Trakya University Journal of Social Science, 15,* 1–18.

Kroet, S. (2017). 'Post-truth' enters Oxford English Dictionary Zyzzyva to replace Zythum as the last word in the dictionary. *Politico.* Retrieved from https://www.politico.eu/article/post-truth-enters-oxford-english-dictionary/

Kurtz, H. (2013). Media's failure on Iraq still stings. *CNN.* Retrieved from https://edition.cnn.com/2013/03/11/opinion/kurtz-iraq-media-failure/index.html

Llorente, J. A. (2017). The post-truth era: Reality vs. perception. Retrieved from https://www.uno-magazine.com/wp-content/uploads/2017/03/UNO_27_ENG_alta.pdf

McIntyre, L. (2018). *Post-truth.* Cambridge, MA: MIT Press.

Melki, J. P. (2013). Sowing the seeds of digital and media literacy in Lebanon and the Arab world. In B. S. De Abreu & P. Mihailidis (Eds.), *Media literacy education in action: Theoretical and pedagogical perspectives* (pp. 77–86). New York, NY: Routledge.

Melki, J. P. (2015). Guiding digital and media literacy development in Arab curricula through understanding media uses of Arab youth. *Journal of Media Literacy Education, 6*(3), 14–28.

Palestine Center for Development and Media Freedoms. (2019). On the challenges of digital rights in Palestine. Ifex. Retrieved from https://ifex.org/on-the-challenges-of-digital-rights-in-palestine/

Penders, B. (2018). Why public dismissal of nutrition science makes sense: Post-truth, public accountability and dietary credibility. *British Food Journal, 120*(9), 1953–1964.

Peters, C. (2013). Even better than being informed. Satirical news and media literacy. In M. Broersma & C. Peters (Eds.), *Rethinking journalism. Trust and participation in a transformed news landscape* (pp. 173–188). New York, NY: Routledge.

Postman, N. (1970). The reformed English curriculum. In A. C. Eurich (Ed.), *High school 1980: The shape of the future in American secondary education* (pp. 160–168). New York, NY: Pitman Publishing Corporation.

Postman, N. (2000). The humanism of media ecology. *Proceedings of the Media Ecology Association, 1*(1), 10–16.

Postman, N. (2010). What is media ecology? Retrieved from http://www.media-eco-logy.org/media_ecology/index.html#WhatisMediaEcology?

Rampersad, G., & Althiyabi, T. (2020). Fake news: Acceptance by demographics and culture on social media. *Journal of Information Technology & Politics, 17*(1), 1–11.

Roberts, D. B. (2017). Qatar, the Ikhwan, and transnational relations in the Gulf. *The Qatar Crisis, 54.*

Rownsley, A. (2020, July 7). *Right-wing media outlets duped by a Middle East media campaign.* The Daily Beast. Retrieved from https://www.thedailybeast.com/right-wing-media-outlets-duped-by-a-middle-east-propaganda-campaign

Saleh, I. (2009). Media literacy in MENA: Moving beyond the vicious cycle of oxymora. *Comunicar: Revista Científica de Comunicación y Educación, 16*(32), 119–129.

Scher, I. (2019). Restriction on press freedom in the Middle East and beyond. *The American Prospect.* Retrieved from https://prospect.org/blogs/tap/restrictions-on-press-freedom-in-middle-east/

Sismondo, S. (2017). Post-truth? *Social Studies of Science, 47*(1), 3–6. doi:10.1177/0306312717692076

Solon, O. (2017). How Syria's white helmets became victims of an online propaganda machine. *The Guardian.* Retrieved from https://www.theguardian.com/world/2017/dec/18/syria-white-helmets-conspiracy-theories

Stephens, N. P. (2014). Toward a more substantive media ecology: Postman's metaphor versus posthuman futures. *International Journal of Communication, 8,* 19.

Twitter Safety. (2020). New disclosures to our archive of stat-backed information operations. *Twitter Blog.* Retrieved from https://blog.twitter.com/en_us/topics/company/2019/new-disclosures-to-our-archive-of-state-backed-information-operations.html

@TwitterSafety. (2020, October 8). *Disclosing networks to our state-linked information operation archive.* Twitter Blog. Retrieved from https://blog.twitter.com/en_us/topics/company/2020/disclosing-removed-networks-to-our-archive-of-state-linked-information.html

Warren, M., & Leitch, S. (2016). The Syrian Electronic Army–a hacktivist group. *Journal of Information, Communication and Ethics in Society, 14*(2), 200–212.

Whitten-Woodring, J. (2009). Watchdog or lapdog? Media freedom, regime type, and government respect for human rights. *International Studies Quarterly, 53*(3), 595–625.

Wilner, M. (2019). Jared Kushner is deploying a data operation to sway Arab media on Middle East peace. *Impact 2020.* Retrieved from https://www.mcclatchydc.com/news/politics-government/white-house/article232878077.html

Woolley, S., & Howard, P. (2017). *Computational propaganda worldwide: Executive summary.* Working Paper No. 2017.11. Retrieved from https://comprop.oii.ox.-ac.uk/wp-content/uploads/sites/89/2017/06/Casestudies-ExecutiveSummary.pdf

World Population. (2020). World population review: Arab countries 2020. Retrieved from https://worldpopulationreview.com/country-rankings/arab-countries

Zarzalejos, J. A. (2017). Communication, journalism and fact checking. In J. A. Llorente & Cuenca (Eds.), *The post-truth era: Reality vs. perception* (pp. 11–13). Madrid: Developing Ideas by Llorente and Cuenca.

Chapter 6

Critical Literacy Is at the Heart of the Answer

Emma Pauncefort

Abstract

2019 was a big year. *The Great Hack* and investigative journalism of Carole Cadwalladr exposed the machinations of Cambridge Analytica. The US senate summoned Mark Zuckerberg to face an extended interrogation on the ways in which Facebook screens content. Greta Thunberg fomented a global 'climate emergency' movement with attacks on lying political leaders. If 2016 saw 'post-truth' rise to prominence as a concept, 2019 was characterised by myriad efforts to champion truth and counter misinformation. And then the COVID-19 crisis hit. The urgency we began to feel in 2019 to address the ills in our society and hunt for a cause and cure has intensified. We now daily ask at whose door we can lay the blame and, from there, what solutions we can implement. For now, we have drawn the battle lines between tech and society and looked to pit governments against technologies which have changed the face of media. But amidst this flurry of activity, we need to stop and ask ourselves: are we setting our sights on the right actors and are we taking the right next steps?

Written in the midst of the COVID-19 pandemic, this contribution responds to the burning debate on how to overcome our current infodemic and immunise against future outbreaks. It offers an alternative narrative and argues for a much more radical course of action. It posits that we have misidentified the root cause of our current post-truth reality. It argues that we are in fact experiencing the extreme consequence of decades of poor education the world over. It champions a shift from drilling young people in so-called facts and figures to developing those deep levels of literacy in which critical thinking plays a fundamental part. This is not to exculpate the Facebooks and Twitters of our time – new tech has no doubt facilitated the dissemination of half-truths and untruths. But it is to insist upon contextualising our current albeit horrifying reality within a much more complex and longer-running societal challenge. In other words, this chapter makes a fresh clarion call for rethinking how we

Media, Technology and Education in a Post-Truth Society, 73–94
Copyright © 2021 by Emerald Publishing Limited
All rights of reproduction in any form reserved
doi:10.1108/978-1-80043-906-120211006

have got to where we are and where we might most meaningfully go next, as well as how, indeed, we might conceptualise the links between technology, government, media and education.

Keywords: Critical literacy; information; fact; censorship; moderation; regulation

'Couldn't you make it more attractive'?

'To whom?' asked Gideon

'Well – the ordinary reader'.

'Oh the ordinary reader. I meant it to be attractive to people who want information'.

–Rose Macaulay, 1920.[1]

This exchange features in Macaulay's novel *Potterism: A Tragi-Farcical Tract*. It glimpses a heated fictional exchange between two journalists with disparate views on their responsibilities as the gatekeepers of information. Here, we watch Gideon, a writer fighting for responsible representation of facts and lived experience, challenging the stance of Peacock, a fellow editor with eyes firmly set on what is good for business. The dialogue encapsulates the main concern of the novel: a biting critique of the conscious blurring of fact and fiction for financial and political gain.

Potterism hit bookshops almost exactly a century ago. And yet it holds timeless pertinence such is the ongoing and, indeed, intensified battle between two camps: one producing whatever content best fills company coffers (notwithstanding public statements to the contrary), even if this means furthering the objectives of bad actors; the other fighting for the use of technologies old and new to disseminate the spoken and written word for the common good.

This pitching of two sides had been painfully evident in 2019. On the morning of 13 December, voters in the United Kingdom woke up to the news that the Conservative Party had won a sliding majority. The swing of seats had been dramatic: the Conservatives cheered a gain of 47 and their main opponents, the Labour Party, commiserated the loss of 59. The Scottish National Party, another key adversary, might have won over an extra 13 constituencies in Scotland, but the fact remained that the Conservatives were now firmly in government and so, claimed a triumphant Boris Johnson, had the mandate of the people to 'Get Brexit done'.

This is how I was going to start this piece. 2019 had felt like a big year. A central figure from the Vote Leave campaign was now incumbent in government. This had been a campaign which, as Netflix's *The Great Hack* revealed, had concealed shady dealings with the now disgraced British political consulting firm Cambridge Analytica. This had also been a campaign which had oiled the wheels of political rhetoric with – to take Macaulay's cue – 'attractive' phrases like never before; the emotive slogans rehearsed by those on both sides of the debate had meant that many had voted with their hearts rather than their heads.[2] What better a springboard to advocate the need for critical literacy education? Little did I know what would be coming just around the corner.

I write in the midst of the COVID-19 pandemic, a pandemic which has been accompanied by a terrifying 'infodemic'.[3] No sooner do we digest one episode of our current drama, another season, complemented by gut-wrenching bonus material, flickers tragically on our radars. We are faced with the Great Flood of bad information. We find ourselves at the heart of a deluge that threatens to have consequences of biblical proportions. Whilst the everyday business of education has been disrupted like never before, our current moment has brought into sharp, agonising focus the real education crisis we, as global citizens, are currently facing: a dearth of deeper, socially embedded literacy skills.[4] The answer? Critical literacy instruction. Not simply, however, as yet another contiguous scheme of learning. Nor as a stand-alone measure. Instead, the answer is to ensure critical literacy instruction sits within the foundations of a timeless education for all and, in turn, at the heart of joined-up efforts to manage the creation and consumption of information in our bewildering C21st information ecosystem.

Drawing on my experience of working at the intersection of secondary and tertiary education in the United Kingdom for nearly a decade, my aim here is to outline the rationale for such an urgent, connected course of instruction. I am not the first to make this clarion call. Nor, I hope, will I be the last. But the crisis in which we find ourselves warrants its rearticulation within the mix of measures already instigated by government, technology firms, media and education outfits, some of which have only emerged after mounting internal and public pressure. The COVID-19 experience demands examination of how we can reinforce existing school curricula whilst veritably preparing young people for C21st society. Our alarm signal requires reconnection with the contentious 'skills versus knowledge' debate. And it entails a review of why government regulation, content moderation by people and platforms, public campaigns and media/information literacy initiatives, albeit welcome, cannot alone tackle this crisis but must instead operate alongside the prioritisation of deep education.

The starting point for this call is our current infodemic. This is not, however, to suggest that our need for critical literacy is as novel as the virus we face. The information challenge global society is now staring down is, at its heart, nothing new.[5] Nor is it a transitory hazard. From that moment when humans first started to communicate, the race was on to develop the skills to unpick the information others present to us; the race was on to turn unrelenting information obstacles into stable information opportunities. Our current age is furnishing us with many a highly charged term – 'post-truth', 'fake news' to name the main contenders.[6] These are, however, but new labels for age-old concepts, albeit now being experienced and commented upon more widely than ever before.

In other words, the clarion call I make here is hundreds, if not thousands, of years overdue in its vigour. But come finally it must, with the overarching COVID-19 infodemic as our catalyst, and the infodemic's characteristics a driving case in point. Thus, with as much circumspection as is possible when commentating on a crisis from within its midst, it is to our current lived experience that I first turn.

The COVID-19 Infodemic – A Catalyst and Case in Point

> 'A regular Potter melodrama', said Gideon. 'It might be in one of
> your mother's novels or your father's papers. That just shows,
> Jane, how infectious a thing Potterism is. It invades the least likely
> homes, and upsets the least likely lives. Horrible, catching disease'.
>
> –Potterism

History does not just repeat itself; it continues unrelenting. A century on from Macaulay's diatribe against media falsities and the individual's complicity in the creation and dissemination of poor information, the epitome of 'Potterism', we find ourselves fighting – to mirror the language employed by world leaders since the onset of the crisis – for the health of society on multiple fronts.

The level of poor information that has accompanied the COVID-19 pandemic has been staggering. Such has been the torrent unleashed that commentators have struggled to offer suitably forceful metaphors. We have been blessed with the reported spectacle of swans and dolphins 'returning' to Venetian canals. We have been horrified by the vision of army tanks entering London. These are but a snapshot of the myriad shades of inexact or unverified information consumed recently by readers across the globe.

The spreading of false information has at times proved inadvertent, as was the case with the Venice story (Daly, 2020). In other instances, the dissemination of misleading information has clearly been intentional. Regrettably, the COVID-19 drama has amply staged political manoeuvring, grimly enlivened with partial storytelling that has not only distorted public messaging but also aggravated fragile diplomatic tensions (the blame game that played out between Trump's White House and China is our prominent example here). Sometimes the motivation has been less clear. A tweet dated 18 March 2020 claiming that the army was taking over London was quickly disproved by the Twitter community: one account holder identified the accompanying image as taken in Tiananmen Square during the student protests of 1989; another individual tweeted: 'are you for real? If you're joking put a smiling emoji at the end if not FFS!'. This disbelief was not, however, widely shared; the story proliferated across the platform and media outlets. The following morning, the Twitter account for *The Daily Star*, a UK tabloid newspaper, reported with an accompanying picture of a policeman and soldier: 'London on coronavirus lockdown by weekend as army moves into "city of super spreaders"'. The proverbial cat had been let out of the misinformation bag. In all these cases, the problem was less that poor content had been shared, but that readers, many readers, engaged with it, and, for the most part, with unquestioning faith in the yarn being woven.

The level of poor content and engagement with it is great cause for concern. The COVID-19 infodemic has not, however, germinated a new problem. If we pair a report on COVID-19 misinformation with world-class thinking on misinformation published in the wake of 2016, the year in which the toxic convergence of power, personality and politics had been catalogued in the UK EU referendum and the US Presidential election, we find common themes: the power of statements by public figures and the speed with which social media promulgates poor information, and the preference amongst those looking to disseminate it to lean on 'reconfigured true content' rather than deepfakes.[7] This finding again corresponds with accepted understanding and experience (and re-emphasises the extent to which the term 'fake news' really is a misnomer).[8] As we are seeing time and time again, it is hard to create billows of smoke without even the smallest fire.

In other words, the COVID-19 infodemic has deplorably rehearsed the whole gamut of bad information and further exposed the complex ecosystem that has grown up around it. This spectrum takes in three broad, overlapping categories: misinformation ('defective information or 'mistakes''); disinformation ('deceptive information or 'hoaxes''), which includes material that is 'politically motivated' or is, in other words, propaganda; and malformation ('damaging information or gossip') (Kivenen, 2020). In Claire Wardle's conceptualisation, 'information disorder' can be defined further according to seven levels of content that are differentiated according to the level of harm intended. These levels, in order from 'low harm' to 'high harm', include 'satire or parody' (an inclusion marking the complexity of information disorder), 'false connection', 'misleading content', 'false context', 'imposter content', 'manipulated content' and 'fabricated content' (Wardle, 2019, pp. 10–11).[9]

It can prove a challenge determining which category should be assigned to bad content. To take our above examples, this is straightforward in the case of the Venice story – this is a typical case of 'false connection', defined as 'when headlines, visuals, or captions don't support the content'.[10] The appropriate category is, however, less evident when it comes to the army in the London story. If the tweet was in fact meant humorously, then we could possibly place it near the 'satire or parody' label; if not, then our next option is to assign the label of 'manipulated content', defined as 'when genuine information or imagery is manipulated to deceive'.[11] Intention therefore counts for much and, without knowledge of it, we are left unsure as to the best categorisation and, in turn, how we might best react.

Nevertheless, aside from the truism that it is rarely possible to define socio-cultural phenomena neatly, the above taxonomies remain extremely important. They bring welcome clarification to the 'fake news' problem in moving us beyond a term that clouds public understanding. The term 'fake news', itself political in origin, is a label that has become heavily politicised (Wendling, 2018). Since its emergence in 2016, it has morphed into a protean category readily deployed to rebuff unwelcome content by political leaders and disappointed speculators, amongst others, and even to redefine, and thus discredit and undermine, the entirety of the media sector (Wardle, 2019, p. 7).[12] Importantly, by honing in on the particular characteristics of our 'information disorder', the categories proposed by Wardle and others alert us to the tentacular reaches of poor information. We should not be discouraged by any seeming mismatch between theory and practice. Rather, we should appreciate how this highlights the complexity of the information range available to us, not just in relation to COVID-19, but across all human knowledge and both online and offline.

Meanwhile, experience of the COVID-19 infodemic remains extremely important. It has proved yet again how we, the reading public, like a good story and how, they, the authors of bad content, often play on our emotions and our deep-rooted fears (Douglas, Sutton, & Cichocka, 2017). It is without doubt another unleashing of the standard information warfare to which we have become – or need to become – accustomed (boyd, 2017). Above all, this infodemic has highlighted the urgency of required action and has piloted what forms part of this action might take.

There has been some movement in the right direction. In the United Kingdom, the BBC, for example, has gone to perceptible lengths to reconfigure programming to raise public understanding with regard to misinformation. Meanwhile, there have been concerted efforts by online platforms, from Apple to Google to Canva and even to Facebook, to strike out as socially responsible leaders in our digital world, albeit in some cases following mounting pressure both internally and externally.[13]

I will tackle the case of social media in greater detail in the ensuing section. I am particularly interested in the shifts in position summer 2020 precipitated and the increasing focus of governments looking to step in. My position nevertheless remains one of concern: neither of these developments bring us closer to an anti-dote, as I will explain.

To Regulate or Not to Regulate, That Is the Question

'Lord Pinkerton would say, learn human nature as it is and build on it. Exploit its weaknesses, instead of tilting against them. Accept sentimentality and prejudice, and use them.'

–Potterism

In his opening remarks to the hearing Social Media Influence in the 2016 US Election on 1 November, 2017, the vice chairman of the Senate Intelligence Committee, Mark Warner, captured the double-edged sword of technological expansion over the past 30 years (United States Senate/Select Committee on Intelligence, 2018, p. 5.). 'The social media and innovative tools each of you have developed', he stated, addressing the CEOs lined up before him, 'have changed our world for the better'. Facebook, Twitter and Google have 'transformed the way we do everything [–] from shopping for groceries to growing small businesses'. Soon, however, Warner's remarks changed course. With quasi-classical epideictic flourish, he tempered his initial bestowal of praise with his ensuing comments. The Committee, he was at pains to underline, felt strongly that, collectively, the companies had not done enough to manage the 'dark underbelly' of the 'ecosystem' they had created (United States Senate/Select Committee on Intelligence, 2018).

Many a household name, and now for many, a household lifeline, derive from tech. Think GAFA (Google, Amazon, Facebook, Apple) as well as the Skypes, Twitters and Zooms of our time. The relatively short history of these tech tools makes their prominence in our daily lives all the more awesome. In 2019 Facebook, for example, reported 2.38 billion users or, in other words, counted amongst its monthly active users over a third of the global population (Roser, Ritchie, & Ortiz-Ospina, 2015, 2019). We have become a highly networked and connected society with possibilities previous generations could barely have imagined. This has been the boon of tech.

Yet this boon has been accompanied by the bad, as Warner flagged in his address. The quick expansion, take-up and the resultant power of these platforms have together gifted productive channels and a lamentably robust infrastructure to bad actors, with social media in particular offering a fertile nursery ground for poor information. A portal to a third of the population is very enticing indeed and has to date been amply exploited for better and for worse. To take 2016, 2019 and the COVID crisis as examples, we have witnessed critical moments in global history, not just accompanied, but characterised by staggering levels of false information.

In response, Facebook in particular has been summoned repeatedly by government authorities over the past few years. The 2017 US hearing, however, is of particular interest here in that it marks a moment in which the aftermath of a crisis brought to the fore two intersecting antidotes for poor information: government regulation and content moderation. The hearing marked a moment in which the seeming fallout between tech and society ignited debate as to who the bad actors really are – are they those who misuse tech tools, or those creators who allow a powerful ecosystem they have developed to kindle antisocial activity? The concern in 2017 centred round Google, Twitter and Facebook's repeated demonstration of 'a lack of resources, a lack of commitment, and a lack of genuine effort' and hence the recognition that regulation might be required to force companies to moderate content (United States Senate/Select Committee on Intelligence, 2018, p. 56.). In the summer of 2020, we witnessed a startling shift in the words and actions of these companies, with resources, commitment and genuine effort strikingly becoming de rigueur, and investment in whole-hearted pandering to sentimentality and prejudice apparently becoming passé. Nevertheless, the same stumbling blocks we saw back in 2017 that threatened successful administration of regulation and moderation remain.

To start with the question of government intervention, the regulation of technology is fraught with difficulty, not just for the US government but any democracy. Taking 'regulation' to indicate 'the intentional use of authority to affect behaviour of a different party according to set standards', Brownsford, Scotford and Yeung have underlined the challenge at hand. The speed of technological change has left legal frameworks furlongs behind, struggling to keep up. 'In this context', they warn, 'the contours of legal and regulatory action are not obvious, nor are the frames for analysis' (Brownsford, Scotford, & Yeung, 2017, pp. 4–6.). There are, they qualify, 'many ways in which technological innovation is legally disruptive' (Brownsford et al., 2017, p. 8.). This is not to say that regulation is impossible. Wins in the regulatory arena include the EU's GDPR legislation and parallel laws in other jurisdictions. Such intervention has started to tackle the data privacy issue – a significant challenge ushered in by technological advancement and, of course, intimately connected with the information issue.[14] Moving beyond these measures soon, however, becomes highly problematic.

Even if the law could be brought up to speed, government involvement in how technology firms operate and, specifically, how they control content treads a fine line between management and censorship of information. This is no new dilemma. Variously in the name of public decency, morale and national security, governments the world over have long made it their business to control access to information and ideas both in war and peacetime. To control information is to control public opinion; to control public opinion is to wield political power (as, indeed, Macaulay starkly underlined). Previously, the bid to stem the flow of information focused on printed publications – novels, newspapers and the like. With the growth of other media and the emergence of new technologies – television, radio and, of course, the Internet and mobile technologies – the challenge has become all the greater but not insurmountable; shutting down information channels is sadly not confined to Bradburian or Huxleian fiction.

From state-controlled closed 'internets' (think North Korea, China, Iran) to complete Internet shutdowns (think India and Kashmir) to flagrant attempts to curb press freedoms and freedom of speech (cue Belarus, Singapore, Brazil and the Philippines, not to mention jurisdictions which pride themselves as democracies), it is no wonder that a statement from the Internet Society in December 2019 warned of rising restrictions to Internet access worldwide (Internet Society, 2019). Nor should we be surprised that NGO Reporters Without Borders (RSF) has mobilised to track attacks on responsible media more closely (Reporters Without Borders, 2020).

Against this background, fervour for regulation of digital platforms is on the rise. Dot Everyone's 2020 report on digital attitudes relayed that 58% of the UK public feel the tech sector operates with too little regulation, with similarly around half of respondents hopeful that government and independent regulators will take action (Miller, Kitcher, Perera, & Abiola, 2020). Yet we still lack the clarity we need for this to happen, namely, agreement on where regulation ends and censorship begins. In the context of the COVID infodemic, we have been warned of how problematic it is for public authorities to counter and debunk misinformation, especially when the core subject matter of that bad information relates to their own actions (Brennen, Simon, Howard, & Nielsen, 2020). Government action can soon smack of the Trumpian approach to journalism, that is shouting 'fake' when not favourable. The predicament faced by those debating government regulation in democratic jurisdictions is the following: too far one way and legislation will be little more than a damp squib; too far the other, then we move into those realms of control more characteristic of authoritarian regimes. There are meanwhile considerations of which we should remain acutely aware in our current economic climate: who will be the winners and losers of such measures? As Stephanie Rieger's deck *Regulate the Web* reminds us, regulation will most likely hurt small and new businesses who will struggle to cover the astronomical cost of compliance; Big Tech will meanwhile smile smugly on, comforted by their extensive resources and clout.[15] Regulation does not, then, offer a clear panacea. This is clearest when we scrutinise the core element in the plan of action it advocates: content moderation.

To Moderate or Not to Moderate, That Is the Other Question

The backdrop to this antidote again resides within that thorny issue of where we should draw the line between free speech and censorship. We also face the equally troublesome question of whether social media companies are platforms or publishers. These twin issues have long fuelled the lines of defence harnessed by social media companies, especially Facebook, to exonerate themselves from charges of inaction and irresponsibility. Here we could quote many an exchange between Zuckerberg and government authorities and news outlets between 2016 and spring 2020. We could also point to Facebook's breakneck u-turn between May and August 2020. In the space of three months the platform dropped its long-held position of hesitancy (and expediency) when it came to moderating political output. In its place came many a proclamation of its unfailing commitment to safeguarding the health of society and the democratic process through rigorous content moderation across the board.[16] What a difference a summer of coronavirus, Black Lives Matter protests and political campaigning makes, not to mention the added pressure of an advertising boycott (here I am referencing the #StopHateForProfit campaign which, as of September 2020, boasts the backing of over 1,100 businesses and 100 non-profits) and internal revolt at Facebook. The outlook I first painted on drafting this essay in April 2020 need not, it now happily turns out, have been so bleak; exploiting prejudice in the name of free speech is now under sustained attack from multiple quarters.

And yet, there is still much cause for concern. Even with expanded energy and efforts, and even if it were to be written into law, content moderation offers no straightforward solution. The reasons why could be the subject of an essay in its own right (and indeed forms the subject of supplementary work to this essay). For now, I would like to expand upon my earlier discussion of information categories and complexity. Here, we reach the crux of the content moderation conundrum – the grey middle area of information and the very human role in content creation and consumption – and return to the main thrust of this essay: that education must lie at the heart of an answer to managing C21st information channels.

The warnings of the real challenge posed by information when it comes to applying moderation techniques sit within the reports of information disorder experts and behind even the triumphant statements heralding progress from the likes of Facebook. One substantial issue is volume. We have little way of knowing the exact amount of information online.[17] Nor can we account accurately for the proportion of poor information. What we can extrapolate, however, from the data available to us and the commentary linked to it is that the levels and nature of content moderation required overwhelm not just man but also machine.

Here is not the place to go into detail about the use of artificial intelligence in this sphere (this will also form the subject of future work). What is worth noting at this point is that the impossibility of applying neat categories to different forms of information means we are working way beyond the current capabilities of any program or algorithm. It also means that we have even further to go in terms of clearing up related moral quandaries (the debates surrounding driverless cars offer an interesting parallel). As Wardle (2019, p. 24) has counselled, 'Computers understand true and false, but misleading is full of grey'. The repeated problematic experiences of Facebook in applying machine learning to content moderation have shown the extreme limitations of algorithmic moderation.[18] Equally, the December 2019 report from UK-based fact-checking organisation Full Fact following participation in Facebook's Third Party Fact-Checking Programme documents the extensive improvement, particularly with regard to information categories, required if, for example, Facebook's initiative is to have deeper-reaching impact (Full Fact, 2018). Clearly, technology has a role to play, not least in protecting human moderators from exposure to violent content and contracting PTSD (Newton, 2020; Facebook, n.d.b). But it seems unlikely we will reach a point in the near to mid future at which we will be able to hand over our moderation woes to automation and guarantee a review of all content. For now, we are forced to rely heavily on human intervention. And here, we start to unearth the real limitations of current moderation practices. We also start to come back to how the content consumer and their individual competences offer the real site of a solution.

Two troubling consequences of relying on manpower are what have been termed the 'illusion of truth effect' and the 'implied truth effect'. The 'illusion of truth effect' is a phenomenon whereby older social media users who are repeatedly told content is false convert that memory a few days later to remember that content as true (Brashier & Schacter, 2020). The 'implied truth effect', meanwhile, plays out when we as users accept any unchecked content as uncontentious or unproblematic, or, in other words, 'true' (Pennycock, Collins, Bear, & Rand, 2019). In his May 2020 BBC interview, Zuckerberg proudly pointed to Facebook's COVID-19 record of responding to 7,500 notices of misinformation and issuing 50 million warning labels on posts, and with positive outcomes (Jack, 2020).[19] Research into the two aforementioned effects tells us, however, that the possible unconscious morphing of falsity into truth as a result of selective moderation and labelling should put us on our guard, especially when we are dealing with the current volumes of poor information in the context of current moderation methods. In January 2019, Full Fact were quick to underline that fact-checking is no 'magic pill'. As their blog post cautions: 'Fact-checking is slow, careful, pretty unglamorous work – and realistically we know we can't possibly review all the potentially false claims that appear on Facebook every day'. It is, they qualified, 'a step in the right direction, and a chance to tackle misinformation that makes a real difference to people's lives' (Full Fact, 2019). But a mere step it remains. Fast forward to April 2020 and we received this statement from Cristina Tardáguila, Associate Director of the International Fact-Checking Network: 'Covid-19 is the biggest challenge fact-checkers have ever faced' (Brennen et al., 2020, p. 2). Research, albeit currently limited, and commentary together remind us not to be too quickly won over by Facebook's updates.

Clearly, then, regulation and moderation can only succeed with the involvement of the critical human reader; the individual who undertakes their own due diligence every time they are faced with content. This has long been recognised by those in the business of fact-checking, as well as by governments themselves. The Code of Principles to which all members of the International Fact-Checking Network are required to adhere stem from the belief that fact-checking by organisations is but one line of defence.[20] Checks and balances to manage human bias run through each of the five principles. The partnership between fact-checker and content consumer is otherwise confirmed in the requirement that fact-checkers undertake each check with a clear methodology so as to allow readers to 'replicate' their work.[21] This collaborative effort is widely acknowledged by organisations. As Full Fact note, the reason many items end up in the moderation queue for fact-checkers in the first place is down to user engagement through flagging posts (Full Fact, 2019, pp. 9 and 25). This positioning of the individual within high-level action meanwhile tallies with the view of legislators, as evidenced by Warner's comments back in October 2017:

> It will take all of us – the platform companies, the United States government, and the American people – to deal with this new and evolving threat... We all need to take a more discerning approach to what we are reading and sharing, and who we are connecting with online. (United States Senate/Select Committee on Intelligence, 2018, p. 6)

Governments, profits and non-profits have achieved some level of consensus: the individual has a responsibility to provide both the first and last line of defence.

The question remains: how do we empower individuals so that they are able to exercise this responsibility, so they are able to navigate the material left unlabelled and verify that which *has* been reviewed, to make informed political and health decisions and not be drawn in by false stories of hope, even in circumstances such as our own? Here, I finally cue critical literacy.

Critical Literacy Education Fit for Societal Purpose

> 'Well, what's the remedy then?' He said, wearily, 'Oh, education, I suppose, Education... We should train them, educate them, teach them to think, see that they know something – know it exactly, with no blurred edges, no fogs. Be sure of our facts, and keep theories out of the system like poison...'
>
> –Potterism

This exchange between characters Jane and Gideon, two 'anti-Potterites'-turned-lovers, features near the end of Macaulay's *Potterism*. It marks a crescendo of lamentations on the ills of the information ecosystem of 1920, an ecosystem driven by the voraciousness of a reading public for information confirming their beliefs rather than challenging them, and propelled by a grim publishing machinery that happily whetted this appetite. For Macaulay, the outlook was gloomy. Gideon, the one character who embarks upon a bold and perilous discovery for the 'truth', meets his end whilst doing so. Effecting a sea change in opinion and embedding a desire to read and relay reality, whatever the cost, felt nigh on humanly impossible.

In 2020 and beyond, we face parallel challenges. With the threat of misinformation firmly on the radar, a tin lining of COVID-19, we have finally left the starting block and begun to nurse our information ecosystem to a decent level of health. The decisions and reactions of the likes of Twitter and Facebook now face daily scrutiny. No longer can even the biggest players passively feed off the user desire for clickable, sensational content. Much more, however, remains to be done, especially if we want to shift from being reactive to proactive and veritably nurture C21st global citizens. As with many of society's ills, education holds the key.

Here, however, I advocate for a very particular type of education: an education that sets us up for active participation in society instead of passive reception of the status quo and the content that props it up. I advocate for an education that makes us critical consumers of media and emboldens us to contribute to a shared envisioning of a better future for society. I advocate for an education that does not dispense with the acquisition of knowledge within subjects that have long formed the backbone of education systems – the Sciences, the Humanities, the Arts – but encourages us to tease out synergies between disciplines as part of the daily course of our study. Above all, I advocate for an education that links up our learning with our lived experience. This education is critical literacy education.

There are countless obstacles, many of them political, to its implementation. Yet, I believe that critical literacy alone has the power to square the circle between providing a rigorous and empowering C21st education and offering an administrable measure to combat infodemics present and to come.

Up until this point, I have made no mention of critical thinking, perhaps to my readers' surprise. Pull up any treatise advocating C21st education and you are likely to find an insistence that today's young urgently need 'critical thinking' skills. The problem is there is little consensus as to what this skill set actually embodies. Here is not the place to discuss the genesis and complex development of 'critical thinking' within education, a term and practice which continues to divide critics as to its definition and implementation. It is, however, important to document the obvious overlap with critical literacy and how it privileges, as I will come to explain, the scrutiny of information so that individuals can respond meaningfully to content. The World Economic Forum's recent definition of critical thinking as 'the ability to identify, analyse and evaluate situations, ideas and information in order to formulate responses to problems' (World Economic Forum, 2015, p. 3) makes this link clear.

In adopting the term 'critical literacy', I am drawing heavily on the work of Allan Luke whose name has become synonymous with the critical literacy movement. Over nearly four decades of research, practice and publications, Luke has heightened the call to broaden our understanding of literacy in response to fast-changing modes of human communication. He has brought intellectual movements and the attention on discourses and how socio-political forces can shape knowledge to bear on education. He has encouraged us to look beyond our conventional understanding of literacy and practices within national borders; to be bold in what we cover in the name of literacy.[22] Building on the legacy of Paulo Friere, his aim has always been to allow children to progress from '"reading the word" to "reading the world"'.[23] Luke has been consistently clear on marking the distinction between the fixed, passive practice of conventional literacy and the wide-ranging, activist practice of critical literacy. In his hands, critical literacy encapsulates the 'cultural and linguistic practice' par excellence that ought to be exercised by every global citizen.[24]

Luke's work has been infused increasingly with a tone of urgency. In 2012, this was in the wake of the Wikileaks scandal; in 2018, this was in the wake of the US and UK votes I referenced above. In 2018 he declared that our era is facing an 'epistemological crisis'. It is hard to conceive of suitably forceful language to describe 2020. It is meanwhile difficult to emphasise enough the centrality of education in bringing us back from this existential precipice. As Luke has remarked, 'Technology per se didn't cause these problems, nor does it in-and-of-itself have the capacity to solve or fix them'.[25] We are reminded to concentrate our efforts elsewhere.

Critical literacy instruction has previously enjoyed some glimmers of support from policy makers.[26] Yet just when it is needed more than ever, its implementation is under threat, and not from the quarters we might expect. The threat in fact originates in the growing belief, buoyed by a particular trend in education research, in education ministries around the world that education should be knowledge-rather than skills-based. This belief is, as I will show, founded on misguided understanding of the nature of 'skills'. It also misses – to my mind, as well as in the view of others working in our sector – the point of education: to provide a toolkit that sets an individual up to live successfully as an upstanding global citizen. In our current 'epistemological crisis' where the line between truth and falsity has – to take Gideon's words – 'blurred edges and fogs', now more than ever we need to look hard at how education intersects with our efforts to safeguard society.[27]

My aim here is to outline the steps I believe we need to take to build on the strong foundations afforded to us by critical literacy exponents such as Luke. These steps involve reviewing what we mean by skills and how critical literacy fits within this, as well as envisioning how we can expand upon Luke's practice by drawing upon thinking in two areas: literacy criticism on the one hand and recent moves to remedy the role played by unconscious bias in our daily decisions on the other. At this point, I want to recognise the strong foundation on which I am building: namely, the inspiring number of what are variously labelled media, information, digital literacy initiatives often spearheaded by non-profit organi-sations, together working unflinchingly to respond to our current information crisis. It has been heartening to chart the accelerating efforts of such work over the past six months. I have meanwhile been glad to join the foot soldiers through my collaborative work with The Commonwealth of Learning, Vancouver, and The Commonwealth Centre for Connected Learning, Malta, through The Digital literacy Lab for Educators initiative. However, we – myself included – are yet to overcome a damaging, predominating perception outside our critical/media/information bubble: the view that such instruction sits beyond standard educa-tion; that it is an optional extra to be considered once content-heavy programmes of study have been completed. The final piece of this clarion call, which I bookend with a snapshot of the national curriculum in England as a trial run in moving from theory to practice, seeks to inch us closer to reaching this long-time, unat-tainable goal. First to delve briefly into the skills controversy.

The 'skill' and 'competency' labels receive much attention in the grand artic-ulations of C21st education reform. Our education systems are, the narrative goes, built for the First Industrial Revolution. Now, it continues, we need to make them fit for our Fourth Industrial Revolution and beyond. This call has been translated in multiple quarters as an appeal to do away with knowledge. Hence the founding, funding and subsequent failing of the now much-critiqued Alt-School initiative in San Francisco (Adams, 2019). Hence also the sustained rebuttal of skills-led education as spearheaded by Professor Eric Donald Hirsch Jr in the United States and, in his wake, Daisy Christodoulou in the United Kingdom.[28] If we go back to the core definition of skill in the Oxford English Dictionary, however, and track how this trickles down into reports from the World Economic Forum, we find that, in fact, a 'skill' encompasses the appropriate application of knowledge.[29] Skills are not, therefore, in their very definition and application opposed to knowledge but rather look to ensure its continued relevance. Luke has for long been concerned about the reduction of critical literacy to 'skills and competences'; little wonder given the press skills-based education has received to date, despite its true definition.[30] In advocating an alternative course of education, it is thus imperative we explain how critical literacy stands as an academically embedded practice.

The next step is pushing the boundaries of Luke's critical literacy conceptualisation to ensure its appropriateness for our current context and future challenges. To this end, I look to the field of critical reading. Critical reading, which first emerged from English university faculties in the middle of the twentieth century, has injected welcome conceptual direction into the practice of critical literacy. Here, I want to exert its influence further through exploring the view that reading is always a conditioned practice.

In his survey of 'Theory' movements (New Criticism, New Historicism, Postmodernism, amongst others), Valentine Cunningham explains that there is always an element of the 'simple trio of knowable, thinkable zones' that form the core of the communication experience at play: 'There is', he outlines, 'always and only ever a sender, a message and a receiver'.[31] What is striking in his review of the highways and byways of Theory (with a capital 'T') is the insistence that the reader always plays a role in creating meaning. 'The reader, and so also the reading', he remarks, 'always arrive in some sense preformed, prejudging, prejudiced, predisposed, by ideas about how reading is done, and what to expect from the kind of text which is presented'.[32] The reader, he insists, has never and will never read 'de novo'.[33] His argumentation here drives at underlining how we as readers come to content preconditioned by one critical movement or another, whether we are aware of it or not. Here, I would like to generalise this notion of pre-conditioning and bring it to bear on critical literacy.

Critical literacy is traditionally a practice that looks to unpick the agendas of content creators. In 1990, Luke and Freebody offered the 'Four Resources Model' to broaden existing literacy activities and deliver on this objective by creating the following roles for readers: 'code breaker', 'meaning maker', 'text user' and 'text critic'.[34] Each of these roles encourages the reader to look at how a text behaves within broader value systems and how it might then exercise influence over us and other readers.[35] This social embedding, which ensures that connection between the classroom and society, is the difference between what Luke sees as the inward-looking practices of critical thinking and the outward-looking, contextualised practice of critical literacy (Luke, 2018, p. 176).

This aspect remains vitally important. In our current context, I believe, however, that we additionally need to bring under review the agendas of content *consumers*, conscious or otherwise. Many of us might now think twice before buying a children's book depicting boys as scientific heroes and girls as fashion hunters. We might also consider what biases come into play when we read a job candidate's name. In stopping to reflect on the thinking shaping our actions we should fall within the remit of critical literacy. We have, in other words, a duty when advocating critical literacy development to bring into the educational fold the wide-ranging work on unconscious bias, first brought onto our radar in 1998 and since expanded into a range of possible biases (Greenwald, McGhee, & Schwartz, 1998).[36] This concern features prominently now in corporate training programmes. And yet we have failed to join the dots and incorporate the same instruction earlier within education delivery when it is equally, if not more important. This is not least the case given the additional channels many of us use to acquire our information: friends and family, whom we tend to unquestionably trust, and social media, with which we tend to superficially engage.[37] In so doing, we can hope to effect a closing of the gap between critical literacy and the latest conceptualisation of critical thinking as 'a willingness to question the beliefs and motivations of others, as well as one's own' (Zammit, 2019, p. 4).

This understanding of literacy is a far cry from what is currently offered in schools in many geographies, including in England. Yet there is room for hope, especially when we dive into the cogs and bolts of critical literacy and uncover the potential it offers to promote *intra*-curricular thinking, teaching and learning.

If we take the example of the curriculum outlined in England for Key Stage 3 and Key Stage 4 (ages 11–16) as last updated in 2014, we can excavate the synergies across subjects and between conventional schooling and critical literacy practice. In English, students are required to 'understand and critically evaluate texts'.[38] In History, the requirement is to understand 'how different types of historical sources are used rigorously to make historical claims' and 'to discern how and why contrasting arguments and interpretations of the past have been constructed'.[39] In Computing, students are required to become 'responsible, competent, confident and creative users of information and communication technology'.[40]

What this snapshot reveals is the extent to which management and manipulation of content runs through what we ordinarily teach in the classroom. The corollary of this is that any scheme of learning that helps a student understand how to interact with content, no matter what it is or where it features, promises a path to academic success whilst coaching in transferable knowledge and practice. In other words, this snapshot points to how critical literacy can provide the foundation for what Christodoulou refers to as 'domain-specific knowledge' (Christodoulou, 2013, p. 68). Without this skill, we cannot, I would further argue, expect students to usefully know what to do with the discipline content they are introduced to, that is – to stretch Bloom's conception of mastery learning – to become masters of the knowledge they acquire.[41]

There is hope but much work clearly remains. It is a curiosity that despite no explicit mention in the individual programmes of study for English at Key Stage 3 and Key Stage 4 in England, we often introduce the dichotomy between fact and opinion in the classroom. This often gets articulated as a fact-versus-fiction choice, including in some recent education programming from the BBC.[42] Yet, as the experience of our current infodemic has amply evidenced, we are often dealing with a spectrum. Once faced with 'real' information, we find that much content hovers somewhere between what we could term 'fact' and 'fiction', in that grey middle area, that area which challenges and often thwarts the efforts of moderators, man or machine. Clearly, we do not want to get caught up in post-modernist debates about the subjectivity of language. However, neither should we espouse the view, firmly held by Christodoulou, that there are many areas of knowledge that are 'immutable'.[43] Currently, by encouraging young people to think of information as falling into one category or the other, we fail to nurture a con-nected approach to information and to conceive of knowledge within the broader context of society. We equip young people with heuristics that become redundant as soon as they step out of the school gate or click online. We do little to encourage a considered approach when encountering material in new media contexts, including social media. In a 'brave new communications ecology' such as ours, one which has upturned long-existing models of authority and information frameworks, we need now more than ever to develop a holistic approach to education within our broader ambitions of striving for a better society.[44] Critical literacy instruction sits at the heart of this.

Conclusion

> 'Potter forever', he said. He added. 'It's symbolic. Potters will be forever, you know. They're so strong...'.
>
> –Potterism

In November 2019, Tim Berners-Lee announced the launch of the Contract for the Web. Led by the World Wide Web Foundation, the initiative aims to co-envision an Internet that returns to its founding mission: to provide a space for all to share information for the furtherance of human understanding. The contract outlines nine principles to this end: three for governments; three for companies and, importantly, three for citizens. The principles for citizens read as follows: 'Be creators and collaborators on the Web; Build strong communities that respect civil discourse and human dignity; Fight for the Web'.[45] The need is evident; the challenge is huge. As the guiding statement declares, 'it took all of us to build the web that we have. It will take all of us to secure its future'.[46]

The picture I set out painting here is a sombre one. It is a picture of unprec-edented threats to society, the result of unfettered access to publication channels and our limited ability to engage responsibly with the many types and subtypes of information available to us. The flood of bad information and the impact on individual lives unhappily continues, now even emerging from – to borrow Gideon's words again – the 'least likely homes'.[47]

For the future to be brighter, we need to take action now. No single answer offers itself as a magic bullet, as commentators all round repeatedly remind us. Writing in 1999, Luke and Freebody warned that critical literacy is not one of those 'magic bullets... an educational and political solution for all that ails us' (p. 3). An article published before COVID-19 truly hit was mindfully headed: 'Is Media

Literacy the Magic Bullet for Fake News?: stopping misinformation requires social media platforms, journalists, fact checkers, and citizens all to take action' (Ascott, 2020). The solution is indeed complicated, as we are now regularly instructed. A report on COVID-19 misinformation concludes thus:

> ...our findings suggest there will be no silver bullet or inoculation – no 'cure' for misinformation about the new coronavirus. Instead, addressing the spread of misinformation about COVID-19 will take a sustained and coordinated effort by independent fact-checkers, independent news media, platform companies, and public authorities to help the public understand and navigate the pandemic... (Brennen et al., 2020, p. 8)

The key element missing here, as recognised by the author of the aforementioned article and Mark Warner, but not enough of those with the power to effect change, is the need for governments to prioritise critical literacy education. Critical literacy instruction alone, in moving us beyond treating symptoms to treating the root cause of information challenges, is the lynchpin of a healthy information landscape and, in turn, a flourishing global society.

The roadmap is clear. We need to mirror the thinking being applied to the current health and, indeed, the ongoing climate emergency to address what is in fact an education emergency. We are so often told that the only way out of the COVID-19 public health crisis is to find a vaccination and immunise the global population. We are not going to save the environment – to take one example from the climate challenge – by taking plastic out of the ocean, though this is of course an important step. Instead, we need to prevent it from getting there in the first place. Similarly, by placing critical literacy instruction at the heart of a coordinated response to our infected information system and ailing education models, we can at least look to a future with a rebooted web and information ecosystem in which every individual plays a critically literate role as a result of their education. Perhaps Potters need not be so strong and contagious forever.[48]

Notes

1. Macaulay (2004).
2. For a comparative review of the populist language used during the election see Flinders (2019). For an overview of the misleading advertising campaigns launched by both sides of the debate see Panjwani (2019).
3. The information crisis was labelled as such in a speech given by the Director General of the World Health Organisation on 15 February (Ghebreyesus, 2020).
4. In March 2020 UNESCO reported that school closures as a result of COVID-19 was disrupting the education of 290.5 million students.
5. Speaking to the UK newspaper *The Guardian* in 2019, Tim Berners Lee remarked on the existential threat the Internet is facing (Sample, 2019).
6. The adjective 'Post-truth' was declared 'Oxford Dictionaries Word of the Year 2016' (Oxford Languages, 2016).

7. In relation to COVID-19, statements by public figures accounted for 20% of material but 69% of social media engagement (Brennen et al., 2020, p. 1).
8. As Wardle explains: 'Most of this content isn't even fake; it's often genuine, used out of context and weaponized by people who know that falsehoods based on a kernel of truth are more likely to be believed and shared. And most of this can't be described as "news". It's good old-fashioned rumours, it's memes, it's manipulated videos and hyper-targeted "dark ads" and old photos re-shared as new' (2019, p. 6).
9. From this point, I will use the term 'misinformation' interchangeably with poor information for brevity whilst mindful that, strictly speaking, this term refers to one strain of the information disorder.
10. Wardle (2019, p. 19).
11. Wardle (2019, p. 45).
12. From many examples in the political sphere we can cite Trump's response to the outcry following his suggestion on 25 April, 2020, that ingesting bleach might be a cure for COVID-19. In one of his rebuttals he complained of the 'Lamestream Media' who ask 'nothing but hostile questions' and consequently deliver 'nothing but Fake News' (Post Trump, 2020). A similar narrative has grown up in response to attempts, most recently through journalist Jamie Bartlett's podcast series, *The Missing Cryptoqueen*, to uncover the scam which is the cyrptocurrency OneCoin. Such has been the flood of calls of fake news by convinced investors that comedians have begun to parody the backlash (see Veitch, 2019).
13. See, for example, Apple (2020); Facebook (n.d.c).
14. The California Consumer Privacy Act (CCPA) came into force in 2020.
15. See Rieger (2020).
16. A pertinent example here is the dramatic change in content contained within Facebook's (n.d.a) statement 'Fact-Checking on Facebook: What Publishers Should Know'. In May 2020, Facebook had insisted on its commitment to 'free expression, respect for the democratic process and the belief that, especially in mature democracies with a free press, political speech is the most scrutinized speech there is'. It was thus upholding democracy, the statement continued, to leave populations the opportunity to see 'what their elected officials are saying' so they could then hold them accountable. On 12 August, this page was updated with a shortened title 'Fact-Checking on Facebook' and a much revised (and much shorter) statement with all earlier references to the exemption of politics removed.
17. A conservative estimate based upon how much data are held on servers owned by Google, Amazon, Microsoft and Facebook gives us a starting figure of 1.2 million terabytes of data (See Mitchell, n.d.).
18. The Vietnam napalm debacle of 2016 is a prominent example here (See Wong, 2016). See also Thielman (2016).
19. According to Zuckerberg, when users see a warning label on content, 95% of the time they do not click through.
20. See The International Fact-Checking Network (n.d.).
21. See The Commitments of the Code of Principles (n.d.).
22. See the figure 'Multiliteracies: Metalanguages to Describe and Interpret the Design Elements of Different Modes of Meaning' (Cazden et al., 1996, p. 83).
23. Cited in Luke (2012, p. 5).
24. Luke (2012, p. 9).
25. Luke (2018, p. 50).

26. See Chapter 1 in Luke (2018) for use of the model in Canada and Quebec.
27. Preface, Luke (2018).
28. Hirch is the educationalist widely identified as the indirect architect of the Common Core curriculum in the United States. See Christodoulou's treatise on a knowledge-based education, *Seven Myths About Education.*
29. The Oxford English Dictionary defines 'skill' as the 'capability of accomplishing something with precision and certainty; practical knowledge in combination with ability'. This marrying of ideas and activity is taken up in the World Economic Forum's (2018) report. Skills (n.d.), the report outlines, 'are used to apply knowledge to complete tasks' (p. 5).
30. See Chapter 14 in Luke (2018).
31. Cunningham (2002, p. 29).
32. Cunningham (2002, p. 4).
33. Cunningham (2002, p. 5).
34. See Luke and Freebody (1999), for an updated review of the model first introduced in 1990.
35. Luke and Freebody (1999, p. 176).
36. The work of The Board of Innovation and description of 16 different cognitive biases, albeit meant for a workplace setting, has much to offer here (Pinder, n.d.).
37. For a snapshot of this phenomenon, see Shearer (2018).
38. Department for Education (2014, p. 18).
39. Department for Education (2014, p. 95).
40. Department for Education (2014, p. 85).
41. Bloom originally put forward his view of 'learning for mastery' to encourage a new approach to learning: focusing on the mastery of a set block of content within a subject before progressing to more advanced work. The practices he suggested to support this would, he insisted, ensure no student was left behind (1981).
42. BBC (2020).
43. Christodoulou (2013, p. 55).
44. See Luke, preface, 2018; Wardle (2019, p. 14).
45. See the homepage.
46. See 'About' section, Contract for the Web (2020).
47. See Full Fact's review published in August 2020 just a few days after the news story hit headlines of the claim reported by the BBC and many other outlets that misinformation has directly led to hundreds of deaths.
48. The author wishes to express deep gratitude to Dr Cassandra Gorman for her insightful feedback on drafts of this contribution and for long being a willing sounding board for the thinking underpinning it.

References

Adams, S. (2019). Zuckerberg-backed AltSchool gives up on schools and focuses on tech. *Forbes.* Retrieved from https://www.forbes.com/sites/susanadams/2019/07/01/zuckerberg-backed-altschool-gives-up-on-schools-and-focuses-on-tech/#2da13531c5b1

Apple. (2020). Ensuring the credibility of health & safety information. Retrieved from https://developer.apple.com/news/?id=03142020a

Ascott, T. (2020). Is media literacy the magic bullet for fake news? The Interpreter. Retrieved from https://www.lowyinstitute.org/the-interpreter/media-literacy-magic-bullet-fake-news

BBC. (2020). Learning English. Retrieved from https://www.bbc.co.uk/learningenglish/english/course/fakenews

Bloom, B. (1981). *All our children learning: A primer for parents, teachers, and other Educators.* New York, NY: McGraw-Hill.

boyd, d. (2017). The information war has begun. Retrieved from http://www.zephoria. org/thoughts/archives/2017/01/27/the-information-war-has-begun.html

Brashier, N., & Schacter, D. (2020). Aging in an era of fake news. *Current Directions in Psychological Science, 29*(3), 316–323. doi:10.1177/0963721420915872

Brennen, S. J., Simon, F. M., Howard, P. N., & Nielsen, R. K. (2020). Types, sources and claims of covid-19 misinformation. Reuters Institute for the Study of Journalism. Retrieved from https://reutersinstitute.politics.ox.ac.uk/sites/default/files/2020-04/ Brennen%20-%20COVID%2019%20Misinformation%20FINAL%20%283%29.pdf

Brownsford, R., Scotford, E., & Yeung, K. (2017). Law, regulation, and technology: The field, frame, and focal questions. In R. Brownsford, E. Scotford, & K. Yeung (Eds.), *The Oxford handbook of law, regulation and technology* (pp. 3–40). Oxford: Oxford University Press.

Cazden, C., Cope, B., Faircloud, N., Gee, J., Luke, A., Luke, C., … Nakata, N. M. (1996). A pedagogy of multiliteracies: Designing social futures. *Harvard Educational Review, 66*(1), 60–92. doi:10.17763/haer.66.1.17370n67v22j160u

Christodoulou, D. (2013). *Seven Myths about education.* Oxford: Routledge.

Contract for the web. (2020). Retrieved from https://contractfortheweb.org/

Cunningham, V. (2002). *Reading after theory.* Oxford; Malden, MA: Blackwell.

Daly, N. (2020). Fake animal news abounds on social media as coronavirus upends life. *National Geographic.* Retrieved from https://www.nationalgeographic.co.uk/ animals/2020/03/fake-animal-news-abounds-social-media-coronavirus-upends-life

Department for Education. (2014). The national curriculum in England: Key stages 3 and 4 framework document. Retrieved from https://assets.publishing.service.gov. uk/government/uploads/system/uploads/attachment_data/file/840002/Secondary_ national_curriculum_corrected_PDF.pdf

Douglas, K. M., Sutton, R. M., & Cichocka, A. (2017). The psychology of conspiracy theories. *Current Directions in Psychological Science, 26*(6), 538–542.

Facebook. (n.d.). Fact-checking on Facebook. Retrieved from https://www.facebook.com/ business/help/182222309230722

Facebook. (n.d.). Hateful memes challenge and data set for research on harmful multimodal content. Retrieved from https://ai.facebook.com/blog/hateful-memes-challenge-and-data-set/

Facebook. (n.d.). Keeping people safe and informed about the coronavirus. Retrieved from https://about.fb.com/news/2020/06/coronavirus/

Flinders, M. (2019). UK election 2019: This is what populism looks like when done by the British. *The Conversation.* Retrieved from https://theconversation.com/uk-election-2019-this-is-what-populism-looks-like-when-done-by-the-british-126733

Full Fact. (2018). Full Fact to start checking Facebook content as third-party factchecking initiative reaches the UK. Retrieved from https://fullfact.org/blog/2019/ jan/full-fact-start-checking-facebook-content-third-party-factchecking-initiative-reaches-uk

Full Fact. (2019). *Report on the Facebook third party fact-checking programme.* Full Fact. Retrieved from https://fullfact.org/media/uploads/tpfc-q1q2-2019.pdf

Full Fact. (2020). We don't know whether "misinformation" killed 800 people. Retrieved from https://fullfact.org/health/800-killed-misinformation/

Ghebreyesus, T. A. (2020). Munich security conference. World Health Organisation. Retrieved from https://www.who.int/dg/speeches/detail/munich-security-conference

Greenwald, A. G., McGhee, D. E., & Schwartz, J. L. K. (1998). Measuring individual differences in implicit cognition: The implicit association test. *Journal of Personality and Social Psychology, 74*, 1464–1480. doi:10.1037/0022-3514.74.6.1464

Internet Society. (2019). Policy brief: Internet shutdowns. Internet Society. Retrieved from https://www.internetsociety.org/policybriefs/internet-shutdowns

Jack, S. (2020). Facebook's Zuckerberg defends actions on virus misinformation. *BBC News Online*. Retrieved from https://www.bbc.co.uk/news/business-52750162

Kivinen, K. (2020). Tips for home-school students searching for reliable information [Blog post]. Retrieved from https://kivinen.wordpress.com/2020/03/20/tips-for-home-school-students-searching-for-reliable-information/

Luke, A. (2012). Critical literacy: Foundational notes. *Theory into Practice, 51*, 4–11. doi:10.1080/00405841.2012.636324

Luke, A. (2018). *Critical literacy, school and social justice*. New York, NY: Routledge.

Luke, A., & Freebody, P. A. (1999). Map of possible practices: Further notes on the four resources model. *Australian Literacy Educators' Association, 4*(2), 5–8.

Macaulay, R. (2004). *Potterism: A tragi-farcical tract*. Urbana, IL: Project Gutenberg. Retrieved from http://www.gutenberg.org/ebooks/11163

Miller, C., Kitcher, H., Perera, K., & Abiola, A. (2020). *People, power and technology: The 2020 digital attitudes report*. Doteveryone. Retrieved from https://www.doteveryone.org.uk/report/peoplepowertech2020/

Mitchell, G. (n.d.). How much data is on the internet? *Science Focus*. Retrieved from https://www.sciencefocus.com/future-technology/how-much-data-is-on-the-internet/

Newton, C. (2020). Facebook will pay $52 million in settlement with moderators who developed PTSD on the job. *The Verge*. Retrieved from https://www.theverge.com/2020/5/12/21255870/facebook-content-moderator-settlement-scola-ptsd-mental-health

Oxford Languages. (2016). Word of the year 2016. Retrieved from https://languages.oup.com/word-of-the-year/2016/#:~:text=After%20much%20discussion%2C%20debate%2C%20and,to%20emotion%20and%20personal%20belief

Panjwani, A. (2019). The facts behind Labour and Conservative Facebook ads in this election. Full Fact. Retrieved from https://fullfact.org/election-2019/ads/.

Pennycock, G., Collins, E., Bear, A., & Rand, D. (2019). The implied truth effect: Attaching warnings to a subset of fake news headlines increases perceived accuracy of headlines without warnings. *Management Science. INFORMS, 66*(11), 4944–4957. doi:10.1287/mnsc.2019.3478

Pinder, M. (n.d.). 16 cognitive biases that can kill your decision making. *Board of Innovation*. Retrieved from https://www.boardofinnovation.com/blog/16-cognitive-biases-that-kill-innovative-thinking/. Accessed on May 26, 2020.

Reporters Without Borders. (2020). RSF launches Tracker 19 to track Covid-19's impact on press freedom. Retrieved from https://rsf.org/en/news/rsf-launches-tracker-19-track-covid-19s-impact-press-freedom

Rieger, S. (2020). Regulate the web: Free expression, harmful speech, and the future of the internet. Retrieved from https://docs.google.com/presentation/d/1Nmc5ZlbO3nQf8DRmUIa4lxzFR4woeaFv0OIQMF8QcDo/edit?ts=5f39b908#slide=id.p

Roser, M., Ritchie, H., & Ortiz-Ospina, E. (2015). Internet. *Our World in Data*. Retrieved from https://ourworldindata.org/internet

Roser, M., Ritchie, H., & Ortiz-Ospina, E. (2019). World population growth. *Our World in Data*. Retrieved from https://ourworldindata.org/world-population-growth

Sample, I. (2019). Tim Berners-Lee unveils global plan to save the web. *The Guardian*.

Shearer, E. (2018). Social media outpaces print newspapers in the US as a news source. Retrieved from https://www.pewresearch.org/fact-tank/2018/12/10/social-media-out-paces-print-newspapers-in-the-u-s-as-a-news-source/

Skill. (n.d.). Oxford English dictionary. Retrieved from https://www.oed.com/view/Entry/180865

The Commitments of the Code of Principles. (n.d.). Poynter. Retrieved from https://ifcncodeofprinciples.poynter.org/know-more/the-commitments-of-the-code-of-principles. Accessed on May 30, 2020.

The International Fact-Checking Network. (n.d.). Poynter. Retrieved from https://www.theguardian.com/technology/2019/nov/24/tim-berners-lee-unveils-global-plan-to-save-the-internet https://mediabiasfactcheck.com/?s=Poynter. Accessed on May 30, 2020.

Thielman, S. (2016). Facebook fires trending team, and algorithm without humans goes crazy. *The Guardian*. Retrieved from https://www.theguardian.com/technology/2016/aug/29/facebook-fires-trending-topics-team-algorithm

Trump, D. [@realDonaldTrump]. (2020). What is the purpose of having White House news conferences when the Lamestream media asks nothing but hostile questions, & then refuses to report the truth or facts accurately.... *Twitter*. Retrieved from https://twitter.com/realDonaldTrump/status/1254168730898173953

UNESCO. (2020). 290 million students out of school due to COVID-19: UNESCO releases first global numbers and mobilizes response. UNESCO. Retrieved from https://en.unesco.org/news/290-million-students-out-school-due-covid-19-unesco-releases-first-global-numbers-and-mobilizes

United States Senate/Select Committee on Intelligence. (2018). *Open hearing: Social media influence in the 2016 U.S. Election S. HRG. 115-232*. Washington, DC: US Government Publishing Office.

Veitch, J. [@veitchtweets]. (2019, October 3). This @JamieJBartlett spreads FAKE NEWS. Belief in #onecoin ecosystem and truly attain your goals. Do not trust him. *Twitter*. Retrieved from https://twitter.com/veitchtweets/status/1179702999549120512

Wardle, C. (2019). First draft's essential guide to understanding information disorder. *First Draft News*. Retrieved from https://firstdraftnews.org/wp-content/uploads/2019/10/Information_Disorder_Digital_AW.pdf?x76701

Wendling, M. (2018). The (almost) complete history of 'fake news'. *BBC News Online*. Retrieved from https://www.bbc.co.uk/news/blogs-trending-42724320

Wong, J. C. (2016). Mark Zuckerberg accused of abusing power after Facebook deletes 'napalm girl' post. *The Guardian*. Retrieved from https://www.theguardian.com/technology/2016/sep/08/facebook-mark-zuckerberg-napalm-girl-photo-vietnam-war

World Economic Forum. (2015). *New vision for education: Unlocking the potential of technology*. Geneva: World Economic Forum. Retrieved from http://www3.weforum.org/docs/WEFUSA_NewVisionforEducation_Report2015.pdf

World Economic Forum. (2018). Towards a reskilling revolution: A future of jobs for all. Geneva: World Economic Forum. Retrieved from http://www3.weforum.org/docs/WEF_Towards_a_Reskilling_Revolution.pdf

Zammit, L. (2019). Fostering Critical Thinking Skills through the teaching of Ethics in Maltese Schools. Understanding the Post-truth Society Conference, 10–11 October. Malta: Commonwealth Centre for Connected Learning.

Chapter 7

Societal Reorientation via Programmable Trust: A Case for Piloting New Models of Open Governance in Education

Walter Fernando Balser, Steve Diasio and Taylor Kendal

Abstract

This essay proposes the need to infuse *open innovation (OI)* and *open source (OS)* principles and technologies into schools as a means of tackling many of the most pervasive challenges in education, and by extension, society at large. It is argued that the principles of OI and OS, which are rooted in innovation management and software development, respectively, may be applied to the way we conceive of and approach organizational governance structures related to schooling, particularly in regard to harnessing innovation, updating management processes, and codifying new systems of trust. Whereas OI offers a novel approach to knowledge flow and the open exchange of ideas, communities rooted in OS principles breed tangible and generative effects through peer network democratization. These emergent, digitally defined networks have been proven to maximize innovation potential, expand collaboration, and enable the propagation of highly durable systems of trust and transparency, all catalytic and essential if we are to realize a future learning economy which favors equity, distributed systems, and common goods over profit, centralized decision-making, and proprietorship. It is within this framing that we articulate the core tenets of both OI and OS translationally as a means of stimulating thinking about how core principles of "openness" and the distributed technologies they enable may help to build common ground in an ever-evolving education and information ecosystem.

Keywords: Open innovation; open source; programmable trust; open governance; trust systems; distributed technologies

Media, Technology and Education in a Post-Truth Society, 95–110
Copyright © 2021 by Emerald Publishing Limited
All rights of reproduction in any form reserved
doi:10.1108/978-1-80043-906-120211007

Openness, as a broad paradigmatic approach, has increasingly become an area of interest for scholars across a wide range of disciplines and industries. Recent research into "open" or "openness" has focused on the changing knowledge landscape of long-established and conventional methods, processes, and techniques across different industries and organizational structures. As a result, many industries and institutions are seeing radical, previously unimagined, and often unmanageable, transformation. Through this transition, openness has been largely tied to two rapidly growing research streams: open innovation (OI) within the business management literature and open source (OS) within the software and distributed developer movement. These advancements have quickly spread to replace increasingly dated approaches to closed or constrained models of "innovation" and sequentially phased waterfall methods and processes in software development.

Coined by Chesbrough (2003), OI has been defined as "the use of purposive inflows and outflows of knowledge to accelerate internal innovation, and to expand the markets for external use of innovation, respectively." The IO paradigm assumes that firms can and should use external, as well as internal knowledge and ideas, to push new products, services, and ideas to existing and new markets (Chesbrough, 2006). It has been well documented that an intentional focus on OI accelerates product innovation in large, medium, and small enterprises (Brunswicker & Vanhaverbeke, 2015; Diasio, 2016). The realized benefits have led to the principles of OI being adapted to existing services as a means of escaping the commodity trap of product development (Chesbrough, 2010). More recently, OI's influence has expanded to a wide range of practices including: open business models (Chesbrough, 2012), open models of intellectual property management (Germeraad & Vanhaverbeke, 2016), open models of decision support (Diasio, 2017), and as an important approach for governance through open government initiatives and urban innovation approaches (Lee, Almirall, & Wareham, 2016); all helping us understand how openness can transform social structures and improve how we govern and improve the quality of life for all citizens, both locally and globally.

Likewise, conceptual models grounded in OS allow for the emergence of a broad set of values from which projects, products, and initiatives (often digitally mediated) can evolve through the collective embrace of open exchange, collaborative participation, rapid prototyping, radical transparency, and community-oriented development (opensource, 2018). Those who support OS are no longer the hackers and misfits operating at the cultural fringes. They are the majority, building many of the most powerful systems and applications that now dominate, for better or worse, many modern societies. Over the past 10 years, OS has moved from an academic curiosity to a mainstream focus [...], and there are now [hundreds of] thousands of active communities, spanning a wide range of applications (Crowston, Wei, Howison, & Wiggins, 2012).

OS communities and networks, driven by collective contributions to ever-complexifying open-source software (OSS) repositories like GitHub, are introducing an entirely new suite of emergent phenomenon and social structures. Recent studies in open-source organizations clearly show the need to explore not only OS but also the *sustainability* of its communities (Hata, Todo, Onoue, & Matsumoto, 2015). While challenges remain with respect to transferability and sustainability of these emergent networks to other contexts, we believe OS approaches as both a tool and a philosophy can help educational organizations build common, more durable epistemic frameworks for a post-truth society. As Michael J. Casey, founder of Steambed Media, noted at the *Understanding the Post-truth Society Conference* in Valletta, Malta,

> we really need to find a way for communities and civil society to come together and form opinions about facts in a structure that is consistent with the decentralized way in which the world is heading. (Casey, 2019)

Based on this premise, an argument could then be made that the education marketplace, which has experienced increased fragmentation and interest from outside sectors in recent years, is primed for OI and OS approaches to solving its most pervasive challenges. This chapter introduces a broad lens from which to view educational leadership and governance in the context of OI, and specifically that this is a means towards "strategically managing the sharing of ideas and resources among entities to co-create value" (Johannsson et al., 2015, p. 175), and similarly, that OS communities offer tangible use cases where collections of individuals and firms contribute to the provision of a public good by freely sharing their innovations with other community members (Von Krogh & Von Hippel, 2006). It is the thesis of this essay that both of these approaches, if applied collectively to education, may represent a new conceptual view of the field as "open," perhaps serving as a catalyst to enable critical shifts to a system that has remained relatively walled and fundamentally unchanged for nearly a century.

While questions remain about the transferability of OI and OS principles to other nontechnical sectors, the increasing commercialization of the schooling space demands further inquiry. Driven largely by external forces, this chapter considers the following questions: What might be demonstrative examples of OI and OS thinking in the current context of schooling? What, if any, benefits might be realized in adapting OI and OS principles and policies to the domain of education? What might be definable traits, or orientations, of an "open leader"? How might orientations toward openness support educational organizations in a hyperdecentralized, post-truth society?

Open Innovation Relevance in a Decentralized Schooling Marketplace

The concept of openness is not new; however, its adoption within monolithic organizations and institutions has been a more recent phenomenon. This transition offers a unique perspective into how organizations deal with pressure to change as a result of the dynamics of a new impending reality. Much like within education, firmly rooted institutions across a range of domains have faced pressures to change in the wake of globalization, technological advancements, resource constraints, and a decentralization of the knowledge landscape. Many organizations and institutions that were once dominant have dwindled or died as a result of not changing or adapting to the new environment (Blockbuster, Kodak and Nokia being prominent examples).

A growing body of literature within the management and innovation space may provide insight into how openness has supported the change process and how these approaches may become increasingly relevant in an environment where truth is opaque and operating autonomously but interdependently is the new normal. OI and its foundational principles have been leveraged in many areas to create value for a wide range of stakeholders by opening up the boundaries to knowledge flows, that in turn, accelerating change that otherwise would not have been possible in a conventional closed paradigm approach to innovation. Open and smart cities have adopted underlying OI principles to tie innovation to public access of data and infrastructure, driving solutions in urban settings (Bakici, Almirall, & Wareham, 2013a, b). It is here, through openness, where traditional hierarchical institutions and governments have unlocked resources, in the form of open databases, empowering citizens to solve problems in their own community through novel management of citizen data (Lee et al., 2016). OI assumes that organizational innovation activities are more like an open system than the traditional (twentieth century) vertically integrated model (West, Salter, Vanhaverbeke, & Chesbrough, 2014, p. 805). This has extended to Open Government initiatives, popularized by President Obama (Executive Office of the President Memorandum, 2009), that supported citizen-led initiatives to drive policy and change at the level of the federal government.

For the education sector, the shift to OI – as opposed to industrial closed-thinking – better aligns with a modern education marketplace that is vastly different than it was decades ago. Defining school-related services as a commodity to be bought, sold, and traded in educational markets (Ellison, 2012; Heilig, Brewer, & Adamson, 2019) is as controversial as it is ideological; however, for the purpose of this essay, we define marketplaces in an OI context as a means to capture and exchange value in a data-rich, informationalized economy (Bingham, Spradlin, & Safari, 2011). Today, in a blended-capital paradigm (Balser & Coleman, 2020), there are tens of thousands of agencies working in the schooling marketplace, many of whom did not exist even a decade ago. In most urban public schools, there is a good chance that many services will not be delivered by the school itself, but rather through a vast network of third-party organizations fulfilling a wide range of needs that local communities demand (Bathgate & Silva, 2010). The integration of external actors into traditional "walled" institutions (Anderson-Butcher et al., 2010) has become commonplace in many cities, especially in environments that have been historically deprived of social services and innovation (Oliviera & Breda-Vasquez, 2012). In these communities, clustering resources has helped to empower local actors, particularly marginalized groups, and to engage in public policymaking and decision-making (Moulaert, Martinelli, Swyngedouw, & Gonzalez, 2005; Oliviera & Breda-Vasquez, 2012, p. 24). The impetus for decentralizing the provisioning of services is only likely to accelerate as private capital enters the public schooling marketplace at an accelerated rate. In 2018, venture capital in the education sector was over $1.4 billion (Wan, 2018), a 1000 percent increase over the last decade, and philanthropic giving to education reached nearly $60 billion (Giving USA, 2018), second only to religion, with much of it coming from a growing list of powerful philanthropic foundations.

Adding to the complexity, leaders operating in an education industrial complex must contend with a checkered history of attempts to integrate external influences in schools (Picciano & Spring, 2013; Hess & Addison, 2019). In recent years, urban schools have faced a wave of interventions from outside sectors that are often and perhaps rightfully perceived as dominant and contextually out of touch with local needs. Examples might include: the infusion of metrics-driven accountability measures inspired by business schools (Cuban, 2004; Gelberg, 2007); incorporation of design-thinking principles from engineering schools into school improvement strategies (Scheer, Noweski, & Meinel, 2012); and most recently, embedding Improvement Science processes rooted in the healthcare industry as a means of driving school-wide improvement and measuring teacher effectiveness (Hannan, Russell, Takahashi, & Park, 2015). These examples highlight the "peculiar demands" (Ellison, 2012, p. 6) of an educational marketplace where school improvement, vis-a-vis product improvement, is a process ridden with conflict because power is distributed (all too often unequally) among individuals, groups, and organizations possessing dissimilar values and misaligned incentives (Datnow, 2000).

Unlike other industries where *absorptive capacity* between sectors can transfer systems and norms from one sector to the next, helping firms maintain a competitive advantage (Murphy, Perrot, & Rivera-Santos, 2012), in education, influence often moves in one direction with outsiders exerting control and seeking to institute their values on school leaders (Trachtman, 1994). Therefore, rather than creating a homogeneity of values across multiple industries (DiMaggio & Powell, 1983), outside-in interactions with schools are often founded under adverse circumstances where educators are seen as failing (Hoff, 2002). This may be further exacerbated with the proliferation of emergent intermediary organizations, particularly philanthropic foundations, many of which are influencing product development and management processes in schooling at unprecedented frequencies. The steady stream of outside forces entering previously isolated markets has helped fuel a climate of domination and resistance (Burawoy, 1991), placing school leaders in a perpetually protective stance (Beabout, 2010; Bradshaw, 2000). To jaded and skeptical educators, merely viewing an evolving education ecosystem *through an open lens* does little to assuage the real concerns of elites acting as "policy patrons" and an ever-widening array of deep-pocketed outsiders influencing the education game (Heilig et al., 2019, p. 340).

In aggregate, this marks the need for a new infrastructure where inflows and outflows of knowledge and resources interact in an ever-evolving education supply chain (Purifoy & Smith, 2018), making an OI perspective all that more relevant. For example, OI allows us to conceptualize expanded partnerships with local agencies not as a means of building deeper community ties but as effective management principles. Viewed through an OI lens, "partnerships" are not just a moral imperative to empower diverse community voices; they are part of a dynamic interfirm ecosystem where a multitude of clients and agencies interact to meet market demands and where knowledge sharing takes place through a cocreative process involving multiple firms and an external community (Sims & Seidel, 2016). Viewing the education ecosystem from this perspective, by presenting "insiders" and "outsiders" as essential parts of an intimately coupled OI system, could help us find common ground between currently polarized reform/antireform camps. "It is the practice of linking outside-in and inside-out by working in alliances with complementary companies during which give and take are crucial for success" (Gassmann & Enkel, 2004). If we revisit the words of Casey (2019) in a post-truth, hyperdecentralized society, "truth will be a negotiated phenomenon" (Fig. 7.1).

Open Source Relevance in Knowledge Societies

The transition from the industrial age to the information age has forced institutions, including educational organizations, to transform into information or knowledge societies (Cardoso, 2005). Specifically, "there is an emerging trend in viewing organizational culture, in general, and innovation and creativity, in particular from a network perspective" (Zou & Yilmaz, 2011, p. 55). The implications of the network phenomenon on schools cannot be overstated. Shirky (2008) notes that as the costs of coordinating and transacting between groups have collapsed, traditional institutional processes that provided advantages in the past may actually impede progress today. Like a root system, as networks expand, their complexity grows at an exponential rate greater than the size of the network itself. In our current educational context, one could argue that the more ideas,

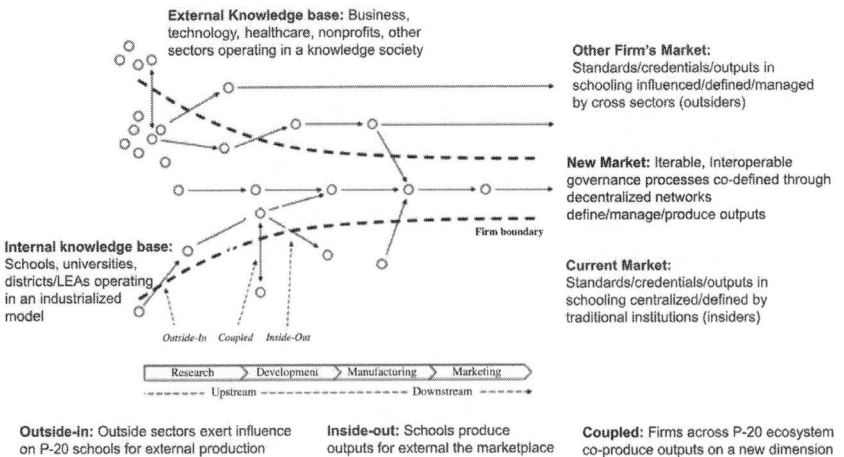

Fig. 7.1. Open Innovation Funnel in Schooling Context. *Source:* Adapted from Jang, Hyejin, Lee, & Yoon (2016).

interventions, agencies, and roles we introduce into a schooling system (a network), the more likely they are to fail under the weight of complexity – absent change in the underlying systems that govern the affected network. Put another way, one cannot promote *ideas, innovation,* and *creativity,* all common discourse in school reform, without first creating processes, or better yet, a foundational ethos adequate to capture the resulting energy. Innovation is often stifled as groups of individuals become centralized; creative output increases at a diminishing rate up to a point, and beyond this point, the tendencies toward centrality inevitably constrain innovation potential (Zou & Yilmaz, 2011, p. 54).

Approaches pioneered by OS communities are most relevant here as they do not offer yet another idea or technical tweak to ingrained infrastructures (Heifitz, Linksy, & Linksy, 2009; Martínez Arbelaiz & Correa Gorospe, 2009), nor do they promote infusing one sector's processes or ethos in a manner that may or may not be analogous to schools. Rather, OS, as a frame of reorientation, suggests a focus on fundamental principles that lie at the heart of governance and power, and we aim to contend, at the center of rebuilding trusted and transparent systems of collaborative organizational cultures. Unlike the intentional and structured legacy hierarchies of our traditional system of education, where informed intelligence reigns, OS networks rely on emergence, supported by consensus and implicit governance structures (Capra, Francalanci, & Merlo, 2008; Di Tullio & Staples, 2014). Organizations rooted in OS ethos promote governance mechanisms that evolve organically rather than through hierarchical predetermination. These governance mechanisms organize and surface generatively and form emergent network structures (Sadowski, Sadowski-Rasters, & Duysters, 2008). Governance mechanisms more often evolve dynamically within OS communities, not through hierarchical predetermination.

The notion of openness and its relation to schooling could mark a shift in discourse around education; yet, this will require a critical examination of the implicit rules and principles shared by all members in a schooling organization (Martínez Arbelaiz & Correa Gorospe, 2009 p. 52). For example, in OS communities, outcomes are not predetermined through a clear plan, but instead, are often left open for interpretation and negotiation by anyone at all evolutionary stages. Rigorous peer adoption processes invite participants with varying decision-making styles and expertise to decide as a community whether to accept or decline a contribution (Zou & Yilmaz, 2011). As with other open systems, the organization lives and deals creatively with change and thrives in – as opposed to tolerates – complex and ambiguous situations (Banathy, 1991). This mirrors the characteristics of double-loop learning organizations (Argyris, 1982) that challenge conventional wisdom and find new purposes, carve out new niches in the environment, and develop increased capacity for self-reference, self-correction, self-direction, self-organization, and self-renewal (Kemp, 1991). These approaches also neatly follow the first rule of change management which states that you cannot change an organization unless its structure lets you promulgate new policies, implement those policies, and assess their outcome (Grier, 2016).

Yielding this kind of authority to a group is natural in OS communities but antithetical to many educational institutions. Professional learning communities (PLCs), academic departments, subject area experts/supervisors, and other constructs move schools implicitly into spaces of informed intelligence and hierarchy where only specific people have ultimate power and authority. To make the kind of transition for which we are advocating, it is necessary to shift perspective from a *one-to-many* toward a *many-to-one* orientation (Betts, 1992). A many-to-one orientation also has pedagogical implications as infinitely more resources could be accessible to all students, only one of which is the teacher. This idea, which is far from novel, can accurately be characterized as an adaptive shift, moving from an emphasis on instruction to an emphasis on learning (Katz & Kahn, 1969). If we agree such a reorientation is needed, how can we proceed in a manner that respects all parties involved, teachers and students most importantly? Amid the COVID-19 pandemic and recent proliferation of asynchronous, digitally mediated learning, many are struggling, rightfully, to make such a transition. Nearly every institution of education is in need of instructional technology infrastructure and support. It has become clear that schools and educators standing alone are not prepared to bridge the many-to-one digital divide, let alone be expected to bridge it equitably for all students. This opens yet another door to the critical importance of the ideas we hope to seed for discussion.

Another area where OS-based frames may surface alignment with schooling is in how we define value, merit, and incentives. In OS networks, like education, motivation does not come solely from market-derived incentives and logic, but instead through intrinsic factors and value derived from creation, creativity, and novelty (Hernández, 2016). OS communities constitute collections of individuals and firms that contribute to the provision of a public good by freely sharing their innovations with other community members (Von Krogh & Von Hippel, 2006). The focus is not on monetizing, although that certainly happens, but on collective action and iteratively evolving products that serve the greater good. While examples vary widely across OS communities, they all share certain traits, including voluntary membership and meritocratic governance processes that allow motivated participants to seek and obtain leadership roles (O'mahony & Ferraro, 2007). In doing so, contributors may capture important intrinsic benefits including enjoyment, elevated reputation, better career prospects, learning, and access to valuable resources (Hertel, Niedner, & Herrmann, 2003; Lakhani & von Hippel, 2003). This is consistent with research that suggests the urgent need to focus on internal accountability measures (as preceding external accountability) if lasting improvement in student outcomes is to be achieved (Fullan, Rincon-Gallardo, & Hargreaves, 2015).

Toward New Orientations and Programmable Trust

Schools are inherently open systems (Katz & Kahn, 1969), yet, if this is true, it appears that we have spent the last half century moving away from their natural disposition. This is why, we are making the case for a fundamental shift – or recalibration, depending on your view – toward the natural state of how teachers, students, professors, deans, principals, chancellors, and community stakeholders are otherwise inclined to interact with one another. Though not exhaustive, the translational examples we provide here demonstrate the breadth and depth of OI and OS influences on institutions. We lay the groundwork for understanding how core principles of openness have disrupted other sectors with the intention of providing a path toward building new, though perhaps innate, orientations for leaders in a knowledge society. Next, we introduce orientations to better align our aspirations for openness with our actions within the schooling landscape. Beyond proposing a method or program, such as distributed leadership in schools (Camburn, Rowan, & Taylor, 2003), this is a call for addressing the unconscious rules and assumptions that govern the entire domain of education, and in turn, the essence of school leadership and flow of activities in the schools, districts, campuses ultimately affected (Fig. 7.2).

Thinking along a philosophical continuum of *open* versus *closed* orientations reminds us that we cannot add to the litany of demands placed on schools; this is a call on leaders, and society broadly, to make a choice with regards to what we truly value. Indeed, schools have operated from a fantasized position in regards to opportunity costs as new priorities are added onto the last intervention with little consideration for scarcity (Buchanan, 1969). In this fantasized setting (the modern educational policy landscape) "everything counts" equally with little regard to

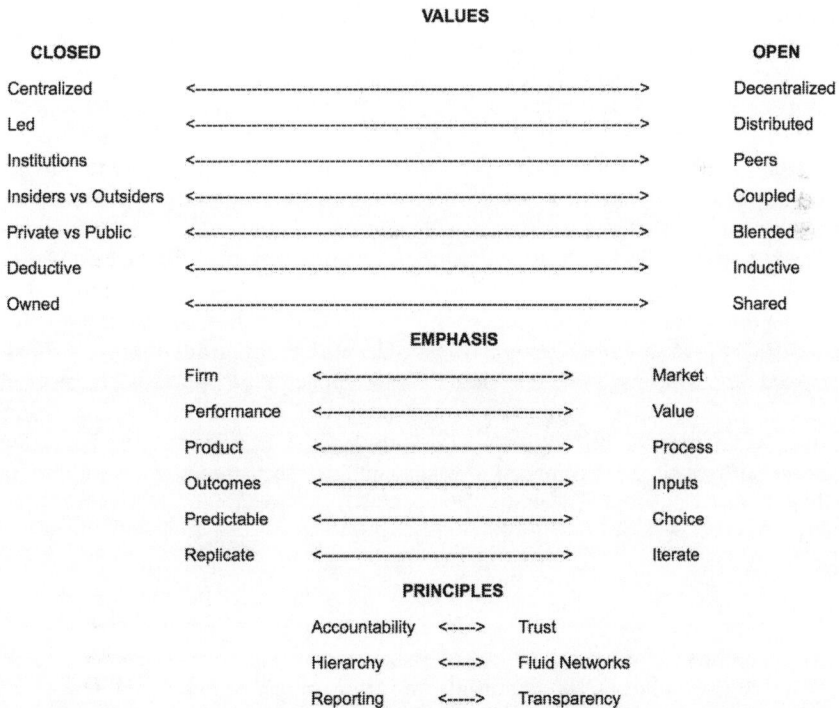

VALUES

CLOSED		OPEN
Centralized	<-->	Decentralized
Led	<-->	Distributed
Institutions	<-->	Peers
Insiders vs Outsiders	<-->	Coupled
Private vs Public	<-->	Blended
Deductive	<-->	Inductive
Owned	<-->	Shared

EMPHASIS

Firm	<-->	Market
Performance	<-->	Value
Product	<-->	Process
Outcomes	<-->	Inputs
Predictable	<-->	Choice
Replicate	<-->	Iterate

PRINCIPLES

Accountability	<----->	Trust
Hierarchy	<----->	Fluid Networks
Reporting	<----->	Transparency

Fig. 7.2.   Closed–Open Orientations: Unconscious Rules Driving Schooling.

better alternatives that may be sacrificed. We contend this is partly due to a centralized system or "grammar of schooling" (Martínez Arbelaiz & Correa Gorospe, 2009; Senge, 2012; Tyack & Tobin, 1994) which is incapable of hearing, never mind vetting and prioritizing, the best ideas in real time. Given this, it is no surprise that most reforms have not only failed to produce the intended outcomes at scale, but in fact may have indirectly led to schools moving away from organically generated solutions that would have already solved persistent challenges. The tensions between social innovation and institutionalization are well documented. Grassroots movements have been prone to bureaucratization and often progress through a life cycle which involves increased formalization, professionalization, and sometimes cooptation into the established political system (Moulaert et al., 2005, Ch. 4).

The lack of interoperability has had debilitating effects on scaling social innovations, most recently in education-based investments. What worked in one setting, the reasoning goes, should work in another. The challenge, however, is that schools operate in dramatically nuanced environments with locally unique challenges. With recent technological advances, fueled by crisis and legacy, an interoperable education system where protocols are built intentionally towards the common good might be surfacing, albeit slowly. The emergence of "web 3.0" innovations such as distributed ledger technology (DLT), decentralized autonomous organizations (DAOs), quadratic voting/funding, and Trust over IP, just to name a few, are indicators that we ought to take serious these notions of OS governance and programmable trust in all contexts, but certainly education. Such advances in "digital trust technologies," and related open standards, are quickly maturing and seem poised to help to support a post-truth reorientation. Through the combination of OI/OS-driven innovations, a near infinite array of intersecting data points and self-executing instructions can now be coded into existence. These new "smart contracts" can then sit idle, resistant to change or censorship, until triggered by predetermined, community-oriented criteria. Blockchain-based applications and self-sovereign digital identities are, in a sense, known treasures waiting for keystones to help unlock their potential. Perhaps most importantly for education policy, there will soon be precedents that bring attention to OI/OS-inspired applications and their potential to impact even the most traditional monolithic institutions. Within society at large, OS communities and networks driven by collective contribution (i.e. GitHub, Wikipedia, and Java) are becoming the default repositories of public knowledge, making the case for transferability to education all that more appealing for an industry obsessed with replicating what others have done and scaling innovations (Rees, Mullins, & Bovaird, 2012).

> Today, more than half of all servers run Apache; the internet itself was built on the back of Java, an open source programming language; Wikipedia offers 16 million articles in 270 languages; 70% of phones run Android, and 30% of all websites run on Wordpress. Even the genetic code was mapped using open source. Using this precedent, then, we suggest that teachers, students, and other stakeholders can and will shape the standards,

curricula, assessments, and schools of tomorrow through distributed and open systems – faster, better, and more efficiently. (Kendal & Balser, 2019)

Closing Thoughts

Thirty years on from the earliest calls to build open systems in schools, the arrow of innovation extends perpetually in a similar direction today. In this chapter, we argue that the growing influence of openness is more relevant than ever across the post-truth landscape, with education being no exception. We highlight the role of openness through two research streams. First, we introduce OI and the role knowledge flows have had in accelerating new products, services, and ideas to market. Next, we introduce OS as a way to understand governance and coopreation in a decentralized environment. In connecting OI and OS to the education landscape, we offer a framework for (re)orientations that help us view an emerging, more open paradigm. These orientations call for a shift from closed models of education to more open mindsets; ones in which knowledge, capital, and markets emerge and thrive alongside but beyond conventional approaches to learning environments. Moreover, we provide use cases of how openness is maturing across sectors and demonstrate its potential to influence an ever-changing learning and leadership landscape. On the institutional level, an open orientation provides capabilities for organizations to adapt and iterate in response to competitive forces that threaten their survival. It is here where collaborating and cocreating can be seen as mechanisms to not only provide greater value but also share costs, while reducing risks in a new reality filled with the ambiguity and opaque truth. Institutions that orient toward openness may find new capabilities that allow for rapid evaluation of information, knowledge, and negotiated truths. Such orientations will also enable new forms of more durable governance via programmable trust, allowing institutions to fluidly adapt to both the needs of their constituents and the surrounding environment. On the individual level, an orientation towards openness provides a sort of mental dexterity that is inclusive to ideas, where knowledge and perspectives are embedded into a collective and collaborative DNA. With an orientation towards openness, individuals view ideas as fluid, malleable, and unfixed. Simple notions become tools of ultimate agency; potential energy to be combined and arranged with other ideas and knowledge, within institutions, for the benefit of society, and across time. The combination and impact of an open orientation for systems and individuals has still broader ramifications for society – particularly where norms and values of communities are transferred.

Further, adopting this orientation may no longer just be about achieving a competitive advantage, but may in fact be an existential imperative. Never have the tensions between learning and innovation been more stark than during the global crisis and pandemic of 2020. A virus has laid bare the fragility of many of our social systems, perhaps education most clearly, and shown how far separated our *innovations* have grown from their underlying infrastructures. There are many examples of how nations, states, and governments, in order to save lives and avoid disaster, have turned to OI as the primary mechanism to enable the manufacturing of needed supplies (ventilators, personal protective equipment (PPE), swabs, vaccines, etc.). As a result of this reorienting towards openness, time was condensed and rapid supplies of critical equipment was made possible. Previously, unimagined collaboration emerged and bridges between disparate groups, nations even, were built. Unfortunately, in nearly every educational context, solutions involving virtual meetings and digital curricula were instituted in real time with few institutions having time to address the deeper questions around trust, transparency, and autonomy that these technologies enable. Without objective mechanisms for sifting through, nevermind assessing, the tsunami of solutions being introduced, student needs were arguably left at the mercy of chance. You could say that the pandemic only added additional unvetted layers to the patchwork of software solutionism; yet, our firmware as organizations, as markets, and as a society has remained unchanged. Whereas software can and should evolve rapidly, *firmware* is more foundational, helping to instruct its underlying hardware and, therefore, constrained by the machine itself. In a very human sense, then, our instructions (i.e. firmware) to operate autonomously, with integrity, and to navigate an infinite information ecology and discern truths are limited, or perhaps defined by, the institutions and markets – the hardware – we currently inhabit.

Central to our interest in exploring new models of OI and open governance in this context is a shared hope that we can offer a *reorientation*; an *upgrade*, so that organizational leaders can preserve democratic structures in schools where they exist, as well as help to construct them where they do not. We view this as essential if we are to realize knowledge societies/economies where ever-evolving technological advancement can present both challenges *and* solutions. These orientations act as a marker for further inquiry and investigation into how openness-based knowledge flows for market creation and openness-based governance models for organizational behavior can responsibly and democratically drive education innovation. While open systems in schools are not necessarily new, we now have a suite of technology, complemented by a growing list of effective use cases, allowing us to imagine entirely new models of trust and governance. All we need is a collective paradigmatic shift in mindset – a reorientation – toward openness.

References

Anderson-Butcher, D., Lawson, H. A., Iachini, A., Bean, G., Flaspohler, P. D., & Zullig, K. (2010). Capacity-related innovations resulting from the implementation of a community collaboration model for school improvement. *Journal of Educational and Psychological Consultation, 20*(4), 257–287.

Argyris, C. (1982). *Reasoning, learning, and action: Individual and organizational* (1st ed., A Joint publication in the Jossey-Bass series in social and behavioral science & in management training, and development). San Francisco, CA: Jossey-Bass.

Bakici, T., Almirall, E., & Wareham, J. (2013a). A smart city initiative: The case of Barcelona. *Journal of the Knowledge Economy, 4*(2), 135–148. doi:10.1007/s13132-012-0084-9

Bakici, T., Almirall, E., & Wareham, J. (2013b). The role of public open innovation intermediaries in local government and the public sector. *Technology Analysis & Strategic Management, 25*(3), 311–327.

Balser, W., & Coleman, H. (2020). Beyond the public-private nexus. *Journal of Transformative Leadership & Policy Studies, 8*(2), 34–46. doi:10.36851/jtlps.v8i2.2257

Banathy, B. H. (1991). *Systems design of education: A journey to create the future.* Englewood Cliffs, NJ: Educational Technology Publications.

Bathgate, K., & Silva, E. (2010). Joining forces: The benefits of integrating schools and community providers. *New Directions for Youth Development, 2010*(127), 63–73.

Beabout, B. R. (2010). Urban school reform and the strange attractor of low-risk relationships. *The School Community Journal, 20,* 9–30.

Betts, F. (1992). How systems thinking applies to education. *Educational Leadership, 50*(3), 38–41. Retrieved from http://www.ascd.org/publications/educational-leadership

Bingham, A., Spradlin, D., & Safari, an O'Reilly Media Company. (2011). *The open innovation marketplace: Creating value in the challenge driven enterprise* (1st ed.). Upper Saddle River, NJ: FT Press.

Bradshaw, L. K. (2000). The changing role of principals in school partnerships. *National Association of Secondary School Principals Bulletin, 84*(616), 86–96.

Brunswicker, S., & Vanhaverbeke, W. (2015). Open innovation in small and medium-sized enterprises (SMEs): External knowledge sourcing strategies and internal organizational facilitators. *Journal of Small Business Management, 53,* 1241–1263.

Buchanan, J. (1969). Cost and choice; an inquiry in economic theory. In J. M. Buchanan (Ed.), *Markham economics series.* Chicago, IL: Markham Pub.

Burawoy, M. (1991). *Ethnography unbound: Power and Resistance in the modern metropolis.* Berkeley, CA: University of California Press.

Camburn, E., Rowan, B., & Taylor, J. E. (2003). Distributed leadership in schools: The case of elementary schools adopting comprehensive school reform models. *Educational Evaluation and Policy Analysis, 25*(4), 347–373.

Capra, E., Francalanci, C., & Merlo, F. (2008). An empirical study on the relationship between software design quality, development effort and governance in open source projects. *IEEE Transactions on Software Engineering, 2*(13), 112–142. doi: 10.1109/TSE.2008.68

Cardoso, G. (2005). Societies in transition to the network society. In M. Castells & G.Cardoso (Eds.) *The Network Society: Knowledge and Policy* (pp. 23–67). Washington, DC: Center for Transatlantic Relations.

Casey, M. J. (2019). Interview at 2019 commonwealth for connected learning conference. *Malta.* Retrieved from https://www.youtube.com/watch?v=hI2RQyh8hk8

Chesbrough, H. W. (2003). *Open innovation: The new imperative for creating and profiting from technology.* Boston, MA: Harvard Business Press.

Chesbrough, H. (2006). *Open business models: How to thrive in the new innovation landscape.* Boston, MA: Harvard Business Press.

Chesbrough, H. (2010). Business model innovation: Opportunities and barriers. *Long Range Planning, 43*(2–3), 354–363.

Chesbrough, H. (2012). Why companies should have open business models. *MIT Sloan Management Review*, *48*(2), 22–28.

Crowston, K., Wei, K., Howison, J., & Wiggins, A. (2012). Free/Libre open-source software development: What we know and what we do not know. *ACM Computing Surveys*, *44*(2), 1–35.

Cuban, L. (2004). *Blackboard and the bottom line: Why schools can't Be businesses.* Cambridge, MA: Harvard University Press, ProQuest ebrary.

Datnow, A. (2000). Power and politics in the adoption of school reform models. *Educational Evaluation and Policy Analysis*, *22*(4), 357–374.

Di Tullio, D., & Staples, D. (2013). The governance and control of open source software projects. *Journal of Management Information Systems*, *30*(3), 49–80.

Diasio, S. (2016). Not all that jazz! Jamband as a metaphor for organizing new models of innovation. *European Management Journal*, *34*(2), 125–134.

Diasio, S. (2017). Open models of decision support: Towards a framework. In *ISPIM - International society for professional innovation management proceedings*, Melbourne, VIC.

DiMaggio, P. J., & Powell, W. W. (1983). The iron cage revisited: Institutional isomorphism and collective rationality in organizational fields. *American Sociological Review*, *48*(2), 147. doi:10.2307/2095101

Ellison, S. (2012). From within the belly of the beast: Rethinking the concept of the 'educational marketplace' in the popular discourse of education reform. *Educational Studies*, *48*(2), 119–136.

Executive Office of the President, Office of Management and Budget. (2009, December 8). Memorandum for the heads of executive departments and agencies: Open government directive, Washington, DC.

Fullan, M., Rincón-Gallardo, S., & Hargreaves, A. (2015). Professional capital as accountability. *Education Policy Analysis Archives*, *23*(15), 1–22.

Gassmann, O., & Enkel, E. (2004). Towards a theory of open innovation: Three core process archetypes. In *Proceedings of the R&D Management Conference (RADMA), Lisbon, Portugal.*

Gelberg, D. (2007). The business agenda for school reform: A parallel universe. *Teacher Education Quarterly*, *34*(2), 45–58.

Germeraad, P., & Vanhaverbeke, W. (2016). How to find, assess and value open innovation opportunities by leveraging IP databases?. *Journal of the Licensing Executives Society*, *3*, 154–156.

Giving USA Foundation and Indiana University Lilly Family School of Philanthropy. (2018). Giving USA 2018: The annual report on philanthropy for the year 2017, 63st annual issue/researched and written at IUPUI, Lilly Family School of Philanthropy.

Grier, D. A. (2016). 15 years to open source. *IEEE Computer Society*, 96. Retrieved from https://ieeexplore.ieee.org/stamp/stamp.jsp?arnumber=7756267

Hannan, M., Russell, J., Takahashi, S., & Park, S. (2015). Using improvement science to better support beginning teachers: The case of the building a teaching effectiveness network. *Journal of Teacher Education*, *66*(5), 494–508.

Hata, H., Todo, T., Onoue, S., & Matsumoto, K. (2015). Characteristics of sustainable oss projects: A theoretical and empirical study. In *Proceedings of the 8th international workshop on cooperative and human aspects of software engineering,*

CHASE '15 (pp. 15–21). Piscataway, NJ: IEEE Press. Retrieved from http://dl.acm.org/citation.cfm?id=2819321.2819325

Heifetz, R. A., Heifetz, R., Grashow, A., & Linsky, M. (2009). *The practice of adaptive leadership: Tools and tactics for changing your organization and the world.* Boston, MA: Harvard Business Press.

Heilig, J. V., Brewer, T. J., & Adamson, F. (2019). The comingling of neoliberal ideology, methods, and funding in school choice politics and research. *Handbook of Research on School Choice*, 335–350. doi:10.4324/9781351210447-24

Hernández, L. (2016). Complicating the rhetoric: How racial construction confounds market-based reformers' civil rights invocations. *Education Policy Analysis Archives, 24*(103), 1–34.

Hertel, G., Niedner, S., & Herrmann, S. (2003). Motivation of software developers in open source projects: An internet-based survey of contributors to the Linux kernel. *Research Policy, 32*(7), 1159–1177.

Hess, F. M., & Addison, J. G. (2019). Retrieved from https://www.nationalaffairs.com/publications/detail/busting-the-college-industrial-complex

Hoff, D. L. (2002). School-business partnerships: It's the schools' turn to raise the grade!. *School Community Journal, 12*(2), fall-winter, 63–78.

Jang, H., Lee, K., & Yoon, B. (2016). Development of an open innovation model for R&D collaboration between large firms and small-medium enterprises (SMES) in manufacturing industries. *International Journal of Innovation Management, 21,* 1750002. doi:10.1142/S1363919617500025

Johannsson, M., Wen, A., Kraetzig, B., Cohen, D., Liu, D., Liu, H., …. Zhao, Z. (2015). Space and open innovation: Potential, limitations and conditions of success. *Acta Astronautica, 115*, 173–184.

Katz, D., & Kahn, R. L. (1969). Common characteristics of open systems. In F. E. E. Harmondsworth (Ed.), *Systems thinking*. London: Penguin Books.

Kemp, J. (1991). Systems design of education: A journey to create the future (book review). *Educational Technology, 31*(4), 60–61.

Kendal, T., & Balser, W. (2019). What hackers can teach schools about thriving in a decentralized reality. *Diplomatic Courier*. Retrieved from https://www.diplomaticcourier.com/posts/what-hackers-can-teach-schools-about-thriving-in-a-decentralized-reality

Lakhani, K., & von Hippel, E. (2003). How open source software works: Free user-to-user assistance. *Research Policy, 32*(6), 923–943.

Lee, M., Almirall, E., & Wareham, J. (2016). Open data & civic apps: 1st generation failures, 2nd generation improvements. *Communications of the ACM, 59*(1), 82–89. doi:10.1145/2756542

Martínez Arbelaiz, A., & Correa Gorospe, J. M. (2009). Can the grammar of schooling be changed?. *Computers & Education, 53*(1), 51–56. doi:10.1016/j.compedu.2008.12.016

Moulaert, F., Martinelli, F., Swyngedouw, E., & Gonzalez, S. (2005). Towards alternative model(s) of local innovation. *Urban Studies, 42*(11), 1969–1990. doi: 10.1080/00420980500279893

Murphy, M., Perrot, F., & Rivera-Santos, M. (2012). New perspectives on learning and innovation in cross-sector collaborations. *Journal of Business Research, 65*(12), 1700–1709.

O'mahony, S., & Ferraro, F. (2007). The emergence of governance in an open source community. *Academy of Management Journal, 50*(5), 1079–1106.

Oliveira, C., & Breda-Vazquez, I. (2012). Creativity and social innovation: What can urban policies learn from sectoral experiences?. *International Journal of Urban and Regional Research, 36*(3), 522–538.

Picciano, A. G., & Spring, J. H. (2013). *The great American education-industrial complex ideology, technology, and profit* (Sociocultural, political, and historical studies in education). New York, NY: Routledge.

Purifoy, C., & Smith, J. (2018). Of currency, new gold standards and rocket fuel to coordinate global impact. *Diplomatic Courier*. Retrieved from https://www.diplomaticourier.com/posts/of-currency-new-gold-standards-and-rocket-fuel-to-coordinate-global-impact

Rees, J., Mullins, D., & Bovaird, T. (2012). *Third sector partnerships for public service delivery: An evidence review*. Working Paper. Birmingham: University of Birmingham.

Sadowski, B. M., Sadowski-Rasters, G., & Duysters, G. (2008). Transition of governance in a mature open software source community: Evidence from the debian case. *Information Economics and Policy, 20*(4), 323–332. Retrieved from http://dblp.uni-trier.de/db/journals/iepol/iepol20.html#SadowskiSD08

Scheer, A., Noweski, C., & Meinel, C. (2012). Transforming constructivist learning into action: Design thinking in education. *Design and Technology Education, 17*(3), 8–19.

Senge, P. M. (2012). *Schools that learn: A fifth discipline fieldbook for educators, parents, and everyone who cares about education*. London: Nicholas Brealey.

Shirky, C. (2008). *Here comes everybody: The power of organizing without organizations*. New York, NY: Penguin.

Sims, J., & Seidel, V. P. (2016). Organizations coupled with communities: The strategic effects on firms engaged in community-coupled open innovation. *Industrial and Corporate Change, 26*(4), 647–665.

Trachtman, R. (1994). This issue: Business and the schools—Redefining the relationship. *Theory Into Practice, 33*(4), 210. doi:10.1080/00405849409543641

Tyack, D., & Tobin, W. (1994). The "grammar" of schooling: Why has it been so hard to change?. *American Educational Research Journal, 31*(3), 453–479.

Von Krogh, G., & Von Hippel, E. (2006). The promise of research on open source software. *Management Science, 52*(7), 975–983.

Wan, T. (2018). Fewer deals, more money: U.S. Edtech funding rebounds with $1.2 billion in 2017. *EdSurge News*. Retrieved from https://www.edsurge.com/news/2017-12-19-fewer-deals-more-money-u-s-edtech-funding-rebounds-with-1-2-billion-in-2017

West, J., Salter, A., Vanhaverbeke, W., & Chesbrough, H. (2014). Open innovation: The next decade. *Research Policy, 43*, 805–811.

Zou, G., & Yilmaz, L. (2011). Dynamics of knowledge creation in global participatory science communities: Open innovation communities from a network perspective. *Computational and Mathematical Organization Theory, 17*(1), 35–58. Retrieved from http://dx.doi.org.du.idm.oclc.org/10.1007/s10588-010-9068-0

Part 2
Repurposing Media for the Post-truth Society

Chapter 8

Fact to Fake: The Media World as It Was and Is Today*

Michael Bugeja

Abstract

This chapter explores responsibility in the posttruth era in communication disciplines while documenting the civic and political ramifications of the current news climate in the United States.

Keywords: Journalism; fake news; media ethics; media literacy; responsibility in posttruth era; falsehood

Sixteen years ago, in the midst of journalism excitement about "convergence" – then known as the marriage of legacy and "new media" – I foresaw the future of my profession in the posttruth era and wrote a series of articles about a world without journalism, the world in which we live today.

One such piece was especially prescient. Titled "The Media World as It Is" (Bugeja, 2005, October 3), I accused now-defunct or failing media chains of caring "more about revenue than reputation," purchasing newspapers and broadcast stations "from families that had safeguarded rights in hometowns for generations." Thus began the downsizing of newsrooms to maximize profits for stockholders. Publishers and media executives justified their actions, investing in technology and proclaiming online access would build social networks, democratize news and generally enhance information in two-way flows. Maybe so, I wrote, but that goal "has always hinged on the presumption of readily available and verifiable information."

I also bemoaned the demise of objectivity, which media critics said never really existed. I saw this as enabling the emerging social media era in which journalism

---

*An early version of this chapter was published online to coincide with a conference called "Understanding the post-truth society," organised by the Commonwealth Centre for Connected Learning on the 10 and 11 October 2019.

Media, Technology and Education in a Post-Truth Society, 113–122
doi:10.1108/978-1-80043-906-120211008

no longer would be "top-down" but democratized. Every opinion, post, or viewpoint was just as valid as any published in *The New York Times. The Columbia Journalism Review*, the professional journalism flagship, also saw the same signs in a watershed article titled "Re-thinking Objectivity," citing me on the topic: "My favorite definition was from Michael Bugeja, who teaches journalism at Iowa State: 'Objectivity is seeing the world as it is, not how you wish it were'" (Cunningham, July/August 2003).

In my 2005 essay, describing the media world as it was, I noted that fear and outrage were by-products of an uninformed society. Now that digital media validated and elevated everyone's opinion, especially in the comments section of news reports, the Internet metamorphosed many traditional news consumers into trolls. "Who wants to participate in a media spectacle where audience and other sources, rather than the reporters, instinctively go for the jugular?" I wrote.

> Too often in this environment, the only people willing to speak out – to contribute to the social debate – are those with special interests or with nothing to lose and celebrity to gain.

I went a step further, predicting science no longer would be taken seriously, primarily because it was based on fact.

> Sources who can explain the complex issues of our era, including biotechnology and bioterrorism, often opt out of the social debate. This includes scientists at our best universities. They see the media world as it is ... and so have refrained from commenting on it. Increasingly the new silent majority will not go public with their facts or informed perspectives because, they realize, they will be pilloried for doing so by the omnipresent fear-mongers and sensationalists who provide a diet of conflict and provocation in the media.

A decade after writing that essay, I published two Oxford University Press books about technology and social change: *Interpersonal Divide: The Search for Community in a Technological Age* and *Interpersonal Divide in the Age of the Machine*. These books held that technology – primarily social media – was not only eroding journalistic truth but also undermining relationships and how we treated each other at home, school, and work. Then came the 2016 US presidential election. All of these technological effects intensified. Tweet-driven politics and social media influencers undermined journalism to such an extent that facts had become alternative, and truth was no longer truth. Instead we heard about fake news, hacked servers, hoaxes, and tall tales.

Those elements define the media world as it is today. This chapter analyzes their impact in the posttruth era, documenting the continued erosion of fact-based journalism since the 2016 US presidential election.

Here are definitions to frame the analysis:

- *Fake*: Unknown origin in use as a slang term for "rob" by nineteenth-century criminals (Jones, 2017).
- *Hack*: A thirteenth-century English verb, meaning to "cut with heavy blows in an irregular or random fashion," with a 1963 reference about cutting phone service between the Massachusetts Institute of Technology and Harvard University (Yagoda, 2014).
- *Hoax*: An adaption of the seventeenth-century word "hocus," meaning to "trick" as well as a criminal term, meaning to drug someone (Kelly, 2016).
- *Tall Tale*: Unknown origin about a wildly exaggerated folklore story with the word "tall" associated with the German "toll," meaning "amazing, incredible and extraordinary" (Stake Exchange Network, 2011, June 27).

The etymology of these terms seemingly sums up the state of US media in the posttruth era. Many Americans, fleeced of fact via hacked emails and fake posts, are addicted to incredible tales that affirm rather than inform belief systems.

In the years following the election of Donald Trump, there have been countless reports about fake news, hacked emails, hoaxes, and tall tales. One of Trump's initial proclamations came in a July 2016 news conference, asking Russia to hack Hillary Clinton's 30,000 missing emails: "I think you will probably be rewarded mightily by our press" (Schmidt). Trump has referred on multiple occasions to the special counsel investigation of Robert Mueller into possible collusion with Russia as a "witch hunt" and "the greatest political hoax of all time" (Axelrod, 2019).

As a candidate, Trump was obsessed with size, ranging from the dimensions of his hands to the tally of his inauguration crowd. Case in point: When then Republican presidential rival Marco Rubio joked about the size of Trump's hands, Trump defended that (along with another appendage) in a nationally televised presidential debate. As Politico reported, Trump stated:

> I have to say this, he (Rubio) hit my hands. Nobody has ever hit my hands. I've never heard of this one. Look at those hands. Are they small hands? And he referred to my hands if they're small, something else must be small. I guarantee you there's no problem. (Gass, 2016)

At the time, this comment seemed outrageous; now, Americans have grown accustomed to hyperbolic remarks. The US media reports such claims regularly. As it happens, Trump's hands are in the bottom 15th percentile of average male hands according to a report based on a handprint mold left at Madame Tussauds wax museum in New York City (Soffen, 2016).

According to *The Washington Post*, the president and top aides regularly demonstrate "that no fight is too small, no spat too insignificant," especially "when it comes to discussion of his inaugural crowds" (Sinderbrand, 2017). The *Post* article, titled "How Kellyanne Conway ushered in the era of 'alternative facts'" discussed Trump's assertion that his inaugural crowd was larger than that of his predecessor, Barack Obama. The article focused on an exchange with NBC anchor Chuck Todd in which Conway disputed the charge that the Trump administration lied about the inaugural size. Instead, she asserted, it provided "alternative facts":

> CHUCK TODD: Wait a minute – Alternative facts?
>
> KELLYANNE CONWAY: – that there's –
>
> CHUCK TODD: Alternative facts? Four of the five facts he uttered, the one thing he got right –
>
> KELLYANNE CONWAY: – hey, Chuck, why – Hey Chuck –
>
> CHUCK TODD: – was Zeke Miller. Four of the five facts he uttered were just not true. Look, alternative facts are not facts. They're falsehoods.

Thus entered into our US news lexicon the term "alternative facts," which dictionary.com defines as: "falsehoods, untruths, delusions. A fact is something that actually exists—what we would call 'reality' or 'truth.'"

Amid the Mueller special counsel probe, which investigated possible Trump collusion with Russia in the 2016 presidential election, the president's lawyer, Rudy Giuliani, uttered another iconic claim. In an article titled "'Truth isn't truth': Giuliani trumps 'alternative facts' with new Orwellian outburst," *The Guardian* dissected yet another Chuck Todd interview about the president testifying before Mueller:

> GIULIANI: "When you tell me [Trump] should testify because he's going to tell the truth so he shouldn't worry, well that's so silly because it's somebody's version of the truth, not the truth."
>
> TODD: "I don't mean to..."
>
> GIULIANI: "No, it isn't truth! Truth isn't truth."

The Guardian summed up that moment in one sentence:

> In a world that has given us "fake news", "enemy of the people" – infamously and also to a disbelieving Todd – Kellyanne Conway's "alternative facts", Trump's war on reality had just found its jingle. (*The Guardian*, 2018, August 19)

The reference to "enemy of the people" is particularly revealing. That phrase came in a Feb. 17, 2017 tweet from Trump who proclaimed: "The FAKE NEWS media (failing @nytimes, @NBCNews, @ABC, @CBS, @CNN[1]) is not my enemy, it is the enemy of the American People!"

Citing that tweet, *The New York Times* noted that Trump repeats that phrase when confronted with stories that deviate from his alternative reality (Davis, 2017). That reality, embraced by multitudes at his campaign rallies, defines truth for millions of Americans; reports to the contrary in the mainstream media are labeled "fake." Truth has been turned on its head.

As of this writing (January 2020), *The Washington Post's* fact-checking database stands at 19, 127 false or misleading claims over 1,226 days (Kessler, Rizzo, & Kelly, 2020). The newspaper reported that the coronavirus pandemic triggered a new genre of untruths, including his pronouncement of hydroxychloroquine as a potential cure. His frequent lie (334 times) was the US economy being the best in recorded history.

Tall tales are part of American lore, and Trump has glommed on to that. Whilst campaigning in Iowa in January 2016, he told his most fabulous tale: "I could stand in the middle of 5th Avenue [New York City] and shoot somebody and I wouldn't lose voters (Diamond, 2016)."

In light of claims such as this, *The Economist* drew the connection between Trump and folklore heroes of US history: "His fame may have been incubated on TV and in the Twittersphere but his persona – big, brash, boastful – goes all the way back to the Wild West" with characters like lumberjack Paul Bunyan who created the Great Lakes to water his ox Babe or pioneer Davy Crockett

> ...who told Congress in 1857: "I can walk like an ox, run like a fox, swim like an eel, yell like an Indian, fight like a devil and spout like an earthquake, make love like a mad bull." (Shone, 2016)

The article posits, "The truly American attitude, of course, is to suspect a hoax but still go along with it, just for the hell of it."

That attitude has been exacerbated by social media, where most Americans get their news. According to the Pew Research Center, 68% of American adults rely in part on social media for news, but "are skeptical of the information they see there: A majority (57%) say they expect the news they see on social media to be largely inaccurate" (Matsa & Shearer, 2018). The Pew report notes that Americans turn to social media for news because of ease of use. "'Convenience' is by far the most commonly mentioned benefit, (21%), while 8% say they most enjoy the interactions with other people."

That study affirms the hypothesis of *Vanishing Act: The Erosion of Online Footnotes and Implications for Scholarship in the Digital Age*, which traces the history of communication platforms from stone age to present. As coauthors Bugeja and Dimitrova note, communication on cave rock (drawings) was permanent; to view it, one had to be in the cave at an appointed time. That might be inconvenient. Rock had limited storage space and was not easily portable. However, by the third millennium BC, clay tablets were in use in Babylonian temples, which one had to visit to access. Tablets were less permanent than rock but had more storage space. Then came scrolls of papyrus and vellum, parchment manuscripts, and, finally, books in libraries, all less permanent than rock and clay with increasing space for content and, more important, portability. What drove innovation in each era?

> Throughout history, concerning archives, convenience trumped permanence when it came to fetching something from the archives. Convenience is to portability as permanence is to durability. ... The Internet scrambled all these factors, making physical place insignificant with 24/7 accessible databanks and digital journals and books, owned by others and stored as files on servers. (2010, pp. 11–12)

Although *Vanishing Act* documented disappearing footnotes of primary sources in communication research, endangering social scientific replicability, and recommended what now is in use in most journals, digital object identifiers, the disclosure of convenience as prime factor of innovation holds true today concerning news viewership.

Other factors in *Vanishing Act* also come into play in ascertaining how news media functioned before omnipresent mobile online access – specifically, place. In the 1970s, during the US Vietnam War and Richard Nixon impeachment, viewers assembled in living rooms at a set time to watch network news. Polls in 1972 and 1974 dubbed CBS news anchor Walter Cronkite "the most trusted man in America" (CBS, 2009) to state the facts and sign off with his signature motto: "And that's the way it is." Journalism had great impact in that era, primarily because newspapers and networks had noon and evening deadlines every day with ample time to fact-check sources and citations. People waited until the next cycle for updates and reports. Advertising was ample, too, underwriting newsrooms with all manner of editors and reporters across the country and globe. That no longer is the case.

According to the Pew Research Center, US newsroom employment between 2008 and 2017 dropped by 23%, with newspapers declining by 45%, from 71,000 workers to 39,000 (Grieco, 2018). The decline has spawned so-called news deserts where communities no longer have access to local news and must rely on social media and national newspapers such as the *New York Times*, *Washington Post*, and *Wall Street Journal*. A University of North Carolina study shows that more than 1,300 communities have lost local outlets with 20% of metro and community newspapers (about 1,800) going out of business or merging since 2004 (Stites, 2018).

Readers and viewers living in news deserts rely on social media and national outlets covering politics. Reports there are often partisan, and that has had an impact on voting in recent US elections, according to a recent study. Authors found that

> ...the decline of local newspapers and the "nationalization" of political news are polarizing vote choice: Voters were 1.9 percent more likely to vote for the same party for president and senator after a newspaper closes in their community, compared to voters in statistically similar areas where a newspaper did not close. (Darr, Dunaway, & Hitt, 2018)

The authors note that 1.9% may not seem like much but often is enough to win elections.

In an article titled, "Does Journalism Have a Future," Jill Lepore discusses the cumulative effect of news deserts in the posttruth era: "The broader problem is that the depravity, mendacity, vulgarity, and menace of the Trump Administration have put a lot of people, including reporters and editors, off their stride" (2019). In the age of social media, she observes, legacy news organizations have amended or violated their own editorial standards, contributing to political chaos and allowing Trump's Twitter feed to set the daily agenda. She notes a troubling aspect of journalism's traditional role: The more adversarial the press, "the more broken American public life. The more desperately the press chases readers, the more our press resembles our politics."

The more our press resembles our politics, the more Americans embrace falsehood, seeking affirmation over information.

A recent study documented the impact of falsehood on Twitter. Investigators analyzed verifiable true and false tweets between 2006 and 2017.

> Falsehood diffused significantly farther, faster, deeper, and more broadly than the truth in all categories of information, and the effects were more pronounced for false political news than for false news about terrorism, natural disasters, science, urban legends, or financial information. … Whereas false stories inspired fear, disgust, and surprise in replies, true stories inspired anticipation, sadness, joy, and trust. (Vosoughi, Roy, & Ara, 2018)

The study also noted that contrary to conventional wisdom,

> …robots accelerated the spread of true and false news at the same rate, implying that false news spreads more than the truth because humans, not robots, are more likely to spread it.

A 2019 study explored what age group was most apt to spread fake news on Facebook, finding that political conservatives were more likely to share such reports than liberals or moderates, with users over 65 sharing "nearly seven times as many articles from fake news domains as the youngest age group" (Guess, Nagler, Jonathan, & Tucker, 2019). The study utilized a list of verifiable fake domains that intentionally spread "false election-related stories generating the most Facebook engagement," with results affirming "the tendency of respondents to share articles they agree with." The study documents, in part, the urge to elevate affirmation over information in the posttruth era.

In a *New York Times* opinion piece, psychologists Gordon Pennycook and David Rand analyzed what makes people susceptible to fake news and what, if anything, can be done about it. "In general," they write, "our political culture seems to be increasingly populated by people who espouse outlandish or demonstrably false claims that often align with their political ideology" (2019). The psychologists summarized research that indicates that people who share fake news fall into two categories.

One group claims that our ability to reason is hijacked by our partisan convictions: that is, we're prone to rationalization. The other group – to which the two of us belong – claims that the problem is that we often fail to exercise our critical faculties: that is, we're mentally lazy.

Laziness invites convenience, once again the chief factor in the digital dissemination of fakes, hacks, hoaxes, and tall tales of the posttruth era. That effect will only worsen as big data instantaneously compiles our likes, dislikes, and buying habits, expressed via social media, reducing human beings to nodes in the algorithmic cloud. As Facebook and Google attract more US advertising in 2019 ($129 billion) than traditional media of television, radio, and newspapers ($109 billion), marking the first time ever that this has occurred (Wagner, 2019), the impact this year was felt not only in legacy news outlets but also in online ones like Yahoo, the Huffington Post and BuzzFeed, which downsized reporting staffs, something that media futurists failed to foresee in advocating for digital journalism (Arnold, 2019). That effect also is likely to continue, decreasing the diversity of news outlets and potentially creating *online news deserts*.

There are no short-term fixes. That time has passed. Society at times seems too comfortable being uninformed but friended. Moreover, technology behemoths – Apple, Alphabet (Google), Microsoft, Facebook, etc. – will continue to frame the news agenda, especially without government regulation in the United States.

There is a glimmer of hope in Americans beginning to realize the negative effects of fake news. The Pew Research Center reports that

> ...nearly seven-in-ten U.S. adults (68%) say made-up news and information greatly impacts Americans' confidence in government institutions, and roughly half (54%) say it is having a major impact on our confidence in each other. (Mitchell, Gottfriend, Fedeli, Stocking, & Walker, 2019)

Nonetheless, the study goes on to state that US adults blame politicians and activists more than journalists for fake news, believe journalists have a responsibility to fix the problem, and "think the issue will get worse in the foreseeable future."

Responsibility in the posttruth era also falls to researchers in communication disciplines to document the civic and political ramifications of the current news climate. Perhaps, then, educational institutions will mandate required courses in technology and media literacy in the hope that emerging generations might discern fact from factoid, rightness from rumor, science from fiction, reality from fantasy, hypothesis from hype, and truth from myth.

Note

1. All of these were hyperlinked to the respective Twitter handles.

References

Arnold, A. (2019). As many as 2,100 people have lost media jobs in the past two weeks. *The Cut*. Retrieved from https://www.thecut.com/2019/02/vice-layoffs-buzzfeed-huffpost-media.html

Axelrod, T. (2019). Trump blasts 'Greatest Political Hoax of all time' ahead of Mueller report release. *The Hill*. Retrieved from https://thehill.com/homenews/administration/439460-trump-lashes-out-at-clinton-dirty-cops-dnc-ahead-of-mueller-reports

Bugeja, M. (2005). The media world as it is. *Inside Higher Ed*. Retrieved from http://www.insidehighered.com/views/2005/10/03/bugeja

Bugeja, M., & Dimitrova, D. (2010). *Vanishing Act: The erosion of online footnotes and implications for scholarship in the digital age*. Duluth, MN: Library Juice Press.

CBS News. (2009). Walter cronkite dies. Retrieved from https://www.cbsnews.com/news/walter-cronkite-dies/

Cunningham, B. (2003). Rethinking objectivity. *Columbia Journalism Review*. Retrieved from https://archives.cjr.org/feature/rethinking_objectivity.php

Darr, J., Dunaway, J., & Hitt, M. P. (2018). When newspapers close, voters become more partisan. *Journal of Communication, 68*(6), 1007–1028. doi:10.1093/joc/jqy051

Davis, W. P. (2017). "Enemy of the people": Trump breaks out this phrase during moments of peak criticism. *The New York Times*. Retrieved from https://www.nytimes.com/2018/07/19/business/media/trump-media-enemy-of-the-people.html

Diamond, J. (2016). Trump: I could "shoot somebody" and I wouldn't lose voters. *CNN*. Retrieved from https://www.cnn.com/2016/01/23/politics/donald-trump-shoot-somebody-support/index.html

Gass, N. (2016). Trump on small hands: "I guarantee you there's no problem." *Politico*. Retrieved from https://www.politico.com/blogs/2016-gop-primary-live-updates-and-results/2016/03/donald-trump-small-hands-220223

Grieco, E. (2018). Newsroom employment dropped nearly a quarter in less than 10 years, with greatest decline at newspapers. Pew Research Center. Retrieved from https://www.pewresearch.org/fact-tank/2018/07/30/newsroom-employment-dropped-nearly-a-quarter-in-less-than-10-years-with-greatest-decline-at-newspapers/

Guess, A., Nagler, J., & Tucker, J. (2019). Less than you think: Prevalence and predictors of fake news dissemination on Facebook. *Science Advances, 5*(1). doi:10.1126/sciadv.aau4586. Retrieved from https://advances.sciencemag.org/content/5/1/eaau4586#F1

Jones, P. A. (2017). "Fake" etymology: The story behind one of the dictionary's most intriguing words. *Mentalfloss.com*. Retrieved from http://mentalfloss.com/article/92556/fake-etymology-story-behind-one-dictionarys-most-intriguing-words

Kelly, J. (2016). "Hoax": Just a little etymological hocus-pocus. *Mashedradish.com*. Retrieved from https://mashedradish.com/2016/10/04/hoax-just-a-little-etymological-hocus-pocus/

Kessler, G., Rizzo, S., & Kelly, M. (2020). President trump has made 19,127 false or misleading claims over 1,226 days. *The Washington Post*. Retrieved from https://www.washingtonpost.com/politics/2020/06/01/president-trump-made-19127-false-or-misleading-claims-1226-days/

Matsa, K. E., & Shearer, E. (2018). Most Americans continue to get news on social media, even though many have concerns about its accuracy. *Pew Research Center.* Retrieved from https://www.journalism.org/2018/09/10/news-use-across-social-media-platforms-2018/

Mitchell, A., Gottfriend, J., Fedeli, S., Stocking, G., & Walker, M. (2019). Many Americans say made-up news is a critical problem that needs to be fixed. *Pew Research Center.* Retrieved from https://www.journalism.org/2019/06/05/many-americans-say-made-up-news-is-a-critical-problem-that-needs-to-be-fixed/

Schmidt, M. S. (2016). Trump invited the Russians to hack Clinton. Were they listening?. *The New York Times.* Retrieved from https://www.nytimes.com/2018/07/13/us/politics/trump-russia-clinton-emails.html

Shone, T. (2016). Why America loves a braggart. *The Economist.* Retrieved from https://www.1843magazine.com/ideas/the-daily/why-america-loves-a-braggart

Sinderbrand, R. (2017). How Kellyanne Conway ushered in the era of "alternative facts". *The Washington Post.* Retrieved from https://www.washingtonpost.com/news/the-fix/wp/2017/01/22/how-kellyanne-conway-ushered-in-the-era-of-alternative-facts/?utm_term=.e13addb34e9d

Soffen, K. (2016). Yes, Donald Trump's hands are actually pretty small. *The Washington Post.* Retrieved from https://www.washingtonpost.com/news/morning-mix/wp/2016/08/05/yes-donald-trumps-hands-are-actually-pretty-small/?utm_term=.d97ff35ab923

Stake Exchange Network. (2011). What is the origin of "tall tale?". Retrieved from https://english.stackexchange.com/questions/31737/what-is-the-origin-of-tall-tale

Stites, T. (2018). About 1,300 U.S. communities have totally lost news coverage, UNC news desert study finds. *Poynter.org.* Retrieved from https://www.poynter.org/business-work/2018/about-1300-u-s-communities-have-totally-lost-news-coverage-unc-news-desert-study-finds/

The Guardian. (2018). "Truth isn't truth": Giuliani trumps "alternative facts" with new Orwellian outburst. Retrieved from https://www.theguardian.com/us-news/2018/aug/19/truth-isnt-truth-rudy-giuliani-trump-alternative-facts-orwellian

Vosoughi, S., Roy, D., & Ara, S. (2018). The spread of true and false news online. *Science, 359*(6380), 1146–1151. Retrieved from https://science.sciencemag.org/content/3/359/6380/1146

Wagner, K. (2019). Digital advertising in the US is finally bigger than print and television. *Vox.com.* Retrieved from https://www.vox.com/2019/2/20/18232433/digital-advertising-facebook-google-growth-tv-print-emarketer-2019

Yagoda, B. (2014). A short history of "hack". *The New Yorker.* Retrieved from https://www.newyorker.com/tech/annals-of-technology/a-short-history-of-hack

Chapter 9

Post-news Journalism in the Post-Enlightenment Era

Hossein Derakhshan

Abstract

News, as one of many forms of newspaper output, has long been synonymous with journalism. The "crisis of journalism" is primarily a crisis of the
news as a cultural form. Drawing on Carey (2008), this chapter argues that
news has lost its monopoly as a source of global experience and everyday
drama, and, thus, has lost its commodity value. The decline of traditional
forms of news is transforming journalism, and its democratic function as
vehicle of public conversation, toward long-form, long-term, and affective
narratives.

Keywords: Journalism; globalization; affect; turn inwards; decline of news;
figuration

Journalism has joined the list of endangered professions; teaching it appears to be
a more stable job than doing it. A great deal of high-quality journalism is still
being pursued around the world every day, but the news industry is steadily
shrinking in most parts of the world.

A distinction between *journalism* and *news* has to be made. As Barbie Zelizer
(2004) notes, there is not one hegemonic definition of journalism; rather it is
"comprised of many contradictory sets of people, dimensions, practices, and
functions," (p. 29) which she classifies in five ways: as an institution, as a practice,
as a profession, as a people, and as a text. Notwithstanding the definition of
journalism, news is not equal, but a subset to journalism.

Norbert Elias' (1978, 1982) theory of *figuration* may be useful here: journalism
can be viewed as a figuration which contains several interdependent processes of
which news is a core one, alongside commentary, entertainment, and community.

While the conventional take on news, as a rational, standardized, and
nonfiction narrative form, is more oriented toward the textual dimension of
journalism, news is nevertheless a historical construct. Raymond Williams' (2003)

Media, Technology and Education in a Post-Truth Society, 123–132
doi:10.1108/978-1-80043-906-120211009

theory of television as a *technology*, a *cultural form*, and a *social practice* can provide a suitable framework to study news historically.

Following Smythe (1981), who conditions technology on the audience (and not the other way around), it is fair to say that the invention of the telegraph itself was a response to an audience whose "hunger for experience" (Rutschky, 1980) incited her to "do away with the epic, heroic, and traditional in favor of the unique, original, novel, new – news" (Carey, 2008, p. 17). As Carey (2008) argues, the invention of news was a historical response to specific social and cultural conditions of the middle class in the late eighteenth century.

For the literate middle and working classes at the time, the prevailing trend in literature was grand, aspirational works on one side or detailed provincial or familial news on the other. The upper class had some access to foreign news, but before the telegraph, that news was stale, overly formal, and old-fashioned, mainly imported from the United Kingdom, then at the height of its global power.

The invention of the electric telegraph in the 1830s satiated the Euro-American middle-class's hunger for national and transnational experience with bursts of information in short, staccato messages, which were, ironically, not unlike tweets, but without any express of emotions. Carey explores how the telegraph and its consequent wire services stripped the local and the regional away from the language of news reports and made it flat, standard, and "objective," devoid of style, humor, irony, and satire, turning it into a commodity: "something that could be transported, measured, reduced, and timed" which was bound to "rates, contracts, franchising, discounts, and thefts," similar to agricultural communities (Carey, 1997, pp. 160–161).

The arrival of instant news transported the middle class from a local perspective to a global one, from a generalized view of the world to one full of specifics, and from a world centered on fiction to one grounded in fact. This opening up of the nineteenth-century media world happened alongside the Enlightenment, where myth and religious narrative gave way to scientific methods and rationality. News became how the middle class positioned itself in the expanding wider world and claimed a distinct cultural identity. The news was a historical invention subject to certain conditions, and, as Carey observes, it "will dissolve when the class that sponsors it and its possibility of having significance for us evaporates" (2008, p. 17).

Today, much of those sociocultural conditions have changed, causing a crisis of, in Carey's argument, *cultural significance* and *social sponsorship*. This sociocultural account of the journalism crisis is not about business models, ethics, technologies, or the quality of journalism which have dominated the debate.

The Crisis

In 2018, US newspapers' digital and print circulation dropped to an estimated 28.6 million, the lowest level on the record, since 1940. Their advertising revenue declines 62%, from $37.8 billion in 2008 to $14.3 billion in 2018, while their staff nearly halved (47%) from about 71,000 workers to 38,000 (Pew Research Center, 2019, 2020).

News businesses have been grappling with these imploding business models for more than a decade. New Internet technologies empowered new players – mainly Google and Facebook – that have claimed control of distribution and the advertising revenue that goes with it.

Inspired partly by President Trump, politicians from Burma to Libya and from Syria to Spain now openly attack[1] journalists, calling them "fake" or "biased," accusing them of twisting reality (Brants, De Vreese, Möller, & Van Praag, 2010). Thus, they increasingly bypass news organizations for an unmediated reach to the public through social media or live television. The public, on the other hand, sees journalists as too soft on power or too close to the wealthy and do not trust what they perceive as conflicts of interest.

It is true that some serious news organizations have recently seen increases in paid subscription services. In May 2020, *The New York Times* claimed to have nearly six million digital subscribers.[2] *The Guardian* has now received financial support from more than a million readers around the world. Yet, subscriptions do not directly equate to readership; it is valuable regular income, but it is not clear how much time subscribers spend reading or how many tend to renew their subscriptions.

More significantly, this can be seen as a temporary and unique anomaly, a "Trump bump" of new subscribers who regard this as a monthly fee of the anti-Trump resistance. Subscribers wear their membership as a badge of support for one side of this highly polarized political moment in much the same way as each of us like a comment on Twitter or Facebook without having read the full argument. It is an exhibition of our worldview.

Carey observed that news is not just a product but also a symbol and an identity-linked ritual akin to attending church:

> [R]eading a newspaper [is] less as sending or gaining information and more as attending a mass, a situation in which nothing new is learned but in which a particular view of the world is portrayed and confirmed. (Carey, 2008, p. 16)

The Turn Inwards

Trump's "America first" rhetoric may have unleashed the reign of the most unlikely president of the United States, but it also signified an end to a prevailing theory of the past 50 years: globalization.

It chimes with the faltering of global institutions and geopolitical aspirations: the declining authority of the United Nations (UN), impending regulation of Internet businesses, closed borders, the rise of nationalism, and seemingly intensifying religious and racial prejudices. In recent years, the World Economic Forum has hosted passionate debates contemplating the end of globalization.

"Nations will revert to their natural tendency of hiding behind their borders, of moving towards protectionism, of listening to vested interests, and they'll forget about transcending those national priorities," said Christine Lagarde, managing director of the International Monetary Fund, at the World Economic Forum, Davos, Switzerland (Thomson, 2017). It fits a surging, troubling trend toward protectionism, toward barricading ourselves against the outside world, against "the other" (Steed, 2018).

News, both as a commodity and as a cultural invention, has also been affected by this process of deglobalization, as evidenced by our declining coverage of international news in our media. By 2010, the frequency and space of foreign coverage in four British newspapers and the number of foreign news stories in the United States had nearly halved over about three decades (Moore, 2010). Even wealthy American TV has scaled back on budgets for foreign-based reporting, cutting expensive foreign correspondents and bureaus. Foreign reporting now tends to be limited to issues directly tied to national interests, such as war or terrorism. In 1989, the year the Berlin Wall fell, *ABC*, *CBS*, and *NBC* devoted a combined 4,828 minutes to international news. By 2000, after more than a decade of steady decline, the three networks aired only 2,127 minutes of international news during newscasts (Fleeson, 2003).

Perhaps that shift is related to the end of the Cold War, which was, for decades, the main source of conflict around the world. Yet, the decline continued even after the 9/11 attacks and the consequent global war on terror – which led to the unprecedented occupation of two nation-states in the Middle East and all the related stories of liberation, rebuilding, and insurgency for the Anglo-American media.

This shift away from globalism is both geopolitical and social, as if it is no longer fashionable for the middle class to be part of the wider world. The rise of religious or ethnic prejudices can also be related to this larger trend. It is a move inward, manifesting itself in many ways, including technology. I have written before about how the decline of hyperlinks, and consequently the web, reflects a wider cultural shift from outward to inward, from the global to the local (Derakhshan, 2015).

It oddly fits with the esthetic of the burgeoning craft movement: local food, local wine and beer, local artisan shops, and the rise of handicrafts. Yet despite this trend toward all things local, journalism manages to miss out yet again because there has been no apparent surge of support for local politics or local newspapers. In fact, local newspapers have consistently shrunk and are now on the verge of extinction, implying a lack of wider interest in local municipal elections – and perhaps in the wider process of participatory democracy itself (Masket, n.d.; Sullivan, 2017).

If you asked me how the appetite for the "local" is manifesting itself in the news, I would have a surprising answer: friends and family. Facebook's decision in early 2018 to prioritize updates from friends and family in the news feed (Isaac, n.d.) was both a reaction to political pressure over the spread of disinformation and a hint at what Facebook and its gigantic global audience regard as the most valuable news. "Research shows that strengthening our relationships improves our well-being and happiness," said Zuckerberg, explaining the decision (Zuckerberg, 2018).

But updates about births, deaths, marriages, babies, and other life events of family and friends are the local news for many people. The popularity of Instagram or Snapchat stories (Vázquez-Herrero, Direito-Rebollal, & López-García, 2019; Villaespesa & Wowkowych, 2020) is built around these interpersonal audiovisual diaries about our lives. And this is happening even while, poignantly, the rise of loneliness in an individualistic capitalist economy with collapsing welfare states means that people often live away from their network of family and friends (Yang, 2019).

Celebrity news is another way this "local" interest is manifesting itself. After all, celebrities have become our *de facto* friends and family. Many scholars see celebrity culture as linked to a middle-class desire for social mobility (Sternheimer, 2011), but it could also be understood as a response to the increase of nuclear families and the social epidemic of loneliness (Kim, Kim, & Yang, 2019).

And travel is yet another factor, one that offers some form of global identity for those who are still interested in the wider world. International travel is cheaper and more popular than ever (Dodds & Butler, 2019; Milano, Cheer, & Novelli, 2019). According to the World Tourism Organization (UNWTO), the number of international tourist arrivals in 2017 reached 1,326 million from only 25 million in 1950s, and international tourism receipts went up to US$ 1340 billion in 2017 from US$ 2 billion in 2008 (Duro & Turrión-Prats, 2019). The middle class no longer needs the news to satisfy their global sense of adventure, for they can reach distant cultures and destinations themselves, in person.

News as Drama

News can no longer be seen only as a vehicle for transmitting information. Carey opened our eyes to the key aspect of its global dramatic and ritualistic experience.

When we read a news story about climate change, corrupt politicians, or abusive celebrities, we not only become aware of the details of what has happened but also feel ourselves caught up in the drama of the story. We take sides, and we want our side to win. "It does not describe the world, but portrays an arena of dramatic forces and action," Carey wrote.

As scholars like Michael Schudson (2011) and John Fiske (2010) explored, news is by nature a drama with a calm beginning, a disruption at its core, and the prospect of a resolution at its end.

Schudson notes that journalists always aspired to astonish people at breakfast tables, rather than to help them understand things. They want their readers to ask their partners or colleagues, "Did you hear...?". They want to be the reason people talk.

That function is also now in serious decline. On one hand, consumption of information has become a very private act that could happen anywhere and anytime, thanks to mobile devices. The days when most people would sit to read a morning paper or make time to watch an evening news bulletin have passed. On the other hand, the inventions of cinema, television dramas, and, more recently, binge-watching entire series on Netflix, Hulu, or Amazon have slowly come to dominate the market demand for drama. From *Game of Thrones* to *Orange Is the New Black*, from telenovelas to Turkish soaps, screen drama is now feeding the appetite for what used to be a major appeal of the news.

Moreover, the 24-hour news channels that have managed to build an audience have often manufactured on-screen drama between the host and their guests, something media scholar John Fiske (2010) describes as soap opera for men. Conventional news bulletins, such as *PBS NewsHour*, have consistently lost viewers; *PBS NewsHour* lost more than half its viewership over the past decade, to around one million viewers per night, whereas cable news audience has not declined overall (Strachan, n.d.).

Notifications Are Not News

Just as the telegraph made reporting independent of time and space in the 1830s and the production of news possible from anywhere, it was the shift to mobile Internet and smartphones that freed the distribution of news from the tyranny of location and time. Now, anyone can receive news at any time and in almost any place.

This has led to a bifurcation. On one side, we have notifications – short blasts of information often directly from the newsmakers themselves. Think of tweets by fire or police departments, politicians, or the public relations (PR) departments of big companies. They are bypassing news organizations. On the other side, we have long, collaborative, detailed, and expensively produced reporting and investigations that often take months or years of work. This long-form and long-term journalism is far more expensive and in-depth than the news stories that dominated journalism for a long time, functioning more like nonfiction literature.

Whatever we have between these two is an increasingly less viable form of news. Many newsrooms have spent the past decade pouring time and journalistic resources into churning out 800-word[3] duplicate versions of news stories already on dozens of other news sites, none of which makes financial or strategic sense anymore. The same is true in video journalism, where studies[4] suggest readers respond best to short, two-minute animations or to hour-long in-depth documentaries. Midlength articles making money for some publishers are opinion pieces, not news stories.

The Future of News

Let us admit that news, as we recognized it for two centuries, is dying. It has lost most of its purpose for the majority of the middle class, and its value as a commodity has evaporated. But if news is almost dead, how can journalism – and thereby democracy – survive?

The biggest challenge for journalism is how to stay relevant to a democratic society even while its primary form – news – is disintegrating and while being buffeted by the twin forces of entertainment and propaganda. It is a grim picture and an extremely challenging task, but two recent trends offer some hope: the rise of podcasts and digital video.

Radio, and podcasts in particular, is a hybrid medium. It is still largely word-based and, therefore, capable of empowering rational arguments and elevating serious conversations, but it can also convey depth of emotion. It is somewhere between the typographic form of books and the photographic form of TV as a medium for intellectual engagement, and perhaps this explains why serious, in-depth podcasts and audiobooks are growing in popularity.[5]

Digital video is also gaining momentum. The combination of serious investigative reporting, opinion, and dramatic structure is a promising sign for the future of journalism. Video can both conduct and cultivate passionate public conversations about important policy issues, and for a much wider audience than academic nonfiction books. Ironically, both are reincarnations of existing forms of radio and documentary cinema.

The broader context, however, is bleak. Human civilization seems to be entering a new phase we could call the "post-Enlightenment," where the pillars of rationality and the written word are being structurally replaced by emotions and images. Faith is replacing facts; like buttons are killing links.[6] Television is making a comeback,[7] dominating every aspect of our lives and reducing it all to entertainment, as Postman (1986) warned.

The steady growth of inequality[8] and the collapse of the welfare states have led to a decline of public education and public media around the world. This has incited a departure from the principles of the Enlightenment,[9] in which knowledge and education were used to overcome prejudice and ignorance.

Conclusion

We should pity journalism. It is not only seeing the news at its very heart taken out, but at a time when democracy is outsmarted by entertainment, it is losing its entire purpose. Carey had a line for this, too: "Without the institutions of democracy, journalists are reduced to propagandists or entertainers" (Carey, 2000).

Carey's warning has never sounded truer. He not only assumes that democracy needs journalism; he also believes that journalism and democracy are, in fact, names for the same thing – in essence, they are both forms of a public conversation.

> What we mean by democracy depends on the forms of communication by which we conduct politics. What we mean by communication depends on the central impulses and aspirations of democratic politics. What we mean by public opinion depends on both. (Munson & Warren, 1997, p. 234)

Media scholar Jay Rosen has his own interpretation of Carey's account of democracy:

Journalists earn their credentials as democrats not by supplying information or monitoring the state – although both may be necessary. As energetic supporters of public talk, they should be helping us cultivate certain vital habits: the ability to follow an argument, grasp the point of view of another, expand the boundaries of understanding, decide the alternative purposes that might be pursued. (1997, p. 203).

If, as Carey provokes, democracy and journalism are synonymous with public conversation, it should not be surprising to see them in deep trouble these days. Saving democracy entails saving journalism – or vice versa.

Notes

1. See https://www.washingtonpost.com/news/fact-checker/wp/2018/02/06/president-trump-cries-fake-news-and-the-world-follows/.
2. See https://www.nytimes.com/2020/05/06/business/media/new-york-times-earnings-subscriptions-coronavirus.html.
3. See https://medium.com/bbc-news-labs/beyond-800-words-new-digital-story-for-mats-for-news-ab9b2a2d0e0d.
4. See https://www.huffpost.com/entry/short-form-vs-long-form-video-the-answer-is-sometimes_b_595d275ae4b0f078efd98de4.
5. See https://www.publishersweekly.com/pw/by-topic/industry-news/audio-books/article/73521-audio-publishing-s-internet-boom.html.
6. See https://www.technologyreview.com/2016/11/29/155271/social-media-is-killing-discourse-because-its-too-much-like-tv/.
7. See https://www.niemanlab.org/2017/12/television-has-won/.
8. See https://nymag.com/intelligencer/2017/12/inequality-is-rising-globally-and-soaring-in-the-u-s.html.
9. See https://plato.stanford.edu/entries/enlightenment/.

References

Brants, K., De Vreese, C., Möller, J., & Van Praag, P. (2010). The real spiral of cynicism? Symbiosis and mistrust between politicians and journalists. *The International Journal of Press/Politics*, *15*(1), 25–40.

Carey, J. W. (1997). The dark continent of American journalism. In *James Carey* (NED-New edition, pp. 144–188). Minneapolis, MN: University of Minnesota Press; JSTOR. doi:10.5749/j.ctttsvzt.14

Carey, J. W. (2000). *Journalism and democracy are names for the same thing*. Nieman Foundation. Retrieved from https://nieman.harvard.edu/articles/journalism-and-democracy-are-names-for-the-same-thing/

Carey, J. W. (2008). *Communication as culture, revised edition: Essays on media and society*. London: Routledge.

Derakhshan, H. (2015). The web we have to save. *The Medium*, July, 14. Retrieved from https://medium.com/matter/the-web-we-have-to-save-2eb1fe15a426

Dodds, R., & Butler, R. (2019). The phenomena of overtourism: A review. *International Journal of Tourism Cities*, *5*(4), 519–528.

Duro, J. A., & Turrión-Prats, J. (2019). Tourism seasonality worldwide. *Tourism Management Perspectives*, *31*, 38–53. doi:10.1016/j.tmp.2019.03.010

Elias, N. (1978). *What is sociology?*. London: Hutchinson.

Elias, N. (1982). *The civilizing process*. New York, NY: Pantheon Books.

Fiske, J. (2010). *Television culture*. London: Routledge.

Fleeson, L. (2003). Bureau of missing bureaus: Although television networks have closed many of their expensive foreign outposts, executives say they can cover the world just as well by dispatching reporters from central hubs. But critics say the shuttered offices come at a steep cost to the public. What is the future for foreign news on TV?. *American Journalism Review*, *25*(7), 32–40.

Isaac, M. (n.d.). Facebook overhauls news feed to focus on what friends and family share. *The New York Times*. Retrieved from https://www.nytimes.com/2018/01/11/technology/facebook-news-feed.html?mtrref=www.google.com&gwh=BFBAD3A BECC50DD665998ACC3AAD9234&gwt=pay

Kim, J., Kim, J., & Yang, H. (2019). Loneliness and the use of social media to follow celebrities: A moderating role of social presence. *The Social Science Journal*, *56*(1), 21–29.

Masket, S. (n.d.). The decline of local news is bad for democracy. *Pacific Standard*. Retrieved from https://psmag.com/news/the-decline-of-local-news-is-bad-for-democracy. Accessed on July 6. 2020.

Milano, C., Cheer, J. M., & Novelli, M. (2019). *Overtourism: Excesses, discontents and measures in travel and tourism*. Wallingford: CABI.

Moore, M. (2010). We need more world news, not less | Martin Moore. *The Guardian*. Retrieved from https://www.theguardian.com/media/organgrinder/2010/nov/01/world-news-foreign

Munson, E. S., & Warren, C. A. (1997). *James Carey: A critical reader*. Minneapolis, MN: University of Minnesota Press.

Pew Research Center. (2019). Trends and facts on newspapers. *Pew Research Center's Journalism Project*. Retrieved from https://www.journalism.org/fact-sheet/newspapers/

Pew Research Center. (2020). *U.S. newspapers have shed half of their newsroom employees since 2008*. Pew Research Center. Retrieved from https://www.pewresearch.org/fact-tank/2020/04/20/u-s-newsroom-employment-has-dropped-by-a-quarter-since-2008/

Postman, N. (1986). *Amusing ourselves to death: Public discourse in the age of show business*. New York, NY: Penguin Books.

Rosen, J. (1997). We'll have that conversation. *James Carey: A Critical Reader*, 191–206.

Rutschky, M. (1980). *Erfahrungshunger. Ein essay Über die Siebziger Jahre*. Köln, 197ff.

Schudson, M. (2011). *The sociology of news*. New York, NY: WW Norton & Company.

Smythe, D. W. (1981). On the audience commodity and its work. *Media and Cultural Studies: Keyworks*, *230*, 256.

Steed, C. (2018). *A question of inequality: The politics of equal worth*. London: Bloomsbury Publishing.

Sternheimer, K. (2011). *Celebrity culture and the American dream: Stardom and social mobility*. London: Routledge.

Strachan, M. (n.d.). 'PBS NewsHour' is unexciting and even-keeled, and people are loving it | HuffPost UK. *Huffington Post*. Retrieved from https://www.huffingtonpost.co.uk/entry/pbs-newshour-ratings_n_58bf1228e4b0f0c1cf96db17?ri18n= true&guccounter=1

Sullivan, M. (2017). Tension between Trump and the media? That's nothing compared to journalism's worst crisis. *Washington Post*. Retrieved from https://www.washingtonpost.com/lifestyle/style/tension-between-trump-and-the-media-thats-nothing-compared-to-journalisms-worst-crisis/2017/09/29/0589a8ea-a50e-11e7-b14f-f4177 3cd5a14_story.html

Thomson, S. (2017). *Christine Lagarde to Davos leaders: I warned about the dangers of inequality in 2013 and nobody listened*. World Economic Forum. Retrieved from https://www.weforum.org/agenda/2017/01/christine-lagarde-to-davos-leaders-i-warned-about-the-dangers-of-inequality-in-2013-and-nobody-listened/

Vázquez-Herrero, J., Direito-Rebollal, S., & López-García, X. (2019). Ephemeral journalism: News distribution through Instagram stories. *Social Media+Society*, *5*(4). 2056305119888657.

Villaespesa, E., & Wowkowych, S. (2020). Ephemeral storytelling with social media: Snapchat and Instagram stories at the brooklyn Museum. *Social Media+Society*, *6*(1). 2056305119898776.

Williams, R. (2003). *Television: Technology and cultural form* (New ed). London: Routledge. Retrieved from https://www.dawsonera.com/guard/protected/dawson.jsp? name=https://lse.ac.uk/idp&dest=http://www.dawsonera.com/depp/reader/protected/ external/AbstractView/S9780203426647

Yang, K. (2019). *Loneliness: A social problem*. London: Routledge.

Zelizer, B. (2004). *Taking journalism seriously: News and the academy*. Thousand Oaks, CA: Sage Publications.

Zuckerberg, M. (2018). *Facebook*. Retrieved from https://www.facebook.com/zuck/ posts/10104413015393571

Chapter 10

How Can Wikipedia Save Us all?: Assuming Good Faith from all Points of View in the Age of Fake News and Post-truth

Toni Sant

Abstract

The world's most popular noncommercial website is built on five pillars, which include an assumption of good faith and ensuring all points of view are included in every encyclopedia article. How does this pan out in the day-to-day reality of fake news and the ever-growing climate of post-truth? How apt are mechanisms established by Wikipedia over a decade ago in the face of unreliable news sources and beliefs based on gut feelings and emotions rather than verifiable evidence? Active editors of Wikipedia firmly believe that this open online encyclopedia and other wikis operating under the same value system are lifeboats for truth seekers in a post-truth society. The mechanisms established over many years for sharing open knowledge through this online platform are even more useful now than they may have been in previous times, even though this too is understandably debatable.

Keywords: Wikipedia; open knowledge; verifiability; fake news; post-truth; truth mechanisms

You presumably know that Wikipedia is an online encyclopedia. You probably also have an opinion about how reliable Wikipedia can be as a source of information. To set an appropriate tone for this provocation, I ask simply: how do you use Wikipedia? I don't aim to answer that question for you. However, I will assume that, like most people reading this, you look things up on Google and that, when you do, on the right side of your screen you get an information box for

Media, Technology and Education in a Post-Truth Society, 133–143
Copyright © 2021 by Emerald Publishing Limited
All rights of reproduction in any form reserved
doi:10.1108/978-1-80043-906-120211010

some of the things you look up, which is populated with data that come from Wikipedia. You sometimes click on that because it's quite big and possibly more attractive than anything else that comes up in the search results. This is very probably one way you regularly end up on Wikipedia. It is frequently your first source of information. Even if we do not click on the links that take you to it, we are all Wikipedia readers through our Google searches.

The first word in the question at the heart of the title of my contribution here is also how. The answer to the question changes if we change the meaning of "use" in the simple query: how do you *use* Wikipedia? Did you know that anyone can write or edit Wikipedia? Have you ever written or edited Wikipedia? If you have never contributed to its content, do you know how this is done? Indeed, anyone can create and edit Wikipedia articles for all to see. However, this does not mean that it is an unregulated information space. The key thing to keep in mind, as far as what I'm proposing here entails, is that Wikipedia is a collaborative repository of information.

If Wikipedia articles are created through collaboration, what is created can arguably be considered to be true by consensus. However, if something is deemed to be true by a community of thousands, if not millions, that does not make it universally true. Determining truth by majority vote is also not a way to determine whether something is actually true or not. A majority of people may hold a belief to be true but that does not automatically make it true – if an assumption or belief is held on information that is not widely held to be factual from different perspectives. Truth and facts are related but facts are not held by belief or assumption but proven in a verifiable manner, such as by repeatable scientific experiment or a widely agreed standard that holds true in other unrelated circumstances.

Relativity and perspective sit opposite to objectivity and universalism. Nevertheless, there are also different perspectives on the same fact. Is it six or is it half a dozen? They are both true and one does not exclude the other. There are just different ways to say the same thing. I mention this to simply highlight different approaches to what is true, what is deemed to be true, and what may seem to be true in more ways than one. Even in science, theories pertaining to chaos, complexity, quantum mechanics, and Heisenberg's uncertainty principle point toward the possibility of relativistic truths.

Declaring Bias

Before proceeding to elaborate more about Wikipedia in the context of fake news and the so-called post-truth age, I should make a disclaimer, which will give you a good sense of how I may be biased when presenting my ideas here. I have done more work for Wikipedia than the average person, and there was a time when I was paid for some of this work, which mostly did not directly involve writing or editing Wikipedia. I have been an unpaid Wikipedia editor since 2010; this is ongoing. I have made about 3,000 edits over a period of a little more than 10 years; that is a very modest contribution compared to the average active

Wikipedia editor. I have created 120 pages on Wikipedia but only 10 of these are actual articles. Although I have indeed created 120 pages on Wikipedia, some of those are discussion pages, some are redirect pages probably associated with name disambiguation (for example, distinguishing the artist Antoine Camilleri from the Vatican prelate by the same name or the Maltese-Australian intersex politician Tony Briffa from the Denmark-based artist who shares his name), and similarly some are disambiguation index pages. In terms of the actual encyclopedia articles I have written, my claim to fame is that I created the English language Wikipedia article for *fatberg*, which is the mass lump of fat that is more frequently being found in sewers beneath large cities.[1] This contribution has now been translated into 12 other languages and the word entered into the Oxford Dictionaries in 2015.

I mentioned earlier that I was paid for some of the Wikipedia-related work that I have done. I was a Wikimedia UK employee between 2013 and 2015, which means that I worked for the Wikimedia Foundation's chapter in London. The Wikimedia Foundation is a nonprofit organization that administers Wikipedia and several other associated projects such as Wikinews, Wiktionary, Wikidata, Wikimedia Commons, and Wikibooks, to name a few. I was paid to organize Wikimedia's education program in the United Kingdom. This work involved going into schools and more often universities to teach students and teachers how to edit Wikipedia. Ostensibly we encouraged students to write Wikipedia rather than cite Wikipedia. "Don't cite Wikipedia, write Wikipedia" was indeed one of our slogans. This chimed well with the teachers and lecturers, particularly because for the most part there has been great resistance by educators in encouraging students to engage with Wikipedia. Dariusz Jemielniak, an elected member of the Wikimedia Foundation board of trustees, is a strong proponent of the idea that it's high time for academia to not only acknowledge the quality of Wikipedia but also promote its use in active ways as part of the curriculum across all disciplines (Jemielniak, 2019). He has studied open collaboration projects for the past decade and previously published an extensive ethnography of Wikipedia (Jemielniak, 2014).

One other thing to add to my disclaimer is that since 2016 I have been a founding trustee of the affiliated user group of the Wikimedia Foundation in Malta and that is Wikimedia Community Malta. This user group is a registered nonprofit organization. In Malta, this type of association is called a voluntary organization, elsewhere they are called nonprofits or charities. In any case, I mention all this so that I make my bias as transparent as possible when proceeding to present my perspective on Wikipedia. I know that while I may try to be as objective as possible in my writing, I am still very subjective in my thinking about Wikipedia. This is all inflected by my experiences working directly on Wikipedia and related projects. These realities and these truths that I believe to be real lead me back to the title question: How can Wikipedia save us all?

Wikipedia and Fake News

How did I come to construct the title question? The way I have intended to tackle it is without nostalgia for what can be called "the regular world" – a world before fake news became as prevalent as it is now. In what ways can Wikipedia save us now? I am not particularly sure that that is how we are best served looking at this question. I do not necessarily want to approach it in a way that is too literal. At the risk of making a grandiose statement, I do not know that Wikipedia can save us from fake news but I have good reason to believe that it is a beacon of hope in an otherwise quite hopeless world.

Let us attempt to take a closer look at some of the ways that Wikipedia can save us from fake news. A good way to do this is to turn to what are known as the five pillars of Wikipedia.[2] Not unlike the distilled fundamentals of some major religions – the Judeo-Christian Ten Commandments, the five pillars of Islam, or the noble eightfold path of Buddhism – there are immutable principles around which the whole system revolves.

The first of the five pillars of Wikipedia simply states that Wikipedia is an encyclopedia. This is mostly to say that it is not a publisher of original thought, not a dictionary or a directory, not a means of promotion or a soapbox, not an indiscriminate collection of information, and the list goes on.[3] Suffice it to say that "Wikipedia is not any of a very long list of terrible ideas."[4] In the context of fake news, it is quite useful to remember that Wikipedia is not a news site. The Wikimedia Foundation, which runs Wikipedia, also runs a news site. It is called Wikinews and it operates on the same software and on the same core values as the encyclopedia operated at Wikipedia.[5] Although Wikinews is not Wikipedia, significantly, for the context of what I am generally presenting here, it is written from a neutral point of view. This is the second of the five pillars of Wikipedia. I will elaborate on this shortly after I have outlined the other pillars, particularly because this concept is embedded in the subtitle to this essay.

The third pillar is that Wikipedia is free content that anyone can use, edit, modify, share, and distribute. This gives two meanings to the word *free*. It is free as in *gratis*: a free beer or a free lunch. It is also free as in *liberty*: free as a bird. Generally speaking, content on Wikipedia is published under an open license known as creative commons. Specifically, this creative commons license only reserves some rights, rather than all rights the way copyright works. The main rights reserved by the license favored by Wikipedia are attribution to the creator/s and ensuring that they require copies or adaptations of the work to be released under the same license as the original.[6]

The next pillar demands that Wikipedia editors treat each other with respect and civility. This is another aspect of the way the title question I posed here is framed. This pillar assumes there is good faith among people who collaboratively develop this online encyclopedia. The fourth pillar demands that there is no mudslinging or point scoring between Wikipedia editors. This is not to say that there are no disagreements among editors. There are several editors who embrace diverging points of view on specific topics. Nevertheless, they are expected to treat each other with respect and civility. For the most part, this really works. When it does not, Wikipedia has an effective mechanism to deal with problematic disagreements or misbehavior. This is known as the Arbitration Committee and its remit is dispute resolution in a manner that is final and binding.[7]

The final pillar is one I am particularly fond of, as it tickles both my political and spiritual bones as an anarchist and a Buddhist, or perhaps merely a lapsed nihilist: Wikipedia does not have any firm rules. I think it is more precise to reiterate this as Wikipedia does not have *many* firm rules. This is because Wikipedia actually has some policies that are nonnegotiable and therefore quite firm.

Turning back to the essential concept of embracing a neutral point of view (the second pillar), it is possibly more practical to think of this as one where all points of view are taken into consideration. In the process, all points can potentially neutralize each other. Aside from being one of the five pillars of Wikipedia, the notion of a neutral point of view is one of the three core content policies.[8] Another core content policy that is closely related to this is verifiability. The basic idea behind verifiability on Wikipedia is that anyone using the encyclopedia can "check that the information comes from a reliable source."[9] This implies that it is less important whether something is true or not than whether it is verifiable. This is where source transparency comes to the fore. We get to transparency not only by having verifiability but also by insisting that sources are reliable. In Wikipedia's way of treating verifiability in a transparent way, whether someone said or did not say something is only relevant if you can verify whether it was said or was not said, rather than whether it's actually true or not that I said something or did not say something. Furthermore, in terms of these three core content policies, since Wikipedia is an encyclopedia, it stands to reason that there's a "no original research" policy at its core.[10] The verifiable sources this encyclopedia is built on must come from others, from elsewhere. It is therefore about what someone else has said and what someone else has produced, rather than what I said or what I produced. Furthermore, they must be reliable. This is very important and we will return to it again shortly.

If you if you look up Wikipedia: Neutral Point of View on Wikipedia (or just WP:POV), you do not just get the policy but also you will see that this policy is nonnegotiable and the principles outlined here and upon which these policies are based cannot be superseded by other policies or guidelines or by editor consensus.[11] This is what I meant when I said that the final of the five pillars claiming that there are not *any* firm rules should rather be interpreted as there are not *many* firm rules. It's not to be interpreted as a circular fallacy, such as a phrase like trust no one – which implies that even that statement itself should not be trusted. This is not a mind game even though it may be considered to be an overwhelming exception or an informal fallacy of generalization. This is a policy that is set in stone, without being considerate for the core values that have made it possible. This is a cornerstone of what Wikipedia is about where there are no firm rules. This is more than a firm rule. This core content policy is not negotiable. Verifiability is very transparently crucial for Wikipedia to work.

Taking a closer look at the ideas embedded in the fourth pillar – civility and respect – the key policy here is assuming good faith. This relates to Hanlon's Razor, which claims that you should "never attribute to malice what is adequately explained by stupidity."[12] For the sake of a common example of applying this to a political figure who may loom large on this collection of writings, we could see how this would work for Donald Trump. Assuming good faith to the former

President of the United States presumes that there is no malice in much of what Donald Trump says but that the many things he says with which so many people disagree are merely utterances that can be attributed to stupidity. This is a very sharp razor and it cuts deep both ways. There is no malice in attributing stupidity rather than malice to any of Donald Trump's utterances as we are assuming good faith on his part. Predating the development of Hanlon's Razor, this concept has been discussed philosophically in a rather eloquent way by Johann Wolfgang von Goethe (1774) in his novel *Die Leiden des jungen Werthers* where he proposes that "misunderstandings and neglect occasion more mischief in the world that even malice and wickedness." Thus, we presume misunderstandings and neglect of civility or respect, and in some cases a lack of modesty or self-awareness. If we believe that malice and wickedness are less frequent than it follows that there is more misunderstanding and neglect when Donald Trump says "in my infinite wisdom" or "I am a very stable genius." For example, that is not wickedness; that is just a neglect of modesty and/or a misunderstanding of the concept of "infinite wisdom or ignorance of what being a 'stable genius' actually means." This is one way of looking at the principle of "assuming good faith" in a post-truth framework that involves a politician like Donald Trump.

Wikipedia's insistence on reliable sources for verifiability is rather more significant in the context of post-truth. Stemming from the strongly held position that verifiability, not truth, is at the core of what is required from Wikipedia editors, we must balance this with the insistence on reliable sources for verifiability. Two essays on this subject contained within Wikipedia itself are rather revealing and quite convincing for anyone seeking to better understand this fundamental approach to the way Wikipedia is built. The first contains general advice on identifying reliable sources.[13] The other provides an analysis of specific examples of sources that appear reliable at first glance, showing how and why they may not be so reliable on closer inspection and further consideration.[14] These guidelines did not crystalize overnight; however, they have been a concern for the Wikipedia editing community since the early years of its inception.

In an email written on September 29, 2003 by Jimmy Wales to the Wikipedia editing community, the online encyclopedia's co-founder proposed the following guidance bringing together ways of looking at all points of view with the importance of expanding only on reliable sources that are verifiable:

If your viewpoint is in the majority, then it should be easy to substantiate it with reference to commonly accepted reference texts;

If your viewpoint is held by a significant minority, then it should be easy to name prominent adherents;

If your viewpoint is held by an extremely small minority, then – whether it's true or not, whether you can prove it or not – it does not belong in Wikipedia, except perhaps in some ancillary article.[15]

From time to time, Wikipedia declares specific news sources to be unreliable. This happens particularly when they regularly carry news reports that are not carried by any other mainstream news source. One such recent exclusion which received considerable mainstream media attention took place in 2017 when Wikipedia banned a popular British newspaper read regularly by millions of people. The Daily Mail was named a potentially unreliable source because it regularly carried exclusive news stories that were not corroborated by any other source that is regularly deemed to be reliable. This delisting did not happen on a whim or because a particular politician deemed it to be a purveyor of fake news. By contrast, CNN is not identified by Wikipedia as a potentially unreliable source, even though the 45th President of the United States leveled this accusation at it more than once. On a much smaller scale, the same goes for the Times of Malta, which has frequently been accused of presenting fake news, particularly by politicians from the government's side who are the subject of alleged corruption or misconduct.

Wikipedia and Post-truth

If you look up "post-truth" on Wikipedia, the first thing you will find is a quote from Sean Illing claiming that post-truth is "the disappearance of shared objective standards for truth."[16] This flies against one of Wikipedia core principles. If there is a common point of view, which may embrace many points of view, then there is a consensus truth, even if this may be built on a compromise similar to agreeing to disagree. One example of this is the politically charged encyclopedia entry on Israel. According to Wikipedia, "Israel" is both the land that the Israelis claim it to be and also an occupied territory of Palestine. Both points of view are true and one does not necessarily exclude the other, unless you side exclusively with either the Israeli or the Palestinian side. The consensus truth approach is to give a wider perspective on this particular situation, and others like it, by presenting more than one point of view when there are diverging, or even conflicting, ideas about the same subject. Another example is "abortion" where both the so-called "pro-life" and "pro-choice" points of view are presented as an integral part on the legal right that some deem to be firmly against their broadly held belief system.

There is no reason to fret about Wikipedia finding itself in any great difficulty as a result of the rise of the so-called post-truth age. Beyond his initial definition of post-truth, Sean Illing holds that "we can never really be post-truth [because] truth is always shifting." Shifting truth is a way to define "subjective truth" or "situational truth" and thus we also need to consider the notion of "absolute truth" in this context. "Absolute truth" equates truth with a definite way to negate the very fact that there are different kinds of truth, which in essence is the definition of "subjective truth." To loosen the dialectic relationship between such overarching ways of looking at things, it is useful to also to think of Wikipedia's take on neutral point of view as one that advocates multiperspectivity. This term is normally applied to fiction to describe stories that employ multiple narrators. However, it applies equally well to an encyclopedia that embraces multiple perspectives to enable a neutral presentation of all points of view about any given subject on which alternative viewpoints are not completely eliminated by the dominant narrative. Around 100 years ago, Horace Kallen (1924) called this approach "cultural pluralism" in an effort to argue against the oversimplification of philosophically complex problems. In other words, the acceptance of cultural pluralism or multiperspectivity can be seen as antidotes to post-truth.

The fact that the Oxford English Dictionary picked post-truth as its word of the year in 2016 is possibly more a matter of zeitgeist than anything else. Significantly, in the English-speaking world, 2016 was the year of both Donald Trump being elected to the White House and a majority of voting citizens in the United Kingdom suggesting to the British Government to adopt what is now commonly known as Brexit, relinquishing the country's membership of the European Union. Both circumstances are mired in accusations of "subjective truth" being presented as "objective truth" while both sides ignored the very idea of a "consensus truth."

Whenever the phrase "according to Wikipedia" is used from a well-developed article about most subjects, this means that what is presented relates to or denotes a consensus of a range of verifiable points of view. This is not a circumstance in which "objective facts are less influential in shaping public opinion that appeals to emotion and personal belief." If this is accepted as a definition of post-truth, then Wikipedia is essentially constructed and operated under policies that are counter to this definition of post-truth. Returning to the example of Israel and Palestine, this is understandably why both sides appeal to emotions with the violence that goes on there and the conflict that goes on in relation to one's personal beliefs as to Israel and Palestine. The same goes for the pro-choice and pro-life arguments in relation to abortion. There are many other examples and instances of this. The ones presented here have been selected as they are among those most widely understood as situations where people with diverging value systems both firmly and rather genuinely believe their version of things to be true.

Beyond the five pillars of Wikipedia and its core content policies, the global Wikimedia Movement (which is even broader than the Wikipedia community) also actively engages in initiatives to ensure diversity (relating to terms such as ethnicity, gender identity, culture, age, nationality, language, ability, orientation, education, political affiliations, religious beliefs, economic background, and many other demographic variables) and inclusion in its projects.[17] This approach has an impact on both the breath of topic covers and the choice of sources. For example, the gender gap and the racial gap among editors are addressed through a number of regular programs that aim to ensure more diversity and inclusion. These include drives such as Art+Feminism, Women in Red, Wiki Loves Pride, and Black WikiHistory Month, among others. Surely this is the organization's way to ensure healthy and robust multiperspectivity.[18]

Doing Something about Fake News

In August 2018, Wired magazine reported on Wikipedia's volunteer-run battle against fake news, which had been brewing for quite some time. If Wikipedia is run mostly (i.e., whenever possible) by consensus, whenever consensus is not possible, it is run by majority vote. Most significant decisions are made through community consultation. There is also a panel of established Wikimedia editors called an arbitration committee used to address dispute resolution in a binding manner.[19] However, Jimmy Wales has attributed this to the even looser nature of the Wikipedia community.

> In this era where we've seen the rise of fake news websites, Wikipedia has had almost no problems with this at all, simply because of our community. It's their hobby to debate about the quality of sources. It's very difficult to fool the Wikipedia community with [fake news].[20]

Asked to apply this as a suggestion to the broader online audience outside the Wikipedia community, Wales proposes that

> ...may be one step that a lot of people can do is to immediately take a more skeptical attitude towards things that you're sharing online. Just take a second and look on a search engine, check some of the keywords and terms, and make sure you're not adding to the problem. Think again. You might be sharing fake news.[21]

The more open and connected people are online, the better the things will be for everyone. Facebook seems to be one of the main trouble zones for the spread of fake news and this is precisely because so many Facebook users share links to stories that claim things that are frequently not fact-checked or based on accepted facts. Links go viral because they seem funny or confirm a widely held belief without any basis. Sometimes it's simply a distorted headline and the actual news story or source it links to says nothing that is asserted in the title.

Recognizing the need to address this significant issue, Facebook itself launched a new feature to provide more context about information that appears on its news feeds in April 2018.[22] This context button includes Wikipedia as a reliable source for verification of other sources precisely because of the way the online encyclopedia is built on citations and the policies associated with the development of stable content about most topics in the English language Wikipedia. While this matter is to some degree or other deemed to be successful with the English language, the same cannot really be claimed for most other languages. Facebook has, however, also provided this feature for some Spanish-speaking countries, France, Germany, Italy, and Poland. The context button became a global Facebook feature by the start of 2019. As Wikipedia continues to improve, in English as well as other major languages, presumably so will this context feature on Facebook designed specifically to provide a tool to combat fake news on the world's most popular social media network.

Conclusion

In this essay I have nonfacetiously proposed that Wikipedia can save us all from fake news by assuming good faith around presenting all points of view in its quest to ensure information is based on verifiable sources that are reliable. Wikipedia proposes a worldview that is broader than most people's personal value system.

It is also important to point out that a number of policy changes have made Wikipedia a more reliable source in itself. Unregistered users are no longer allowed to create new pages. In this way, a profile of whoever creates a page is captured and developed over time, thus providing a good way to measure whether a particular Wikipedia contributor or one of dubious intent. Another useful quality control measure relates to the practice of having most new pages, or heavily edited articles, go through a review by one or more active editors once they are published. There are also a number of automated software devices known as bots that help patrol edited content on the encyclopedia in an effective way, particularly to weed out petty vandalism.

The very fact that an online knowledge platform as open as Wikipedia has some safeguards in place to protect a dangerous free for all attitude from over-taking its contents is rather reassuring. This is not to say stupid individuals, or groups of individuals, will not try to enforce their point of view without ensuring that it is taken in as part of Wikipedia's rather generous stance on neutral point of view. Verifiability from reliable sources can only go so far when we assume good faith. Nevertheless, the more you engage with Wikipedia to better understand how it operates in relation to fake news and notions of post-truth, the more you will see that it has robust mechanisms to protect its readers in ways that social media platforms certainly do not have. Harnessing the power of Wikipedia can be a step in the right direction for any online platform seeking to combat fake news. It can also provide a sobering perspective on the way post-truth can or cannot actually do more than amplify the stupidity, carelessness, or mindlessness with which our societies are afflicted, as they possibly have been for millennia.

Notes

1. See http://en.wikipedia.org/wiki/Fatberg
2. See https://en.wikipedia.org/wiki/Wikipedia:Five_pillars
3. See https://en.wikipedia.org/wiki/Wikipedia:What_Wikipedia_is_not
4. This quote is from https://en.wikipedia.org/w/index.php?title=Wikipedia:BADIDEA
5. Wikinews is available at http://www.wikinews.org
6. Full details available here: https://en.wikipedia.org/wiki/Wikipedia:Copyrights
7. See https://en.wikipedia.org/wiki/Arbitration_Committee
8. See https://en.wikipedia.org/wiki/Wikipedia:Core_content_policies
9. See https://en.wikipedia.org/wiki/Wikipedia:Verifiability
10. This core policy is outlined here: https://en.wikipedia.org/wiki/Wikipedia:No_original_research
11. See https://en.wikipedia.org/wiki/Wikipedia:Neural_point_of_view
12. See https://en.wikipedia.org/wiki/Hanlon%27s_razor
13. See https://en.wikipedia.org/wiki/Wikipedia:Reliable_sources
14. See https://en.wikipedia.org/wiki/Wikipedia:Potentially_unreliable_sources

15. Wales, Jimmy (2003) email available at https://lists.wikimedia.org/pipermail/wikien-l/2003-September/006715.html
16. See https://en.wikipedia.org/wiki/Post-truth
17. See https://en.wikipedia.org/wiki/Wikipedia_community
18. Details about these campaigns can be found on the following Wikipedia pages: https://en.wikipedia.org/wiki/Art%2BFeminism; https://en.wikipedia.org/wiki/Women_in_Red; https://en.wikipedia.org/wiki/Wikipedia:Wiki_Loves_Pride; https://en.wikipedia.org/wiki/Wikipedia:Black_WikiHistory_Month
19. See https://en.wikipedia.org/wiki/Arbitration_Committee
20. NPR, All Things Considered. "Wikipedia Founder Says Internet Users Are Adrift In The 'Fake News' Era" – April 27, 2018. Available at https://www.npr.org/2018/04/27/606393983/wikipedia-founder-says-internet-users-are-adrift-in-the-fake-news-era
21. Wales has actually gone one step further in his attempts to combat misleading news headlines, known as clickbait, which is spread most easily on social network platforms like Facebook and Twitter. Launched in November 2019, WT:Social is a microblogging social network designed as an alternative to Facebook and Twitter. This project follows his unsuccessful attempt to create a for-profit news wiki (not affiliated with Wikinews or any other Wikimedia project) where journalists were employed to work alongside volunteers to improve the quality of reporting on established news outlets. See http://wt.social
22. Helping People Better Assess the Stories They See in News Feed with the Context Button – https://about.fb.com/news/2018/04/news-feed-fyi-more-context/

References

Goethe, J. W. von (1774). The sufferings of Young Werther. *Die Leiden des jungen Werthers*, 14. Translated by Bayard Quincy Morgan.

Jemielniak, D. (2014). *Common knowledge?: An ethnography of Wikipedia*. Stanford, CA: Stanford University Press.

Jemielniak, D. (2019). Wikipedia: Why is the common knowledge resource still neglected by academics? *GigaScience, 8*(Issue 12). December 2019. doi:10.1093/gigascience/giz139

Kallen, H. (1924). *Culture and democracy in the United States* (pp. 126–129) New York, NY: Boni Liveright.

Wales, H. (2003). Retrieved from https://lists.wikimedia.org/pipermail/wikien-l/2003-September/006715.html

Chapter 11

Public Rebuttal, Reflection and Responsibility. Or an Inconvenient Answer to Fake News

Ruben Brave*

Abstract

Information may well be an asset, but the sheer volume of what we have to navigate makes it challenging to determine those elements which are relevant to us. The credibility of news media outlets as our gatekeepers and first form of resistance to polluted information is increasingly questioned. Scientific research indicates that the quality of news offerings from news media outlets would benefit by triangulating news stories with a more diverse set of offerings and, in the process, build journalists' trust or otherwise in the sources of these offerings. Without the network effects of the Internet, false or incorrect information probably would not be such a successful phenomenon. Public opinion is quick to portray social or mainstream media platforms as guilty parties but tends to ignore the equally detrimental ramifications of their exploitation of social capital. A more reflective approach is required. This essay suggests that it is in our interest to reboot our societal consciousness and explore the underlying cybernetical dimensions, even if these appear to be confrontational for interested stakeholders in our current misinformation crisis.

Keywords: Fake news; misinformation; poor journalism; annotation; diversity; network effects

What do we do at Make Media Great Again, also known as MMGA?[1] We collaborate with publishers and community to fight misinformation. We improve the quality of media together with our pool of screened involved readers, viewers and listeners. We have built a transparent system for actionable suggestions from this

---

*Please see http://rubenbrave.squarespace.com/

Media, Technology and Education in a Post-Truth Society, 145–154
Copyright © 2021 by Emerald Publishing Limited
doi:10.1108/978-1-80043-906-120211011

community pool. NU.nl (translated as NOW.nl), with 7–8 million visitors a month, the most important news service in the Netherlands, is our test partner (Brave, 2019). We test with a screened group of critical and knowledgeable (originally mostly NU.nl) readers (called 'annotators'[2]) who offer suggestions to increase the journalistic quality through the balanced use of sources and clearer transfer of information.

And when I talk to my American friends about Make Media Great Again, they all agree what a great potential our endeavour has. But they also say:

Change the name,
change the name,
change the name.

And to be fully honest to a large extent, I must agree with this. Because for some reason, we keep getting enthusiastic emails with subjects such as: 'Yeah let's build that wall!'

But nonetheless, we are not changing the name, not yet....

> In this day and age, our biggest asset is information, but its increasing amount makes it hard to see through. News guides us through the daily disorder which impacts us directly..... (Overweg & Brave, 2018)

My personal wake-up call for the need for MMGA started when I was confronted with 'fake news' on the publicly funded national NOS website, the Dutch Broadcasting Foundation. For some of us, it might not be a surprise that a state-funded medium spreads wrong information, but in the Netherlands, people still put a lot of trust in this institution. The case was quite remarkable. During the election period, the website reported that the frontman of the Labour party was asking questions in parliament about ethnic profiling by the police.[3,4]

After investigating the parliament website and ultimately asking the Registry what these questions actually were, I received an email that the Labour Party had not asked any questions about ethnic profiling. It appeared that a female member of parliament of the Democratic Party with a migration background had asked the relevant questions.[5]

This information could have impacted voting behaviour; it influenced mine.

The specific situation concerning the NOS also seemed to function as a synecdoche. What was salient about the apparent refusal of the NOS editors to rectify the article was that they seemingly chose to turn their journalistic spotlight on a male white, native (Labour party) party leader instead of a female immigrant (social liberal) member of parliament. This did not merely involve the appearance of partiality with regard to a specific political colour but also illustrated the proverbial 'pars pro toto' with regards to the substantive side of the news item concerned – namely institutional bias (specifically with regard to race and/or gender); a cultural phenomenon that was also crucial and with even more detrimental effects in the so-called "Toeslagen-affaire", the Dutch childcare benefits scandal (https://en.wikipedia.org/wiki/Dutch_childcare_benefits_scandal). This was strongly rejected by Giselle van Cann, the NOS vice editor-in-chief, saying she could not identify with the conclusion – namely that the NOS would rather claim that a white, native party leader asked parliamentary questions than a member of parliament of immigrant background. There was no reason for suspicion for a preconceived motive or prejudice; this was just an error. She pointed out that when parties *say that they are going to submit* parliamentary questions, they usually do the same. But the NOS does not have a habit of asking the registry if this has actually been done; they will only verify if they have reason to believe that the questions have not been submitted. The fact that the parliamentary website, a reliable and accountable source, stated otherwise (on multiple occasions) suggests that they did not follow through with that principle.

When I confronted the editor-in-chief, Marcel Gelauf, of the Dutch Broadcasting Foundation and asked if they would at least consider editing the headline of the concerning article, the editor-in-chief responded as follows: '*I'm not going to contribute to history falsification!*'

How curious...!

These days, how can anyone tell what is factually accurate and what is not? What is formulated to reveal and what is written to conceal or even to mislead? These are increasingly pressing questions, especially as a new historical round of disinformation is upon us and 'fake news' is flourishing in all its glory. Can critical readers help in improving the reliability of 'our information'? There was agreement that our society would benefit from better news, yet we lacked the tools to take up ownership of this process and improve this ourselves.

As an open-source movement, MMGA offers transparent tools for journalistic reporting where everyone can contribute. Up to 50,000 readers were involved in our first pilot, with candidates individually selected from the news organization's readers' commentary panel (their forum NUJij). From these readers, more than 300 are now registered as annotators (Fig. 11.1).

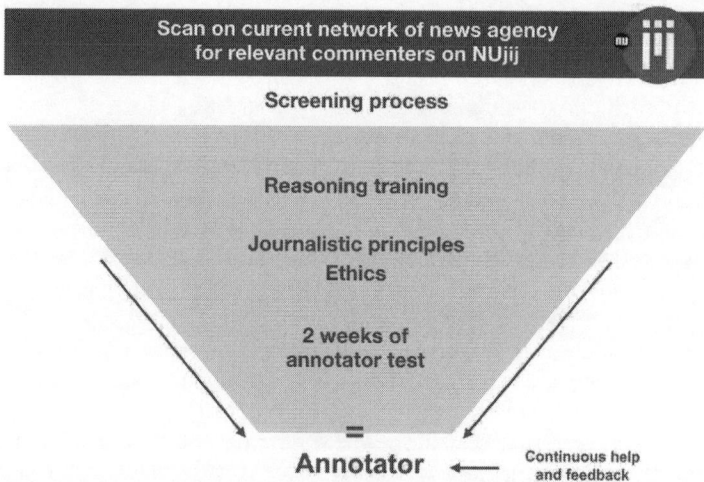

Fig. 11.1.   Screening, Selection and Training Process Overview.
Source: (© Make Media Great Again, own picture) https://drive.google.com/
file/d/1dsCc9sIW37SO5G_vpQgclFX9NYYe_nT1/view?usp=sharing.

And from this group, we selected, screened, and trained knowledgeable and/or critical thinking readers to actually work on annotation assignments.

We believe we are improving the quality of media through annotations. People have unique, diverse views and also relevant knowledge that helps the editorial process and quality. With our digital tools, people are able to detect misinformation, biased language and false contextualization. MMGA annotations are practicable suggestions, labelled notes, directly attributed to words, sentences or paragraphs.[6] They are actionable for the editor, avoid debate based on personal preferences and, if correct, directly trigger a correction within articles.

Editors are free to implement annotations or otherwise.[7] Since these are immediately executable and based on the principle of journalistic objectivity, they overcome the known issue of lengthy debate due to subjectivity that arises with regular reader comments. The system differs from the well-known response form, whereby the reaction usually concerns disagreement with the online paper's opinion or the tenet of the whole article. Annotations focus on specific elements of an article and are structured according to annotation labels. We do not just test the annotation system itself but also determine how those involved respond to and work with it. Furthermore, provided these annotations are clear, factually accurate and presented with proper transparency, they provide the necessary motivation for their immediate implementation, given that doing so will only improve the quality of the work in question.

We are working to improve the credibility of the media and strengthen the bond with their audience. The intention is to contribute to media's credibility at a time when this is being questioned, since media outlets are seen as the first buffer to protect us from wrong information. This fundamental role of media is essential for a proper functioning of democracy, constructive social debate and to fortify social cohesion. The potential of the project goes beyond journalism[8]; any organization or body that provides information as a 'public service' is likely to benefit from its implementation, irrespective of whether these are orthodox governmental institutions or museums. It is vital to lever on the openness of the Internet to facilitate the representation and participation of diverse and hitherto underrepresented groups in media and society at large.

Editorships, newsrooms and the army of opinion leaders typically reveal a skewed distribution in their composition with respect to gender, place of origin and residence, among other things (https://www.newsleaders.org/2019-diversity-survey-visuals). MMGA, with its 'diversity panels', is geared towards more nuanced use of language in journalism and on multiple perspectives in reporting. True quality is arguably impossible without diversity, and this is embedded in the composition of our group of annotators to ensure it is as diverse as possible: men, women, people from various ethnic backgrounds and minorities of all sorts. This minimizes the chance of overlooking particular contexts. According to scientific research (Lehrman, 2019), a more diverse group can improve the quality of news offerings and build trust in the sources of these offerings. Trust is now one of the major issues in mainstream journalism, perhaps the reason why we keep turning to the New York Times, the Washington Post, the Wall Street Journal, the BBC and The Guardian as 'media for the public good', to echo Robert McChesney. Diversity is a means of improving the quality of published content, rather than an end in itself (Awad Cherit, 2009; Kaltzada, 2018).

The fact that media organizations are finally acknowledging the need to fight fake news to maintain their readership's trust opens the door for collaborations. Our intention is not to destroy existing media organizations but to improve the quality of what they produce. MMGA is a cost-effective solution since we mainly work with volunteers and a value-added layer of contributors who create a safety net against misinformation, making it very difficult for 'hardcore fake news' to slip through the net. We collaborate with universities, well-known investigative journalists and impactful media for a maximum reach.

The post-truth reality resurfaced in earnest when I was watching a new TV series: The Man in the High Castle.[9,10]

An American alternate history television series depicts a parallel universe where the Axis powers (Rome–Berlin–Tokyo) actually win World War II instead of the Allies. It is produced by Amazon Studios and based on Philip K. Dick's 1962 science fiction novel of the same name. Coates (2017) states that for a lot of African Americans, the world Philips K Dick sketches has a lot of resemblance with their actual reality (for more general ethical questions on how Western society currently views 'our reality', see Berlatsky, 2017 and Zemler, 2016).

So back to the TV series. While binge-watching, I'm using Facebook and there – *for some reason* – I'm directed to a journalistic looking Facebook post with the purport that Bill and Melinda Gates are not trying to save the world from malaria or polio but are instead testing experimental medicines (on behalf of large pharmaceutical companies) on poor Indian kids ... just like the Nazi's would do![11] I must admit that for a second I felt rage and indignation. This was big news! The world needed to know about this, and I was ready as ever to share this post with my friends and relatives[12] to shine the light on this wrongdoing and work to a fairer, more ethical world.

Then I remembered MMGA's code of conduct,[13] inspired by the journalistic ethical code the Bordeaux Declaration, multiple Dutch guidelines concerning journalism and prevention of improper influence by conflicts of interest, and the Five Pillars of Wikipedia. Our first directive states:

> Your annotations are based on facts for which you can indicate a reliable source (which thus are verifiable and can be held accountable), as completely as possible and regardless of the opinions expressed about this source.

I could not find *one* reliable source backing up the claims made in the Facebook post. So I paused. Much as I felt the urgency to spread this 'news', I did not want to take responsibility for sharing an unverifiable article. I remembered the results of one of the first MMGA tests we conducted concerning our Trustmark on 500 random Internet users. The Trustmark signifies and guarantees that all articles are subject to the audit of an independent community, sources are easily viewable to the public and any alterations to the article are also tracked and viewable by the public (Fig. 11.2).

To create more transparency and trust. From our survey with these 500 readers, 9 out of 10 stated they experience an article with a Trustmark as more

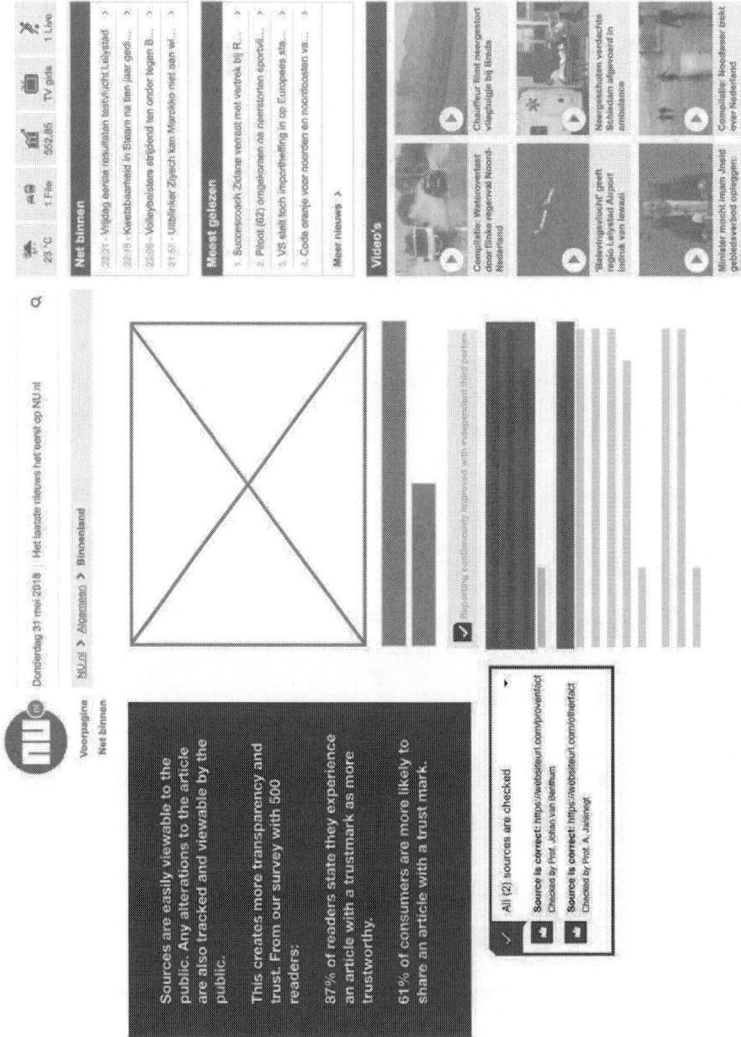

Fig. 11.2.   Test Results Adoption Indication MMGA Trustmark. *Source:* (© Make Media Great Again, own picture)
https://drive.google.com/file/d/1hKtEsvDYbAGPnOvejSmLdMNtxzMtDxmf/view?usp=sharing.

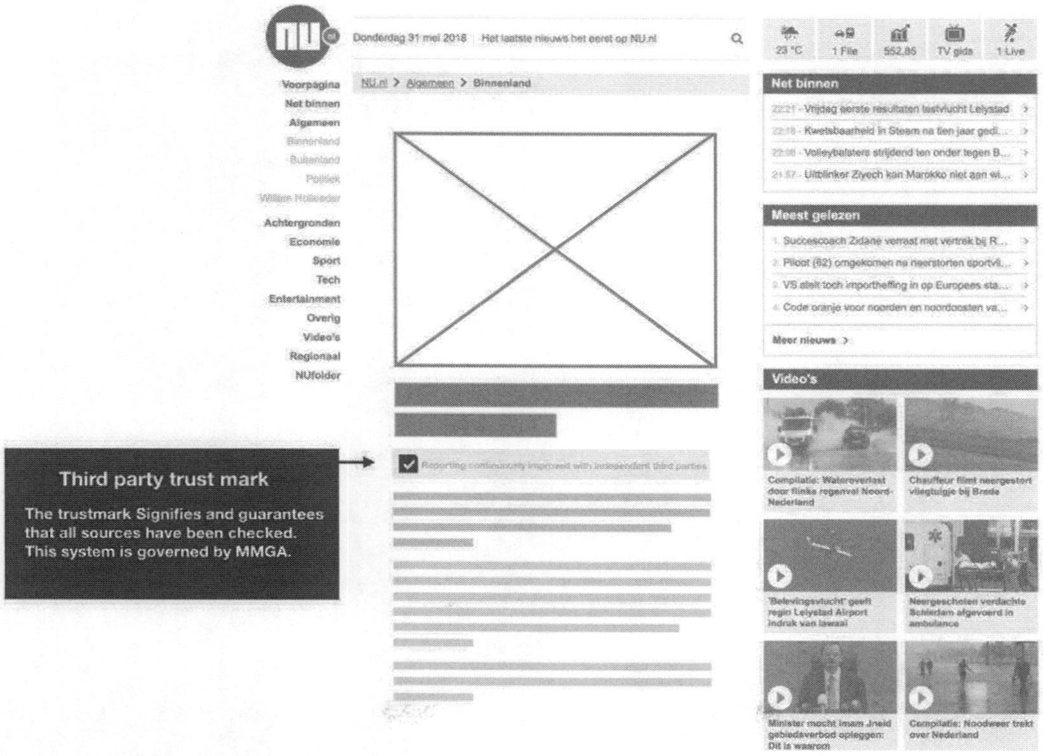

Fig. 11.3. Overall Function of MMGA Trustmark. *Source:* (© Make Media Great Again, own picture) https://drive.google.com/file/d/18J9tuW0B-O5lSqq3tmUM_DFYhv6SA60m/view?usp=sharing.

trustworthy. Also, more than 6 out of 10 were likely to share an article with a trust mark (Fig. 11.3).

What will happen when people become more aware when such trust marks are missing in the article they are reading? Would they be more conscious when they are sharing unmarked articles? Without the network effects of the Internet, wrong information would probably have the same damaging effects as simple 'false gossip' in the contained context of, for instance, a school classroom (Törnberg, 2018). In that utopian Internet version, the risk for so-called 'network corruption' would decrease significantly – since network corruption is a form of corruption in which the interaction of multiple actors within a (social) network results in corruption, but in which the individual behaviour as such is not necessarily corrupt.

We are quick to look at platforms such as Facebook and news media like the Dutch Broadcasting Foundation (NOS) as guilty parties for the fake news problem and equally quick to reach for all kinds of tech-related solutions to save us. Based on my own 'Man in the High Castle' experience, I suggest that self-reflection on our own Internet behaviour will help us make a leap in our societal consciousness if we are going to survive this post-truth era. We are not merely using the technical infrastructure of the Internet, as if it is something outside of us – beyond our own power and responsibility. We are an integral and decisive part, the living nodes, of this global information network and need to act with due

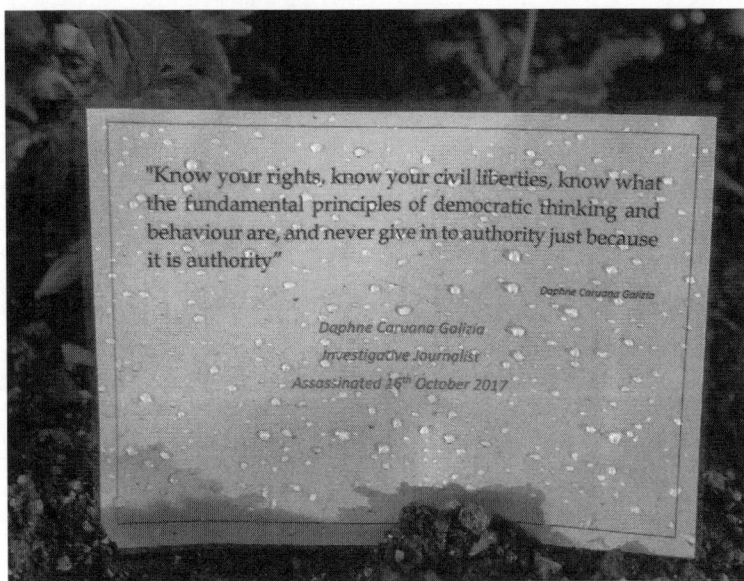

Fig. 11.4.   Quote of Daphne Caruana Galizia at the Protest Memorial in Valletta on the Night before the Conference. *Source:* (© Make Media Great Again, own picture) https://drive.google.com/file/d/17zp2h4lgb-uIt3QKACunms-4EDxVW6VP/view?usp=sharing.

responsibility – or at least start conscious efforts to start learning the online societal role we all share (Fig. 11.4).

The name of our organization stays as it is. It is not just a gimmicky reaction to Donald Trump's original election motto or an indictment of mainstream media. The name reminds us of the easily overlooked fact, another inconvenient truth, that we all individually have to play our part – as reflective and responsible citizens – to make the media great again.

Notes

1. MMGA was set up in 2017 by the Netherlands-based Bema foundation while it was involved in preparations for the European Press Prize. It uses a blockchain-based annotation platform in which screened and trained experts and/or critical thinking readers (with hundreds of registrants) can provide constructive feedback to high-impact news sites concerning the use of sources and other quality aspects of news articles to correct misinformation and combat disinformation. NU.nl and AD.nl, two of the 'Big Four' largest Dutch online news platforms, were early adopters and co-development partners. In 2020, MMGA was acquired by Internet Society Netherlands (ISOC) to become the Internet Society Netherlands MMGA Working Group to jointly combat the global 'infodemic'. Also, see www.mmga.io and https://mmga.pr.co/187643-internet-society-isoc-acquires-make-media-great-again-mmga-to-jointly-combat-globalinfodemic
2. Annotations MMGA brings journalists and audience together through annotations. See https://mmga.io/en/home/annotations/
3. See https://nos.nl/artikel/2108228-pvda-stelt-kamervragen-over-staandehouding-typhoon.html
4. See https://nos.nl/artikel/2108228-pvda-stelt-kamervragen-over-staandehouding-typhoon.html
5. See https://www.tweedekamer.nl/kamerstukken/kamervragen/detail?id=2016Z10648&did=2016D22233
6. See a live demo of the annotation production by an annotator at https://www.youtube.com/watch?v=5IEMiIBPNDk
7. See a live demo of an editorial response to produced annotations at https://youtu.be/cDa-qU9t2WM
8. See http://bit.ly/MMGA-presentation-Q2-2019
9. See https://www.youtube.com/watch?v=zzayf9GpXCI
10. See https://www.npo3.nl/film-en-serie/reviews/the-man-in-the-high-castle
11. See https://www.youtube.com/watch?v=BG8nu4xs3Ck
12. See https://www.youtube.com/watch?v=mYTeeZnf43w
13. Code of conduct annotators: https://mmga.io/en/home/gedragscode/

References

Awad Cherit, I. (2009). *Cultural diversity in the news media: A democratic or a commercial need?* Retrieved from https://www.researchgate.net/publication/241889366_Cultural_Diversity_in_the_News_Media_A_Democratic_or_a_Commercial_Need

Berlatsky, N. (2017). *The man in the high castle: When a Nazi-Run world isn't so dystopian.* Retrieved from https://www.theatlantic.com/entertainment/archive/2015/01/man-in-the-high-castle-when-a-nazi-ruled-world-isnt-so-dystopian/384708/

Brave, R. (2019). *Introducing "public annotations" in journalism.* Retrieved from https://medium.com/@MakeMediaGreatAgain/introducing-public-annotations-in-journalism-e688b04be903

Coates, T. (2017). *The lost cause rides again.* Retrieved from https://www.theatlantic.com/entertainment/archive/2017/08/no-confederate/535512/

Kaltzada, P. (2018). *Why diversity in media matters.* Retrieved from https://ideasforeurope.eu/news/diversity-and-media

Lehrman, S. (2019). *Trust project | 20 may trust summit workshop.* Retrieved from https://n36.08b.myftpupload.com/wp-content/uploads/2019/03/Summit_Report_Hearst20May_ms_sl-1.pdf

Overweg, R., & Brave, R. (2018). *Mission & vision teaser MMGA.* Retrieved from https://www.youtube.com/watch?v=hUVpy6DGvbQ

Törnberg, P. (2018). *Echo chambers and viral misinformation: Modeling fake news as complex contagion.* Retrieved from https://www.uva.nl/en/content/news/press-releases/2018/09/echo-chambers-and-viral-misinformation.html?1571169250873

Zemler, E. (2016). *Creators of the man in the high Castle: There are 'deeply disturbing' parallels.* Retrieved from https://www.theguardian.com/tv-and-radio/tvandradioblog/2016/dec/16/man-in-the-high-castle-season-2-review

Chapter 12

The Kony 2012 Campaign: A Milestone of Visual Storytelling for Social Engagement

Massimiliano Fusari

Abstract

Images had long conveyed politics through forms as varied as private paintings and public coins. If images are storytelling vectors (Fusari, 2017), visual artefacts were intended to re/shape human perception of current events and, consequently, their states of 'being in the world' (Heidegger, 2001); this is the reason why the visual quality of communication might be hard to disjoin from that of 'performativity' (Cartier-Bresson, 2018).

The polysemic (Barthes, 1977), if not fully open (Eco, 1989), quality of visual semiotics complicates identification of any framework of reference and adds to the need for practical and sensible research in digital communication (Fusari, in press).

Since the first US Presidential debate televised in 1968, a new interest surged towards the understanding and production of visual communication of politics. Increasingly so, images (both still and moving ones) have affected, if not thoroughly shaped, understanding of all recent political affairs, particularly so from the 1992's Gulf War onward (Baudrillard, 1995; Kellner, 1992).

The 2012 Invisible Children (IC)'s campaign is here assessed as the milestone marking the potential for global impact acquired by socio-political visual-centred storytelling.

The intertwining of the digital with the visual has yet to be precisely arranged for socio-political storytelling; also, storytelling as a format and approach has increasingly gained relevance, adding new concerns to issues of veracity.

In response, this chapter advances the notion of 'storyline' in conjunction with that of 'storytelling': the resulting taxonomy aims to review specific notions of truth- and trust-fulness from a visual-centred perspective.

The chapter thus explores the requirements for communicating and understanding visual storytelling on digital media; by doing so, it addresses the extent to which 'visual storytelling' might be a notion fit for the job of disseminating today's digital cultures.

Media, Technology and Education in a Post-Truth Society, 155–173
Copyright © 2021 by Emerald Publishing Limited
All rights of reproduction in any form reserved
doi:10.1108/978-1-80043-906-120211012

Eventually, the chapter will question how to *design* visually centred communication formats and, in turn, *engage* these as storytelling of socio-political issues for digital platforms.

Keywords: Visual performance; visual storytelling; digital strategy; visual politics; storytelling; phenomenology

Introduction

Digital media engage material and symbolic projection of one's identity/ies across personal spaces and social communities (among many: Tsatsou, 2009; van der Graaf, 2014; World Economic Forum Report, 2016). Ideas of state and society, of power and politics, have been quickly and consequently evolving. This seems to be particularly impacting processes of representation and self-representation across intertwined and overlapping practices on *visual* media (Fusari, in press).

In today's continuously evolving scenario, the booming number of participants that digital and social media allow in, and empower to fully contribute to the communication game, further complicates understanding and engagement of political relations across societies and cultures, internally, regionally and globally.

Easiness of digital media production echoes immediacy of digital distribution; richness of available platforms reflects personal, social and cultural re/making of content/s (Engadget, 2020). In turn, the 24/7 all-permeating quality of digital communication and the fully personal usage each and every one (*of us*) has of it renders any identification for a consistent pattern truly futile, if not pointless.

As much as education focuses on verbal skill sets delivery, visual literacy development is left mostly, if not uniquely, to art schools (Greenaway, 2008). Furthermore, the same notion of the visual is both extremely difficult to pin down, and harshly disputed (for a basic orienteering see among many: Elkins, 2011; Mangani, Piper & Simon, 2006; Ritchin, 2009).

Visual semiotics, i.e. how that which is seen is interpreted by others, is a research field still coming out of the doldrums. The Saussurean and Peircean traditions are frameworks for verbal analysis that semioticians strive to specifically translate into bespoke visual-led grammars (see for instance: Kress & Van Leeuwen, 1996).

As such, today's challenge might be reframed around the search to *adapt* for the visual, rather than merely *adopt* a grammar of semiotics; in turn, what could be the specific contribution of those with expertise in both the political practice and in visual literacy? Equally crucial, does the 'visual' quality of communication refer to a form, a channel or a dissemination strategy? For instance, is reading a verbal text 'visual' as it goes through the eyes? Does a 'verbal' description visualized in the mind of a reader remain 'verbal' or evolve as a 'visual' ekphrasis? In turn, focusing on different semiotic qualities, is the narration of a painting 'verbal,' 'visual' or 'sonic', or all of them together?

As Eco has long argued for,

> To say that light is a *medium* is a refusal to realize that there are at least three definitions of 'light'. Light can be a *signal of information* [as the result of electricity]. Light can be a *message* [I'm at home];

and light can be a *channel* [to read a book]. In each of these cases *the impact of a phenomenon on the social body* varies according to the role it plays in the communication chain. (Eco, 1995, p. 139, emphasis added)

Unquestionably, at the core of today's digital cultures, and growing, is the centrality the visual quality of communication has acquired. The number of, both private and public, digital images defies sensible assessment, as day-by-day individuals and groups storytell their existence. Whatever the estimate, it can be safely stated that there are more images *produced* in a single year than were ever throughout the whole history of photography (BuzzFeed, 2012).

As the first rule of communication (i.e. who speaks on behalf of whom, representing what?) might be increasingly more complex to clearly frame on digital media, current shifting cultures could finally provide scholars and practitioners with the opportunity to rethink the visual as both a 'practice' and a communicative 'performance'.

What if, for instance, a State Department (SD) spokesperson tweeted as themselves and then repeated exactly the same note as the spokesperson on the SD's official Facebook page? Or the other way around? What is the impact of which precedes what in a dissemination sequence, and consequently, on its analysis? Furthermore, how to assess an image being referred from another source in support of one's arguing? Or incorporated in a TV interview or, again, being shown live at a White House's briefing? In other words, how to draw a line between different *persona*s (Jung, 1990, p. 123) communicating the same, as well as distinct, multimedia message/s on parallel and multiple digital platforms? Furthermore, how do 'audiences' decipher overlapping dynamics engaging the message, the platform and communicative threads of digital actors? Finally, who does still have the time to attentively, consciously, if not, *intentionally*, manage and appreciate all this in today's speeding-up cultures and politics?

If current digital cultures, whatever form they may take, are appreciated as visual/visual-centred/visual-led (Qualman, 2018), should effective visual competency be prioritized over verbal ones? Equally, how/should those who have power in their gift be aware of the strategic use of visual-led communication *and* storytelling practices for political action?

As far back as the early 1990s, Muzi Falconi (2004), with many others, signalled the extent to which communication had already become an autonomous player in the production and consumption of socio-political and cultural values. Thus, as communication becomes so much more than just a tool for the transmission of knowledge, it should be appreciated as knowledge in itself, and, hence, as truly 'agentic' (Bandura, 1999; Coole, 2005).

In turn, as political actors critically engage with the rapid evolution of multimedia formats across digital platforms, it would seem unavoidable for them to incorporate sensible notions of visual storytelling into their political thinking and daily practice. This chapter will therefore review the mission, strategies and implementation of political actors' agenda by reference to two major goals:

(1) To incorporate the visual and emotional qualities of communication for digital practice/s as effective 'storytelling';
(2) To master techniques and visual methodologies for the strategic planning and dissemination of storytelling as socio-political 'storylines'.

This chapter originates from the acknowledged centrality of visual communication, with its own bespoke features, to advance an operational definition of digital politics by means of visual storytelling. To do so, this essay relies on the 2012 IC's groundbreaking campaign to indict Commander Kony. By reference to the media quality of the campaign, the chapter aims to investigate the relation between visual storytelling for socio-political communication to recommend its integrated application as strategic storylines.

By exploring how to strategize media channels and communication operations across online and offline worlds in a target-oriented and responsive manner, the chapter advances a revised framework for the analysis and practice of visual politics on digital media. Final recommendations and identified best practices are suggested as merely temporary takeaways because of the volatile nature of current media developments.

Storytelling as an Agent of Order

As briefly introduced above, digital communication 'is' and 'works' across multiple and overlapping semiotic fields. These features seem to be particularly difficult to strategically manage because of [1] the multi-media and multi-platform quality of the digital; [2] the increased, and continuously increasing, role of the visual and [3] its very personalized usages. As a result, storytelling might be a notion to be revamped to structure some order in today's chaos.

Storytelling is today's buzzword. It is all-pervasive and more and more referred to as the new Holy Grail resolving each and every communication issue. Indeed, 'man is a storytelling animal by nature' (Eco, 1984, p. 509), and storytelling could be rightly appreciated as a pivot, if not the pivot, for all forms and formats of communication, from the visual to the verbal.

Because of its communicative quality, it could be argued that storytelling, by extension, should be approached as a solution equally applicable for cultural and political issues. Though, if everything is a 'story', including, possibly, the same storytelling format, then, as a practitioner, I'm puzzled by what this might signify and, operationally, lead to.

In view of its massive usage, storytelling has been equally referring to the practice of *telling* a story and that of *understanding* one, as much as, frequently, both of them at the same time. Beyond the practices above mentioned, as it were not enough already, storytelling could also be referred to as a process. Even journalism, as acutely noted by Ronson,

> ...walks a line. Journalism is storytelling. We wait around for the best bits – the most engaging, extreme, colourful moments – and

we stick them together, ignoring the boring stuff, turning life into a
narrative. (Ronson, 2012, p. 71)

Though, as he concludes, 'there's shaping a story and there is making things up'.
To bring some clarity, this chapter argues for an epistemological differentiation between the concept of 'storytelling' and that of 'storyline'. Any differentiation between the two notions must not be approached as an academic exercise,
but, instead, intended as a much-needed taxonomy for today's dissemination of
overlapping digital cultures.

For the present context, storytelling is differentiated from storyline as follows:
the former is the final result of multiple media forms, such as, for instance, the
visual, the sonic and the verbal, as combined to purposely communicate. The
latter, 'storyline', is the produced storytelling as strategically disseminated by
means of target-oriented operations; these operations are media-driven and
platform-informed to specifically tailor the storytelling content for distinct, yet
fully integrated, digital storylines.

Both notions incorporate the idea of combining form with content with their
most revealing difference being their consequentiality: one storytelling is translated into bespoke storylines when it is *strategically* disseminated by means of
dedicated operations including, but not limited to, the apt usage of digital
channels and online/offline platforms.

If the above framework is accepted, it consequently follows that all socio-
political actors that are part of today's far-reaching communication system, from
small community centres to international NGOs, from local stakeholders to
United Nations agencies, face the challenge of continuously re/tuning production
strategies to translate (visual) storytelling into strategized storylines. The case
study of the IC's campaign will be used to explore in detail this set of
considerations.

The Case Study

The IC's (2012) campaign has been extensively researched and widely reviewed
from a multitude of perspectives, with contributions assessing its impact across
academic and social fields (Campbell, 2012; Foreign Policy, 2012; Kanczula,
2012; The Guardian, 2012; The Huffington Post, 2012; Tunheim 2012).

Nevertheless, analyses were mostly synchronic to events with public commentators and academic researchers re-focusing on other priorities shortly after
the campaign. In turn, this chapter addresses the IC's campaign from a distance,
using the campaign itself as an opportunity to critically review practices of visual
storytelling.

As such, the chapter will first contextualize the campaign within its wider
socio-political and media framework, then review it by reference to established
grammars of storytelling. Conclusions will recommend a sensible management of
the relation between storytelling and storyline, with a few lessons learnt for
prospective uses.

The IC's Campaign and Its Framework

The IC's campaign officially began on 5 March 2012 with the simultaneous release across YouTube, Vimeo and on the IC's website, of a 29-minute video (hereafter: IC, 2012). For IC, this represented the culmination of years of committed policies of socio-political awareness across a number of international *fora* nationally and globally.

IC's stated aim was to achieve the indictment of the Lord Resistance Army's Commander Joseph Kony, and IC explicitly timed its campaign to coincide with the US Presidential Election year.

IC arguably ran its integrated communication strategy on a double gamble. Firstly, the length of the video went, and still does, against all rules and best practices for online communication. Tunheim (2012) quantified in three minutes the average running time of successful YouTube videos and in four minutes the average running time of the top 10 YouTube videos; IC was surely aware of the dramatically decreasing attention span of audiences (Qualman, 2018): to argue for a visual-driven storytelling of 29 minutes promised to be an endeavour with unpredictable outcomes.

Secondly, IC chose to synchronize the launch with the US' Presidential Election when public interest in political topics might be expected to rise. Though, the same rise in interest could have equally deprived IC of precious prime-time attention, as political news fights for a place on daily news bulletins and across the political debate.

While it is difficult to speculate on which supporting intelligence IC might have relied on for its assessment, it should be argued that IC viewed the communication challenge as an opportunity to wage a media *Blitzkrieg*. IC chose the election year to enforce a deadline-driven approach as its Damocles' sword to leverage on its targeted stakeholders, the Democratic and Republican parties. The menace implicit in this strategy is that failing to engage with the IC's agenda would incur the high cost of losing the primary targeted audience IC was after: US' young voters.

In the author's words,

> ...we need to remind them [US politicians] that, in this election year of fighting and name-calling, no matter what side you are on, this is something we can all agree on. (IC, 2012, 24:04)

By using *tactically* the US' election year, IC built up *strategically* its agenda both nationally and internationally: in turn, the efficaciousness of its engagement policy might be rightly appreciated as truly Kissinger-ian.

Nationally, IC's explicit strategy employed a bottom-up commitment to lobby 20 American public/cultural figures and 12 American political representatives for the arrest of Kony (Fig. 12.1).

To make 'Kony world news by redefining the propaganda we see every day, all day, that dictates who and what we pay attention to' (IC, 2012, 24:50) required the smooth and simultaneous integration of actions both online and offline:

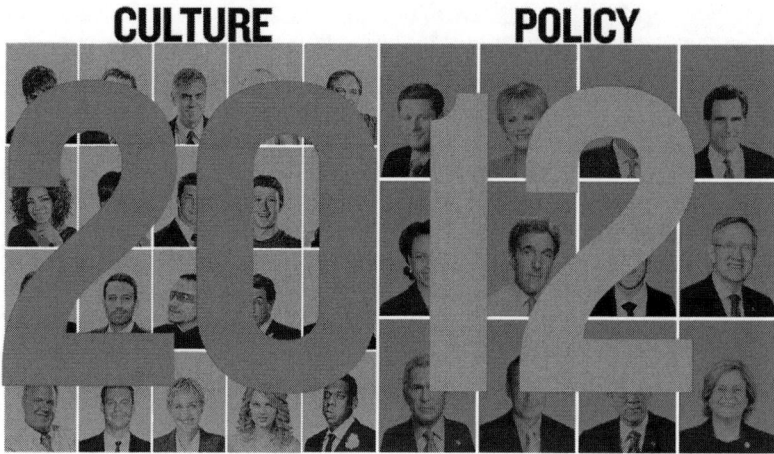

Fig. 12.1.   Cultural and Political Targeted Stakeholders, Screenshot
from Video. *Source:* IC (2012, 23:10).

lobbying the 20+12 public figures was carried out taking full advantage of all digital platforms, or, according to the taxonomy suggested above, by employing multimedia storytelling as strategized storylines.

Using cultural icons as 'influencers' led IC to gain massive coverage and to successfully achieve its leverage attempt: for instance, a tweet from Oprah skyrocketed threads on the topic from 66K to more than nine million in less than 24 hours (The Huffington Post, 2012).

Furthermore, social media actions were not used as an aim in itself (to gain followers and/or likes), but as a fully functional and integrated component to IC's strategic effort, which was meant to culminate with the *Cover The Night*'s appointment.

> [We will] blanket every street in every city till the sun comes up [...]
> we will be smart and we will be thorough [...] the rest of the world
> [...] will wake up with hundreds of thousands of posters
> demanding justice on every corner (IC, 2012, 25:40)

Meanwhile, on 21 March, US senators Inhofe and Coons put forward a resolution

> condemning Joseph Kony and his ruthless guerrilla group for a 26-
> year campaign of terror [...to back up] the effort of Uganda, the
> Democratic Republic of Congo, the Central African Republic and
> the newest country, South Sudan, to stop Kony and his Lord's
> Resistance Army. (Inhofe, 2012)

An official statement pledged support 'for the US' effort to help regional forces pursue commanders of the militia group' across both aisles of the Senate. Incidentally, in a rather surprising example of bi-partisanship during election time Senator Graham stated that:

> *When you get 100 million Americans looking at something, you will get our attention.* This YouTube sensation is gonna help the Congress be more aggressive and will do more to lead to his demise than all other action combined. (Kern, 2015, p. 201, emphasis added)

Through a comprehensive plan articulated with the combined arrangement of multiple actions, the campaign achieved unprecedented success in its reshaping of the public discourse: by incorporating media, channels and platforms as part of the campaigning, IC consistently tailored its storytelling into a series of consistent and strategized targeted storylines. Indeed, the resulting conversations rendered Kony truly famous, as IC had hoped by the sheer force of numbers (the 100 million Americans quoted above).

The campaign proved to be the first one to tactically rely on, and fully use, digital media for online activism, successfully re/framing public and cultural agendas (Kanczula, 2012).

IC's commitment to root its campaign on a community of focused and engaged participants (as argued throughout the video), thoroughly and consistently supported implementation of its agenda through activities on digital media and public channels. IC explicitly reminded viewers that participants in the project should be termed neither participants nor audiences. Instead, IC claimed that, by joining in the campaign, individuals would not 'study but shape human history' (IC, 2012, 28:25): in so doing, they would truly become empowered and efficacious digital actors. By achieving 'real' outcomes, as exemplified by President Obama's letter (see below), IC's dedicated community, the US youth, would feel fully empowered and would therefore commit further to disseminate IC's storytelling.

In turn, IC reiterated its call for dedicated activism by direct reference to the wider flow of global political events, including the unfolding 'Arab Spring', to exemplify the acquired centrality of digital media as tools of accountability (IC, 2012: Teaser).

IC's Campaign under Storytelling Lenses

As stated above, this chapter aims to critically review the communication efficacy of the IC's video as translated into a set of comprehensive storylines. As much as issues of veridicality are crucial to socio-political communication, these lie outside the present realm of intervention. For instance, the above-mentioned Obama letter (see IC, 2012, 18:50) should be critically reviewed in its truth-fulness and trust-fulness as a best fitting example of the difference between 'shaping a story' and 'making things up'.

Visual polysemy has been previously argued in its capacity to turn a single image into multiple and co-existing meaning-making processes (Barthes, 1977). Visual images are indeed semiotically 'open' (Eco, 1989) because of the 'irreducible plural' and the 'overcrossing' of meanings they endlessly generate (Barthes, 1977, p. 159).

The following analysis will combine the storytelling formats of the Narrative Arc and the Hero's Journey. These two techniques will be complemented by reference to basic archetypes and to the three ingredients part of each story 'Theme, Coherence and Plausibility' (Lupton, 2017, p. 36).

Freytag (1894) identified five consequential parts in the analysis of any dramatic work: exposition, rising action, climax, falling action and resolution. Through implementation of the Narrative Arc approach, the following storytelling has been identified and argued for (Table 12.1).

As per the rules of visual communication (Cartier-Bresson, 2018), even the smallest alteration may illicit dramatic changes to *any* storytelling; if even a single photograph carries the potential multiplicity of co-existing messages (Barthes' 'irreducible plural'), the semiotic possibilities for a 29-minute video are virtually infinite.

Indeed, the above Narrative Arc is not the sole possible storytelling, and different ones could be identified via the intersection of alternative *studia* and

Table 12.1. Freytag's Five Consequential Parts in the Analysis of Any Dramatic Work.

Exposition	*00:00–01:55*	Today's world is being re-defined by digital media and its overlapping boundaries. We all have become part of a single community, *and so are you*
Rising Action	*01:55–08:20*	Jacob changed my [Jason Russell's] life. Gavin, 'my son', did the same. I care for Gavin and Jacob and Jacob ran away from Kony. This made Kony personal to me, *and – as we all belong to the same community – this should become personal to you too*
Climax	*10:36–17:10*	Kony's capital crimes Vs. the inaction of the international community. Kony's abductions would have been top media stories if they happened in the United States. Digital media *empower us all* to re/prioritize agendas
Falling Action	*17:10–22:55*	In the past we didn't know or could not act. *Now you know and can make a difference, why wouldn't you?*
Resolution	*23:00–29:10*	Gavin recommends a solution. The strategy is to make Kony visible with clear tactics and operations. *Your actions shape history*

puncta (plural of Barthes' *studium* and *punctum*). These two notions were left overall unclarified, if not unresolved, by Barthes, who would roughly identify the *studium* as 'meanings that are nameable [...] given cultural meanings that we understand at once' (Barthes, 1981, p. 44). The *punctum*, by contrast,

> will break (or punctuate) the *studium*. This time it is not I who seek it out (as I invest the field of the *studium* with my sovereign consciousness), it is this element which rises from the scene, shoots out of it like an arrow, and pierces me [...an] accident which pricks me (but also bruises me, is poignant to me). [...] The *studium* is that very wide field of unconcerned desire, of various interest, of inconsequential taste: I like / I don't like. The *studium* is of the order of *liking*, not of *loving*. (Barthes, 1981, pp. 26–27)

Storytelling's semiotics might be placed at the intersection between multiple and shifting combinations of *studia* and *puncta*, i.e. of different liking and loving emotions. The better a storytelling is arranged in its combination of form by content, the more focused, constrained and finalized its polysemy is: IC's story-telling was majestically arranged, first, and then strategically translated into its consequential storylines as dichotomies on the tone of 'Us vs. them', 'Young vs. old' and 'Commitment vs. apathy', or in other words, of 'Good vs. evil'.

However, visual polysemy should not too easily disregard as 'tamed' for the present context; because of the synchronic quality of the visual (Paivio, 1990), *puncta* perform distinctive storytellings through the highly personalized quality (the loving mentioned above) in the relation between the frame and the viewer. Furthermore, the process might occur both at a quantitative and qualitative level; the former when different audiences look at the same video, with the latter happening as the same audience engages the video at different times, and, hence, within shifting phenomenological states of 'being in the world'.

In reference to Freytag's Narrative Arc, storytelling was identified among multiple potential options available. This recognized storytelling might indeed be questioned by reference to alternative *puncta*, in consideration to chosen events and their lengths. In order to validate the shared analysis, this will be tested against the format of the Hero's Journey.

This approach, like the Narrative Arc, has a long history (Campbell, 1949), often overlapping with psychoanalytic notions of myths (Eliade, 1976) and archetypes (Jung, 1990). Regardless of its different features, what all paradigms share is the notion of 'change' occurring to the main character, the 'Hero'. By storytelling how the Hero becomes other than that which they were before, change makes each and every story both personally relevant and universal.

In short, the format of the Hero's Journey goes as such: an ordinary context is unsettled because of a sudden change requiring the Hero to act upon; by answering their call and leaving the comforts of their past life, the character faces a number of challenges that makes them 'other' and 'more' by the time they return home. Classic examples include *the Epic of Gilgamesh*, Homer's *The*

Odyssey and Dante's *The Divine Comedy*. These stories present an educational journey for *any* audience to learn by personification: this eventually makes even the most distant journey truly memorable as it is relevant to each and every one (Table 12.2).

Lupton argues that the five ingredients of each story are 'Arc, Change, Theme, Coherence and Plausibility' (Lupton, 2017, p. 36). The arc element has been addressed

Table 12.2. Semiotic Strategies: Application of Narrative Arc, Hero's Journey and Archetype.

Narrative Arc	The Hero's Journey	Archetype
Today's world is being re-defined by digital media and its overlapping boundaries. We all have become part of a single community, *and so are you*	The Hero leaves their previous community and becomes one with IC to change the world	*The Young Hero*
Jacob changed my [Jason Russell's] life. Gavin, 'my son', did the same. I care for Gavin and Jacob and Jacob ran away from Kony. This made Kony personal to me, *and – as we all belong to the same community – this should become personal to you too*	Jason cares and has offered himself as an example of social commitment	*The Mentor*
Kony's capital crimes Vs. the inaction of the international community. Kony's abductions would have been top media stories if these happened in the United States. Digital media *empower us all* to re/prioritize agendas	They don't do anything. Where do you stand?	*The Shadow*
In the past we didn't know or could not act. *Now you know and can make a difference, why wouldn't you?*	Seize the Sword and fight!	*The Warrior*
Gavin recommends a solution. The strategy is to make Kony visible with clear tactics and operations. *Your actions shape history*	The final reward	*The Wise Man*

above in its five components. The change component has been similarly assessed, by pinpointing the transformation from the 'Young Hero' into the 'Wise Man'.

The three elements that Lupton adds, namely, the theme, coherence and plausibility, address the extent to which any storytelling would require to be validated as both understandable and valuable. Indeed, IC informed its storytelling with coherent and plausible elements by presenting convincing characters, while crafting a consistent and consequential flow.

Above, the storytelling techniques of the Narrative Arc and the Hero's Journey have been matched and further complemented by reference to some basic archetype figures. The pending issue seems now to pivot on who is the Hero that IC particularly targets to transform beyond the storytelling's most immediate representation.

As the classics dictate, the Hero is someone that does not study history, but rather shapes it. Exactly like Jason was changed by the story of Jacob, everyone engaging the IC's campaign becomes the transformed Hero: Jason's transformation is his viewers' journey: each viewer is the Hero shaping today's events as history and making a difference, globally.

IC's comprehensive storytelling run, undoubtedly, in a very strategic manner through offline and online engagement tactics and very effective follow-up operations: as such, it will be here referred as an effective storyline, which led to a yet unparalleled global impact making Kony truly famous (The Huffington Post, 2012; Tunheim, 2012). All this was majestically complemented, and viewing data unquestionably state so, with a final call to action (IC, 2012, 23:00–29:10), further empowered by the prospect of future actions (IC, 2012, 29:10–30:00).

All three semiotic strategies used above (the Narrative Arc, The Hero's Journey and the archetypes), as completed by reference to Lupton's toolkit, converge on one clearly argued storytelling: you, the US' digital youth of 2012, will be making history by joining *our Quest*.

IC successfully translated its storytelling as storylines to leverage targeted American cultural, public and political (20+12) stakeholders. Once IC gained the ability to shape its storytelling as storyline (see below), those wishing to challenge/criticize/question IC's communication had not the ability, nor the resources, to do so. Furthermore, IC prevented conversations from happening on its platforms, thus forcing confrontational storytellings to argue their counter-narrative/s *elsewhere*.

Eventually, it should be recognized that all oppositional voices challenged IC's storytelling by either reasoning or fact-checking; further, they challenged IC's storytelling through, mostly, if not solely, verbal arguments. In addition, they did so on platforms with a much-limited audience: even for those commenting on Facebook, numbers were infinitely smaller than IC's. As such, IC's rooted and committed community proved the strongest strategic asset at its disposal (Campbell, 2012).

For instance, Kagumire as one of most respected commentators *on* Uganda *from* Uganda had worldwide recognition as expert and scholar on the region, though with a very limited public profile. She still covers socio-political issues of her country and the Region, collaborating with a wide array of political actors and very respected partners (Kagumire, 2012).

Whatever her authority and expertise, she could not digitally compete with IC, as a crude comparison between viewing data on YouTube, as per end of April 2020, indicates: 102M (with 236K subscribers and 1.3M likes) for IC Vs. 637K (with 443 subscribers and 9.5K) for Kagumire. Furthermore, Kagumire would not have had the time, nor, arguably, the resources, to shape a storytelling as visually compelling and emotional-driven as that of IC; like for any chess game, early positioning proved of capital importance.

Publics, 'public opinions' and 'civil societies' are *radically* evolving because of, and through, digital assets and, increasingly more, because of the emotional capital of visual media and storytelling formats. Visual communication, in virtue of its synchronic grammar of communication, has altered verification procedures for issues of trust and accountability: in result, the disjunction of the real from the represented is widening and becoming increasingly un-knowable. This is the reason why the strategic usage of media, channels and platforms to tailor a storytelling as purposeful storylines might be rightly assessed as key to managing contemporary digital cultures.

Conclusions

Smartphones are worldwide more present than toothbrushes (Qualman, 2018). In result, media production and dissemination capabilities fully intertwine with and thoroughly enhance today's social media practices across multiple and overlapping platforms.

In such a context, it could be argued that noticeable and effective communication is at everyone's fingertips because of smartphones' availability and easiness of production; and with it, the very concrete ability to re/shape current cultures through dedicated and focused socio-political activities. Storytelling, thus, can be looked at the empowering toolkit through which digital users have the potential to aptly and strategically plan and pursue their aims.

The amount of visual information being produced on a daily basis is unparalleled and continuously growing. The visual is the object of enormous media production and, consequentially, of digital dissemination; in turn, visual content constitutes the vast majority of all produced, distributed and consumed data (Deloitte Global, 2017).

However, as Toscani argues, to be able (and/or capacitated) to produce a photograph doesn't make one a photographer (Toscani, 2017): in fact, media production skills are not one with media literacy competencies. Indeed, visual communication requires both the practical skills and the sensibility that only education can foster: as such, it asks for the software, i.e. the thinking abilities, possibly more than the hardware, i.e. the camera.

The challenge visual forms bring to current digital frameworks extends from the pre-production phase to the production and post-production, as suggested through the above discussion on the Stop Kony campaign. This impacts current debates on the ontology and epistemology of storytelling, and of visual storytelling, specifically. It consequently changes how we perceive ourselves as 'human beings', and fully informs what we are becoming.

This is the reason why the relation between the real and its interpretations, alongside its disseminations as dedicated stories, continues to gather attention across all digital actors contributing to today's quickly evolving politics of communication.

As each image conveys the potential for multiple and, even contrasting, semiotic spaces and emotional universes, to choose one image over another is already (and should indeed be appreciated as such) a purposeful choice on the real as 'that specific real'.

Alongside with the issue of which real to articulate as what storytelling to be then communicated as a dedicated storyline, decision-making on practices and strategies, processes and policies, do inform all phases of communication. How does the gigantic amounts of pictures endlessly shot worldwide on smartphones change representation and understanding of visual societies? Does it facilitate, or even promote, visual literacy in terms of skills development and/or competencies enhancement? As the world is increasingly narrated visually, is it also better visually understood?

To become effective visual storytellers, one is required to master visual storytelling's production capabilities in its operational and strategic usage; s/he is therefore required to manage the tools and competencies of today's grammars of socio-political engagement across both the media and the socio-political realms.

As the former is thoroughly ineffective without the latter, these skill sets are required to turn storytelling into bespoke storylines, first through the crafting of evocative and consistent storytelling, and then with its strategic dissemination as convincing storylines.

IC engaged the visual form as a powerful communicative tool, and fully adopted aesthetics as its semiotic propeller (Fusari, *forthcoming*). As such, IC's success should be identified in the apt combination of form with content, both at the storytelling and storyline moments.

The majestic quality of IC's storytelling was achieved through a key feature of storytelling techniques, i.e. the effective usage of emotions. As +Acumen, a leading platform on digital literacy, argues, storytelling is 'feelings, nothing more than feelings' (+Acumen, 2019), and this is what makes storytelling templates fully evocative and *therefore* convincing.

The IC's campaign to indict Kony successfully implemented the relation between the emotive component of visual storytelling and its *strategic* usage on digital media as bespoke storylines. This essay explored the relation between the real and the represented, with particular attention to the specific visual literacy requirements, now as much as then, that are required to manage the visual storytelling of politics.

The case study of the IC's campaign, among several other considerations, marked the acquired capability of media, and visual media specifically, to impact with considerable magnitude today's socio-political discourse. IC's unquestionable ability to turn its storytelling into powerful storylines is the reason why IC was chosen as a still relevant case study nine years after its appearance, which is truly a very long time for digital parameters.

The IC's campaign illustrates that the successful usage of the visual quality of storytelling, with its emotional capital for digital media, is key to its dissemination as understood storylines. As Kevin Spacey argues, once storytelling is effective, 'you will have kids forcing media on their peers in a way that any blockbuster movie could only dream of' (Spacey, 2013). Indeed, this trickle-down model was witnessed at every step of the IC's campaign, from the crafting of the storytelling to its dissemination strategies as storylines: US youth was the unstoppable actor forcing IC's agenda on celebrities and political figures (the 20+12) for them to leverage IC's un-negotiated agenda onto Washington.

New actors beyond the State system, what has previously been addressed under the rubric of 'public diplomacy', have surfaced to impact and re/shape cultures, publics and politics worldwide. Their tool to raise, re/direct and possibly re/root cultural paradigms of social changes has expanded to include the apt production, distribution and engagement of (visual) storytelling as understood (multimedia and hence: multisensorial) storylines.

However, activities that are part of today's digital politics continue to shift across evolving forms of engagement on unmapped territories, with no clear direction for analysts or practitioners yet to follow; IC's twin bracelets included in its distributed toolkit or the 'pay as you can' fundraising model/supporting scheme (IC, 2012, 25:15) are very clear examples of bespoke strategies to commit targeted audiences in a sensible way for the target group.

In such a fluid and hybrid scenario, the synchronic quality of visual media challenges the basics of cognitive processes: for instance, to say 'the red rose smells' is different from drawing or picturing a red rose because graphic elements are processed at different speeds and by different areas of the brain (Caviglioli, 2019). Hence, distinct elements within the frame (as well as outside it, for instance: the prospective) are differently prioritized by the audience's mind: the result produces multiple, co-existing and ever-changing cognitive understandings.

Politics and communication rely on, and, in turn, feed human beings; the visual as the adjective to both media and storytelling, identifies a field of highly questioned, massively evolving and exceptionally volatile semiotic engagements: all the above contributes to approach current cultures as 'post-symbolic communication' (Lanier, 2011).

Visual-driven storytelling is increasingly popular and popularized on smartphones: its over-production and consequential re/informing presence endlessly changes forms of public knowledge as communication, understanding and media dissemination of contents.

As much as storytelling was previously recommended as an agent to order visual communication, it should be eventually appreciated that things are not that easy, nor yet already solved: in fact storytelling, as a format of *visual* communication, informs digital politics as *multiplied* shifting representations.

The synchronic (Paivio, 1990) quality of the visual should be therefore recognized as ontological; it should be further appreciated as the definitive argument against the supposed simplicity, easiness or immediacy of this specific communicative form. In fact, the visual is a complex and multifaceted media form that requires literacy skills development and intellectual sophistication (Fusari, *forthcoming*).

The profound mark that IC produced with its Kony 2012 video is yet unmatched and offers a final opportunity for two major takeaways, with both of them becoming increasingly relevant:

(1) crafting a powerful visual storytelling is as challenging as effective when audiences understand it through effective storylines: IC would have never re/ shaped the public discourse *globally* without its 29-minute superb video as tailored into convincing storylines;
(2) turning storytelling into storylines must be consistently arranged through credible, shareable and consistent sets of targeted operations on multiple and integrated platforms.

As media channels and digital platforms acquired an undisputed centrality, their operational management and strategic engagement continues to be at the centre of the communication debate. How to prioritize media forms, digital platforms and the dichotomy between social media and digital networks when communicating politics? What to make of digital actors that overlap and/or re/ shape strategic communication to their advantage? How, eventually, to make sense and respond to trolls?

IC proved the extent to which a compelling visual storytelling has the capability to effectively implement strategized media actions as engaged storylines. Visual storytelling was identified as that which matches the right form for a specific content and, in turn, the right content for the identified media form; its result is then purposely and tactically tailored into dedicated storylines. IC's storytelling chose simplicity and linearity over multifaceted richness; it did so to regiment its sensorially articulated storytelling into a monolithic storyline of Good vs. Evil.

Strategy is indeed pivotal to communicate the real as *that representation* through the tailoring of each and every available medium: the sonic, the visual and the verbal, each of them requires dedicated frameworks and offers the opportunity for the integrated and enhanced engagement of their bespoke features. For instance, silence as the absence of sound, has the ability to thoroughly reframe and re/signify multimedia communication to purposely activate an emotion and achieve an aim.

Similarly, what is referred to as 'negative space' could be purposely used as a communicative feature alongside aesthetic notions of colour, shape, lines, and spaces of composition. In other words, there is no form of communication that cannot be used tactically to achieve a key result.

This brief analysis of what is still – in 2021 – the most effective and impactful socio-political campaign was aimed to specifically evince the centrality of the visual as the form of communication shaping media and politics globally. The visual was pleaded not only as the medium informing today's cultures globally, but as a specific form of communication increasingly crucial to engage with socio-political issues. In addition, visual storytelling was identified as the pivot through which contents are convened as purposeful storylines.

Failing to tactfully and strategically master these elements will continue to make visual communication un-appreciated, un-strategized and overall misunderstood, turning inter-personal and social understanding, as well as appreciation of human and cultural perception, in a prolonged state of crisis (Ryan-Mosely, 2021). This is the reason why approaching an educated and strategic appreciation of the visual medium, and of storytelling as a format of communication, remains, today, more relevant than ever.

References

+Acumen. (2019). Storytelling for change. Retrieved from https://www.plusacumen.org/courses/storytelling-change

Bandura, A. (1999). Social cognitive theory: An agentic perspective. *The Asian Journal of Social Psychology, 2*, 21–41.

Barthes, R. (1977). *Image, music, text*. New York, NY: Hill and Wang.

Barthes, R. (1981). *Camera Lucida*. New York, NY: Hill and Wang.

Baudrillard, J. (1995). *The Gulf War did not take place*. Bloomington, IN: Indiana University Press.

BuzzFeed. (2012). How many photos have been taken ever? Retrieved from https://www.buzzfeed.com/hunterschwarz/how-many-photos-have-been-taken-ever-6zgv

Campbell, J. (1949). *The hero with A thousand faces*. Princeton, NJ: Princeton University Press.

Campbell, D. (2012). Kony 2012: Networks, activism and community. Retrieved from https://www.david-campbell.org/2012/03/16/kony2012-networks-activism-community

Cartier-Bresson, H. (2018). *The decisive moment*. Göttingen: Steidl.

Caviglioli, O. (2019). *Dual coding with teachers*. Melton: John Catt.

Coole, D. (2005). Rethinking agency: A phenomenological approach to embodiment and agentic capacities. *Political Studies, 53*(1), 124–142.

Deloitte Global. (2017). Photo sharing: Trillions and rising. Retrieved from http://www.deloitte.com/TMTpredictions

Eco, U. (1984). *The name of the rose*. London: Vintage Classics.

Eco, U. (1989). *The open work*. Columbia, SC: Harvard University Press.

Eco, U. (1995). *Faith in fakes: Essays*. London: Secker and Warburg.

Eliade, M. (1976). *Myths, rites, symbols: A Mircea Eliade reader*. New York, NY: Harper Colophon.

Elkins, J. (Ed.) (2011). *What is an image?* Pennsylvania: Penn State UP.

Engadget. (2020). Travis Scott's 'Fortnite' concert drew 12.3 million concurrent viewers. Retrieved from https://www.engadget.com/fortnite-travis-scott

Foreign Policy. (2012). Joseph Kony is not in Uganda (and other complicated things). Retrieved from https://foreignpolicy.com/2012/03/07/guest-post-joseph-kony-is-not-in-uganda-and-other-complicated-things

Freytag, G. (1894). *Freytag's technique of the drama: An exposition of dramatic composition and art*. Chicago, IL: Scott, Foresman and Company. Retrieved from https://archive.org/details/freytagstechniqu00freyuoft

Fusari, M. (2017). From the photograph to the meta-image. My practice-led search for a new digital epistemology. In *Proceedings to Immagini?* MPDI, Basel.

Fusari, M. (In press). *Aesthetics as storytelling*. Bristol: Intellect.

van der Graaf, S. (2014). The fabric of social media: An introduction. MEDIA@LSE Working Paper Series.

Greenaway, P. (2008). Rembrandt Ja obvinyau. Holland: 147 minutes.

Heidegger, M. (2001). *Phenomenological interpretations of Aristotle: Initiation into phenomenological research by Martin Heidegger*. Bloomington, IN: Indiana University Press.

IC. (2012). Kony 2012. Retrieved from https://www.youtube.com/watch?v=Y4Mnpz G5Sqc

Inhofe, J. (2012). 33 senators introduce Bipartisan resolution condemning Joseph Kony and the Lord's resistance Army. Retrieved from https://www.inhofe.senate.gov/newsroom/press-releases/33-senators-introduce-bipartisan-resolution-condemning-joseph-kony-and-the-lords-resistance-army

Jung, C. G. (1990). *The archetypes and the collective unconscious*. Princeton, NJ: Princeton University Press.

Kagumire, R. (2012). My response to Kony 2012. Retrieved from https://www.youtube.com/watch?v=KLVY5jBnD-E

Kanczula, A. (2012). Kony 2012 in facts and figures. Retrieved from http://www.guardian.co.uk/news/datablog/2012/apr/20/kony-2012-facts-numbers

Kellner, D. (1992). *The Persian Gulf TV war*. Boulder: Westview Press.

Kern, R. (2015). *Language, literacy and technology*. Cambridge: Cambridge University Press.

King, D. (2014). *The commissar vanishes: The falsification of photographs and art in Stalin's Russia*. London: Tate.

Kress, G., & Van Leeuwen, T. (1996). *Reading images: The grammar of visual design*. London: Routledge.

Lanier, J. (2011). *You are not A gadget: A manifesto*. London: Penguin.

Lupton, E. (2017). *Design is storytelling*. Chicago, IL: Cooper Hewitt.

Mangani, S., Arthur, P., & Simon, J. (Eds.). (2006). *Images: A reader*. London: SAGE Publications.

Muzi Falconi, T. (2004). *Le relazioni pubbliche nelle organizzazioni complesse*. Milan: Lupetti.

Paivio, A. (1990). *Mental representations A dual coding approach*. Oxford: Oxford University Press.

Qualman, E. (2018). Word of mouth. Retrieved from https://www.youtube.com/watch?v=2IcpwISszbQ

Ritchin, F. (2009). *After photography*. New York, NY: W. W. Norton.

Ronson, J. (2012). *Lost at sea – the Jon Ronson mysteries*. London: Picador.

Ryan-Mosley, T. (2021). Beauty filters are changing the way young girls see themselves. Retrieved from https://www.technologyreview.com/2021/04/02/1021635/beauty-filters-young-girls-augmented-reality-social-media/?truid=0d89947977a6b4a1d33c4e5efc907cae&utm_source=engagement_email↪utm_medium=email&utm_campaign=site_visitor.unpaid.engagement&utm_content=04.11.non-subs&mc_cid=fec08796b5&mc_eid=c0ab3bcdd1

Spacey, K. (2013). James MacTaggart lecture 2013. Retrieved from https://www.youtube.com/watch?v=oheDqofa5NM

The Guardian. (2012). Kony 2012 – what's the real story? Retrieved from https://www.theguardian.com/politics/reality-check-with-polly-curtis/2012/mar/08/kony-2012-what-s-the-story

The Huffington Post. (2012). The Kony 2012 Kraziness. Retrieved from https://www.huffingtonpost.com/2012/04/12/kony-2012-viral-infographic_n_1421812.html

Toscani, O. (2017). Photojournalism and digital photos. Personal communication with the author.

Tsatsou, P. (2009). Reconceptualising 'time' and ... PLATFORM. *Journal of Media and Communication*, *1*(July), 11–32.

Tunheim. (2012). Kony 2012 – a triumph of video advocacy. Retrieved from https://www.pinterest.co.uk/pin/142918988145131956/?lp=true

World Economic Forum Report. (2016). Digital media and society. Implications in a hyperconnected era. Retrieved from https://www.weforum.org

Chapter 13

Post-truth Visuals, Untruth Visuals

Ġorġ Mallia

Abstract

This chapter seeks to present a limited overview of some aspects of manipulated and/or fake images that contribute to society 'becoming post-truth'. It
subclassifies levels of manipulation and also presents the finding from a
descriptive survey that gauges perceptions on awareness and recognisability
of fake images. It also presents perceptions of effect on individuals of images
modified for aesthetic reasons and carried by social media. The majority of
respondents seemed affected by this, but with only a minority whose
perception of self was affected. Another result of the survey is that there is a
general mistrust of images not carried by gatekept sources.

Keywords: Fake visuals; image manipulation; awareness of fake images; deep
fake videos; effect on self-perception; mistrust of image truth

Shaping people's thoughts and inclinations has always been one of the primary
roles of the media. This is facilitated, and at the same time made nightmarish, by
the prevalence of largely unregulated social media in a society that has lost its
primary gatekeepers, as newspapers fall and television stations adapt to viewer
and subsidiser demands, modifying content in order to vie for scarce financing.
Professional journalism of both the textual and image-generation type is still
gatekept in the main and is often the one double-sourced, relatively verified fount
of 'truth'. Journalists have the role of verifiers (Martin, 2017, p. 51). But what is
verified has been swamped by what cannot be.

Visuals have often been considered to be more truthful than words. The
symbolic nature of text allows for a wider interpretation than the more seemingly
factual visuals. This seems often to be the case even in courts of law, deeming
interpretation not to actually be necessary – that people see visual representations
as the real thing, a perception of reality. This leads to what Tushnet (2012)
describes as the source of much bad law.

Media, Technology and Education in a Post-Truth Society, 175–187
doi:10.1108/978-1-80043-906-120211013

Given the nature and sophistication of image manipulation software at this stage of technical development, this is a logical conclusion to arrive at.

> The ubiquitous availability of easy-to-use software for editing digital images brought about by rapid technological advances of the 21st century has dramatically decreased the time, cost, effort, and skill required to fabricate convincing visual forgeries. (Shen et al., 2019, p. 439)

This applies both to still images, manipulable through software such as Adobe Photoshop and, most recently, moving images, with Deep Fake technology, that is, 'digital manipulation of sound, images, or video to impersonate someone [...] in a manner that is increasingly realistic, to the point that the unaided observer cannot detect the fake' (Blitz, 2018, p. 61, quoting; Chesney & Citron, 2018). This leads to all sorts of problems, not least legal. Is this a form of expression? In which case, might any regulation of manipulated images (still and moving) fall foul of the US first amendment, to quote one example (Blitz, 2018)? But in a sense, that is the least of our worries.

Referring to Plato's play on reality and illusion in *The Republic*, Bordo (2006) gives an excellent definition of the present state of play.

> For us, bedazzlement by created images is no metaphor; it is the actual condition of our lives. If we do not wish to remain prisoners of these images, we must recognize that they are not reality. But instead of moving closer to this recognition, we seem to be moving farther away from it, going deeper and deeper into the cave of illusion. (p. 79)

Many are aware of this illusory fake truth (to use a litotes), but few know how to cope with it. In fact, one of the most basic questions to be asked is to what extent people who are untrained in manipulation detection, that is, the normal person in the street, can recognise a fake, and how this impacts on their perception of 'truth'. Though the literature is adamant that people have a very limited ability to detect manipulation (Lehmuskallio, Häkkinen, & Seppänen, 2018; Nightingale, Wade, & Watson, 2017).

For still images, the field of photo forensics has developed 'to restore some trust in photographs' (Hany, 2017, p. 78), but this chapter looks beyond professional recognition of what are fake visuals. Given the massive pervasion of social media and the spread of fake images to people who are predominantly not professional photo forensic experts, we may presume a general acceptance of fakes as being truthful. This chapter proposes to present a limited look at the situation as it now stands, also presenting perceptions elicited from data provided by a brief, descriptive survey.

As opposed to the psychological and physiognomic determinants of perception (as in, Zakia, 2008), this chapter is more interested in the recognition of truth, manipulation and faking in images presented in the media, both legacy and social.

The Manipulation Strata

One cannot put all manipulated images into one bag, of course. There are a lot of strata of *faked* or manipulated images. The fact that software can so easily change any aspect of the snapshot… the image grabbed from a moment in reality… implies the presence of scepticism with regard to any published image. And the indications are that viewers are quite easily fooled by forgeries. A study by Schetinger, Oliveira, da Silva, and Carvalho (2017) showed that, though users guessed right around 58% of the time, they only identified 46.5% of the forgeries. Experience and young age of participants affected the results positively. 'The subject's behavior (time, hints, confidence level, etc.) during the study had the biggest impact on the success rate' (Schetinger et al., 2017, p. 150). Though the study is only three years old at the time of the writing of this chapter, given the lightning advances, that was still a time when manipulation software was not as advanced as it is now, so manipulations might not have been as perfect as they can be now. In other words, odds are that if that research was carried out today, the percentages would be different. Research is finding it very difficult to keep up with the speed with which technology advances in these areas.

For the sake of facility of identification, I am sticking to images in the media (and ignoring mediated reality or digital art), sub-classifying the process of media-based manipulated images into three very broad categories, or strata.

Tweaking: post-production of images often resorted to by artistic photographers, this involves the touching up of contrast, saturation, brightness, as well as exposure correction, levelling or curving highlights, midtones and shadows, setting temperature and all the other little tweaks permitted by the software. Cropping can also fall within this category, though I cannot imagine deletion and cloning being permitted by (say) photography competitions. The following is taken from the rules section of the Rise Photography Awards.[1] The content is typical of such competitions.

> Post-production may be used to enhance an image, while retaining the integrity of the photographic capture. Post-production in all categories (excluding the Creative Category) should not take away from the intention of the original capture.

The 'integrity' and 'intention' of the original capture preclude heavy editing, limiting *tweaking* to nothing more than touch-up.

Journalist photographers often tweak photos in this way, at times for the sake of clarity and better reproducibility. I am here talking about what is 'allowed', as opposed to what can be abused of. Minimal tweaking can also lead to the creation of a produced version of the truth. The O.J. Simpson photo on the June 1994 *Time* magazine cover is an iconic example of how minimal tweaking can provide a re-interpretation of an image. The darkening of the mugshot within a racially tense situation, led people to their own conclusions, though the photo-illustrator in charge of that tweak, Mat Mahurin, denied an agenda, insisting he was just dramatising the image.[2] Whatever the intention, the manipulation deviated from the true image 'as taken'. Here it was the context that provided the catalyst for the manipulated image's interpretation. Images never exist in a vacuum, so any changes made need to take all factors into consideration to gauge the extent of the effect of the manipulation.

Aesthetic modification: modification of images using image altering software (such as Adobe Photoshop) in order to smooth, enhance, liquify and generally convert an image into one that only retains the base elements of the original. This has become a very popular practice with regards to images used on social media, and on Instagram in particular. The 'influencer' culture among those who use that platform is often highly dependent on looks, with photos being heavily edited in order to fit a created norm for the profile. Most social media sites have a set of filters that changes the atmosphere of an image, varying depth, age and colour. Filtering of this type is also a feature of almost all phone and tablet operating systems as part of their camera or photo apps, with a lot of shortcuts to changes included along with the more precise tools for users themselves to tweak images. Logically, an enormous amount of third-party apps such as Snapseed, VSCO, Pixlr and Android and iOS versions of Photoshop, are also intended to carry out manipulation on the hoof. Effecting changes within the categories of both *Tweaking* and *Aesthetic Modification* has become the norm, rather than the exception.

Modification of images to enhance aesthetics is a practice that has long been used for the touching up of glamour magazine covers, for example. Images of models are rendered perfect, with blemishes removed and bodily highlights enhanced. Magazines abuse Photoshop, often because celebrities demand that they be protected from exposure to reality (Ives, 2008, p. 24). It used to be called 'airbrushing' in a pre-digital age, since the fine spray of the airbrush was often used to blend skin tones and smooth roughnesses, as well as removing unwanted elements (including human subjects... often, but not exclusively, associated with despotic regime historical re-imagining).

Compositing: Another phrase that would describe the process is 'heavy editing'. In this case, diverse elements coming from different sources are brought together to produce a seamless whole that conveys content that is different from the original components. This is at the core of digital art, and is also what is often used to create the very popular memes that dot social media. These practices converge with the post-truth society when fake images are intentionally passed on as truthful. Even here, one needs to try to understand intention because in the end, as with the fake content in text, it is the intent of the creator that classifies the result. One cannot compare the image of a holiday couple taken in their back garden, superimposed over an image of the Bahamas, with the photojournalist who composites two photos of a soldier calming civilians in Basra in order to create more impact, and Brian Walski was sacked by his newspaper in 2003 for doing just that (Campbell, 2003).

Compositing is not something that was born with the post-truth society. Nor was it only possible with the use of manipulative software packages. Images have been altered since the inception of photography. This was a political and a propaganda tool that was used to hoodwink viewers and to change the perception of reality. Photo montages dot the history of photography, and some of the results became famous photos that everybody believed were real until detective work brought out the truth. One such photo is that of General Ulysses S. Grant on a horse in 1864/65 against a backdrop of the siege of Richmond. This turned out to be a composite of three images, taking Grant's head from one, a horse and horseman from another and the backdrop of the tented headquarters during the siege from yet another (Graham, 2015).

Logically, an enormous amount of out of favour political personages disappeared from (for example) Soviet-era photos through the use of photomontage.

This is easily the stratum of manipulation that creates the greatest threat to truth in media, and which has led to a mistrust of image veracity.

A Survey

An online survey was run as a way of getting descriptive, general feedback about public perception of fake images. The survey was diffused on social media and 526 random, valid responses were elicited online, composed of 56% female, 43% male and 1% other respondents. The age distribution of participants was not even, but nonetheless fit in quite a few brackets. 39% were between 43 and 60 years of age, 24.5% were between 31 and 42 years of age, 14.3% were between 60 and 70 years of age, 7.2% were between the ages of 22 and 30 years, and 4.2% were over 70 years. There were no respondents aged 16 years or under. By far the majority of respondents had a tertiary level of education (81.4%), 14.1% stopped at the post-secondary level and 4.4% at the secondary level of education.

The survey asked questions primarily about still images, but also touched on video portrayal of untruthful content. All three strata discussed above were taken into consideration when posing the survey questions.

Perception on whether visuals are more truthful than text no longer adheres to the old adage and seems to be distributed across the board (Fig. 13.1). A large number of participants are non-committal. This is a clear indication that a

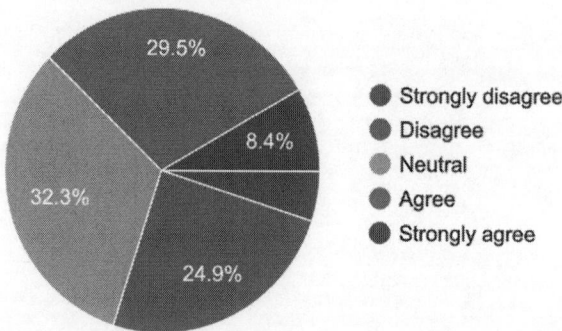

Fig. 13.1.   Visuals Are More Truthful than Text.

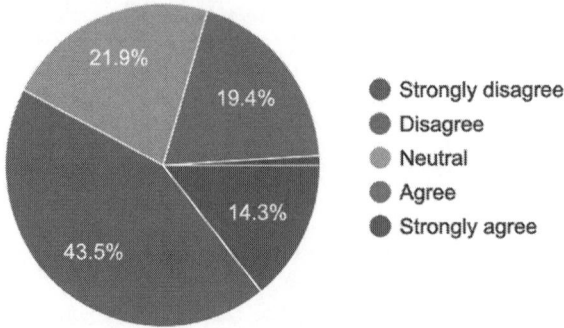

Fig. 13.2.   Visuals Are Less Interpretable than Text.

majority of people no longer trust their eyes when it comes to visuals ... or are at least wary of them.

In fact most respondents think that visuals are at least as interpretable as text (Fig. 13.2). Given the symbolic, very interpretable nature of text, putting the iconic nature of images within the same context is indicative of uncertainty.

There is a general awareness, even by those who might not be cognisant with the methods of manipulation, that photographs can be faked (Fig. 13.3).

There is very slightly less certainty about videos that include people talking (Fig. 13.4), but credibility, even of moving images with sound, is shaky. Definitely a far cry from a time when an image was perceived to be immutable in what it contained and conveyed.

But, being aware of the possibility of manipulation and being able to determine if a photo is a fake are two different things (Fig. 13.5). Only 23% of respondents thought they could recognise a fake photo.

And this general trend grows when it comes to fake videos (Fig. 13.6), with 43.2% of respondents shying away from an answer.

Only 2.7% actually recognised more than 30 fakes (Fig. 13.7). Logically, this does not mean that there are not a lot of these faked items out there, but

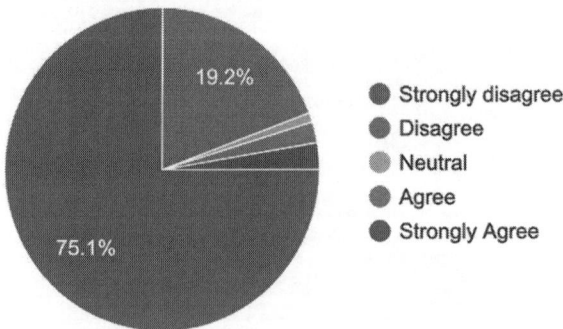

Fig. 13.3.   Photographs Cannot be Faked.

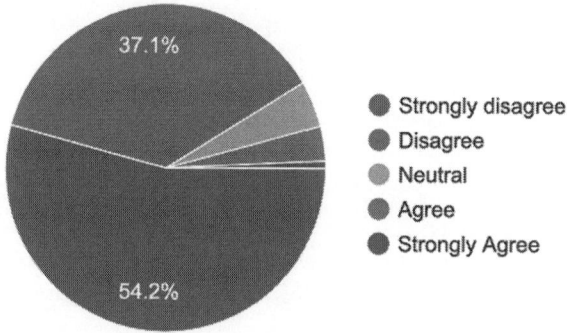

Fig. 13.4. Videos of People Talking Cannot be Faked.

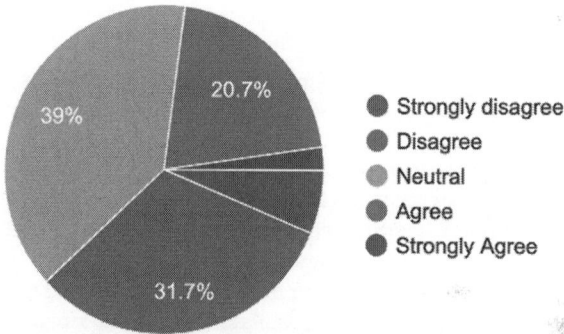

Fig. 13.5. I Can Recognise When a Photo has been Faked.

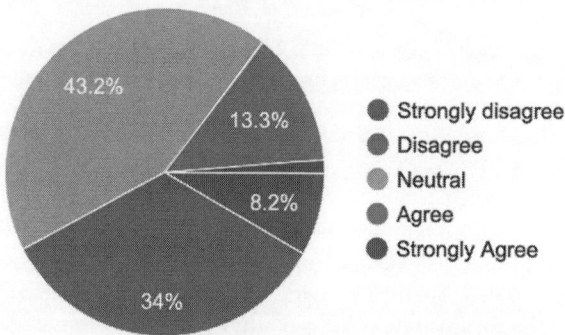

Fig. 13.6. I Can Recognise When a Video has been Faked.

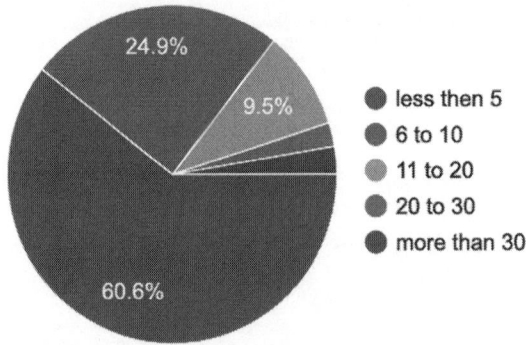

Fig. 13.7.   I Have Seen and Recognised as Fake this Many Fake
Photos/Videos in the Last Month.

corroborates the previous data that most people are incapable of recognising that
such images and/or videos have been manipulated.

Those among the 129 respondents who felt they could recognise fake images,
more often than not stated that they used different types of software to be able to
do so, though quite a few pointed out that not all faked images were very professionally and perfectly done. So, noting imperfections was one way of determining manipulation. This included inverted shadows, colouring mistakes and the
occasional lack of proportionality. Though, inversely, images being 'too perfect'
could also trigger an alarm. Knowing how to use software such as Adobe Photoshop, some thought, could also help in the recognition of areas of manipulation.
The supposition is that knowing what the software can do can show what has
been done. This is problematic, since this presupposes manipulation simply
because the software exists that can do it. Some go to search engines for image
searches to fact-check visuals. It has got to a point that made one participant
write that 'I never believe images on any media unless it's from a reputable
source'.

Pretty much the same reasoning was put forward by the 81 participants who
thought they could recognise fake videos, but also including such unique features
for moving images, such as lip-synching. Most people seem to be fact-checking on
search engines such as Google. What most participants agreed on was that
technology, for example in the creation of Deep Fakes, was advancing to the
point where it was becoming much more difficult to discern manipulation.

Asking respondents if they had manipulated photos/videos themselves (Fig.
13.8), 27.6% said that they had, which, in spite of being an extensive minority,
remains a relatively large number and indicates that the tools for the manipulation of images are quite easily available, as is the will to do that manipulation. 163
participants elaborated on their answer, giving reasons for manipulation that
varied from editing out people to the creation of artistic compositions. Creating
satire is also at times mentioned, but the most frequent reason seems to point at
the milder sort of manipulation: colour correction, brightness, cropping. In other

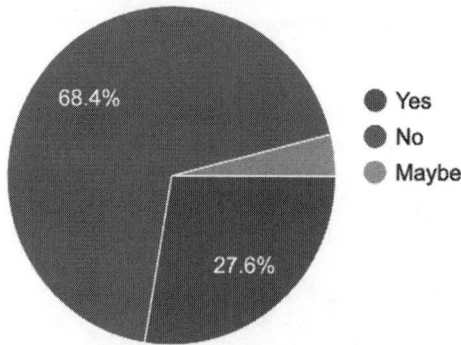

Fig. 13.8.   I have Manipulated Photos/Videos Myself.

words, tweaking. It also seems to be taken for granted that 'Cosmetic retouches are sometimes *de rigueur*, say for glamour imagery'.

A very important part of the survey tried to gauge the participants' personal assessment of affect (Fig. 13.9). While the perception of truth might be overwhelmingly affected, there is no greatly marked difference in their own perception of themselves when confronted by one particular type of manipulation… the one that is most commonly evident on social media. That is, the touched-up photos of beautiful people, done with the intention of eliminating all blemishes and enhancing the aesthetic, as discussed in the section on *aesthetic manipulation* above (Fig. 13.10).

There were 23.9% of participants who said they were affected. This is a relatively big number, meaning that, though many would be aware of the manipulation, though not all, as indicated above, some were still psychologically and emotionally influenced by what they saw.

Very interesting and quite telling were some of the reasons given by those 23.9% who felt their perception of self touched by the manipulated images.

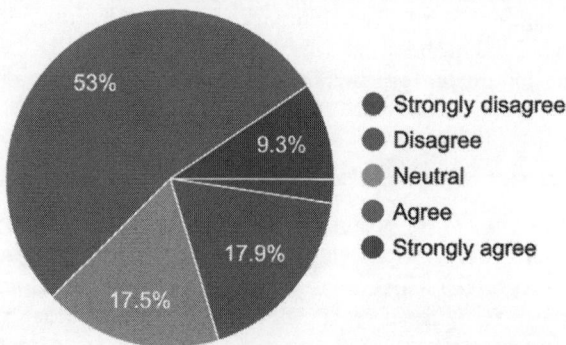

Fig. 13.9.   Fake Images Affect My Perception of Truth.

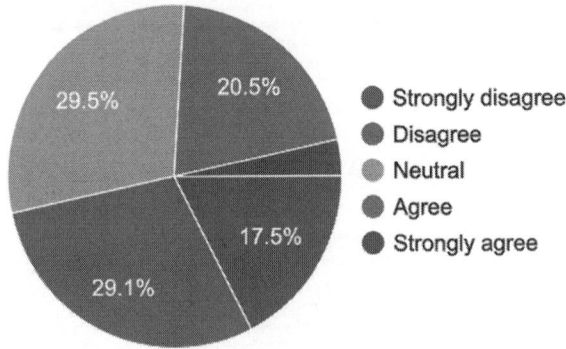

Fig. 13.10. My Perception of Myself is Affected by Touched-up Photos of Beautiful People.

Nothing too deep or psychologically significant, but we are dealing with individuals whose perception of quality of life... potentially leading to sadness, a feeling of inadequacy, is directly linked to the manipulation.

Here are a few examples that are typical, though not entirely representative, of the 100 comments made by participants: 'These touched up photos create an unrealistic standard that I sometimes expect myself to reach'. Also, 'when faced with these perfect renders of what I believe I should look like, I feel horrible; despite knowing that these photos are probably heavily photoshopped'. The strength of manipulated photos goes beyond awareness of origins: 'If you're a person who is struggling with body image, seeing photos of gorgeous women doesn't help. Personally even if I know that they are fake, they still affect me'. Though, there were also instances of the inverse effect, typified by this comment: 'I usually end up feeling better about myself, because I would know that the people in the touched-up photos wish they looked like that too'. This was a very small minority reaction, however. By far the majority reported negative effects of manipulated photos that portrayed aesthetically enhanced subjects.

When asked in an open-ended question where they encountered fake or manipulated images and/or videos, 166 participants singled out social media. A further 176 specified Facebook, and 69 Instagram. Traditional media was also represented, but minimally, which is indicative.

Discussion of the Main Data Results

A strong component of the open-ended answers in the survey was related to viewers being incredulous, suspicious of all images, except for those from sources they believed to be gatekept and reputationally sound. The need for methods that train individuals to recognise fakes is clearly there, if for no other reason than to diminish the incredulity.

There are lots of methods being touted. The 'faceforensics' dataset route proposes an automated benchmark for the detection of facial manipulation, particularly for video fakes such as those created by DeepFakes, Face2Face, FaceSwap and NeuralTextures (Rössler et al., 2019). The literature is full of suggestions of this type. In most cases, deep studies are suggested, looking at the trace left by manipulation (e.g. detecting fake images generated by Generative Adversarial Networks, as in the paper by Marra, Gragnaniello, Cozzolino, & Verdoliva, 2018).

In almost all cases, expert knowledge of the programmes and protocols involved is necessary, but there are cases where 'the man in the street' might be taught enough to be reasonably certain of detecting fakes. A brief article by Stewart (2015), for example, in which simple procedures are suggested, particularly using a reverse image search, is something that was mentioned by a number of participants in the survey. Another brief article by Snelling (2019) looks at how acceptable and commonplace manipulation is, particularly to the younger generation (which he describes as 'generation meme'), but that there are ways of getting to the source of images, provided there is enough visual literacy training.

The implications of so many people being aware of the existence of fakes and as a result not trusting visuals are very negative for news diffusion. This mistrust is rampant, and fake images contribute to the global lack of credibility of, particularly, online resources (Wierzbicki, 2018). The more tools available to those who are not technical experts in the field of image manipulation, the more empowerment to users of online content will have, and the more general trust in visual elements there will be because of the awareness of what makes fake visuals.

A large percentage of participants felt they were affected by fake visuals, although only a relatively small percentage of participants felt they were affected personally by the result of image manipulation in the aesthetic modification stratum. Feedback elicited quite clearly showed quite a large impact on those who were affected, in the main resulting in some distress. The results of a study by Kleemans, Daalmans, Carbaat, and Anschütz (2018), found that

> the common practice of Instagram users to manipulate and tweak their appearance in pictures can have negative consequences, at least for the girls who are prone to make social comparisons. (p. 103)

The fact that that study found that not all girls were affected concurs with the findings of the present research, although the results, in this case, were not cross-tabulated by gender. Terminology used in the majority of open-ended answers in the survey is indicative of the female gender, but this is just speculative as no semantic analysis has been carried out that might have proved gender-specific language.

This is only a very minor side-effect of manipulated visual use in online media, but it is the most rampantly used modification for, in the main, purely personal reasons. That is, as distinct from agendas that are potentially motivated by, among others, political, economical, minority-denigrating (as in racism, homophobia, ethnicity, tribalism, etc.) intentions. The O.J. Simpson case referred to above would, for example, pertain to the latter. With 3.6 billion social network users in 2020 (statista.com), with Facebook having 2.6 billion monthly active users, according to that social network's own statistics, and 1 billion monthly Instagram users (according to Instragram's own statistics), the personal aspect definitely cannot be ignored. I am singling out these two social networks because it was clear from the survey that they are the most used by those who participated.

Young people in particular (Beacom, 2017) are seeking audience gratification through a self-presentation that deviates from reality.

Conclusion

This has been a cursory look at one narrow aspect of what manipulated or outrightly fake images contribute to the post-truth society in which we live. This chapter has tried to subclassify still image/video manipulation into three broad, overlapping strata, increasing in the severity of the shift from actual to constructed reality. It has presented data from a descriptive survey, gauging perception of individuals regarding their awareness of the presence of fake images/videos, their ability to recognise these as such and the effect one type of manipulated image might have on self-perception.

One takeaway from the chapter is the awareness of increased mistrust in images that do not come from known, gatekept sources.

Visuals are only a small, albeit quite important, part of the manipulable constructs that deviate from what would generally be accepted as truth. However, because of the way they were traditionally perceived as being steadfast presenters of reality, their fall from grace has left an indelible mark on present-day society.

Notes

1. See https://risephotoawards.com/
2. See http://www.alteredimagesbdc.org/oj-simpson

References

Beacom, C. (2017). Behind a screen: Self-presentation amongst Maltese young people on social media. Unpublished, B.Psy (Hons). Dissertation, University of Malta.

Blitz, M. (2018). Lies, line drawing, and deep fake news. *Oklahoma Law Review, 71*(1), 59–116.

Bordo, S. (2006). Never just pictures. In S. Manghani, A. Piper, & J. Simons (Eds.), *Images: A reader*. (pp. 78–81). London: SAGE Publications.

Campbell, D. (2003). US war photographer sacked for altering image of British soldier. *The Guardian*. (Thursday, April 3, 2003). Retrieved from https://www.theguardian.com/media/2003/apr/03/pressandpublishing.Iraqandthemedia

Chesney, B., & Citron, D. (2018). Deep fakes: A looming crisis for national security, democracy and privacy? *Lawfare*. (Feb 21, 2018). Retrieved from https://

www.lawfareblog.com/deep-fakes-looming-crisis-national-security-democracy-and-privacy

Graham, K. (2015). Fake photo of Ulysses S. Grant has fooled people for a century. *In Digital Journal.* (October 3ċ, 2015). Retrieved from http://www.digitaljournal.com/a-and-e/arts/fake-photo-of-ulysses-s-grant-has-fooled-people-for-a-century/article/448098

Hany, F. (2017). How to detect faked photos. *American Scientist; Research Triangle Park, 105*(2), 77–81.

Ives, N. (2008). Despite talk of ethics codes, airbrushing is here to stay. *Advertising Age.* 79.16: 24. Web.

Kleemans, M., Daalmans, S., Carbaat, I., & Anschütz, D. (2018). Picture perfect: The direct effect of manipulated Instagram photos on body image in adolescent girls. *Media Psychology, 21*(1), 93–110. doi:10.1080/15213269.2016.1257392

Lehmuskallio, A., Häkkinen, J., & Seppänen, J. (2018). Photorealistic computer-generated images are difficult to distinguish from digital photographs: A case study with professional photographers and photo-editors. *Visual Communication, 18*(4), 427–451. doi:10.1177/1470357218759809

Marra, F., Gragnaniello, D., Cozzolino, D. and Verdoliva, L. (2018). Detection of GAN-generated fake images over social networks. In *IEEE conference on multimedia information processing and retrieval* (pp. 384–389). Retrieved from https://ieeexplore.ieee.org/document/8397040

Martin, N. (2017). Journalism, the pressures of verification and notions of post-truth in civil society. *Cosmopolitan Civil Society: An Interdisciplinary Journal, 9*(2), 41–55. doi:10.5130/ccs.v9i2.5476

Nightingale, S. J., Wade, K. A., & Watson, D. G. (2017). Can people identify original and manipulated photos of real-world scenes? *Cognitive Research: Principles and Implications, 2*(30). doi:10.1186/s41235-017-0067-2

Rössler, A., Cozzolino, D., Verdoliva, L., Riess, C., Thies, J., & Niesner, M. (2019). FaceForensics++: Learning to detect manipulated cacial images. Retrieved from openaccess.thecvf.com

Schetinger, V., Oliveira, M. M., da Silva, R., & Carvalho, T. J. (2017). Humans are easily fooled by digital images. *Computers & Graphics, 68*, 142–151.

Shen, C., Kasra, M., Pan, W., Bassett, G. A., Malloch, Y., & O'Brien, J. F. (2019). Fake images: The effects of source, intermediary, and digital media literacy on contextual assessment of image credibility only. *New Media & Society, 21*(2), 438–463. doi:10.1177/1461444818799526

Snelling, J. (2019). What's Wrong with this Picture? *School Library Journal*, p. 18–22. (February 2019).

Stewart, S. (2015). A tale of two images. *The Quill*, 22–24. (May/June 2015).

Tushnet, R. (2012). Worth a thousand words: The images of copyright. *Harvard Law Review, 125*(3), 683–759.

Wierzbicki, A. (2018). *Web content credibility*. New York, NY: Springer-Verlag.

Zakia, R. (2008). Perception, evidence, truth, and seeing. In M. R. Peres, M. Osterman, G. B. Romer, N. M. Sturart, & J. T. Lopez (Eds.), *The concise focal encyclopedia of photography* (pp. 239–249). New York, NY: Focal Press, Taylor and Francis.

Chapter 14

Reflections on the Visual Truth and War Photography: A Historian's Perspective

Anna Topolska

Abstract

In order to discuss visual truth both from the epistemological and ethical perspective, this essay focuses on the nature of photographic image and its complex relationship with human perception and ethics in Western culture. It argues that this relationship is similarly complex to that of history and reality it represents and points out that the ethical approach to truth is most constructive for society. By looking at the most politically, ethically, and ideologically engaged category: war photography, the author analyzes how images are constructed and used in various contexts. The text provides a background of history of war iconography but focuses on the examples from the twentieth and twenty-first century: the Vietnam War, the Balkan conflict, the war in the Persian Gulf, the war in Iraq, and the war in Syria.

Keywords: Visual truth; war photography; historical truth; ethics; semiolog; visual epistemology

Julianne H. Newton discussing in 1998 the problem of visual truth and journalism said:

> We must never give up the goal of understanding, recording, interpreting and discussing in various ways our various worlds simply because we now believe there is no such thing as absolute, objective TRUTH (Newton, 1998, p. 9, original underlining).

Twenty years later, debates on the question of visual truth continue to mix ethical and epistemological categories. We can agree that, from the epistemological point of view, it is not possible to talk about some absolute visual truth, even in the case of traditional photography, let alone the digital form – but about

Media, Technology and Education in a Post-Truth Society, 189–201
doi:10.1108/978-1-80043-906-120211014

interpretations of the world. However, these interpretations have various intentions. And here the debates begin trying to judge which image is justified and represents the truth and which is not. Because of this complex situation, to help audiences of visuality decide which image is worth believing, it is crucial to analyze how images are constructed and used, even those that are a simple reflection of a fragment of the world, such as traditional, nondigital photography. For that reason, this essay focuses on the nature of photographic image and its complex relationship with human perception and ethics in Western culture, choosing to look at the most politically, ethically, and ideologically engaged category: war photography. I argue that this relationship is similarly complex to that of history and reality it represents.

In the process of recognizing the world, sight is one of the most important senses. Thanks to it we establish our place in the world before describing it with words. There is a mutual relationship between perception and imagination. Our previous perception experiences, which shape our visual images of the world, transform into imaginations functioning in our memory which, recalled by associations, precede our subsequent experiences (Gombrich, 1990). The iconosphere that we live in influences what and how we see the world, and the ways we see the world influence the kind of visual space we create around us. The same is the process of circulation of photographic images in Western culture. Therefore, the notion of what constitutes visual truth turns out to be problematic from the very beginning. And it has two aspects.

On the one hand, we have the myth of visual truth of photography which results from the very nature of it – traditional, analog photography – where the image imprinted on photosensitive material is a direct result of light and the presence of the photographed object. And even though nowadays we mostly deal with digital images – often manipulated – this myth still comes back. It is related to the witnessing, experiential, aspect of seeing in general. On the other hand, we are increasingly aware that photography, and the iconosphere around us, is just another language that is used to communicate. Visual communication, I believe, occurs at the intersection of ideology (which is mythologized) and aesthetics, understood after Baumgarten as perception, which is historically and culturally conditioned. We see through a set of what I call *visual topoi*, which simplify our understanding of the world that surrounds us.

The twofolded nature of photography, the medium which focuses my interest here, consists in the fact that, on the one hand, it is – at least in the case of analog photography – or it is believed that it is, as I said, a reference to the reality which once was in front of the camera and, on the other hand, in the fact that it uses signs, therefore is a language. The latter was already noticed by the semiologists of the 1950s and 1960s, such as Roland Barthes. He spoke about the mechanism of mythologization in which images have two levels of interpretation: sign and myth. They rely on specific patterns and comprehensible signs that convey meaning not only by their content or context but also through reference to other images in the culture at large. Photographs, then, can refer to iconic narratives or cultural myths. So, the most important here is the way the content is conveyed, not the content as such. Because this process of mythologization naturalizes history, the meanings are read by the viewers as something obvious. The duality of photography was accurately described by the German philosopher Siegdried Kracauer who noticed that photography has a lot in common with history (Kracauer, 1995). He understood both of these cultural phenomena as a method of description of reality, as phenomena at the intersection of epistemology and aesthetics, on the one hand trying to reach the truth and represent it and on the other hand reaching for patterns and forms of this description to give it particular shape. Both photography and history "touch" reality, which is impossible to be represented faithfully. Tools of description of this reality are needed, or verbal tools or visual ones. Photography "touches" reality through its technological side and evidences of past presence. History uses sources that document the past; however, in both cases, a form of communication is needed: a frame, a sign, a narrative, or a context. According to Kracauer, the work of historians should consist in maintaining balance between these two tendencies, which he calls realistic and formative.

Nevertheless, even though we are aware that we cannot tell exactly what the past was, at least because of the fact that we have to focus on selected events and cannot describe them all, we still speak about historical truth. It should be the goal we pursue even if we are aware it is not achievable. A historian and philosopher of history, Jerzy Topolski, wrote in his last theoretical book, addressed to young adepts of history, *Introduction to History* [Wprowadzenie do historii]:

> (...) purse the truth, that is: develop your source basis, improve the method of your research and of narrative practice, put in the first place evaluation based on the ethics of the group of scholars, at the same time do not avoid bold conceptions broadening the scope of discussion. Also, do not think that your truth is the only one valid (...), fight with the pressure of the only truth, as behind such truth there are always someone's interests (Topolski, 1998, p. 160).

In the same book, he points out that we cannot have access to the past reality. In his opinion, while we can speak about truthfulness of single-base sentences, which are based on the information from the sources, we cannot say the same about the whole narrative. However, some argue (Wrzosek, 2010) that the belief in the truthfulness of single-base sentences and access to the past through historical sources is merely historians' nostalgia for the past and its experience, and its truthfulness is only decided in confrontation with the already existing historical narratives (so interpretations of the past). But I think that does not change the fact that historians have also a nostalgia for the historical truth, and once it turns out to be impossible to be reached in the epistemological dimension (which happens in Topolski's theory on the narrative level), they turn to the ethical understanding of it ("put in the first place evaluation based on the ethics of the group of scholars" – Topolski says), what I also would like to do in my considerations of the visual truth. Ultimately, in fact, neither history as knowledge nor visual representations of the world exist outside the human community in which the role ascribed to such phenomena is, we want it or not, to regulate discussion and provide sense to human existence (on many levels). Once we are devoid of the notion of truth in general, the foundations of the tissue of that community are shaken.

Visuality has a similarly complex relationship with the reality it represents, as history. Even though we can say that a photograph is an accurate reference to a fragment of reality, the whole context in which it is used gives it the meaning. There also are instances when a photograph which is used is not necessarily coming from the context which is discussed in the narrative in which it is placed or is a deliberately selected fragment of the context and not necessarily the most representative one. In such situations, it is not necessarily the whole narrative which is false: the photograph might be used as a metaphor or a symbol, which does not diminish the importance of the whole message or its validity and truthfulness. Visual truth is, then, conditional. It also is an ethical category here – it should be the ultimate goal of the authors of visual narratives (who should embrace the ethics of the journalist profession), as it is that of historians. However, they are aware that it cannot not be reached (on the epistemological level) and that there might be several, equally valid, versions of it. The audiences, in turn, should be aware of the fact that a language is used to create visual messages and look for their intentions, even though our perception mechanisms make us prone to trust visuality in general.

War Iconography

In the history of visual arts, war is a laudable topic, a pretext for presentation of the triumph of a state or a leader. Works of art depict great acts, a victory over the enemy. They would show justice, generosity, and greatness of the leaders of commemorated wars. War is treated as a decoration, often depicted in the convention of a tournament skirmish (as, for example, in the painting of Uccello's *The Battle of San Romano*). Such images were often commissioned by public edifices to serve propaganda purposes. In the seventeenth century, the opposite tendency emerged in painting, what Foucault called "counterhistory" – depicting the suffering of civilians during wars. The cycle of graphics of Jacques Callot's *Misfortunes of War* inspired by the reality of Lorraine during the Thirty Years' War, through Goya's *The Disasters of War*, and the paintings of Gericault or Delacroix (*The Massacre at Chios*) up to *Guernica* of Picasso are examples.

Documentary photography also began to be a part of this trend and to refer to people's sensitivity to human suffering. History of war photography goes back as far as the Crimea War – the photographs of Roger Fenton from 1853 to 1856 – and the American Civil War – the photographs of Timothy O'Sullivan from the Gettysburg battle in 1863, but it was the war in Vietnam (the so-called first media war) which, reported visually on a daily basis, showed the unexpected influence which can be made on the society by showing them suffering of civilians (especially of the opposite side). The media were not showing images of defeat of Americans, but focusing on victories to create the impression that everything was under control. The most known is the photograph by Huynh Cong Ut from June

1972, entitled "Accidental Napalm," which depicts a group of children running and screaming, accompanied by a few soldiers (the most terrified girl is naked), and which became one of the icons of the antiwar movement.[1]

Hariman and Lucaites aptly stated in their book *No Caption Needed* that power of photojournalism lies not in the indexical accurateness of a photo but in the fact that it can go beyond into the realm of ethics and promote, for instance, as in the recalled example, values of democratic society. First, they write: "Photojournalism might be the perfect ideological practice: while it seems to present objects as they are in the world, it places those objects within a system of social relationships and constitutes the viewer as a subject within that system. These relationships – including the relationship between media producer and audience – are arbitrary, asymmetrical relations of power, yet they are made to appear natural as they are articulated through the unexceptionable signs of the real world" (Hariman & Lucaites, 2007, p. 2). So, on one level, photography may use the aforementioned myth of visual truth of photography, which takes advantage of the "realistic" – in the words of Kracauer – aspect of analog photography, in order to support biased one-sided views. But then they add: "But there may be more to the story. The images standing out above the billions of other images scattered through media space cannot be exempt from the laws of power, but they may be reflecting other forms of social, political, and artistic consciousness as well. Perhaps they are works of art, more specifically, of public art grounded in the experience and aspirations of a democratic society and oriented toward the problems and rewards of ordinary life" (Hariman & Lucaites, 2007, p. 2–3).

But knowing this power of photojournalism, it was possible, in the following decades, to exploit it more in a more deliberate way. The wars ongoing in the 1990s, the first Gulf War and the war in the former Yugoslavia, differ in their iconosphere. During the war in the Persian Gulf in the 1990s, no images of suffering were shown, to avoid reactions similar to that of the Vietnam Era. Instead, technological power of the United States was emphasized, and photographs showing this technological aspect dominated the media.[2] There are images of attacking planes, aviation photographs showing hit targets from above meant to underline the precision of US bombers and that they were only targeting military objects. There are no images of civilians, no victims. Instead, there were images of the natural catastrophe which was caused by Iraq, the leaders of which ordered to light the oil wells in Kuwait. Media were using the sources shared with them by the military who managed and limited access to the information. Journalist David Levi Strauss (1991) said:

> The generals of the Vietnam era who conducted the Operation Desert Storm, realized that modern technologies of communication make it impossible to conduct war in an open way. The war of today needs to be hidden behind the impermeable veil of propaganda – no images of death, no destruction, no puddles of blood after raids (…), no orphans, no gangrene or naked little girls burnt by napalm.

Ultimately, due to its visual narrative, the war was nicknamed Video Game War. And that refers to the issue of truthfulness of its image and questions that image's relationship with the reality. Nevertheless, we cannot say that aviation photographs of the Gulf War are less accurate in their "realistic" (again in the words of Kracauer) aspect than the photograph of the naked girl in Vietnam. What is undermined here is the whole narrative – not the "single-base sentences" of Topolski – and the one-sided character of it, as well as the avoidance of confrontation with the ethical dimension of conducting a war. Such visual coverage poses a question about the "reality" of the war as such, which by many – exemplified by Jean Baudrillard – was believed to be a simulation of a war, the purpose of which was opposite – not to conduct a war. Baudrillard wrote: "There is one more problem for those who believe that this war really happened: how is it possible that a real war did not create real images?" (Baudrillard, 2006, p. 108). And then: "Electronic war does not have, precisely speaking, any political purpose *sensu stricto*: it serves as a preventive electric shock which is supposed to safeguard from the outbreak of a future conflict" (Baudrillard, 2006, p. 112).

The Balkans

On the other visual extreme, there is the war in the Balkans, which commenced around the same time. In photography, the war is very bloody and the suffering of civilians is omnipresent. Symptomatic is the way in which Tadeusz Mazowiecki, a special emissary of the United Nations for human rights in the territory of the former Yugoslavia, began the introduction to his reports from 1992 to 1993:

> Last summer, we all were shocked by the news which came from Bosnia and Hercegovina. The world saw the photos of gaunt people standing behind the wire fences of concentrations camps, of burnt houses in villages and towns, shelled temples, heard information about raping women and killing children (Mazowiecki, 1993, p. 9).

Mazowiecki refers, first of all, to the photos which have strong war connotations of a previously decided moral meaning. The photographs of "gaunt people standing behind the wire fences of concentrations camps" are a direct reference to the most iconic war photographs in the European history – the ones taken during the liberation of the Nazi concentration camps in 1945. Photographs with such background are made indisputable for the public opinion. This, on the one hand, is of course motivated by intentions related to the protection of human rights and thus morally justified, but, on the other hand, such images are clearly constructed to have such effect, they are not accidental, they quote other images to reinforce their message, and they are rhetorical statements. And that has to be very carefully taken into consideration when deciding about visual truthfulness of an image.

It turns out, from the analysis of all the photographs from the Balkan conflict which appeared in three weekly magazines: the European edition of American *Time*, German *Der Spigel*, and Polish *Wprost*, that there are actually some repeating patterns, the *visual topoi* that I already mentioned – such as "mother with child," "child with a gun," "funeral," "dead bodies," etc. These images work as Barthes' myths and create specific narrative about the war. Its general image was that of the suffering of civilians, first Bosnians and later Albanians. NATO and UN forces were presented only in a very positive way. We can read from these photographs a justification of any intervention of NATO (especially in Kosovo) – in a few cases in a very direct way, for example, by showing Albanians holding banners: "Help, NATO, help" (Time, 1998a). Another way of conveying the message about justified intervention is publication of images such as the photo depicting dying people in a bloodstained hall of a hospital or the photo from Kosovo meaningfully entitled "The massacre of the innocents" depicting killed children, with a caption "Will NATO strike this time?" (Time, 1998b). The NATO action in Kosovo was preceded by many photographs of Serbian crimes. Support of the public opinion, and avoiding antiwar protests, seemed very important. When we look at particular sides of the conflict, we can see a black-and-white vision. Photos in *Time*, *Der Spiegel* and *Wprost*, were more balanced but still followed the same tendency. Serbs were mainly shown as aggressors, killing, destroying, and committing ethnic cleansing. In general, there were more photos of civilians but these which depicted soldiers showed Serbs. There is only one photo of Muslim soldiers in the Time magazine in the entire analyzed period. The photo is captioned "Jubilation at least" and shows them in a very positive context while they are celebrating a victory (Time, 1994). This black-and-white image of the military forces was supported by the photographs of civilians. They were generally Bosnians, Croats, and Albanians and were depicted as victims. We cannot learn from these magazines much about the victims of the other Serbian side. In "Time," there are only few such examples, like a photograph of a crying widow of a Serbian policeman (Time, 1998c). *Der Spiegel* and *Wprost* are a bit more balanced but still the major part is the same: suffering citizens are mainly Bosnians, and soldiers are Serbs.

The most common of the *visual topoi* which builds up that view is the image of a mother with a child. It is actually an image which comes back in the visual coverage of most armed conflicts; however, in the reports from the Balkan conflict, it was particularly exploited. In European iconography, this motif is closely linked to Christianity and depictions of Virgin Mary with baby Jesus. In this context, motherhood means highest sanctity and love, warmth, and child's safety in the mother's arms. It is also one of the main archetypes of womanhood in Western culture. There have been hundreds and thousands of such iconic paintings and sculptures in the European history of art for many centuries (such as Rafael Santi's "Madonna Tempi" from 1507).[3] There are also instances when an image of Madonna with the infant Jesus became central to national myths or identities, like in the case of Poland where Black Madonna of Częstochowa is believed to be not only the protectress of child Jesus but also of the entire nation and proclaimed the queen of Poland by the king John II Casimir Vasa in 1656. As in other cases of images of Madonna with Jesus, the main meaning refers to the protecting powers of mothers.

In the iconography of the Balkan conflict as depicted in the press, images of mother with child appear usually to illustrate articles concerning refugees, when this pair is framed from a larger group of people – for instance, the cover of *Time* from April 12, 1999 depicting Albanian refugees from Kosovo.[4] The mother with a little baby in her arms seems as if she leads a group of refugees at the same time breastfeeding her baby. Her sight is directed forward, not only with courage and determination but also bitterness and sadness. The caption to this image again refers to potential intervention of the West into the conflict and says: "Are ground troops the answer?" The question seems rhetorical here, as the answer to it is the photograph.

In all of the cases, of course, the portrayed woman and the child were really in front of the camera of a photojournalist who decided to capture the scene, but who was also conditioned in his/her seeing by the iconosphere in which he/she was educated, in which the archetype of mother with child is strongly rooted and visualized. As Gombrich (1990) observed, we see what we have previously known. The pictures cited are, through their reference to objects' existence and presence in the captured moment, not only realistic but also, one can say, true. In the indexical meaning and according to the mechanism by which photography operates, Roland Barthes (Barthes, 2013) would say they are signs in which the *signifiant* is the image of a woman and a child we see, and the *signifie* is understanding it, according to captions given, as a Bosnian or Albanian mother with her child in the war which takes place in the Balkans. This is the level of sign. On this level, we comprehend just that. But employing all the aforementioned cultural meanings takes the pictures to the next level, according to Barthes, the level of myth. There, our sign becomes an empty form, a *signifiant* of the myth, while all that cultural meanings and references to the entire visual history constitute a new *signifie*. Taken together, they create a myth where the sign of the first level – a Bosnian/Albanian mother – is merged with the broader connotations of the *signifie* of the myth. Thus, the message is universalized and a particular historical moment is naturalized. The viewers are ascribing broader meanings to the case which is illustrated by that particular photograph. Bosnians and Albanians are then unequivocal moral winners of the situation, as no-one would discuss with the power of the Holy mother and her call for help. This way, the captions which prepare the public opinion for NATO's intervention become indisputable. Moreover, repetition of such images over the entire analyzed decade of different phases of the Balkan conflict reinforces it even more in the viewers' vision of that war. And, in fact, NATO's bombing of Serbian targets met with no antiwar protests in Europe.

But there were also other *topoi* with similar messages contributing to the overall image of the war in Western press – little boys with guns, pictures of funerals, old women in front of their ruined homes – signifying another archetype of womanhood in the Western culture: the guardian of home fireplace, here lamenting over her ruined home referring here to the entire country. There were not only images of everyday life under siege but also pictures of dead bodies referring to the oldest tradition of depicting suffering of civilians in war iconography which goes back, as aforementioned, to seventeenth century Europe. One of the images belonging to this category is the photograph depicting dead bodies of children lying among shrubs and cloths, entitled "Massacre of Innocents," from "Time" from

October 12, 1998, which additionally refers to the Biblical tradition, again recalling religious connotations. "Massacre of Innocents" is an event described in the Bible, in the Gospel of Matthew (2:16–18), according to which the king of Judea Herod the Great, wanting to get rid of the threat of newly born Jesus, orders to kill all male children below the age of 2. In Christianity, it is believed, although the event is by scholars considered a legend (Maier, 1998), that these killed children were the first Christian martyrs in the name of Jesus. Moreover, it is also a highly visual topic, as multiple paintings were created throughout the history of European art, with the most famous of Peter Rubens from 1611 to 1612. In it, like in the photograph from *Time*, murdered children lie on the ground among some clothes. The photograph under discussion is an illustration to the article beginning with the words: "More deaths in Kosovo produce more cries of outrage from the West. Will NATO strike this time?" Again, here, the good side and the bad side are clearly defined, and, what is more, the good side is given religious connotations which indirectly make them equal to martyrs. The image and all its cultural references and hitherto history of visual representations of the chosen topic leave the viewer with no arguments against, as the illustrated historical moment of the war in Kosovo is here universalized and taken to the level of main symbols of Western Christianity. This way, the authors of the photograph, not only the journalist which took it but also the editors of the magazine who chose the context for it, address Western viewer's deepest beliefs and moral standards and their visual imaginarium imprinted by education.

The general visual image of the Balkan conflict in the Western eyes is then a one-sided mythology, despite single pictures of victims of the other side found in the representative weeklies. The question is if we can talk about visual truth here. One the one hand, it is difficult to accuse the photographers of manipulations, especially that the war was portrayed in the pre-digital era. We can safely say that the captured events and scenes really happened. Also, very often photographs were motivated by journalist ideals and ethical standards both of the profession and of being an emphatic human. Once again referring to Kracauer (1995) and Topolski (1998), we can say that the pictures are true in their foundations. However, the narrative they became a part of, the entire context of other pictures, articles they illustrate, and captions that accompany them, shed a whole new light on them. The truth that the visual narrative of Western press is proclaiming has a pretension to be the only one. Its goals are political. There is a conflict here between being a witness of an evident violation of human rights by Serbs – what was emphasized in the previously recalled words of the UN emissary – accompanied by the feeling of relief which is provided to the viewer by a possibility of NATO intervention, and lack of representation of the atrocities committed by the other side of the conflict. Visual truth turns out to be conditional once again.

Abu Ghraib

The war in the former Yugoslavia might be the last media war in traditional meaning, where the art of creating politically desired images was perfected. It can also be called the last media war. In Iraq, journalists are no longer exclusive reporters of war events. The development of the Internet also undermines the role of paper press and changes the modes of communication and information flow, symptomatic of technological developments and cultural shifts. As in the 1910s/ 1920s, the invention of the 35-mm camera, easily portable, popularized photography and photojournalism and made it possible to report events on a daily basis and without long exposure times; in the 2000s, popularization of mobile phone and small affordable digital cameras took away from journalists their monopoly on visual news and developed so-called citizen journalism, especially in the form of citizen photojournalism. As Bowman and Willis (2003) wrote:

> The venerable profession of journalism finds itself at a rare moment in history where, for the first time, its hegemony as gatekeeper of the news is threatened by not just new technology and competitors but, potentially, by the audience it serves. Armed with easy-to-use Web publishing tools, always-on connections and increasingly powerful mobile devices, the online audience has the means to become an active participant in the creation and dissemination of news and information.

Citizens provided live visual coverage in the case of the 9/11 attack on the World Trade Center in New York, contributing to the iconosphere of Western culture. Soldiers also became authors of visual records of war, very often using cameras as just one more weapon. In 2004, the world was shocked once again by war photography, in a similar way than during the war in Vietnam, as photographs of prisoners of war kept in custody in Abu Ghraib, Iraq, and tortured by American soldiers occupying the country began to circulate, disseminated by the soldiers committing the acts of torture themselves. They were first showed on the CBS television on April 28, 2004 and a few days later published in *The New Yorker*.[5] Despite reports of the International Committee of Red Cross, journalists, and protests of other humanitarian organizations about tortures carried out by Americans in Iraq, there was little interest from American authorities or US public opinion. Susan Sontag (2004) noticed in her famed text that it was the photographs which made it "real" to them. People were not prepared for this form of activity, taking photos, done by soldiers, despite the fact that photographs taken by perpetrators of their victims go back to the Second World War and Nazi photographs and to the photographs of lynching in America which were made to serve as trophies. But in the digital age, their dissemination accelerated and became global. Pictures again proved to be more likely to be trusted to reveal the truth than words.

The discussion, however, was not about the truthfulness of the pictures as such, but about the story behind them and their context. Were they representative for only a small number of sadistic events, or where they representative for the entire system employed by the American administration in the war on terror? The investigations were carried out, which proved a systemic character of the doings exemplified by the photographs. However, the discussion among the public opinion remained ongoing, despite more and more evidence, not necessarily visual. Mark Danner argues that the power of the photographs was two-edged. He writes:

> (...) though the photographs first announced Abu Ghraib to the world and gave impetus to the investigation of what happened there, as the months passed and more evidence accumulated the images have increasingly had the opposite effect, helping to block a full public understanding of how the scandal arose and how what Americans did at Abu Ghraib was ultimately tied to what they had been doing in Afghanistan, Guantánamo, and elsewhere in the "war on terror" – and, finally, to what officials had been deciding in Washington. (Danner, 2004, p. xiii)

So, an image can both reveal and conceal the truth. The truth, as this example shows, can be a matter of choice. The agreed truthfulness of a photograph in its indexical meaning opens up a political discussion. But that is already a symptom of a new mode of society – the post-truth society where the choice of what one wants to believe is political, not grounded in evidence, which, in the public discourse, can be now ignored and brought down to mere interpretation of reality.

Images Today

Images today continue to be susceptible to the rules of the past: they have those same semiotic levels, and most people still believe in the myth of visual truth and the witnessing aspect of photography, no matter what interpretations of them they choose to believe. We increasingly deal with what philosopher Wolfgang Welsch (1998) called anesthetics, which is the result of more and more prevalent presence of images in our lives. When we Google "Syria 2020," we will find hundreds of photographs showing war destruction.[6] Images like this have connotations referring to the imagery of the Second World War and cities such as destroyed Warsaw or Dresden. They also bring to mind similar photographs from the Balkan conflict. When, in turn, we Google "Syria refugees," we will get hundreds of images of Syrian people traveling on foot across the world with their belongings or staying in refugees' camps. These photographs also bring to mind previous similar images, the closest of which are those from the former Yugoslavia. However, while on the one hand the audiences of these images subconsciously read these visual references, they do not care any longer. Public opinion is no longer shocking, nor does it necessarily feel any empathy for the victims of that war, as the reactions of parts of European societies and some governments in recent years have shown.

We have been subjected to so many similar images that we have become immune to them: on the one hand, the images lose their power to inspire action, and we in turn take what we see for granted, and we do it more subconsciously. Visuality has become so inherent to our everyday experience, particularly through the mass take-up of social media, that people absorb images in a noncritical way that they do not inspire them to any reaction any longer. Anesthetics is the mode of contemporary visual communication. Today, aestheticization happens as anaesthetization – the state resulting from an excess of experiences and content present in culture and from their schematization, leading to intensification of the experience of the world and then, in effect, to indifference to too many stimuli to paralysis of sensitivity. In such a state, receivers are unable to critically decode images seen around and are more vulnerable not only to the "natural" tendency of images to simplify the world but also to conscious manipulations which happen in the realm of digital iconosphere. In such cases, in turn, even the indexical reference of an image is nonexistent and the image itself is a mere simulation. Nevertheless, the myth of visual truth of photography and the nature of human perception make people instinctively believe such images. It is particularly important then to raise the issue of visual truth, not to say that it is gone or was never here, but to develop visual literacy and critical approaches to visuality and reinforce ethical standards in creation of visual narratives.

Notes

1. See http://www.apimages.com/metadata/Index/Watchf-AP-I-VNM-APHS021000-Vietnam-Napalm-1972/e674e44489a54fbca89b41a7d821b89e/168/0
2. See https://commons.m.wikimedia.org/wiki/File:Gulf_War_Photobox.jpg#
3. See https://commons.m.wikimedia.org/wiki/File:Tempi_Madonna_by_Raffaello_Sanzio_-_Alte_Pinakothek_-_Munich_-_Germany_2017.jpg
4. See http://content.time.com/time/magazine/0,9263,7601990412,00.html
5. See https://commons.m.wikimedia.org/wiki/File:Abu_Ghraib_17a.jpg#mw-jump-to-license
6. Example: https://www.gettyimages.com/detail/news-photo/an-aerial-view-of-the-buildings-destroyed-by-the-assad-news-photo/613097156

References

Barthes, R. (2013). *Mythologies*. New York, NY: Hill & Wang.

Baudrillard, J. (2006). *Wojny w Zatoce nie było*. Warsaw: Wydawnictwo Sic!.

Bowman, S., & Willis, C. (2003). We media: How audiences are shaping the future of news and information. The Media Center at the American Press Institute. Retrieved from http://www.hypergene.net/wemedia/weblog.php

Danner, M. (2004). *Torture and truth. America, Abu Ghraib, and the war on terror*. New York, NY: The New York Review of Books.

Gombrich, E. (1990). Obraz wizualny. In M. Głowiński (Ed.), *Symbole i symbolika*. Warszawa: Czytelnik.

Hariman, R., & Lucaites, J. L. (2007). *No caption needed. Iconic photographs, public culture, and liberal democracy*. Chicago, IL: The University of Chicago Press.

Kracauer, S. (1995). *History. The last things before the last*. Princeton, NJ: Markus Wiener.

Levi Strauss, D. (1991). Bezkrwawa wojna, Fotografia 6x9. 5, vol. X–XII.

Maier, P. L. (1998). Herod and the infants of Bethlehem. In R. Summers & J. Vardaman (Eds.), *Chronos, Kairos, Christos II: Chronological, nativity, and religious studies in memory of Ray summers*. Macon, GA: Mercer University Press.

Mazowiecki, T. (1993). *Raporty Tadeusza Mazowieckiego z byłej Jugosławii*. Poznań-Warszawa: Fundacja "Promocja Praw Człowieka – Badania i Nauczanie" and Agencja Scholar.

Newton, J. H. (1998). The burden of visual truth: The role of photojournalism in mediating reality. *Visual Communication Quarterly, 5*, 4.

Sontag, S. (2004). Regarding the tortures of others. *New York Times*, May 23. Retrieved from https://www.nytimes.com/2004/05/23/magazine/regarding-the-torture-of-others.html

Time. (1994, November 14). *Time Magazine, 144*(20).

Time. (1998a, June 22). *Time Magazine, 151*(24).

Time. (1998b, October 12). *Time Magazine, 152*(15).

Time. (1998c, April 6). *Time Magazine, 151*(13).

Topolski, J. (1998). *Wprowadzenie do hitorii*. Poznań: Wydawnictwo Poznańskie.

Welsch, W. (1998). Estetyka i Anestetyka. In R. Nycz (Ed.), *Postmodernizm. Antologia przekładów*. Kraków.

Wrzosek, W. (2010). Źródło historyczne jako alibi realistyczne historyka. In J. Kolbuszewska & R. Stobiecki (Eds.), *Historyk wobec źródeł. Historiografia klasyczna i nowe propozycje metodologiczne*. Łódź: Wydawnictwo Ibidem.

Chapter 15

It Is Time for Journalists to Save Journalism

Lina Zuluaga and Phillip D. Long

Abstract

The current environment of misinformation is causing expensive and negative consequences for society. Fake news is affecting democracy and its
foundations, as well as newspapers and media companies that aim to combat
this "pandemic." In order to effectively provide accurate information, these
companies are in need of a workforce with specific attitudes, skills, and
knowledge (ASK). However, several studies show that students either do not
have those ASK or have poorly developed them, indicating the need for
better media literacy skills. Given that such skills are often not taught in
school, nor is there a way for students to efficiently obtain them and tangibly
show them to future employers, we propose a model[1] that enhances the way
students learn and how we measure such learning. Journalism students –
enrolled in liberal arts, general studies, and humanities – have the potential
to be upskilled and become the new critical thinking and fact-checking force
needed to neutralize misinformation and foster a healthy society. Our model
applies learning science and behavioral research on feedback and intrinsic
motivation to foster students' ASK through a digital apprenticeship model
that uses structured activities together with mentorship and feedback. Students participate in the creation of digital products for the journalism and
news media industry. This prepares them for the types of tasks they will be
required to perform in the job market. The digital apprenticeship matches
students with the proper mentor, peer, and professional network. Students'
work is compared against professional news media production to generate
feedback, improve quality, and track progress. During the digital apprenticeship, students receive the ASK-*SkillsCredit,* a digital badge, which serves
as a "nutritional" fact label that displays how students created the media
content, the level of efficacy of the apprenticeship, and the standard of
journalism quality of the piece. Lastly, we propose to enhance existing

Media, Technology and Education in a Post-Truth Society, 203–221
Copyright © 2021 by Emerald Publishing Limited
doi:10.1108/978-1-80043-906-120211015

learning management systems to capture and promote a learner's profile data and expose aligned opportunities in news media outlets.

Keywords: Working-based learning; tutoring; apprenticeship; digital learning; blockchain; certifications; news media industry; career readiness

Introduction

The current environment of misinformation is causing expensive and negative consequences for society. Dov H. Levin, a Carnegie Mellon scholar, has researched the historical record for both overt and covert election influence operations (Shane, 2018).

> At least 27 countries have had some sort of election manipulation by fake news. People made their decision based on manipulated media targeted at moving their feelings, instead of providing them with the means to make an informed decision.

There were allegations of fake news that exacerbated polarization in social perceptions in the 2016 US presidential election (Allcott & Gentzkow, 2017). Fake news of any kind weakens democracy by diminishing social trust and spurring intense partisanship. Moreover, fake news also imposes a social cost to citizens who are facing growing barriers to knowing and comprehending the state of world affairs.

The issue of fake news is also affecting the newspapers and media companies that aim to combat this "epidemic." To effectively provide accurate information, media outlets are in need of a workforce with attitudes, new tech skills (Strada Institute, 2019), and knowledge that journalists do not have or which are poorly developed. Research on students from middle school through college across 12 states in the United States found that students did not know how to find the sources for the information they were reading, nor how to determine if the sources were credible and unbiased (Wineburg, McGrew, Breakstone, & Ortega, 2016). The results from such studies demonstrate that students need better media literacy skills. However, such skills are not often explicitly taught in school, nor is there a way for students to obtain them and tangibly show them to future employers.

Huckle and White (2017) propose 'Provenator,' a blockchain application to verify digital content. However, in their paper they readily acknowledge that technology is not enough: human skills are needed. Using the BBC as a case study, they show how, in complicated contexts such as the Syrian conflict, journalism depends on specific human skills that technology cannot replace. Technology has helped the BBC reach places their journalists cannot access due to security issues. However, in order to validate the "user-generated content," journalists have had to learn a new set of skills.

Not all newspapers or media outlets have had the opportunity, or the means, to build the workforce needed to provide efficient fact-checking. Some have tried to do so with technology, but technological only solutions have not necessarily solved the problem – and in some cases are likely to have exacerbated it. Facebook, for instance, while countering the propaganda in the run-up to the 2016 US election found that its algorithms were not always spotting fake stories (Huckle & White, 2017). To curate the news items appearing on its platform, Facebook claims it has to rely on human editors.

These technologies, though a resource for verifying authenticity of a story, will only be capable of providing a partial solution to the problem of fake news. Full fact-checking and corroboration takes human skills such as "evaluating information" (Wineburg et al., 2016).[2] The traditional meaning of information literacy is being challenged to consider changes in technology, format, delivery mechanism, the collaborative nature of information sharing, affective learning, and more.[3]

Given this context, we propose a model to close the gap between what news companies need and the skills journalists must acquire in college. The model describes a way to bring journalism students and media companies together in order to strengthen integrity in the process of content production and reduce misinformation. In turn, students will be given a real-world challenge that prepares them for a global career. Additionally, the model proposes the insertion of traceable metadata to verify the students' acquired level of attitudes, skills, and knowledge (ASK).

Why Does This Problem Matter? Key Attributes of the Problem

We have to accept that "democracy requires more effort than just casting a vote every few years" says Moises Naim, former executive director of the World Bank (Naim, 2019). That is why newspapers and media companies play a vital role in contributing to functional and sustainable societies. In a way, journalism and the mass media industry act – or should act – as democracy's immune system (Newmark, 2013). Just as the immune system protects the human body from the harmful effects of foreign invading organisms, journalism and the mass media industry should protect democracy by efficiently and accurately identifying fake news that threaten the well-being or functioning of the body politic. Once misinformation is identified, news outlets together with other actors (such as those in higher education) should work to target those threats, exposing or isolating them and, if necessary, eradicating them before they can damage democracy.

Taking this notion as the basis of our argument, we find a compelling reason to diligently work toward nourishing the news and media world and engaging in that purpose with other stakeholders. Goldin and Katz (2007) describe in the book *The Race Between Education and Technology* the incapability of the education system to keep up with the pace of the technological progress. Running economical analysis of decades of data, it is evident that advanced technologies were not embedded in the education offer. Universities play a key role in the pipeline for the new workforce, yet are not adapting quickly enough to the changing demands of the job market, with the result that students are not developing sufficient capability for the needed skills. For instance, as reported by the Georgetown University Center on Education and the Workforce, some 43% of college grads are underemployed on their first job (Korn, 2018) and "the majority of entry-level jobs require a rich mix of formal postsecondary education along with high-quality work experience, preferably matched to an individual's career pathway or postsecondary field of study" (Carnevale & Smith, 2018, p. 7).

Some universities still believe that:

> ... [it] is wonderful and important for employers to develop their employees' skills, but colleges and universities need not take notice, because these efforts are irrelevant to collegiate education goals and purpose. They think assessing skills cannot and should not be done outside the context of the subjects one should study in college. (Neem, 2018)

Yet, out of the 56.7 million Americans that were in the freelance economy in 2018, 93% of those with a college degree considered training to be more relevant to their work than their degree (Edelman Intelligence, 2018).

The system focuses primarily on a unidirectional delivery of knowledge (conventional), but students also need to acquire skills "in context," and they also need to learn social skills and attitudes that enable them to collaborate with others. As noted by Bransford, Brown, and Cocking (2000), the actual learning process crystallizes when students can relate their skills to specific contexts where they can be used. This may be a reason why direct training was more useful for freelancers with a college degree, given that they received knowledge directly linked with a task.

Another challenge is that, traditionally, universities have been designed in silos. The pressure to maintain specialized departments has contributed to a diminished capacity for interdisciplinary education, interdepartmental collaboration, relevant application and knowledge exchange, both within the university and with external stakeholders. Such absence of a fluid flow of information, knowledge, and talent between higher education areas and recruiters – governments, small businesses, think tanks, companies – has significant consequences. Students may be missing out in acquiring important skills because they are taught in a different department or because the academy is unaware of the demands of the job market. Even if college students possess the ASK needed in the workplace – or workspace in a freelance digital economy – and could contribute in the construction of valuable content, there is a lack of transparent, verifiable information on students' interests, learning outcomes and content creation abilities; for instance, current transcripts report on student "seat time" (the number of hours completed) as opposed to learning outcomes or subject mastery. Important indicators, such as the number of hours of writing, or the number of papers mentored by professors actually written, are not reflected in transcripts. Indeed, to develop concrete ASK and demonstrate these achievements, students need a system of mentors, peers, and a professional network to review, measure, and endorse their effort and level of expertise in a trustable way.

A Real-life Example

In 2018, the Inter-American Development Bank (IADB) in Washington, DC, implemented successfully some elements of the model presented in this paper, by using a TalentoLab structured activity in an online small and private online course, SPOC, called Communicating Effective Educational Policies. Universities' presidents, journalists, economists and philanthropists were the learners grouped based on complementary skills, and they were guided in an one-to-one tutoring activity to publish a news report using interactive data software. The activity used working-based-learning and formative assessment.[4]

In this respect, we focus on the need to exchange information between universities and media outlets and discuss the characteristics that would enable a fluid collaboration between them to allow students to secure the requisite skills for the job market and demonstrate their achievements in a practical and traceable way.

For us, the new basic currency in the digital society comprises the Attitudes, Skills and Knowledge (ASK) a human possesses. Our interest is in investigating how universities may contribute to the development of this currency for each student and alumni in a lifelong learning ecosystem.

What Others Have Done

In the following section we describe the solutions others have presented. Later we will explain our model and its benefit compared to existing solutions.

Digital Badges

Badges were used in the Army and the Boy Scouts (and today, Girl Scouts) to highlight levels of achievement. Digital badges are a "representation of an accomplishment, interest, or affiliation that is visual and available online, containing metadata including links to the context, meaning, process, and result of an activity" (Gibson, Ostashewski, Flintoff, Grant, & Knight, 2015). According to Shields and Chugh (2017), digital badges are quickly becoming an appropriate, easy, and efficient way for educators, community groups, and other professional organizations to exhibit and reward participants for skills obtained in professional development or formal and informal learning. However, digital badges do not necessarily incentivize learners to engage in positive behavior or identify progress in learning and content trajectories. Badges are not always attached to a larger assessment system where students can cobuild activities visible to others (i.e., employers, mentors, and peers) or in which third parties may rank ASK between badge holders.

Reflecting the interest to connect education and the workplace, in 2011, the US Secretary of Education announced the launch of the HASTAC/MacArthur Foundation Badges for Lifelong Learning Competition. In 2015, in collaboration with the Mozilla Foundation, the state of California started a coalition of the community college system, state government, and business community to provide input on digital badge assessments for the "Top 10" 21st Century Skills – Adaptability, Analysis/Solution Mindset, Collaboration, Communication, Digital Fluency, Empathy, Entrepreneurial Mindset, Resilience, Self-Awareness, Social/ Diversity Awareness.

Kudos

In 2016, Sharples and Domingue from the Open University (OU) published a paper on educational reputation currency, which they named "kudos." The "badge" concept was repurposed as a unit in a Student Learning Passport, which contains information about what students have learned and how they have acquired specific skills. More recent OU research focuses on experiments to add OpenLearn badges to a private blockchain.[5] Blockchain technology can be deployed as a tool to track intellectual work and leverage a nonfungible token that represents intellectual currency. As the OU's learning platform, OpenLearn hosts over 800 free courses and attracts over five million visitors per year; this provides an opportunity for OU to build their Open Blockchain in which all transactions are time stamped and are cryptographically signed. The transactions are peer-to-peer in principle. No host institution is required for the awarding of accreditation. Future work will integrate badges from other institutions including FutureLearn and optionally place badges onto the public Ethereum blockchain.

The Open University continues to be involved in numerous research projects looking at the applicability of blockchain to build transparency in course records. However, rankings, course grades, digital badges, credentials, degrees, and e-portfolios are all subject to a systemic weakness, in defining the level of competence work has to demonstrate in order to complete a task or a class. The digital and freelance economy makes it more challenging to keep pace with all forms of education design and their signs of completion. A codesigned system between education and the workplace could eliminate the time lag between the skills in demand and the current curriculum.

Our Application of the Model

Even though both the digital badges and kudos systems address some of the issues associated with tracking students' learning, they lack a trusted verification of ASK. They may represent the academic knowledge a student is meant to learn, but "valid or important knowledge now is different from prior forms of knowledge, particularly academic knowledge" (Bates, 2015, quoting Downes 2007). Knowledge is increasingly not static but dynamic, and it is difficult for colleges to nurture the needed ASK underlying professional performance.

We propose a digital apprenticeship bridge that allows students, universities, and recruiters to both track and compare the dynamic ASK among participants. Our application of the model focuses on the development of a career in journalism and news media outlets, whereby students, universities, and newsrooms may secure a mutual understanding of the value of the artifacts learners create during their apprenticeship. Our model brings together mentoring, through an apprenticeship, with technology, in order to promote: (1) lifelong learning; (2) a method to teach students skills that are currently needed in the job market; and (3) a solution to track and value students' ASK in a collaborative way between academics and employers using blockchain. Our proposal enhances the way we measure students' learning by embedding a formative assessment, based on learning science and behavioral research on feedback and intrinsic motivation, into structured activities (apprenticeship model). Existing learning management systems (LMSs) are leveraged to match students with the proper mentor, peer, and professional network to deepen their current ASK.

For the education–workplace connection to function, universities should include a system that articulates courses, curriculum, and assessment to enrich the metadata of the digital badge. This enables other institutions and employers to secure a tangible description of students' competencies. 63% of Americans believe what employers, facing difficulty in recruiting, have known for some time – there is a skills shortage in the workforce. This requires innovative thinking and resolute changes in public policy.[6] Economists, demographers, and political leaders are increasingly concerned that the next generation of workers will not be able to fill millions of new jobs across the United States. The combination of a generational and demographic change in the workforce and a technological revolution in the economy is conspiring to create a skills and talent pipeline gap that could leave jobs unfilled. Between 2002 and 2016, the shares of US jobs that require substantial digital knowledge rose rapidly, mostly due to large changes in the digital content of existing occupations (Muro, Liu, Whiton, & Kulkarni, 2017).

Advancement in technology also expands access to learning opportunities by making it possible to study and learn independent of time and place. There is an increased offering of open educational resources (OERs), online courses, credentials, certificates, and badges with the potential to become stackable and be transformative to close the digital skills gap.

A Korn Ferry report in 2018 stated that technology, media, and telecommunications (TMT) will fall short of 4.3 million workers worldwide by 2030.[7] The digital skills gap is already hampering digital transformation in 54% of companies, with the gap widening: the TMT industries may already be short of more than 1.1 million skilled workers globally. Fast forward to 2030, and that deficit may reach 4.3 million, or 59 times Alphabet's entire workforce. In total, these shortages are predicted to cost the TMT industries $449.7 billion in unrealized revenue.

Students will participate in the creation of content products for the journalism and news media industry. The ASK-*SkillsCredit* badge serves as the requisite standard or "nutritional" label of the student's media content that is verified and secured on the blockchain. Students' work will be compared against professional news media production to generate feedback to improve quality and to track progress and effort. This will create a marketplace of talent and content that is vetted by mentors, peers, and news media professionals. As digital apprenticeships are designed for lifelong learning, learners continue to receive training recommendations automated by the system based on new skills in demand in the marketplace. Learners are guided from universities to the workplace to become the new force to neutralize fake news and foster a healthy society.

To secure ASK-*SkillsCredit* – the new currency to trace ASK acquired – students will be assigned to a mentor in the journalism field or a news organization. The learning interactions will take place through LMSs. The outcomes generated from such interactions (actual journalism work) are reviewed by the mentor, who determines the student's competency on the basis of a formative assessment methodology. The badge, the ASK-*SkillsCredit,* reflects the level of progress.

We believe that this model will have a positive impact on lifelong learning, curriculum updates, and ASK verification.

Lifelong Learning

Our digital apprenticeship model is not a regular internship, or a sum of work experiences disconnected from the learning journey of the student. Rather, it combines the evidence from the effectiveness of tutorial learning and the power of the contextual and experiential learning in the workspace.

In 1984, Bloom observed that the *tutoring process demonstrates that most of the students do have the potential to reach this high level of learning. I believe an important task of research and instruction is to seek ways of accomplishing this under more practical and realistic conditions than the one-to-one tutoring, which is too costly for most societies to bear on a large scale.* Bloom's revolutionary founding continues to be applicable to current adaptive learning technologies.

As illustrated in Bloom (1984), the achievements of students engaged in a tutorial instruction are comparably higher than regular learning (in a standard classroom) or mastery learning.

> (1) Conventional. Students learn the subject matter in a class with about 30 students per teacher. Tests are given periodically for marking the students.

> (2) Mastery Learning. Students learn the subject matter in a class with about 30 students per teacher. The instruction is the same as in the conventional class (usually with the same teacher). Formative tests (the same tests used with the conventional group) are given for feedback followed by corrective procedures and parallel formative tests to determine the extent to which the students have mastered the subject matter.

(3) Tutoring. Students learn the subject matter with a good tutor for each student (or for two or three students simultaneously) This tutoring instruction is followed periodically by formative tests, feedback-corrective procedures, and parallel formative tests as in the mastery learning classes, It should be pointed out that the need for corrective work under tutoring is very small. (Bloom, 1984, p. 4)

To stimulate student interest in the digital apprenticeship, we design activities and interactions based on Harlow's (1950) experiment results and Pink's (2011) explanation of the three basic drives: 1. *biological drive*, when humans and other animals ate to satiate their hunger, drank to quench their thirst, and copulated to satisfy their carnal urges; 2. *external drive*, based on rewards and punishment and is extensively used in traditional education and business incentives; and 3. *intrinsic motivation*. The third drive reveals how performing a task provides an intrinsic reward, this satisfaction activates the self motivation to keep performing the task for the sake of learning better how to improve on the perform of the task. Our application of the model connects the role of the tutor showing how to perform the task (I do), then the tutor and the learners perform the task together (we do), and finally, the learners should perform the task themselves (you do). They gain the self confidence and the clarity on the task and gain intrinsic motivation to keep going with this lifelong learning skill. All this happens in the context of structured activities or real-world challenges (working-based-learning). Digital games, for instance, are practical applications of this research on the third drive, and we propose to do the same with the digital apprenticeship, with students retaining the interaction with tutors and seeing their progress in the performance of specific tasks in their ASK dashboard.

Teaching Students the Skills Needed in the Job Market

In order to close the existing gap between the skills students acquire and the skills needed in the job market, our method proposes that students engage in real-life work, tutored and mentored through the digital apprenticeship; this is essential to understand and gain the skills needed to secure meaningful and gainful employment after graduation. Levering on Raish and Rimland (2016) and Wineburg et al. (2016), we can integrate such labor market skills in demand into the curriculum by adding the digital apprenticeship, that includes structured activities were learners gain metaliteracy skills such as: communication; problem-solving; synthesizing information; evaluating information (a critical skill to combat fake news and the cornerstone of civic online reasoning); and media and digital literacy. We propose to use existing technology to increase feedback interactions in order to boost students' ability to gain such skills and create a space where this information can be evaluated.

In the study *Saving the Associate Arts (A.A.) Degree,* Schneider and Sigelman (2018) acknowledge the importance of programs that add elective skills-based courses or embed high-value, industry-recognized certifications into the courses of colleges and universities study. According to federal data cited in the same study, community colleges awarded over 670,000 associate degrees during the 2014–2015 academic year. Around 289,000 (over 40 percent) of associate degrees awarded by community colleges in the United States were in a single field of study: liberal arts, general studies, and humanities. Digital skills are not included in the tradition curriculums. The study recommends three ways to increase the wage opportunities: (1) identifying the marketable skills that are most in demand in local labor markets – and communicating that information to students; (2) embedding these marketable skills in the curricula of A.A. programs; and (3) establishing strong ties with local employers, both to increase awareness of needed skills and to provide avenues for students into employment. Skills-credits courses are exemplified throughout the study.

Our application of the model will insert the digital apprenticeship in the curriculum of liberal arts programs. This will be the avenue to bring industry certifications into the structured activity tutored by real-world skilled experts.

We believe that learners can get training and be ready earlier to earn. For example, Salesforce,[8] a leading CRM tech company, owns a Learning Management System (LMS) called Trailhead, which releases "digital badges" to acknowledge the level of competency of learners completing courses on Digital Marketing, Data Visualization,[9] etc. News media industry, and in the Creative and Culture Industry (CCI), those skills are in high demand,[10] that is why in our application of the model we embed that type of industry certifications into the digital apprenticeship, and into the liberal arts program's curriculum.

Assessment and Verification of Attitudes, Skills, and Knowledge (ASK)

To track the ASK gained by students during the digital apprenticeship, the model builds a visual and dynamic badge dashboard that pulls data from the apprenticeship and from other data sources that universities gather from formal or informal learning interactions during the students' journey to enrich the mentor/student match for the apprenticeship, and intentionally embed a formative assessment. Part of our model focuses on the belief that the ASK-*SkillsCredit* represents a more comprehensive, dynamic, and market-responsive proposition compared to standard resume. Specifically future employers will be able to evaluate the actual competences candidates possess and identify the work performed in acquiring those skills.

The ASK-*SkillsCredit* Dashboard

Our model proposes that the Universal Learner Record (ULR), in development by Arizona State University (ASU) and piloted in a collaborative proof of concept with Salesforce could be leveraged to capture and promote a learner's profile data and expose aligned opportunities in the digital apprenticeship bridge between the university and the news media outlet (Komarny, 2019).

The ULR data model is incorporated into a blockchain and can be accessed directly from the Lightning™ user interface or via an open API to generate an

ASK badge. The student's record is updated, and the credential made available for release in the online version of the media outlet. In the process, the student benefits from the following standard blockchain features:

(1) Immutability – the unchangeable nature of the records committed to the blockchain
(2) Encryption and Merkle hashing – records are locked or "chained" together such that any attempt to alter any record can be easily discovered; and when discovered, any further commitment of records to the system is stopped until the situation is resolved.
(3) Distributed design – no one institution is responsible for maintaining a learner's record. It is a shared responsibility between all partners of the permissioned network to make the design more sustainable and resilient.
(4) Linked to the ASK badge assertion by a Content Identifier (CID) to the student's work stored in an associated publicly accessible distributed peer-to-peer file system (IPFS), providing the most robust strategy for future proofing and guaranteed availability of this information.[11]

The Civil Media company (n.d.) is a news media company already using block-chain and digital currencies. They are in need of a pipeline of a "newsforce" of talent. That is why we will implement the digital apprenticeship bridge between news media companies and higher education institutions. The dashboard is the architecture of data points traced when applying our model and articulated with the existing ULR and accessed by students via their LMS at their institution, for their particular curriculum and course. The collaboration between universities and newspapers in this shared effort will enable the following:

(1) Students to match mentors and tutors for skills development (fact-checking, diversity checking, and fostering digital and media literacy skills);
(2) Verification of those skills (Wilson, Kurzweil, & Alamuddi, 2018);
(3) Showcase of skills in an e-portfolio[12] to offer visibility of student profiles to potential employers, such as the mass media industry;
(4) Position the e-portfolio as a repository for recruitment and assessing value for monetary compensation.

The ASK-*SkillsCredit* badge will be updated with the following:

(1) Academic credit: credit validated by universities or academic institutions that prove acquired ASK. It measures the level of competency of ASK.
(2) Publishing and reputation credit: recognition of authorship by news outlets for a published piece. It measures if students satisfactorily apply their ASK in a journalistic job task.
(3) Monetary value credit: skills become valuable credit in the market, with students' acquired skills rendered tangible and comparable. In a freelance economy, value credit shows reputation and can eventually be converted into monetary rewards.[13]

Fig. 15.1 provides the data points that pulled with the ULR generate the student ASK baseline diagnosis before entry in the digital apprenticeship. It connects the institutional, curricular, and course elements of the three areas for learning design (attitudes, skills, and knowledge).[14]

The *Attitudes* column meaningfully articulates data collected in the admission process, such as students' motivations, interests, and passions. With this information, we can match students with networks that enhance their attitudes through mentoring, volunteering, and a buddy system. Data points could come from the admission center, career center, alumni, and well-being center.

The *Skills* column measures tutoring interactions and outcomes: time, frequency, and evidence of learning in media production and digital skills.

The *Knowledge* column traces updated sources of interdisciplinary information to provide theory related to journalism and communications, which will complement students' practical work. This includes professor's traditionally assigned grades and the latest scientific research produced in papers, reports, MOOCs, and interactions with a PhD network, such as Academia.edu members.

Our project architects a complete learning framework for the digital apprenticeship bridge to news media outlets.

The attitudes component of the Digital Apprenticeship: to support the career pathway from learners going from colleges to newsrooms is composed by a baseline assessment connected to the formative assessment along with the traditional study program.[15,16] Preferences exist not only in these built-in forms shared with other living beings but in distinctly human ways (Banaji & Heiphetz, 2010). Since attitudes guide behavior and intentions drive contribution, our model helps learners know themselves better and identify the team or organization that best complements them.

The skills component of the Digital Apprenticeship is composed by a performance analysis of "best in class" journalists such as the Pulitzer Prize awarded Katie Kingsbury and by an adjustable list of microcredentials (stackable certifications such as the Salesforce one mentioned before) that are curated from existing technologies in high demand, among them:

> Basic digital tools: Google IT; Digital marketing and fundraising: Salesforce; Data visualization: Tableau; Datasketch; Video editing: iMovie; Adobe Premiere and Final Cut Pro; Data Cleaning: OpenRefine; Text mining: Voyant; SameDiff; and HathiTrust Research Center; Journalism, audience and information veracity or fact check: Poynter ACES Certificate in Accurate, Audience-Focused Editing. BBC Apprenticeships[17]

The knowledge component of the Digital Apprenticeship is based on academically researched theories, including: mass communications (Marshall McLuhan); gatekeeping theory (Kurt Zadek Lewin); multimodal discourse and interaction analysis (Frederick Erickson); microaffirmations (Mary Rowe); connectivism (George Siemens), memes-cultural genes (Richard Dawkins); and on emerging theories on fact-checking and practice (Dong, Kementsietsidis, & Tan, 2016).[18]

Level	Attitudes	Skills	Knowledge
Instituti onal	GRIT-Resilience and counseling Lifelong admission center	Apprenticeship Center (work study hours)	Content Curation Center (MOOC and Digital Content)
	Career Development Center (Outplacement, soft skills)	On-the-Job human resources partnership center	Design Studio (Editing and multimedia conversion)
	Mentorship and Alumni Center	Bank of Projects Center/Entrepreneur/ Writing Center	Research Center Connection (Source of: new knowledge, new readings, new syllabus)
	Community Engagement Center	Incubator	Center for Learning and Teaching
	Well-being Center	Venture	Academic Success center
Curricul um	Institutional team checklist and edits	Co-designed work breakdown structure and 7 version of final project assessment	Updatable syllabus-MOOC and online module-Creative
	Growth mindset methodology for assessment	Cross-cutting courses-Intercultural Knowledge and Global Thinking**	Learning type activity
	Civic engagement** and ethical reasoning**	Integrative Learning**	VALUE Rubrics**
Course	Counselor or academic advisor 30 minutes every 2 weeks scheduled	Job Description – on-the-job learning	Learning Analytics
	Volunteering activity-Foundational and skills for Lifelong learning	e-portfolio	Apprenticeship Teaching Module
	Student representative (making the most of College or U resources)-Learning Type, Background and Interests-Teamwork**	Peer to peer tech tutor	Content/Critical Reflection framed as ppt for Learning Community-Based on Problem solving**
	Buddy System-tutoring disability peer or high school mentee-Teamwork	Streaming platform (more than 100.000 students are able to attend a class) online tutor	Interdisciplinary written reflection-research assistant-Inquiry and data analysis

**Tune of VALUE Rubrics with Essential Learning Outcomes.
Scalable with technology

Fig. 15.1.   Checklist of the TalentoLab' standard methodology that incorporates labor market data to the learners collected data at the institutional, curriculum and course level.[19]

The learning framework of our model embeds immutable and discoverable metadata to address most of the common problems of the current skills verification, such as the following:

(1) Skills assessment: skills assessment is not purposefully designed to be understood beyond the specific course or program of study.
(2) Context-bound definitions: even if skills are assessed in a way that can be understood beyond the course, there is not a direct, trustable, and accessible platform to verify them.
(3) Skill ontologies: skills are named differently across the education system and in the workplace. Learning objectives and job post descriptions use different names to describe the same skills or achievements they seek. The Partnership for 21st Century Skills is currently building a common language for universities and the industry (Raish & Rimland, 2016).[20] EMSI, BGT, INGENIA and other skills taxonomies are using AI to make the data comparable.[21]
(4) Skills monetary value: skills are not matched nor compensated appropriately. The educational system and the culture and creative industry lacks a comparable assessment system that accurately labels the skills the student possesses to facilitate the career transition, nor uses at its capacity big data analysis on labor trends to match or guide student's career choice to maximize their skills value. Nor facilitates the global flow of talent and digital content production.

Part of the issues described above is caused by a lack of collaboration between companies and education/training providers. It is also for this reason that we propose a model that enhances such collaboration in order to fulfill the needs of lifelong learning and career readiness in the context of a freelance and digital economy.

Why Universities Should Matter

There are four key areas of higher education for which this model brings convenient opportunities for revenue and progress: career and student success, internationalization and applied research.

Career and Student Success

In the context of the digital and freelance economy, career and student success will depend on the ability of universities to instill habits to nurture intrinsic motivation, facilitating students' skill of learning how to learn. Our model includes lessons learned from working-based-learning, one-to-one tutoring activities and formative assessment designed to foster the lifelong learning skill. In addition, vocational skills (in the form of the digital apprenticeship) embed within university knowledge can foster career and student success.

Internationalization

International student enrollment in the United States has dropped precipitously in recent years.[22] Our project offers a meaningful intervention with the potential to engage international students through digital apprenticeship[23] as pathways that allow student/ mentor-tutor-professor interaction beyond frontiers. Newsrooms and universities will collaborate by enrolling in the digital apprenticeship in an existing LMS in the cloud.

Applied Research and the Good Pandemic

Richard Dawkins, the prominent evolutionist and author, introduced the concept of "memes," the cultural equivalent of genes:

> Ideas and concepts, from fashion to music, take on a life of their own within society and, by propagating and mutating from mind to mind, affect the progress of human evolution. (Rafferty, 2010, p. 214)

Social evolution and strong democratic institutions are common goals of news media and universities. The construction of knowledge and applied research is instilled by memes, cultural units of information spread by social interaction and engagement. Two institutions, news media companies and universities, historically have received the public trust and responsibility for the structure of knowledge and meme propagation. Our digital apprenticeship implementation requires the knowledge produced by professors and the evidence-based research taught in universities; real-world and skilled tutors, along with kind, mindful and empowering mentors. These agents can level and clear the avenue for closer collaboration between newsrooms and universities.

Conclusion

Fake news are the symptom of a sick society and a targetable threat to democracy. The journalism industry plays the role to spread or to confront fake news. Communications and journalism students, the future operators of media outlets, need drastic changes in the education they are provided by higher education institutions if they desire to become effective agents to neutralize fake news and foster a healthy society.

We encourage schools and news media outlets to become our partners in order to create a new force and source of "time tested trusted news" (Benioff, 2019) and foster a healthy society. We have seen that, in order to create such a force, we need to embrace lifelong learning, effective feedback (professor, tutor and mentor), and contextual learning (working-based-learning). However, this is not a task for just one agent – the university – but rather of many stakeholders that may contribute to the problem or the solution: tech companies, social entrepreneurs, students, and recruiting companies. The corollary holds that the Attitude, Skils, and Knowledge (ASK) journalists need to strengthen and encourage vibrant democracies can only be instilled in a collective effort led by journalists themselves. From that perspective alone, it is also time for journalists to save journalism.

Notes

1. This model is the first application of the standard methodology designed at the Georgetown University's TalentoLab and recognized in 2018 by the US Department of Education as one of 25 innovations that will reshape the workforce training and the career readiness structure in the education system. This copyrighted methodology combines work-based learning and formative assessment when implementing the following attributes of the method: 1) ASK: traceable metadata to verify the students' acquired level of attitudes, skills and knowledge; 2) ASK skills credits: academic, reputational and digital currency credits owned by a learner and certified in a blockchain credential; 3) TalentoLab Structured Activity: real-world challenges translated into the education world in the form of work-based learning activities that are designed and evaluated at the course level across disciplines and university programs; e.g. The digital apprenticeship is an application of this model and it is described in this paper; 4) EFAS: Entrepreneurial Formative Assessment ensures that these activities are aligned with national and international standardized assessments.

2. Also see 'Evaluating Information: The Cornerstone of Civic Online Reasoning'. Stanford Digital Repository at: https://purl.stanford.edu/fv751yt5934

3. Make and Jacobsen (2011), Reframing Information Literacy as Metaliteracy, College and Research Library, 62–78 as cited by Raish and Rimland (2016).

4. See https://ds-specials.netlify.com/educacion-latam/

5. See https://www.open.edu/openlearn/

6. See https://www.shrm.org/about-shrm/press-room/press-releases/pages/skills-gap-research-workplace-immigration-report.aspx

7. See https://www.kornferry.com/content/dam/kornferry/docs/article-migration/FOWTalentCrunchFinal_Spring2018.pdf

8. Salesforce is the popular customer relationship management system used to manage sales, marketing, and fundraising campaigns.

9. In 2016, more than 27,000 jobs were available to community college graduates that asked for Salesforce skills. On average, these jobs pay $64,000 per year – $24,000 above the median salary for an Associate Arts degree. The demand for Salesforce skilled talent is growing. The numbers reveal that this demand is set to create 3.3 million jobs in the Salesforce ecosystem by 2022. IT roles that require Salesforce skills carry an 11 percent salary premium. (Tenorio, 2018)

10. See https://www.cio.com/article/3188348/7-salesforce-certifications-that-will-advance-your-career.html

11. The ASK Badge is linked to a journalist's work. The link is a hashed CID (content ID) that connects the creative work the media journalist produces (article, picture, etc.) to the ASK Badge, where the work itself is stored in an associated IPFS system. The work is by definition in a public place, but if the link to it is hashed to the blockchain, any change at all to the file that is uploaded to IPFS and then linked to the chain will be detectable. We acknowledge that solving these issues will require time. For instance, there needs to be a system for verifying that a journalist's content is original, even when it has been transformed into a format other than that in which it is stored in the IPFS. Just converting it to HTML from text is a change that would make it no longer verifiable by our standards. So the content in IPFS must be in the format that the news media distributes to the world.

12. Still to be developed: links to content displayed in an e-portfolio to its corresponding object in an IPFS distributed file store.
13. When students enter the labor market with the badge earned through the institution's journalism mentorship program (connecting the artifacts created during that program to the ASK badge), their ULR needs to be activated so that work undertaken for their employer can be linked and endorsed by the employer. An alternative approach is to create a work-approved token issued by the employer.
14. ASK is an acronym of the copyrighted standard methodology designed by TalentoLab at Georgetown University. Working paper (c) 2017–2021.
15. In a future iteration, we plan to have a freeform text written by the student in the ULR. We have a link to the written text that has been uploaded into the public IPSF distributed file store. Analysis can be conducted via natural language processing of that text, but the format of the output and the specific components of the data structure to be captured in the ULR or elsewhere still have to be determined.
16. Preferences characterize every living organism; without them, plants would not turn toward the sun, nor cockroaches scamper away from it. Human preferences exist not only in these built-in forms shared with other living beings but in distinctly human ways, such as the consciously molded attitudes we convey through artistic expression, the moral codes by which we judge our worth and our failings, or the words we craft to describe imagined utopias. The group that gave this concept scientific birth in the early twentieth century chose attitude as the name to refer to such preferences. So intently did the pioneers focus on a study of attitudes that the field of social psychology came to be synonymous with the study of this single concept (Banaji & Heiphetz, 2010, p. 348).
17. See https://www.bbc.co.uk/careers/trainee-schemes-and-apprenticeships
18. This chapter proposes that historical data (also called long data) hold the key to understanding when facts are true.
19. Fig. 15.1 is the description of the sources of data that will be displayed in a dashboard linked to the ASK badge. This figure also describes the system to articulate silo departments in an education institution and to bridge useful information to human resources professionals. More information in the standard methodology created at Georgetown University's TalentoLab.
20. The transition from an industrial age to an information age has led to a change in how we think about processing information and what it means to learn and know.
21. EMSI's mission in higher education is to connect students, education, and work by providing data and analytics that help colleges and universities make smarter decisions and create successful strategies. See https://www.economicmodeling.com/higher-education/
22. The Institute of International Education showed that Intensive English-language programs, which are designed for foreign students coming to the United States, and are the predictive information to anticipate university enrollment, are down 35 percent from their 2015 high. Dozens of programs, including those at the College of New Jersey, California State University at Los Angeles, and the University of Houston's downtown campus, have closed (Fisher, 2019).
23. Zuluaga, L., & Vegas, E. (2016) Teachers without boarders: the potential of the Pacific Alliance to improve effective learning in Latin America. Inter-American Development Bank Digital Blogs, Education Division, Education in Focus.

References

Allcott, H., & Gentzkow, M. (2017). Social media and fake news in the 2016 election. *Journal of Economic Perspectives, 31*(2), 211–236. doi:10.1257/jep.31

Banaji, M. R., & Heiphetz, L. (2010). Attitudes. In S. T. Fiske, D. T. Gilbert, & G. Lindzey (Eds.), *Handbook of social psychology* (pp. 353–393). Hoboken, NJ: John Wiley

Bates, T. (2015). Is the nature of knowledge changing? In *Teaching in a digital age*. Open Text. Chapter 2: The nature of knowledge and the implications for teaching. Retrieved from https://opentextbc.ca/teachinginadigitalage/chapter/section-2-4-does-technology-change-the-nature-of-knowledge/

Benioff, M. (2019). We need journalism to elevate humanity. Retrieved from https://time.com/5700913/marc-benioff-journalism-humanity/

Bloom, B. (1984). The 2 sigma problem: The search for methods of group instruction as effective as one-to-one tutoring. *Educational Research, 13*(6), 4–16. Retrieved from https://www.jstor.org/stable/1175554?seq=1#page_scan_tab_contents

Bransford, J., Brown, A., & Cocking, R. (Eds.). (2000). *How people learn: Brain, mind, experience, and school*. Washington, DC: National Academy Press.

Carnevale, A., & Smith, N. (2018). *Balancing work and learning: Implication for low-income students*. Georgetown University Center for Education and Workforce. Retrieved from https://cew.georgetown.edu/cew-reports/learnandearn/

Dong, X., Kementsietsidis, A., & Tan, W. (2016). A time machine for information: Looking back to look forward. *ACM SIGMOD Record, 45*(2), 23–32. doi:10.1145/3003665.3003671

Edelman Intelligence. (2018). Freelancing in America 2018. UpWork.

Fischer, K. (2019). How international education's golden age lost its sheen. *The Chronicle of Higher Education*. Retrieved from https://www.chronicle.com/interactives/2019-03-28-golden-age

Gibson, D., Ostashewski, N., Flintoff, K., Grant, S., & Knight, E. (2015). Digital badges in education. *Education and Information Technology, 20*(2), 403–410. doi: 10.1007/s10639-013-9291-7

Goldin, C., & Katz, L. (2007). *The race between education and technology: The evolution of U.S. Educational wage differentials, 1890 to 2005*. The National Bureau of Economic Research. doi:10.3386/w12984

Grech, A., & Camilleri, A. F. (2017). *Blockchain in education*. Publication Office of the European Union. doi:10.2760/60649

Harlow, H. F. (1950). Learning and satiation of response in intrinsically motivated complex puzzle performance by monkeys. *Journal of Comparative and Physiological Psychology, 43*(4), 289–294. doi:10.1037/h0058114

Huckle, S., & White, M. (2017). Fake news: A technological approach to proving the origins of content, using blockchain. *Big Data, 5*(4). doi:10.1089/big.2017.0071

Kelly, A., & Schneider, M. (2012). *Getting to graduation: The completion agenda in higher education*. Baltimore: Johns Hopkins University Press.

Komarny, P. (2019). Future of learning platforms. First let's acknowledge that the future is already here. Retrived from https://medium.com/@philkomarny/future-of-learning-platforms-1ccd60cd552c

Korn, M. (2018). Some 43% of college grads are underemployed in first job. *The Wall Street Journal*. Retrieved from https://www.wsj.com/articles/study-offers-new-hope-for-english-majors-1540546200

Make, T., & Jacobsen, T. (2011). Reframing information literacy as metaliteracy. *College and Research Library*, *72*(1). doi:10.5860/crl-76r1

Muro, M., Liu, S., Whiton, J., & Kulkarni, S. (2017). Digitalization and the American workforce. Retrieved from https://www.semanticscholar.org/paper/Digitalization-and-the-American-Workforce-Muro-Liu/e713d45a5e1b38f9a36ea193ee539d18d3c a4684

Naim, M. (2019). A booming market for charlatans, We have to accept that democracy requires more effort than just casting a vote every few years. *El Pais*. Retrieved from https://elpais.com/elpais/2019/01/09/the_global_observer/1547030862_215361.html

Neem, J. N. (2018). Skills don't matter (outside their context). Inside HigherEd. Retrieved from https://www.insidehighered.com/views/2018/02/23/skills-disconnected-academic-programs-shouldnt-matter-colleges-opinion.

Newmark, C. (2013). Who, what, when, where, why, and how. *Columbia Journalism Review*. September/October, 2013. Retrieved from https://archives.cjr.org/cover_story/who_what_when.php

Pink, D. (2011). *Drive: The surprising truth about what motivates us*. New York, NY: Riverhead Books.

Rafferty, J. (Ed.). (2010). *New thinking about evolution*. New York, NY: Rosen Education Service.

Raish, V., & Rimland, E. (2016). Employer perceptions of critical information literacy skills and digital badges. *College and Research Libraries*, *77*(1), 89. doi:10.5860/crl.77.1.87

Schneider, M., & Sigelman, M. (2018). *Saving the associate of arts degree*. American Enterprise Institute. Retrieved from http://www.aei.org/publication/saving-the-liberal-arts-making-the-bachelors-degree-a-better-path-to-labor-market-success/

Shane, S. (2018). Russia isn't the only one meddling in elections. We do it, too. *The New York Times*. Retrieved from https://www.nytimes.com/2018/02/17/sunday-review/russia-isnt-the-only-one-meddling-in-elections-we-do-it-too.html

Sharples, M., & Domingue, J. (2016). The Blockchain and Kudos: A Distributed System for Educational Record, Reputation and Reward. In K. Verbert, M. Sharples, & T. Klobučar (Eds.), *Adaptive and adaptable learning. EC-TEL 2016. Lecture notes in computer science* (Vol. 9891). Cham: Springer. doi:10.1007/978-3-319-45153-4_48

Shields, R., & Chugh, R. (2017). Digital badges-rewards for learning? *Education and Information Technology*, *22*(4), 1817–1824. doi:10.1007/s10639-016-9521-x

Strada Institute. (2019). Robot-ready. Human + tech skills + EMSI. Retrieved from https://www.stradaeducation.org/report/robot-ready/

Tenorio, L. (2018). The demand for Salesforce skilled talent is HUGE… It's time for you to get in on the action! Retrieved from https://medium.com/trailhead/huge-demand-for-salesforce-talent-3bb30c597b39

The Civil Media Company. (n.d.). The civil white paper. Retrieved from https://civil.co/white-paper/

Wilson, M., Kurzweil, M., & Alamuddi, R. (2018). *Mapping the wild west of pre-hire assessment: A landscape view of the uncharted technology-facilitated ecosystem*. Ithaka S+R. doi:10.18665/sr.310761

Wineburg, S., McGrew, S., Breakstone, J., & Ortega, T. (2016). *Evaluating information: The cornerstone of civic online reasoning*. Stanford Digital Repository. Retrieved from http://purl.stanford.edu/fv751yt5934

Part 3
Future-proofing for the Post-truth Society

Chapter 16

Karl Marx and the Blockchain

Devraj Basu and Murdoch Gabbay

Abstract

Blockchain is often presented as a technological development; however, clearly it is not only that: the 'Blockchain buzz' exists in the context of current social and political developments. In this essay, we analyse blockchain technology and its social and political context from a perspective of Marxist economic theory. Since arguably the last great inflection point in society and technology was analysed by Marx in terms of labour and capital and since we seem to be experiencing a shift in the balance between these forces today, it makes sense to revisit the Marxist ideas and apply them to the current situation, to see how well they still apply and if necessary to update them for current events.

Keywords: New factor of production; labour versus capital; blockchain technology evolution; data-driven value creation; Marxian economic theory; technology and society

Bitcoin and Distributed Ledger Technology

Consider Blockchain

In 1991, blockchain was just a research idea (Haber & Stornetta, 1991), which was commercialised as a digital timestamping service called *Surety* in 1995.[1] In 2008, a design for a cryptocurrency called Bitcoin was introduced by Satoshi Nakamoto (an alias) (Nakamoto, 2009). It went live on January 2009.

On 10 October 2010, Bitcoin traded at 10 cents/bitcoin. By 29 February 2011, it was at 1 USD/bitcoin. By 1 April 2013, it reached 100 USD/bitcoin. Bitcoin scraped 1000 USD/bitcoin at the end of 2013, fell back, but then rallied and reached 19,783 USD/bitcoin on 17 December 2017. Unsurprisingly there came a crash – but Bitcoin was not wiped out and its reputation was not utterly destroyed: it survived and at time of writing, Bitcoin trades at around 10,000 USD/bitcoin

Media, Technology and Education in a Post-Truth Society, 225–241
Copyright © 2021 by Emerald Publishing Limited
All rights of reproduction in any form reserved
doi:10.1108/978-1-80043-906-120211016

(for a trading volume of roughly 10 million transactions per month). That is a 100,000-fold increase in value in 10 years.

It is not just as a store of value that blockchain technology has shown resilience; it has shown real influence. Innumerable elaborations on the underlying ideas have been spun off. Some are foolish; some are fraudulent; and some are sensible. However, it is clear that at the time of writing, the world is awash with a soup of cryptocurrency-related businesses, startups, research projects, and initiatives. And more generally – since a cryptocurrency is just a special instance of a distributed ledger – the cryptocurrency soup is just one well-known eddy in a cauldron of blockchain-based distributed ledger ideas.

Our Question Is: Why?

This is not to ask just why blockchain has seen growth and resilience – though this is part of the question. Our question is: why has blockchain-based tech *in particular* seen this interest?

There is no shortage of plausible future tech: biotech, fintech (financial technology), quantum tech, 3D printing tech, battery tech, space tech, renewable energy tech, machine learning tech and so forth. It is unclear that blockchain technology will be more important for human progress or offer a clearly better return on investment (ROI) than (say) biotech, fintech or machine learning. Indeed, these are all experiencing their own booms – and deservedly so because they have a pedigree of delivering concrete benefits and profits.

What does blockchain have that (for instance) machine learning does not?

A Word on Terminology

We may use the terms *blockchain* and *distributed ledger technology* (DLT) interchangeably, but in fact they mean slightly different things:

- a *blockchain* is a (usually distributed, usually cryptographically assured) chain of blocks (the technical term is *Merkle tree*), whereas
- a *distributed ledger* is a database that exists on (i.e., is distributed over) multiple locations (but not necessarily secured on an actual blockchain).

So technically, the git version management system is a blockchain, and a RAID 1 hard drive array is a distributed ledger. In practice, the terms blockchain and DLT are used to refer to a cryptographically secured block-structured distributed ledger, usually with some element of peer-to-peer communication and consensus. If we write 'blockchain' or 'DLT', we mean one of them – along with a general hint that DLT is intended in a slightly more general sense than blockchain. A *cryptocurrency* is then a currency whose ownership ledger is distributed on a cryptographically secured blockchain.

A Carnival of Incompetence

Blockchain has a history of error, fraud and incompetence so outrageous[2] that even for the cynical reader it is worth recalling a selection of examples:

- *2011* Bitomat kept its wallet on an ephemeral Amazon EC2 server. Being 'ephemeral' meant that when the server restarted, it would restart with empty discs. They restarted the server. 17,000 BTC got wiped.
- *2012* Bitcoinia was a 16-year-old's first serious PHP project. It quickly got hacked, and because the admin had reused their password on other secure sites, this led to a wave of further hacks. 18,547 BTC got lost.
- *2011–2014* 850,000 BTC were syphoned out of the Mt. Gox exchange.
- *2015* AllCrypt was run on a MySQL server that also ran WordPress. This is the security equivalent of building a bomb shelter with patio doors. It did not end well.
- *2016* Loanbase did the same thing.
- *2017* Zerocoin had a basic error in its code; == (is equal to) instead of = (make equal to). Coins could be spent twice, and were.
- *2019* QuadrigaCX founder Gerald Cotten died (or possibly absconded), leaving his laptop with 190 million USD in crypto assets locked under a password that only he knew.

Q. What Is DLT Good for? A. Not Much, and Yet...

The list above, tragicomic as it is, cautions against dismissing the interest in blockchain tech as a mere mania. Yes, it is a mania, and full of fools, but if this were only about manic foolishness, then presumably – after 10 years' nonsense like the above – the field would fall into disrepute and the fools would move on to the next thing.[3]

Instead, interest in DLT has only increased. After each disaster the investors piled back in, with renewed determination. Blockchain projects have multiplied and the headline value of Bitcoin has failed to go down the drain.

Yet we struggle to find use cases for DLT on a scale to justify such optimism. This is not to say that *potential* use cases are inconceivable or elusive: on the contrary, plausible *potential* use cases abound. What is difficult, even today, is to find *proven* use cases.

In fact there are only two cardinal successes so far, and both are crypto-currencies: Bitcoin and Ethereum.[4] In terms of demonstrated usefulness and functionality, Bitcoin and Ethereum are of interest only as stores of value.[5]

This is a circular and self-referential answer to the question of why DLT has value: Bitcoin and Ethereum have value because everyone agrees they have value. While perhaps satisfactory for an investor, it does not address the fundamental academic question of *why*.

At this point we should perhaps mention that we make no claim that DLT cannot create value, have applications and demonstrate fundamental ROI beyond Bitcoin and Ethereum as a store of value.

But the intensity and persistence of the mania surrounding this technology, are striking: a technology with no use cases aside from itself, and with a ten-year history of abject failure, corruption, and people getting fleeced, refuses to die and instead stimulates continued interest and investment. Investors have not (all) moved on to the next fad. Researchers (including the authors) remain active in the sector. Businesses display patience and continued interest.

Why?

The Economic Ideas of Karl Marx

To try and arrive at a fresh understanding of what is happening, we will consider some economic and political theory and a little history.

Karl Marx was an economist, political theorist and socialist revolutionary.[6] The first two aspects of his work interest us most here.

In Marx's seminal essay *Wage Labour and Capital* (*Lohnarbeit und Kapital*) of 1849 (Marx, 1849), Marx defined a *factor of production* as a unit in an economy.[7] He identified Labour and Capital as two major factors of production:

- *Labour* is work: digging ditches, childcare, writing articles, teaching, consultancy and so forth.
- *Capital* is assets: buildings, tools, factories, dollars, bitcoin, rights (such as copyright or land rights) and so forth.

Marx observed that Labour and Capital are fundamentally in opposition:

- Labour wants labour to be expensive and assets to be cheap.
- Capital wants labour to be cheap and assets to be expensive.

This is a simple but not trivial observation: that there is a chain to creating value, and each party in the value chain has an incentive to maximise their benefit.

For society to function, these imperatives must find an equilibrium:

- Labour – meaning people who work – must be paid enough to invest in themselves and their families.
  If this were not to happen, then society would implode, because nobody would have money to buy capital items, pay for services and nurture the next generation of educated and productive citizens.
- Capital – meaning people who own stuff – must be paid enough that owning and maintaining stuff is worthwhile.
  If this were not to happen, then society would implode, because nobody would have an incentive to take care of things or to invest in the future to maintain and develop the tools, tangible and intangible, which humans need.

Marx's basic argument was that this equilibrium is unstable and unsustainable:

- Competition would lead to increases in worker efficiency.
- For an individual worker, greater efficiency is generally good – an Internet connection, for instance, helps these authors to efficiently research and teach. This is a good thing, which, e.g., the authors' students value and the authors' university employers can monetise.
- However, for the system *as a functioning whole*, the effects need not necessarily be so positive: if we can obtain the same productive output from fewer workers, then the value of work overall may drop, unless more work can be invented.

In Marx's day, 'work' meant digging ditches (to put it crudely).[8] But, the world only needs so many ditches. Therefore, if, e.g., thanks to a mechanical digger, the same number of ditches can be dug by 10% of the workforce and suppose also that with new teaching technology universities can teach the same number of students with 10% of the professors, then 90% of this workforce becomes redundant. This is not just in terms of a particular individual no longer having a specific employment but also in terms of the systemic economic relevance of including working people in the system.

They are not needed; and things that are not economically needed have no economic value. Even if we put on our callous capitalist hats and set aside the inhumanity and social damage of the unemployment experience, this also destroys the value of capital itself: because, if the people are not needed, then neither are the capital assets to maintain them as humans.

Thus if the value of labour collapses, then so does the value of capital, and Marx's analysis of the system as a whole, viewed as an economic machine inhabited by humans, is that it will increase in efficiency, shed labour, shed capital, implode and collapse.[9]

In short, Marx's observation was that the capitalist system, in and of itself and even taken purely in terms of its own internal logic, is unstable and inherently self-contradictory.

The historical record is unclear whether he was right. Capitalism has not collapsed yet, but that does not mean it won't. We certainly have no grounds to be smug.[10]

We will argue that in a sense, the remarkable recent persistence of interest in DLT reflects an awareness of, and is a response to, the problems described above; but we are not yet ready to describe how. First, we must survey some recent economic history.

Labour versus Capital: A Tug of War

A simple test to see where the balance of power lies between Labour and Capital is to look at inflation:

- If inflation is high, Labour is powerful and can command ever greater wages.
- If inflation is low, Capital is powerful and can hold wages down.

From a perspective of Marxian economics, inflation is quite a reliable indicator of the balance of power between Labour and Capital. If this balance of power shifts too far in one direction or another, central banks can try to manipulate the resulting inflation, or lack of it, by controlling the money supply. However, since the financial crisis of 2008, attempts to create inflation have been ineffective – which suggests that the traditional (monetarist) view of inflation may not be so applicable to a world with globalised finance and supply chains (el Erian, 2016).[11]

With this test in mind, we will sketch the context of the current interest in blockchain tech by looking at the broad sweep of inflation over the past 80 years since the end of the Second World War.[12] We will split this into three eras:

- Era 1, 1945–1979: from the end of the Second World War to the elections of Margaret Thatcher (1979–1990) and Ronald Regan (1981–1989).
- Era 2, 1979–2008: from the Thatcher/Regan era and the corollary administrations which followed through to the 2008 financial crisis.
- Era 3, 2008–today: the reality our teenage University students enter as working adults.

In 1945, both Labour and Capital were significantly depleted after the disasters of the first half of the twentieth century. Social solidarity in their wake was high, and it was agreed that both Labour and Capital required investment.

Capital was scarce, but Labour was in even greater demand because

- labour is required to produce capital, but capital is not required to produce labour,[13] and
- with depleted capital, labour was relatively unproductive and therefore more of it was required.

The 1950s and 1960s were good times to be at work, and because there was plenty of demand for labour to go around, workers could build capital and increase efficiency and see this reflected in rising paycheques.

And, it is not just about wages: society valued Labour and was willing to speculatively invest in skills and education. For instance, the Servicemen's Readjustment Act of 1944 (the G.I. Bill) was described as a reward for war service – which it was – but its deeper meaning was an investment in labour skills and education (for example, free university education). Another influential example of post-war investment in Labour has been the UK's Open University (1969), which has inspired open universities in many other countries, e.g., in Israel (1974).[14]

Jumping ahead just for this paragraph from the United States in 1944 to the United Kingdom in 1998 (in the middle of our Era 2 above): university education, which until then had been free, became not-free as tuition fees were introduced.[15] These were modest at first but the precedent had been set and fees rose to a maximum of 9,000 pounds a year in 2010 (this was after the financial crisis, at the start of our Era 3).

In our analysis this social signal should alert us that something important has happened, because tuition fees are – in fact – not tuition fees at all, but instead they are a targeted tax on Labour; workers are welcome to join the workforce and add productively to the economy, and all society asks of them in return is to pay a modest upfront tax of 36,000 pounds (assuming a four-year course) against future earnings. What could be regressive about that? The contrast with the Era 1 attitude could hardly be starker.[16]

In the 1970s, something changed: wages stopped rising. This was a decade of strikes; Marx would say that productivity gains had finally started to eat into the value of Labour. Fewer workers were required, but they continued demanding the wage increases of previous decades, but now, just as Marx predicted, Labour lacked its old leverage. Social unrest followed.

Something had to give, and between 1979 and 1981, the balance of power swung to Capital – which was terrified of inflation, this being one thing that can really eat into the value of a capital asset.

An ideology was required to justify the falling value of work and workers, and this was promoted as *individualism*. Exaggerated symbols of independence developed, such as Madonna's *Material Girl* and Arnold Schwarzenegger's body. These myths were of people who did not need anybody's help and were strong and rich and successful because of it; and they were held up as icons of a new capitalism. But the actual effect was to break the power of Labour, since if everybody is in it for themselves, then they are not in it for one another and they can therefore collectively be exploited more, paid less and/or fired – and, as per the ideology, it's their own fault for not working hard enough, not being entrepreneurial enough and not wanting it enough.[17] The Thatcher era right to buy of council properties (Murie, 2015) was part of this too: making it possible for workers to take ownership of their homes turned them into holders of capital and thus gave them a stake in the new system.

Over the following 30 years to 2008, the value of capital shot up. In retrospect we see that this postponed the problem, but it did not solve it, and the financial crash of 2008 was of a piece with the strikes of the 1970s:

- In the 1970s, the ROI in Labour either flattened out or became self-defeating. In a rush to maintain returns, the system became unstable. With Labour weakened and discredited, political power shifted to Capital.
- In the 2000s, a similar process took place with Capital; the ROI in capital flattened out or became self-defeating, and in a rush to maintain returns, the system became unstable – the precise mechanism was that Capital borrowed money and leveraged it, but the deeper driver here was that Capital had run out of ways to earn real returns and so it invented imaginary ones.

We now see the problem: where can the pendulum swing next?

Nostalgia versus the Future

When society is in difficulty, people can either be realistic and analytic about their difficulties or they can look to vivid fantasies of escape. These fantasies are quite revealing:

- *Go back to the 50s and 60s!* White men were real men; the world was ruled by Christians; and women and children and black people knew their place.
  Much of the current US politics has retreated to this space.
- *Go back to the 70s!* Workers united to face down evil capitalists. Yes, it did not come out so well for the workers then, but this time will be different.
  This current has not met with electoral success in either the United States or the United Kingdom, though it may remain relevant as a pigeonhole into which to stereotype proponents of a more socially conscious capitalism.
- *Go back to the 80s!* This is like going back to the 50s and 60s, but with more tech and funkier suits.
  Baby boomers are particularly prone to this fantasy, because the 80s were good to them, especially if they bought property.
- *Anarchy and authoritarianism* are all jumbled up in a single item of political opportunism.
  This would be amusing, were it not for the election of so many outrageously unfit politicians in 2016–2018, along with an enabling retinue of crooks, fanatics and thieves, all anxious to carve up what is left of the pie before (they fear) the music will finally stop.
- *Zoom to the future, usually with new tech – like in Star Trek!* But perhaps without the aliens, or the warp drive, but the point is: tech will solve our problems.[18]
  The dreams of blockchain lie here. Viewed in context as an escapist fantasy, they are not clearly more dangerous than the alternatives – and at least as a fantasy it is forward-rather than backward-looking, which matters.

It is now important to appreciate that blockchain is not just any old techno-utopian escapist fantasy. It is also a concrete technology, with specific technical qualities, which make certain promises, not all of which are unreasonable.

Consider what Labour and Capital most fear:

- Labour worries that resources will continue to be co-opted by Capital. This is valid since it has been a pattern for the past 40 years – that is, wealth inequality has trended up (Roser & Ortiz-Ospina, 2016).[19] Most recently, the United States leaned shamelessly into this with the Tax Cuts and Jobs Act (TCJA) of 2017, in which wealthy Americans essentially agreed to cut taxes on the wealthy and thus allocate more of the pie to themselves.
- Capital worries that Labour, fed up with stagnant wages and aggravated by regressive taxation and lagging and biased social investment, may decide the game is hopelessly rigged and rise up and confiscate assets – either through progressive taxes and political reform or through theft and destruction. Or, perhaps a corrupt government will take advantage of social instability and loss of legitimacy to concentrate wealth in a new elite, as has happened in history before. These fears too are reasonable.
- Both Labour and Capital, again with good reason, fear a currency collapse whose real costs may be unable to avoid or inflict upon somebody else.

Here, Bitcoin makes some relevant promises: in particular, it promises anonymity and independence from government. Thus

- Labour projects onto this an ideal of a libertarian currency that is accessible to all, cannot be co-opted and (implicitly) promises financial independence from a corrupted and discredited elite.
- Capital projects onto this an ideal of a stable and secure asset that cannot be inflated away or confiscated by a vengeful mob come to grab their share.
- Both Labour and Capital like the idea that Bitcoin cannot be inflated away. One Bitcoin will still be one Bitcoin tomorrow, whereas a dollar may be worth only 50 cents.

Blockchain's Promise

In fact, Bitcoin is not anonymous[20,21]: patterns of Bitcoin ownership resemble those of other capital assets (Outumuro, 2020), and Bitcoin is volatile, liable to theft and difficult to transact in.

However, fiat currencies share many of the same features: they can also be not anonymous, unevenly distributed, volatile and liable to theft. Libertarians particularly emphasise here institutional theft by inflation – it is unclear how rampant theft of cryptocurrencies by hackers is any better, but at least it's not by a *government*. As Satoshi wrote:

> The root problem with conventional currency is all the trust that's required to make it work. The central bank must be trusted not to debase the currency, but the history of fiat currencies is full of breaches of that trust.

So in relative terms, Bitcoin may not seem that bad, and in any case the utopian *promise* is there, even if the reality has not caught up just yet.

And here is why cryptocurrencies have captured the collective imagination.

It is not just that we live in uncertain times. There seems a sense in which we may be at the end of an economic arc, which started in 1945, inflected in 1979 and has reached some endpoint since 2008, where increases in productivity of Labour and Capital have stalled or become counterproductive *at the same time*.

There seems nowhere to turn, the system is wobbling and the key component of *trust* in that system is ebbing away.

If so, then this is an arc which Marx predicted. The endpoint of his prediction was a social collapse which may yet happen, and (so the fear) we may be trapped on this trajectory by an economic logic which we struggle to escape.

Fantasies of escape to a golden age are obvious nonsense, and even their proponents, wilfully blind as they may be, are aware of this at some level, which accounts for the stridency of much of current politics. Next to this, cryptocurrencies promise a way out which is not obviously any more crazy than anything else, and *this* is why Bitcoin has bounced back from one disaster after another, and why research and investment continue to flow to blockchain tech, trying to make it work.

Yes, many of the other techs from Section 'Bitcoin and Distributed Ledger Technology' have proven capable of generating ROI within the current system – but as Marx argued, beyond a certain point just increasing the productivity of individual components in an economy does not necessarily make the economic system as a whole stable or more productive, so just delivering ROI does not in itself address the deeper worry.

What no tech can currently promise is an escape from this contradiction, which Marx observed embedded in the system itself – no tech, that is, except for blockchain. That promise, however tenuous, is specific to our time.

The problem is blockchain technology does not actually deliver. It is, for now, mostly vapourware (cf. the discussion in Section 'Q. What is DLT good for? A. Not much, and yet...').

So in summary so far: we have argued that blockchain promises, but does not yet deliver, a modern technological fix to a specific social and economic problem which was predicted by Karl Marx back in 1849 and which, arguably, the world economy has been stuck in for the decade since 2008.

We will argue next that since Marx's time, there have been two developments which he could not have foreseen and which may have modified the rules of the game:

- The rise of the digital economy, and specifically of intangible assets that can be infinitely copied at near-zero cost, which must therefore be protected by copyright.
- The rise of data as a new factor of production.

We will discuss the technology first.

Blockchain as a Technology in the Digital Economy

The Tech

For Marx, technology was as much a problem as a solution. As discussed, it increases worker efficiency to the point that having workers becomes systemically unnecessary, so that capital becomes unnecessary, so that the economic system implodes.

On the face of it, the digital economy makes this worse than Marx could have imagined. Moving electrons around is extremely low cost; it is no harder to make a million copies of a program than one. A small number of good programmers can move many electrons, and one reason for the concentrations of wealth which we have seen is surely just down to social policy failing to distribute the exceptional productivity of computer programs.[22]

A concrete example gives a feel for the numbers that can be at play: in 2017, Facebook bought WhatsApp for 19 billion USD. At the time, WhatsApp had 55 employees. Some of this money was set against projected future earnings, but the fact remains that on a per-capita basis, the market judged that each WhatsApp employee had created 350 million USD in current or future value.

For this reason Capital loves the digital economy. Once you have copyright control of a program or film or a patent, you have an economic perpetual motion machine and need to do little more than sit back and rake in the profits.[23] Labour is effectively removed from the equation – aside from perhaps having to feed and clothe the families of no more than 55 programmers.

Labour also loves the digital economy. It brings comfort and increased productivity – provided you have the necessary skills, of course. If not, you may have a problem.[24]

'Technology', however, is a broad term, and blockchain tech has some quite unusual features which may not be generally appreciated.

Let us look at the core technology that had to be harnessed in order to start off the revenue streams of some companies that are now worth hundreds of billions of USD:

- Facebook is fundamentally based on a labelled graph. *Graph* here is in the mathematical sense of a connected object with *nodes* (dots) joined by edges (lines); a Facebook landing page, with icons of people on a map of the world and connected by lines, sums it up.
  The mathematical notion of graph is a first-year undergraduate topic: it is not hard.
- The Google PageRank algorithm is, fundamentally, an advanced undergraduate project or perhaps early-stage PhD.
- Amazon is 'just' a database, and MS-Dos Windows, and MS Word are fairly simple programs.

This is not to say that Facebook, Google, Amazon and Microsoft are based on simple systems; on the contrary, scaling up from the initial product to the worldwide firms we know today it is technically very complex.

Nor is this to say that creating such companies was simple and easy. Far from it, there were more failures than successes.

Our point is that if we assume the course is set, that the winning formula was found and that whatever wisdom or luck that was required has been added to the mix – in other words, if we assume we have won this particular lottery – then the fundamental *conceptual* requirements of getting the tech started were not great.

Contrast this with, for example, ARM, Intel and Airbus. The tech required to fabricate chips or aircraft is rocket scientist level from the start; it requires specialists with years of training and specialist managers able to manage them, and if things go wrong, then people get very excited and have government enquiries.[25]

To put it another way, you cannot start a chip fabrication business in your garage, but you can start a trillion dollar software company – or at least you could have 10 or 15 years ago (nowadays the incumbents would buy you up or crowd you out, but that is a different debate).

Blockchain in its infancy is more like Airbus than Amazon. To start a revenue stream based on DLT requires expertise, research and special management which simply has not yet been assembled in the sector. Consider that a company wishing to generate a revenue stream from a cryptocurrency product must commit to solving mathematical problems that are

- fundamentally hard,
- in a safety-critical context,
- for consumer use.

It is ambitious, and may be impossible, to satisfy all three of these criteria simultaneously in an *initial product*.

Part of the difficulty is that this not only requires specialised programmers and mathematicians to invent and implement a new body of mathematics but also requires processes and qualified managers who do not exist yet because the field has not matured; potential regulatory changes to provide a legal framework into which users can escape if and when things go wrong (because they always do); and a programme of public education to educate a population who (as a general body) may still be storing their PaS5w0rds on post-it notes stuck to the monitor.

A Prediction

Based on the analysis above, we would like to offer a prediction, just for the sake of argument.

The killer apps and real impact of blockchain will not appear first as front-end consumer applications.[26] They will appear in backend applications, developed by large institutions (banks, or logistics companies, or large tech companies) for internal use or for use with their institutional peers.

These will be organisations with deep pockets and long experience of managing extreme complexity who can afford to engage (and if necessary to create) a small army of highly specialised programmers, lawyers, computer scientists and mathematicians to develop a product that requires a PhD just to switch it on safely.

In other words, in spite of the success of Bitcoin, we predict that blockchain tech will behave economically more like rocket science and less like cash and will democratise only later, if at all.

A Few Words on Data

On the face of it, Data is just an asset. By this view, owning data is like owning any other capital asset.

However, Data has the potential to become a factor of production in its own right; an actor on a level with or even ruling over Labour and Capital.

What is the difference? In practice, we propose that the difference between an asset class and a factor of production is that the former only demands maintenance, whereas the latter tends to actively pull itself together into a self-serving entity:

- Labour is people. People flow together because humans are social.
- Capital is ownership of things. Things demand care to remain operational, increase in value and to not be stolen. This gives holders of capital as a group an incentive to flow together to cooperate and protect their wealth.
- Data in its modern forms looks like an asset for input, e.g., to machine learning and AI algorithms, but it is not just that: Data requires curation to harvest and clean it and infrastructure to process it, and it displays potent networking effects; a database that is twice as large is (crudely put) four times as useful. These properties give data a form; it tends to want to flow together into a single entity, just like Labour and Capital do.

It will be a social and regulatory question whether Data becomes a capital asset or a factor of production on a par with Labour and Capital, and if the latter, whether it will be an equal, a subordinate or the master of Labour and Capital.

This is relevant to our Marxian analysis because it is one pertinent way in which the world which Marx was thinking in differs substantively from the world which we now inhabit. There may be a new actor in the drama, and how they could influence the story is not yet understood. We leave a fuller analysis to future work.

The Way ahead

If Marx were around today, we suspect he would have liked crypto, at least in principle. The promise of Bitcoin to allow Labour to mine coin and thus take control of the means of production of what one might call *cryptocapital* is a relevant and clearly Marxian dream – though sadly it is *only* a dream.[27,28]

By looking at the world as Marx did in 1849, we have obtained an analysis of why blockchain tech has been so uniquely resilient in 2008–2020 and what it really promises for the future: namely, an escape from Marx's logical contradiction as outlined in Section 'The Economic Ideas of Karl Marx'.

We can now turn to a natural corollary question: could Blockchain actually save us from the trap that Marx identified? Perhaps.

In blockchain's favour, it does not generally destroy jobs, and it renews incentives to invest in Labour, because designing, implementing and managing these systems is skilled work, in highly specific ways.

Making blockchain-related technologies work implies significant investment in logic and formal methods[29]; tens and perhaps hundreds of thousands of highly qualified programming and management jobs; the democratisation of high-level, high-assurance programming languages and the skills to use them; much work in communication and education; entire new areas of mathematical research, regulation and legal specialisation; and, arguably, the rise of a new breed of hyper-technical companies employing programmers with skills that are currently expected only of the highest-level graduates. In other words, Blockchain means employment, innovation and investment in skills, and this will increase the value of Labour.

Importantly, Blockchain is at the same time creating capital, albeit of kinds not seen before – including but not restricted to Bitcoin. This may relieve some of the tension between Labour and Capital which (by our analysis) has so destabilised the world for the past 10 years.[30]

It is worth pausing to compare and contrast the profile of blockchain tech with that of machine learning/AI tech, which at first glance appears similar in that it is also very mathematical and computer-intensive. It too requires highly qualified labour, though perhaps not as much of it. However, the underlying technology does not need to be democratised in quite the same way; its incentive is to resist rather than promote the creation of legal frameworks (which increase costs) and its raw input capital is Data (often from surveillance capitalism) which is *harvested*, not *built*. In short, there is a possible incarnation of blockchain tech, if it is ever created, which will want a community of active and informed citizens using and innovating with its products to create economic output while protected by well-considered legislative frameworks – whereas machine learning seems to want to harvest data from a herd of humanity which uses its products via controlled portals in *de facto* walled gardens, while operating in a legal void except for those laws required to protect the incumbents' datasets and IP.[31]

So it may be that working towards even a fantasy of a blockchain-based solution to the stagnation since 2008 may in itself usefully help to escape it – regardless of whether it actually works for the purposes originally intended. At a human and social level, that would be good enough.[32]

A remarkable confluence of technologies is necessary for blockchain to work, including cryptography, computer science, mathematics, law, communications infrastructure and public education. To be useful, this combination must diffuse and democratise, and it is impossible to predict the effects this will have – not just on society but also on the technology. As blockchain spreads, it will evolve.

To democratise and diffuse, this technology will require a broad coalition: from a pair of professors writing in Scotland to an Ethiopian coffee farmer; all parties will be trying to solve their own individual problems, and if the tech is to be truly useful, it will need to assume different yet compatible forms, working within sensible social and legal structures yet to be devised. This democratisation and diffusion is likely to change the tech beyond recognition, and what started as a techno-utopian dream may transition to be the backend of a bank and then go elsewhere and assume forms that we would hardly recognise.[33]

One thing that seems likely – and of which we hope that Marx would approve – is that if we can make this happen, then it will require a lot of work and a lot of infrastructure. That would be Labour and Capital working together again – and that, in and of itself, would be cause for hope.

Notes

1. It's still running.
2. Thanks to Gerard (2017, p. 36). for collecting many of these examples.
3. The honest and competent operator will find that it is technically very difficult to deliver blockchain safely and usefully to end users (so while carefully trying to do so, risks being shoved aside and crowded out by dishonest, incompetent ones).

There are deep reasons for this, which we discuss in Section 'The Tech' and Section 'A prediction'.

4. Apologies to the cryptocurrencies we left out. At time of writing, Ether's market capitalisation is one-tenth that of Bitcoin and it is the largest of the so-called *altcoins* (crypto other than Bitcoin; Ripple is next, with a twentieth). We mention Ethereum in particular because of its widespread cultural influence, due to its adoption and its emphasis on smart contracts, which has sparked many projects and elaborations ....

5. ...but smart contracts, while interesting (especially to a logician/programmer, such as the second author) are not yet a *proven* functionality. They deserve their own essay which we leave for future work.

6. US lay readers please note: in Europe, 'socialist' is not an insult and may even be a compliment.

7. Means of production: https://en.wikipedia.org/wiki/Means_of_production#Related_ terms. Accessed on July 9, 2020.

8. It would be unfair to fault Marx for failing to anticipate the digital economy. More on this in Section 'Blockchain as a Technology in the Digital Economy'.

9. ...but not serving them; we have our *callous* capitalist hats on here, for the sake of this argument ....

10. At this point this article could suggest that a more socially conscious and humane economic system might also be a more stable and sustainable one. This suggestion is reasonable and worth exploring (and has been explored by other authors, such as Mazzucata (2018)) – but not in this essay. We need to follow a different thread.

11. So that is *two* things a capitalist's money cannot buy: love and inflation.

12. This analysis is US/UK-centric, which is a simplification but a reasonable one, because the dollar is the world's currency and because thus far the main drivers of blockchain technology have also been US/UK-centric.

13. Raising children is necessarily labour-intensive, but not *necessarily* capital-intensive.

14. List of open universities: https://en.wikipedia.org/wiki/List_of_open_universities. Accessed on July 9, 2020.

15. ...by a UK Labour government, we might add.

16. This is in England. Scotland has no tuition fees.

17. To be clear, Thatcher and Regan were trying to solve real problems. Labour *was* worth less; the strikes could *not* continue; and something *did* need to be done.

However, the human cost of the adjustments was lasting and non-negligible, and this cost fell mostly on Labour instead of Capital. The way the ideology blamed its victims for their victimhood was as elegant as it was cruel, and the repercussions and costs of this injury and insult resonate to this day – and not only for Labour: once asset ownership was more important for income than the labour contributed, this devalued the caring professions like childminders, doctors and nurses. Now the coronavirus pandemic (which flared up during the preparation of this article) has thrown a particularly graphic light on how professions that are economically irrelevant as measured by GDP can become a matter of life and death and how even if we only care about GDP, failing to account for the value network in which that one economic measure is embedded can become self-defeating.

In retrospect, one could certainly try to devise exits from the 1970s situation which in the long term might have been more equitable and economically beneficial.

This concern is relevant today because we are now seeing elements of the strategy replayed; e.g., with the so-called *gig economy* and individualistic slogans such as *be the CEO of you*. These are not necessarily all bad – a gig may be a welcome earner for, e.g., an individual with some energy and free time – but we have seen in our lifetime what the systemic consequences can be of promoting as a cool lifestyle choice a business model that is great for Capital and terrible for Labour and can therefore not claim ignorance this time around.

18. Marx would have countered that tech *is* the problem. We return to this in Section 'The Tech'.

19. Also see https://www.equalitytrust.org.uk/how-has-inequality-changed. Accessed on July 9, 2020.

20. Bitcoin Magazine. Is Bitcoin anonymous? https://bitcoinmagazine.com/what-is-bitcoin/is-bitcoin-anonymous. Accessed on July 9, 2020.

21. It is pseudonymous, which sounds like 'anonymous' but means something quite different.

22. Microsoft, Apple, Amazon and Alphabet were worth roughly 1 trillion USD each in January 2020, and Alibaba, Facebook and Tencent about half a trillion USD – see list of public corporations by market capitalization: https://en.wikipedia.org/wiki/List_of_public_corporations_by_market_capitalization#2020. That really is a lot of money. Accessed on July 9, 2020.

23. *Copyright trolls* practice the purest form of this business model, incurring just the fixed costs to acquire the patent and then enjoying very low marginal costs. This impressively combines being a malevolent and parasitic modern piracy, with being an elegant distillation of an essential truth of the digital economy.

24. ...and so may society. We still need waiters, nurses, teachers and childminders. The problem is figuring how to pay them, which was part of Marx's critique.

25. Yes, the Wright brothers worked out of a bicycle shop, but that was over a 100 years ago and they were aiming for a prototype plane, not a socially transformative global cryptocurrency. The two things are different.

26. This is not to say that consumer applications will not exist; just that they will be made for the sake of it and not actually be that important, except perhaps for public education and diffusion of the ideas.

27. The actions of the US Federal Reserve in the coronavirus pandemic have reminded us how the means of production of capital in the United States (and thus in the world) are operated to serve an oligarchic elite. It would not be prudent to stake one's life and livelihood on an expectation that Capital will share the pie, because it won't.

28. Mining Bitcoin has long ceased to be democratic; most is now mined in huge centralised 'Bitcoin farms' or by distributed malware.

   For the record, Bitcoin is a proof-of-work system (proof-of-stake is inherently different). The industry is aware of this issue and attempts are being made to design cryptocurrencies that do not reward centralisation so much. (If the reader has tried to buy a graphics card in the past five years, that price spike you may have noticed was due to crypto mining – and now graphics cards are used for AI. But we digress.)

29. This is the second author's professional specialisation.

30. Thanks to the reader who astutely pointed out that Marx might say here that this can only be temporary. No doubt, but a breathing space is still space to breathe,

and all other things being equal, a technology that promises to create both labour and capital is better than one that does not.

31. This is not to say that machine learning and AI are bad – just that it is not the case that all tech is the same, just because it's tech. Each technology has its own character, and the gist of this article is an analysis of the specifics of Blockchain tech through a lens of Marx's theories.

32. A related discussion of blockchain as a *convening technology* (in the music industry) is in Baym, Swartz, and Alarcon (2019) – meaning a technology which may or may not actually work on a technical level but which serves to 'galvanise goodwill and to imagine a specific shared potential future, together with implications that have value beyond any ultimate success of the technology around which they convene'.

33. A portion of this larger point is made in detail in (Swartz, 2017) observing that the technology may in large part evolve from being *radical* to being *incorporative* (fitting into existing technical structures).

References

Baym, N., Swartz, L., & Alarcon, A. (2019). Convening technologies: Blockchain and the music industry. *International Journal of Communication, 13*, 402–421.

el Erian, M. (2016). *The only game in town: Central banks, instability, and avoiding the next collapse.* New York, NY: Penguin Random House. ISBN 978-0812997620.

Gerard, D. (2017). *Attack of the 50 foot blockchain: Bitcoin, blockchain, Ethereum & smart contracts.* North Charleston, SC: CreateSpace Independent Publishing. ISBN 978-1-974-00006-7.

Haber, S., & Stornetta, W. S. (1991). How to time-stamp a digital document. *Journal of Cryptology, 3*, 99–111. doi:10.1007/BF00196791

Marx, K. (1849). *Lohnarbeit und Kapital [Wage labour and capital].* Retrieved from https://www.marxists.org/archive/marx/works/1847/wage-labour/index.htm. Accessed on July 9, 2020.

Mazzucata, M. (2018). *The value of everything.* New York, NY: Public Affairs. ISBN 978-0-241-34779-9.

Murie, A. (2015, November 11). The right to buy: History and prospect. Retrieved from http://www.historyandpolicy.org/policy-papers/papers/the-right-to-buy-history-and-prospect. Accessed on July 9, 2020.

Nakamoto, S. (2009). *Bitcoin: A peer-to-peer electronic cash system.* Retrieved from https://bitcoin.org/bitcoin.pdf

Outumuro, L. (2020). A comprehensive analysis of Bitcoin's current state. Retrieved from https://medium.com/intotheblock/a-comprehensive-analysis-of-bitcoins-current-state-b41dc2a4dc44. Accessed on July 9, 2020.

Roser, M., & Ortiz-Ospina, E. (2016). Income inequality. Our world in data. Retrieved from https://ourworldindata.org/income-inequality

Swartz, L. (2017). Blockchain dreams: Imagining techno-economic alternatives after Bitcoin. In M. Castells (Ed.), *Another economy is possible* (pp. 82–105). Polity Press. ISBN 978-1509517206. Retrieved from https://www.wiley.com/enus/Another+Economy+is+Possible%3A+Culture+and+Economy+in+a+Time+of+Crisis-p-9781509517213

Chapter 17

Two Sides to Every Story. The Truth, Post-truth, and the Blockchain Truth

Joshua Ellul, Alex Grech and Gordon J. Pace

Abstract

One of the rallying cries of the blockchain community is that of immutability: the irreversibility of the past, the absolute truth which, once stored, remains there forever. The technology was designed with this foundational pillar in mind to ensure that changes to history are inordinately expensive and practically impossible to execute – and increasingly so, the further in the past the event which one intends to manipulate lies. This platonic view of absolute truth is in stark contrast with a world of manipulated truth, and it is not surprising that it is being revisited as a means of combating fake news. We argue that claims to the absolute nature of the blockchain are at best exaggerated, at worst misrepresented or even 'fake news'. We discuss implicit centralised points of trust in blockchains, whether at a technological, social or governance level, and identify how these can be a threat to the 'immutable truth' stored within the blockchain itself. A global pandemic has unleashed an unprecedented wave of contradictory positions on anything from vaccines and face masks to 'the new normal'. It is only natural that the pursuit of blockchain as a placebo for society's 'truth' problems continues.

Keywords: Blockchain; interoperability; governance; immutability; blockchain truth; tamperproof data

The Truth, Post-truth and the Blockchain Truth

Although the notion of the blockchain is irremediably intertwined with that of *immutability* and transitively (or by inference) with that of *truth*, the Bitcoin white paper (Nakamoto, 2009) which proposed the algorithms behind blockchain never uses these two terms.[1] Instead, the paper repeatedly speaks about *trust*. At the surface, the paper sets out a concrete problem, that of providing 'peer-to-peer [...] electronic cash [that] would allow online payments to be sent directly from one

Media, Technology and Education in a Post-Truth Society, 243–253

Copyright © 2021 by Emerald Publishing Limited
doi:10.1108/978-1-80043-906-120211017

party to another without going through a financial institution', and provides a technical solution. It does not seek to discuss or assess alternative design or architecture, but simply describes the solution and reads more like technical documentation than an academic paper. And yet, as one digs deeper, one finds that the real underlying theme is that of addressing the slow demise of trust in central authorities. Enabling the storage and transfer of cryptocurrencies is but one application of the solution presented in the paper, but a domain salient at the time of publication, since it was doing away with financial institutions – a type of point of trust readers were all too aware of just after the 2008 financial crisis. However, the payments angle is nothing other than a red herring, as the paper goes on to present a technical solution to store information in a manner which cannot be tampered with, yet without the need of a centralised point of trust.

Achieving trust requires having the means for immutable records. As long as the records were produced and stored by single-independent entities, governments, banks, media houses or large corporations, the truth was one-sided, written by guardians of the ledger. Blockchain, despite doing away with the need for trust, ensured consistency of the data across a network of users by providing a technological mechanism for cryptographically locking past records in a manner such that they cannot be changed. In the context of Bitcoin and other cryptocurrencies, these corresponded to historical transactions that no party can delete or otherwise modify. Cryptographic signatures ensure that only the owner of the asset can initiate such a transaction, the consensus mechanism between participants on the network ensures that attempts to spend more than one has, or otherwise cheat or enter into some fraudulent transaction, never accepted, and the block-based storage of past transactions ensures that what is written and accepted is there to stay. In a centralised solution, it takes but one party (the central one) to lie for the records to show false claims, but in a decentralised solution, no single party has that power. This is what led to the notion of the blockchain as a storage of *a single democratic truth*.

In this paper we argue that this notion of correctness corresponding to truth is nothing but an illusion at different levels. Not only can the information stored immutably be false, but also the very notion of immutability breaks down on various levels.

Parallels with the Truth (and Blockchain)

Blockchain systems are often touted to be repositories of unchanging truth, in that if a business process makes use of a blockchain, then the information stored within is irrefutable or immutable. This is partially correct, in that data once recorded in a blockchain cannot be changed (excluding the caveats we identify further below). However, this does not mean that the information recorded is necessarily representative of the truth. As the adage goes, 'garbage in, garbage out', and the mechanisms provided by blockchain can only to a limited extent recognise garbage. The level of truthfulness of blockchain is much deeper than just the information recorded within.

The Blockchain Truth versus the Truth

Much of the popular literature on blockchain conflates the notions of immutability and truth. The properties and qualities of the medium do not necessarily correlate with the quality of the content stored therein. What is set in stone need not be any more reliable than what is scribbled on paper. And yet, part of this conflation arises from a legitimate observation. As a ledger, a medium of storage of transactions, the blockchain is designed in a manner that ensures only transactions which follow real world notions of property can be notarised on the blockchain, i.e., one can only spend one's own assets, one cannot spend more than one has, one cannot spend a resource twice (double spending), etc. In addition, the decentralised consensus manner in which these invariants are achieved ensures that no party can single handedly record transactions in violation of these basic principles. In this sense, the transactions of digital assets as written on a blockchain *do* contain a degree of truth with respect to these underlying axioms characterising property.

This form of *internal* consistency or truth provides certainty regarding the ownership of assets recorded on the blockchain. However, this still provides no guarantees regarding *external* consistency – verification of the information written on the blockchain with respect to 'information from the real world'. The veracity of the claim that a particular party A transferred 30 bitcoins to party B can be determined using the blockchain – but not that party A transferred a number of bitcoins to party B equal to the temperature in Celsius at the time of the transaction in a particular location.

This weak link, the bridge between the digital information stored on a blockchain and empirical information from the real world, becomes even more pertinent when one uses blockchain systems to execute smart contracts.[2] Although smart contracts working solely on the digital assets native to the underlying blockchain have been shown to be useful, e.g., the notion of token ownership and management facilitated by smart contracts has been one of the most successful use cases on Ethereum, with various initial coin offerings depending on such smart contracts. However, many smart contracts need to extend their reach beyond the blockchain: confirmation of user identity, readings from the real world, actuation of devices in the real world, etc. The centralised nature of many such points in the real world means that the truth of the data recorded about such interaction is much less well-founded than that of the internal information. For instance, a reading from a sensor in a particular location is, by its very nature, centralised and the rest of the network cannot attest to or confirm such data.

It is worth highlighting the parallelism with the mathematical modelling of real world events and phenomena, where the mathematical conclusions arising from the model can be based on indisputable *deductive reasoning* (just as one can conclude things about internal blockchain transactions and computation), whilst the fidelity of the model with respect to the real world depends on *empirical, inductive reasoning* following the scientific, as opposed to the mathematical method (just like the interaction of the blockchain with the real world).

In the rest of the paper, when we refer to blockchain truth, we are limiting our discussion primarily to internal truth – that is, the consistency and soundness of the transactions and records of smart contract interaction and computation on the blockchain.

The Blockchain Truth versus the Blockchain Truths

Without going into the details of proof-of-work algorithms used in traditional blockchain systems, at an abstract level, the system ensures not only that any node (or computer) in the network will add the next block of new entries to the blockchain but also that the node that does add the next block has spent considerable resources to do so and that other nodes will only accept such a block if validated to be a sound one, i.e., it contains only valid transactions. This ensures that the particular node is disincentivised from maliciously adding invalid transactions, as not only would it have spent resources in vain, given how the decentralised system works – the other participating nodes would also detect the erroneous transactions and reject the malicious block proposed.

Blockchain proof of work, whilst providing such assurances, comes with a level of uncertainty. There is no guarantee that only one node will find a new block. This is further compounded by the communication lag between parts of the network, with the result that at any point in time there could be multiple versions of the blockchain – one with a new block that you can see and another with a block that I can see. Both blocks contain valid transactions and may contain transactions that are in both blocks; also some transactions appear in one block but not in the other. In the long run, only one of the blocks may prevail, meaning that the other will be discarded. When such a divergence occurs, a partition (sometimes called a temporary fork) will occur in the network, with some nodes seeing one version and others seeing another version. The strategy used by blockchain to address such situations is to accept the longer chain, the block in the version of the blockchain which happens to be extended first. If both are, once again, independently extended at the same time, neither is discarded until one of them is extended before the other. Although this can be indefinitely extended, it becomes increasingly improbable with each extra block, ensuring that eventually one version will win over the other. Proof of work thus guarantees that the version of the blockchain adopted is the one in which the majority of resources have been spent. In the long run, one is thus guaranteed a single consistent 'truth' written on the blockchain, but until then, different branches coexist, potentially leading to seeing recorded transactions which may not remain recorded in the long run. Consider what happens if you see a transaction written into a block confirming that I paid you for some goods, which you hand over to me, only to later realise that due to another concurrently created block that block never makes it into the blockchain in the long run.

Due to the potential of such temporarily erroneous records, a transaction is typically not considered to have been recorded immutably until it appears nested deep enough, with a number of newer blocks added after the block in which it appears. Many systems that interact with Bitcoin wait for 6 blocks to consider a transaction to be immutable.[3] Indeed, for different blockchains, the number of blocks one should wait until a transaction is considered to be immutable varies (based upon the statistical impossibility of there still being a partition in the network).

In some ways, this process of establishing the content written on a blockchain has some parallels in the way knowledge and truth are perceived or constructed offline. New knowledge may be reviewed by individuals who may verify it to be consistent with their world view. However, other independently developed new knowledge, possibly inconsistent with the other, may be developed and accepted by a different community. What is perceived to be true from one's perspective may not be so perceived by another. Logic dictates that as more new knowledge is developed building upon earlier knowledge, one of the alternatives will prove to be more useful in building a body of knowledge and thus be accepted over its alternatives: it would have been validated. This corresponds directly to the notion of proofs (even in the mathematical and scientific sense) to require a social act of acceptance:

> A proof becomes a proof only after the social act of 'accepting it as a proof.' This is as true for mathematics as it is for physics, linguistics, or biology. (Manin, 1977)

In the same way, as in the case of blockchain, the more new knowledge or proofs are built on the old ones, the more the old ones can be seen to be socially accepted and thus 'true'.

This correspondence between blockchain established transactions and knowledge can be extended to socially accepted 'facts' or beliefs. In an interesting parallel, this can be extended to geographically local established facts or beliefs. Peer-to-peer networks such as blockchain systems tend to aim for geographically close nodes to be connected to each other and to be less likely directly connected to those that are geographically more distant. This is due to nodes preferring connections that are faster, and the closer a node is to another, the higher the likelihood its connection is faster. This means that such partitions may result in geographical partitions of versions of the blockchain (for those moments of time when such a partition occurs), which mirrors the manner in which local views and beliefs may develop independently, requiring time to spread and further utility of a subset of such views for convergence to occur.

A blockchain is able to process transactions and reach consensus across the various participating nodes through a well-defined protocol – rules that specify how messages between nodes should be structured by the sender, communicated between nodes and interpreted by the receiver. A protocol is effectively a language, with its syntax and semantics. And similar to a language, nuances can often result in misinterpretation and miscommunication, whether in the spoken language or in the digitally communicated protocol. Unlike natural language, computer communication protocols include features meant to deal with communication channel failures, e.g., loss of messages, corrupted messages and out of order delivery of messages. In addition, the protocol on a blockchain system also ensures that transactions recorded should follow standard axioms of ownership, e.g., double spending of one's cryptocurrency is disallowed. However, changes to the code which follows such a protocol may feature unintentional bugs or possibly even intentional malicious behaviour. The difference in what is allowed by the protocol of those using the updated code and those who have not updated the code used on their node may result in misunderstandings, with different versions of the truth, from which a blockchain could branch into a partitioning of the network, called a hard fork, such that neither side of the partition would recognise or accept the other's updates due to the two sides speaking a different dialect of the protocol. One of the better known such protocol divergences on a popular blockchain was disclosed in 2018 with code fix CVE-2018-17144.[4] An update to Bitcoin Core (an open-source implementation of the Bitcoin node) resulted in a bug which removed checks to ensure that no double-spending occurs, with the possibility of miners being able to create fake Bitcoin, thus inflating the otherwise controlled amount of available Bitcoin. Were it not for the vulnerability having been identified early and fixed, incompatible extensions of the blockchain could have arisen.

Until now, we have discussed how forking of a blockchain can arise from technological features. However, a fork may not only be driven by protocol and implementation initiatives but also by social forces with choices made by node owners. If the community prefers to make certain changes to history as recorded on the blockchain, there can be a (social) choice of adopting technology to force such a change, and all nodes choosing to adopt such technology will start operating in a new blockchain world with its history rewritten.

The cryptographic mechanisms underlying blockchain still limit what changes can be made to the history. One method is to have the various participating nodes agree to drop a number of the most recent blocks and to restart tracking transactions from a particular point in the past. This could be seen as erasing the most recent pages of history so that the event is seen to never have taken place. Another way to achieve this and keep intact other events that took place in the same blocks (or pages) is to retain all of the previous history and then add new records which act as corrections to the previously recorded events. The infamous DAO hack (Mehar et al., 2019) is a commonly cited example of this, which resulted in part of the Ethereum community choosing to undo part of the past to compensate for a hack in a smart contract executing on the platform which resulted in substantial amounts of funds being lost.[5]

These scenarios illustrate how different versions of the 'truth' can be recorded on the blockchain. Some of the information will differ based on which part of the network one is communicating with. While the algorithms used in blockchain accept that temporary forks are inevitable and have built-in techniques to deal with them, permanent forks lie outside the scope of such algorithms and result in the underlying blockchain being duplicated, which raises further issues of where the truth actually resides.

The Blockchain versus the Blockchains

Let us return for a moment to the DAO hack fork. The fork arose after a discussion within the Ethereum community. One part of the community considered that the unfortunate event happened due to the logic written in the code, and since code is law, the network should continue to operate without implementing any changes to circumvent consequences of the hack. The other side deemed that the Ethereum platform could suffer reputational damage due to the hack, and although changing such data would go against the ethos of decentralised smart contract logic, it would be better to intervene just the one time. So, the participating nodes agreed to add hard-coded corrections to update the various accounts involved to retain their original balances before the event took place.

This led to a split of the community, with some continuing notwithstanding the hack, whilst others adopted a policy (and node implementation) supporting the obliteration of history, resulting in two distinct (and non-interoperable) Ethereum blockchain systems. The natural question is – which is the true Ethereum blockchain? Whilst the ethos behind such systems is meant to decentralise power, in practice we see that there are aspects of centralised power that can influence recorded truths. Whilst the system remains democratic in the sense that anyone can choose to run a mining node which can make choices in regards to what decision should be made in such instances, in reality many users are just passive users of such systems. Also, whilst any user could publicly lobby and push for a certain decision to be made, in reality it is a limited number of figure heads that tend to sway public opinion. What are the consequences of allowing for majority or popularity to control historical truths and events? When a network forks in two, as in this case, a user will now have access to two versions, with their digital assets replicated on both versions. This could result in the aggregated value of the two versions of digital assets to be more than the original true value of the digital assets; more so, the duplication and division of the networks could result in the true value of the original digital assets losing their value. Whilst (many) centralised systems do allow for the public to disagree in direction, the outcome is (more often than not) for a centralised controller to take the community forward. As can be seen in such decentralised systems, when differences of opinion occur, this can more easily result in divisions of communities. Would it be more suitable to have a single widely accepted version of the truth which was driven by a centralised controller or potentially many different versions of the truth which are driven by differing communities' opinions? If the aim were to be to strive towards the common good, which route would be in the right direction? Decentralisation does not always necessitate for the common good to emerge (Ellul & Pace, 2019); however, does it necessitate for the truth to emerge? If so, does the truth necessitate the common good?

In such scenarios where a fork leads to the creation of a new blockchain, it is indeed a debatable question as to which emergent blockchain is the true one. The most natural answer is that the version of the blockchain which continued extending on the original one, or with the original node software, should inherit the identity of the original. However, one has to consider that (1) in some circumstances, the branching may occur in such a manner that both branches of the fork leave the history unchanged and both adopting updated (but distinctly so) node software; and (2) the majority of the community may choose to adopt the version which changed the history. This latter was the case with the DAO hack, where only approximately 10% remained faithful to the original blockchain.

Indeed, this forking into alternative blockchain realities and hence alternative underlying truths can be reminiscent of Borges' *Garden of Forking Paths* (Borges, 1941), in which reality branches into different options, or the many-worlds interpretation of quantum physics. However, one distinction is the existence of the alternative paths in the same reality, allowing for access to either, or possibly even both branches, putting us more at the level of the author or reader in Borges' fiction. One may, in fact, perform asset transfers in any surviving branch of a blockchain, effectively doubling one's assets upon a fork, even if the branching typically would result in loss of value for such assets.

Trust in the Blockchain as a Decentralised Governance System? Not Now. Not yet

Attempts to identify 'systems of resistance' to mitigate the worst excesses of the post-truth society tend to gravitate around the regulation of large social media platforms. As an example, consider the proposed European Digital Services Act: at face value, the legislation will replace the current framework established by the e-Commerce Directive with an updated regulatory framework for digital services with revised rules for the Single Market for Digital Services. In practice, it is a thinly veiled instrument to restrict the dominance of gatekeeper Silicon Valley platforms in certain markets and tackle the spread of hate speech, fake news and associated harms for society, public discourse and democracy.[6] The effectiveness of central governance instruments such as the proposed legislation – or the General Data Protection Regulation (GDPR) – to eradicate illegal and damaging forms of online content, at this juncture, is questionable.

The corresponding hope in the affordances of the blockchain has much to do with the blockchain as a 'trust machine' which can reinforce the basic tenets of democracy and human decency. Such claims tend to be based on its potential as an *infrastructure for consensus* – at face value, for large groups and organisations to reach agreement on and permanently record information *without a central authority*. These claims have extended to the blockchain being associated with an ecosystem for a fair, inclusive, secure and democratic digital economy, with writers contemplating the sociopolitical implications of blockchain-driven decentralisation (Lyons, 2018, 2020). Such optimism is not restricted to academics or researchers. Small nation states have been actively exploring how to apply or change existing laws and regulations to blockchain's new realities. In 2018, Malta enacted a regulatory framework for blockchain, cryptocurrencies and distributed ledgers, signalling the island's intent to go against the grain in Europe and introduce technology-specific legislation.

And yet, decentralisation is not necessarily a comfortable bed fellow for governments and policy-makers, despite their declared enthusiasm for DLT and the blockchain. The trust machine is meant to facilitate trust in facts, information without powerful intermediaries, a *verifiable, immutable single point of truth* – while democracy and the politics of representation remain very much rooted in centralisation, as opposed to the automation of peer-to-peer transaction platforms. If we look at the blockchain's affordances for decentralised governance through a praxis lens, we may well be disappointed with the evidence collected from relatable use case studies. The more high-profile, efficient applications of the blockchain for public governance purposes – such as the much-lauded 'e-Estonia – the most advanced digital society in the world' – tend in practice to be centralised systems: in Estonia's case, the blockchain is a private, military-style, centralised system run by organisations with a direct relationship with the Estonian government. Even in the case of low-key initiatives, such as in the case of systems for the accreditation of education credentials using the public bitcoin blockchain (Grech & Camilleri, 2017), the 'garbage in/garbage out' analogy remains. If the initial certificate that is notarised on the blockchain by the issuer of the certificate has been tampered with, there is little that the blockchain may do to rectify the mistake.

The blockchain's inability to independently validate truth as an input variable appears to limit its applicability as a fix for vagrancies of the post-truth society. Yet, the organic crisis unleashed by COVID-19 has also left nation states scrambling for solutions in STEM as opposed to the rhetoric of populist leaders. The dystopian views of a future society governed by 'under-the-skin surveillance systems' (Harari, 2020) and AI or concerns about China social engineering surveillance systems that compute citizen social credits are being muffled by a renewed trust in the affordances of the machine – to keep us safe and to determine whom to trust and whom to 'socially distance'. When the machinery of democracy appears to be incapable of reporting the most basic facts – determining who is infected and who is not – putting our trust in automation and decentralised technologies may well appear to be a means to navigate to some semblance of 'a future'.[7] A society governed by smart contracts, no matter how seemingly rudimentary, mundane and flawed, may be a preferable vision of the future to the chaos of this moment. If we cannot trust democracy for the governance of the truth, let's delegate this to the machine – imperfect as it may be.

The democratisation project and the blockchain will simply not go away. The European Blockchain Services Infrastructure (EBSI) initiative is a utopian project in the making: European governments, along with the EC and the European Court of Auditors (having come together as part of the European Blockchain Partnership), are building their own Europe-wide blockchain for cross-border government services. By design, the initiative is starting with a limited number of use cases, with the intention to scale up over time into a comprehensive platform, from a test bed for a generic 'European self-sovereign identity' capability into a longer-term roadmap to make EBSI interoperable with other government and – crucially – commercial blockchain platforms. Interoperability, the holy grail facilitated by blockchain, is of course not dependent on the machine – but on the bona fide intentions of policy-makers to learn about technology and regulate it through the simple expedient of using it themselves on a cross-border basis. EBSI is a 'build it, and they will come' project.

The utopian dream may well accelerate, or flounder, in the post COVID-19 days.

Concluding Remarks

Claims that the blockchain will contribute to a better society because of an underlying taxonomy that facilitates the immutability of data are premature. The blockchain – public, private or hybrid – cannot deal with the simple garbage in/garbage out challenge, and absolute decentralisation remains infeasible and perhaps even undesirable. Yet the technology continues to be seen as a hammer looking for a nail. So while COVID-19 has ignited dystopian fears of surveillance societies, the intentions of researchers and policy-makers continue to position blockchain as a technology for the public good – or for the service of post-democracy societies. Time will tell where it will be successfully deployed for beneficial societal use. However, it is clear that in the immediate short term, it can provide sufficient means to ensure data have not been tampered with. Though it does not provide a direct solution to eliminating fake news and untruths, for any event, it is the perfect tool for recording the two sides to that story.

Notes

1. Blockchains are distributed digital ledgers of cryptographically signed transactions that are grouped into blocks. Each block is cryptographically linked to the previous one (making it tamper evident) after validation and undergoing a consensus decision. As new blocks are added, older blocks become more difficult to modify (creating tamper resistance). New blocks are replicated across copies of the ledger within the network, and any conflicts are resolved automatically using established rules (Yaga, Mell, Roby, & Scarfone, 2018, p. 49).
2. Smart contracts are automated or self-enforcing contracts that can be used to exchange assets without having to place trust in third parties. Many commercial transactions use smart contracts due to their potential benefits in terms of secure peer-to-peer transactions independent of external parties. Many commonly used smart contracts are vulnerable to serious malicious attacks which may enable attackers to steal valuable assets of involving parties (Yu, Al-Bataineh, Lo, & Roychoudhury, 2020).
3. See https://en.bitcoin.it/wiki/Confirmation – Accessed on August 2020.
4. See https://bitcoincore.org/en/2018/09/20/notice/.
5. Decentralised Autonomous Organisation.
6. See https://www.digitalsme.eu/the-digital-services-act-and-the-role-of-social-media-platforms/.
7. In April 2020, the EU organised a European-wide hackathon with the aim of identifying tech startup solutions to the COVID-19 pandemic. See https://www.euvsvirus.org/.

References

Borges, J. L. (1941). *The garden of forking paths*. London: Penguin Modern. Reprint, 2018.
Ellul, J., & Pace, G. (2019). Blockchain and the common good reimagined. The Common Good in the Digital Age conference. The Vatican City State.

Grech, A., & Camilleri, A. F. (2017). *Blockchain in education. Joint research Centre science for policy report.* European Commission. Retrieved from https://publications.jrc.ec.europa.eu/repository/bitstream/JRC108255/jrc108255_blockchain_in_education%281%29.pdf

Harari, Y. N. (2020). The world after coronavirus. *Financial Times.* Retrieved from https://www.ft.com/content/19d90308-6858-11ea-a3c9-1fe6fedcca75. Accessed on March 20, 2020.

Lyons, T. (2018). Blockchain innovation in Europe. Consensys AG on behalf of the European blockahin observatory and forum. Retrieved from https://www.eublockchainforum.eu/sites/default/files/reports/20180727_report_innovation_in_europe_light.pdf

Lyons, T. (2020). How the EU is using the blockchain. Retrieved from https://www.ledgerinsights.com/how-the-eu-is-using-blockchain-to-build-a-citizen-centric-european-internet/

Manin, Y. I. (1977). *A course in mathematical knowledge for mathematicians.* New York, NY: Springer-Verlag. ISBN 978-1-4419-0614-4.

Mehar, M. I., Shier, C. L., Giambattista, A., Gong, E., Fletcher, G., Sanayhie, R., . . . Laskowski, M. (2019). Understanding a revolutionary and flawed grand experiment in blockchain: The DAO attack. *Journal of Cases on Information Technology, 21*(1), 19–32.

Nakamoto, S. (2009). Bitcoin: A peer-to-peer electronic cash system.

Yaga, D., Mell, P., Roby, N., & Scarfone, K. (2018). *Blockchain technology overview.* Gaithersburg, MD: National Institute of Standards and Technology. Retrieved from https://nvlpubs.nist.gov/nistpubs/ir/2018/NIST.IR.8202.pdf

Yu, X. L., Al-Bataineh, O., Lo, D., & Roychoudhury, A. (2020, May). Smart contract repair. *ACM Transactions on Software Engineering and Methodology, 1*(1), 32. Retrieved from https://arxiv.org/pdf/1912.05823.pdf

Chapter 18

Decentralised Verification Technologies and the Web

Allan Third and John Domingue

Abstract

The Internet, the Web and social media have radically transformed a number of core pillars of our social fabric. The way billions of citizens work, interact and socialise is underpinned by our global network infrastructure. Unfortunately, we have also seen a number of negative effects from this transformation. As has been widely publicised, undesirable impacts include the spread of disinformation and fake news; attacks on democratic elections and the 'weaponisation' of personal data. This article describes some of the technological approaches that are being taken to address some of the above issues. At the core of these technologies are notions around decentralisation. With blockchains it is possible that citizens can create their own 'self-sovereign' identity – the digital equivalent of writing one's name onto a piece of paper – and acquiring verification through blockchain-based techniques. An approach to alleviating the 'weaponisation' of personal and sensitive data is to give citizens their own data store. Initiatives such as Sir Tim Berners-Lee's Solid allow users to store, manage and control their own data according to any personal preferences or constraints. We believe that a combination of personal data stores and blockchains will lead to a new type of resilient communication and collaboration mechanism, whereby personal rights and empowerment are enhanced and transparency at the community level is integral.

Keywords: Blockchain; self-sovereign identity; Linked Data; decentralisation; personal data; trust

The Internet, the Web and social media have radically transformed a number of core pillars of our social fabric. The way billions of citizens work, interact and socialise is underpinned by our global network infrastructure. Unfortunately, we have also seen a number of negative effects from this transformation: the spread

Media, Technology and Education in a Post-Truth Society, 255–269
doi:10.1108/978-1-80043-906-120211018

of disinformation and fake news; attacks on democratic elections and the 'weaponisation' of personal data. We argue that among the factors behind these phenomena, a key role is played by the *centralisation* of data and of digital identity and the consequent *alienation* of data and digital identity from its subjects. The decentralisation of data and identity has the potential to increase transparency and to empower individuals with regard to their digital lives, mitigating against the problematic phenomena just described. Rather than control and management residing under a central, usually large, company or authority, the locus is instead with the individual user or community. This paper describes some of the technical approaches that are being taken to address some of these issues. A combination of blockchain technology, self-sovereign identity (SSI) and personal data stores has the potential to form a new type of resilient communication and collaboration network, whereby personal rights and agency are enhanced, and transparency at the community level is essential.

What's Wrong on the Web?

Misinformation, the abuse of personal data and, consequent to both of those, the manipulation of democracy are by no means the only social issues to be found on the modern Web, but they are significant and, we believe, can be addressed or mitigated by the use of decentralised verification technologies. All three have received extensive discussion elsewhere (Del Viacrio, Zollo, Cadarelli, Scala & Quattrociocchi, 2017; Farrell, Piccolo, Perfumi, Alani, & Mensio, 2019; Fernandez & Alani, 2018; Koulolias, Jonathan, Fernandez & Sothirchos, 2018; Reveley, 2013). We provide some illustrative examples and draw a few conclusions about some of the factors underlying them.

In the current, centralised, model, Web services are provided by a small number of typically very large corporations. For an individual to access a service, they generally need to sign up for an account with the central provider, which serves as their digital identity for interactions with the service. Personal data needed for account and service provisioning and data generated using the service, alone or in conjunction with other services and other users, are stored on servers maintained and controlled by the provider. Multiple services from the same provider may reuse the same digital identity, but with different service-specific sets of personal data about the individual, leading to an accumulation of significant datasets on the provider's servers. The Guardian journalist Dylan Curran, in exploring Google's storage of personal data, downloaded 5.5Gb of data relating to him.[1] Accessing services from a different provider requires a different account and involves sharing personal data with that provider, which may independently accumulate over time and across its different services.

This is a simplistic picture. Technologies such as federated authentication and various forms of cookies allow providers to track activities and collect data across different providers. Federated authentication (e.g., using a Facebook account to log in to a third-party site) reduces the multiplicity of digital identities, but does so at a cost of centralising digital identity further in the hands of the account provider.

What does this mean in practice? Individuals gain relatively convenient access to Web applications, often for free, although the distinction between free and paid does not affect the data and identity concerns under discussion. Providers are able to aggregate large volumes of data about individuals and, over many users, large populations. Analytics over these large datasets of personal and behavioural data can provide significant financial value in terms of targeted advertising and personalisation of services (such as allowing the personalisation of, say, which social media posts and news stories a user is exposed to). There are two well-attested phenomena. The first is the 'social bubble' effect. When the content users see is affected by content they and people with similar patterns of activity have interacted positively with in the past, this can lead to increasing homogenisation of perspectives to which they are exposed; when it comes to, say, political views, this may lead to a polarisation of positions as alternative opinions come to seem artificially strange or outlandish due to lack of exposure. The social bubble effect has been cited as a factor in widespread surprise at the result of the UK Brexit referendum (Del Vicario, Zollo, Caldarelli, Scala, & Quattrociocchi, 2017). Social bubbles can also lead to the amplification of misinformation, including so-called 'fake news' and conspiracy theories. Examples of fake news which has been circulated on Facebook include that the US Democratic politician Nancy Pelosi used social security funds to pay for an impeachment enquiry into President Trump, that her son was involved with the Ukrainian gas industry and that Trump's father was a member of the Ku Klux Klan.[2] Several conspiracy theories are also held to have gained, or regained, global prominence due to social bubbles from the (originally spoof) theory that Finland is a hoax, the flat Earth theory, to the dangerous autism-phobic 'antivax' theory and the various conspiracy theories about the COVID-19 infection (MacDonald, 2015; Mohammed, 2019).[3] None of this is to say that biased exposure to different perspectives or to misinformation is a new phenomenon, simply that they can be, and have been, significantly amplified by a Web in which predictions based on huge volumes of personal and behavioural data are used to determine what content people are shown.

The second phenomenon to follow from the centralised aggregation of these data is its deliberate manipulation for economic or political gain. Perhaps the most well-known example of this is the Cambridge Analytica scandal, in which data about the online behaviour of voters in the United Kingdom and United States were bought by a data analytics company and used to develop highly targeted political advertising and social media campaigns to sway voters in a particular direction.[4] It is widely believed that these campaigns, particularly in the presence of strong social bubble effects, influenced the results of the 2016 Brexit referendum and the 2016 US presidential election.

There is an extra dimension to the manipulation or weaponisation of personal data in this way, in that it involved data being used by a third party (Cambridge Analytica), purchased from Web providers such as Facebook, without *transparency* with the data subjects about the uses to which their data were being put, by an entity with whom they had no direct relationship. Add to the mix the lack of transparency about Facebook's own internal processes and individuals are likely to have had little awareness of how their data were ultimately being processed.

Mass aggregation of data and lack of transparency of processing represent problems with centralised data at Web scales. Having digital personal data held and controlled by providers whose interests do not necessarily align with the data subjects removes individual control and opportunity to understand how it is used. In many ways, the individual is *alienated* from their own data in a Marxist sense (Reveley, 2013): it stems from their own activities but they cannot control how it is used or who profits from it. The same can be said for digital identity. If identifying oneself online relies on a digital proof from a third party, as with data, then control is lost over how one's identity is used online – as with data. In face-to-face interactions, we segment our identities depending on the context – professional personas and social ones are demarcated from each other (to give a very coarse-grained example; of course, the distinctions and expressions of identity vary considerably more subtly than this). If, however, an application requires sign in with, e.g., a Facebook account, then one is potentially exposing one's entire Facebook identity. While it is possible to limit what is revealed by choosing certain *types* of information to hide in, say contact lists or posts, such filters are not *content*-based: one cannot choose to reveal only professional contacts, for example. In a sense, this is a different form of centralisation: the identity presented by each digital account contains the total of all data on that account. Segmenting digital identities by having multiple accounts, or dividing one's activity in different spheres of life between different online services, is possible but impractical, imposing a memory and management burden on the user.

The result is that it is very difficult to know who is making use of data about which aspect of any digital identity, in terms of tracking data and activities, or correlating multiple identities for the same person. The same themes of aggregation, lack of transparency and consequent lack of control and alienation apply to identity as well as data. Strictly in technical terms, of course, digital identity is simply a special case of personal data, but the activities and meanings around identifying oneself are particularly important to people, and many tasks are reliant on identity (e.g., many financial activities). Most significantly, to be able to talk about controlling who can access personal information at all presumes a notion of 'who' and an ability to distinguish one actor from another.

Decentralised Technologies

There are three families of technology which we argue can provide an alternative infrastructure for the Web to mitigate or avoid some of these problems. We introduce them briefly here. A number of references are made to *Linked Data* and to *Valuable Personal Data* (*VPD*). In brief, the concept of Linked Data is to make data integration practical at Web scales. By its structure, Linked Data in the form of RDF is self-describing, in the sense that each piece of data is represented in a way that also includes its schema and ways to determine its semantic relationships with other pieces of data.[5] In particular, RDF terms are URIs and can typically be dereferenced to retrieve a machine-readable description of their semantics, which may be further specified in shared machine-readable documents known as *ontologies*. This allows software which operates on RDF data to parse its intended meaning. When multiple data sources use common vocabularies to talk about the same types of entity and relation, data integration and interpretation across multiple sources become relatively straightforward. There already exist vocabularies for a very wide range of topics – from describing people and their relationships (FOAF) to time and location (W3C) to events, educational achievements and many more. This form of Linked Data is flexible, open and expandable. At the time of writing, there are an estimated 1,260 of datasets containing 16,187 links in the Linked Data cloud, and standards and libraries such as JSON-LD and LDflex make RDF available in developer-friendly formats.[6,7,8] We use the term VPD to refer to a specific subset of personal data where the data subject can derive significant value from sharing it with selected third parties, provided the third party trusts its content. The prototypical example would be an educational qualification – it is personal data regarding the subject, and the subject can share it with others in order to gain value from a better job or access to further educational pathways. This type of data can pose a problem when it comes to control of personal data: we would typically like to say that all personal data should be under the control of its subject, but with VPD, subjects can have an incentive to modify its contents falsely, so there is a legitimate interest of third parties in the ability to trust its contents and provenance. This concern might then suggest that it cannot be under its subject's control. One of our goals here is to demonstrate the potential to satisfy both requirements.

Distributed Ledger Technologies

The key concept of a distributed ledger technology (DLT) is that of a shared append-only timestamped list of records, with no single entity in control. By 'append-only', we mean that once a record has been added to the ledger, it remains there as it is, immutable and undeletable. Perhaps the most well-known example of a distributed ledger is the cryptocurrency network, Bitcoin, and its underlying blockchain data structure is perhaps the most well-known DLT.

A blockchain network is made up of a set of nodes. In the fully decentralised case, such as Bitcoin or Ethereum (Nakamoto, 2008; Wood, 2014), anyone can create a node and join the network. The ledger (the blockchain data structure itself) is duplicated, potentially in full, across every node. When any participant wants to submit a new record, it is added to the pool of records. The network then follows a pre-agreed *consensus mechanism* to select a particular node to be responsible for updating the ledger. Various consensus mechanisms are used, from the high-energy consumption *proof of work* used in Bitcoin, in which nodes race to solve a hard computational problem, to *proof of stake* (Saleh, 2020), which is somewhat similar to nodes placing a bet on which node is to be selected next. However it is chosen, the selected node picks a set of records from the pool to form a *block*, which is added to the chain of blocks forming the ledger. Crucially, each block contains a cryptographic signature (a *hash*) of its predecessor.[9] In combination with the open duplicability of the ledger, this means that any attempt to edit the contents of earlier blocks will be detectable by any node. It can be shown that as long as no one entity or cartel controls more than 50% of the nodes in a blockchain network, this mechanism is fair, and ledger contents are immutable in all practical senses, with no need for any central 'control node' to ensure this. This is in contrast with traditional ledgers held by banks, in which the sources of trust for historical records are the bank, its reputation and relevant financial laws.

Blockchain networks such as Ethereum have included processing as well as data in their architecture. A piece of executable code can be added as data to a blockchain, at which point it, like any other data, can be treated as immutable. If a user or community is satisfied that the code correctly and safely performs a certain task, then anyone can call the code on the blockchain to perform that task and trust that it will do so as expected.[10] In Ethereum, such 'smart contracts' are executed by every node on the network so that outputs and execution traces can be cross-checked, but work is ongoing into ways to achieve the same trust with a smaller number of executing nodes (Kocovski et al., 2019). This opens the possibility for trust-critical data processing to be carried out using DLTs. Community-verified libraries of smart contracts could promote the reuse of known safe functionalities. Such approaches, coupled with techniques such as tamperproof execution logs certifying that a service has not broken any data usage conditions in processing, could provide many options for more trustworthy computing.

It might be assumed that the open and shared nature of blockchain data would make this technology incompatible with several data protection principles – in particular, it might seem as if data cannot be private and that subjects would be unable to exercise a 'right to be forgotten' with immutable data. If data themselves are directly added to the blockchain, then this indeed would be the case. There are, however, ways to gain the advantages of being able to demonstrate that data have not been modified without having these problems. One approach is to put data only on a private blockchain network, which is not open to the public, in which case both privacy and deletion/alteration can be possible, but data can still be verified/alterations detected if the private blockchain regularly puts the hash of its most recent block as a record on an immutable public blockchain. A simpler approach would be simply to store data wherever is private and convenient and to put a hash of its contents, at whatever granularity is needed, on an immutable public blockchain. Anyone with whom the data are shared can verify its contents, but the data themselves are not public and can be deleted at will. We refer to this approach as *anchoring* of data in a DLT, with the hash as the *anchor*.

Self-Sovereign Identity

The idea for SSI arose in opposition to the model described earlier (Tobin & Reed, 2016). Rather than registering for a digital identity in the form of an account provided and controlled by someone else, SSI approaches enable individuals to create and control their own digital identities directly, in the form of some kind of cryptographic token which can be self-generated and which, with the appropriate infrastructure, can be used to prove relationships or claims pertaining to the holder of the token. These might include a relationship to an organisation (such as 'employer-employee'), a country ('citizen') or a service (e.g., 'user'). This corresponds more closely to the ways in which various forms of identity are shared non-digitally.

At its core, identifying yourself digitally frequently corresponds to proving that you possess a secret that no one else should, such as a password or access to a specific email address. In case the secret is a password, it is necessary for at least one other party to know the password, or at least its hash, in order to be able to vouch to others that the pre-agreed secret is known. An asymmetric public-private keypair has many of the properties required, with no need for secret sharing or prior agreement. If someone can access your public key, then they can verify that a message was signed using your private key without ever needing to know what your private key is. Public-private keypairs can be uniquely generated by anyone. A document containing a public key and machine-readable descriptions of how to interact with the holder of the corresponding private key is able to serve as a form of *decentralised identifier* (DID).[11] Services which support it can challenge a user (or potential user) to prove control of such an identity, verify the response and choose to grant or deny access to the service on that basis.

The DID draft specification defines how to handle identity in this general way. A DID is a URL (e.g., did:eth:a97cbd3254c) which can be resolved by a specific protocol (in the example, 'eth' names a DID resolver based on the Ethereum blockchain) to retrieve a document containing cryptographic details and interaction endpoints for an identity. The DLT plays the role of providing a verifiable source of (public) cryptographic details. Compliant software can resolve DIDs and use them to support secure communication between DID-bearing parties.

A key part of the value of DIDs comes from their relationship to Verifiable Credentials (VCs) – another W3C standard, which defines a model for sharing claims about a subject, in the form of Linked Data, alongside metadata for verifying their authenticity, such as a cryptographic signature, or the address of a blockchain record containing their hash or some more advanced cryptographic data such as a Merkle proof or a Zero-Knowledge Proof (ZKP) (Goldreich & Oren, 1994).[12,13] A ZKP is a way of sharing a specifically chosen piece of information in such a way that the recipient can verify it cryptographically without learning more than necessary about a data subject. The stereotypical example is that of proving one's age to, say, buy alcohol. This could be achieved by sharing the date of birth, but that contains more information than needed to verify the actual relevant question 'is this person above the required legal minimum age for this transaction?'. A ZKP would in this case allow the construction of a proof of age which did not reveal the subject's date of birth to the verifier to minimise exposure of personal data.

To implement privacy-preserving SSI with DIDs and VCs, individuals can create a new DID for each different party they interact with (or even more fine-grained, if desired) and share, via VCs, the minimum identifying information needed or desired for that interaction – presenting the relevant public persona much as with face-to-face interactions.

The obvious objection from service providers might be that it is possible for people to lie more easily the smaller set of personal data they share - and there are occasions where this matters, for example, if a site needs to know if someone has certain legal rights or if it has legal obligations of its own. Leaving aside, of course, that the current model provides no particular guarantee that users are telling the truth, there are very flexible ways to deal with this. Suppose that Alice wants to use the Bobble service, and Bobble needs to know that Alice is in fact her real name.[14] Alice can use a DID and her real-world ID (e.g., driving licence) to communicate with an official government body where she lives, represented by Charlie. Charlie agrees that Alice is who she says she is and issues a VC confirming it. Alice can then issue a second VC from the DID she uses to interact with Bobble, containing the claim that Charlie represents her government and that it endorses Alice's claim to her name. Bobble can verify this VC without needing to know the DID she used with Charlie or needing to see her physical identity.

Self-Sovereign Data

The third technology we will discuss is that of personal data pods, specifically, their implementation in the Linked Data Platform standard, such as the Solid project led by Sir Tim Berners-Lee (Sambra et al., 2016). The key idea is that data should be stored with its owner, with Web applications being granted fine-grained permission to access parts of it as desired by the owner, with permission revocable at any time. Individuals would have a 'pod' (or more than one) which they can organise as they wish containing resources that can be public, private or shared with specific access controls. Data stored in a pod can be shared or made accessible according to standard protocols and data models so that different users, service providers and pod implementations can interoperate smoothly. Fig. 18.1 below shows the intended shift in paradigm, with applications becoming *views* over data held by each user.[15]

In addition to putting data control into the hands of individuals, this approach also allows the reduction of duplication across similar or related services – with a single set of, e.g., calendars stored in the pod and external scheduling applications with appropriate, and variable, visibility over them, or a wishlist, from which different online shops could provide a personalised list of only the items they stock. For these scenarios to work most effectively, each application must understand the way that the data it interacts with are represented and, most importantly, how it is to be understood. Solid and Linked Data Platforms generally originate, as the name suggests, in the Linked Data community and are based around the RDF data model. There is, therefore, a practical ecosystem for developing applications able to interact with Linked Data Platform based pods.

An important aspect of the data pod concept is that the pods are *portable*; no one is tied to a particular implementation or host, and data and pod URIs should be able to move and rehost as the user desires.

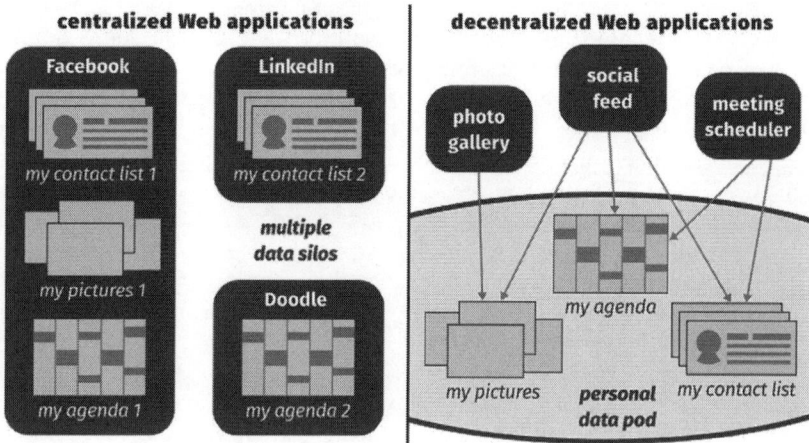

Fig. 18.1.   Decentralised Web Applications as Views Over a Personal Data Pod. *Source:* Verborgh (2017).[21]

A Decentralised Web

The fundamental architecture of the Web as it stands is decentralised. The communication protocols, such as DNS and HTTP, are standard and open. Anyone with the resources can create a Web server and publish pages, data and applications without needing centralised permission or support to do so. The centralisation that we see nowadays is not inherent to the Web itself, but has developed on top of it, as a result of social and economic factors, as well as certain technological ones. Computing began with monolithic machines in small numbers and with no or limited connectivity between them. Single-user applications running on a single machine with data locally were the norm. As the cost of computing and storage fell and more powerful and networked hardware became available, the extension to multi-user and distributed computing came by adaptation of the single-user applications and services. The model we have now is a successor to this. In developer terms, it was an obvious step that to use Google's services, one would need to register with Google so that they could manage your digital identity for accessing their servers, which would be running applications which could only access your data if it was in some sense local to them – either local to server storage or local to a database controlled and structured by the service provider. Alongside this, where VPD is concerned, the lack of trust on the part of service providers for user-hosted data is also a factor. This technical history, combined with the clear economic advantage such companies are able to derive from aggregating users' personal data, is part of why the current situation is as it is.

A further factor, we believe, is the lack of a technical trust layer for the Web. Encryption secures communication channels and their endpoints but does not guarantee anything about the content of communications. And the standard approaches to digital identity are not built with privacy and autonomy in mind.

Let us consider instead the possibility of a more decentralised Web, built on the existing infrastructures but taking advantage of the technologies we have described here and developed according to a model that is decentralised from the beginning rather than extending a single-user model. In particular, imagine the following within the context of system that resists the affordances of the so-called post-truth society:

(1) **SSI is the default**. There are widely adopted standards for SSI and most Web-based interactions involving identity are conducted using DIDs and VCs, backed, where relevant, by DLTs.

(2) **Self-sovereign data is the default**. Web application providers no longer host large data centres in which they hold personal data about users of their applications. Instead, following mutual identification with SSI, an application is granted appropriate permissions to the relevant user's personal data pod (and only to the relevant contents inside). Applications are views over the data.

(3) **Data and processing are transparent and verifiable**. DLTs are used to provide a trust layer for data and processing. VPD are anchored to a DLT: its subject controls who can see and use their data, and for what, but can demonstrate using the DLT anchor that they have not edited or manipulated it inappropriately. Similar guarantees can be made by data processors – users can trace how their data have been handled and where it has gone in a manner which can be verified using DLTs. Note that in both cases, data and processing, this does not necessarily mean making everything public; data can be anchored anonymously using hashes, and processing can be traceable with, e.g., anchoring execution logs and the use of smart contracts for key operations (e.g., data deletion) where trust is important.

There are other, dependent, requirements. We may imagine, for example, a marketplace of providers of personal data pod hosting.

What do we gain from this? Through the widespread adoption of self-sovereign approaches, individuals' alienation from their own digital identities and data (and what happens with these) is mitigated. They are able to manage how they present themselves online in a manner more similar to face to face. We would conjecture that the increased similarity to physical social presentation might therefore lead to a digital society which better fits human cultures and customs, which, after all, developed through physical socialisation in the first place. The ability to trace the processing of data verifiably affords more scrutiny, and therefore control, over how personal data are used and how it can be aggregated and could allow open and community verification of behaviours of actors such as service providers. And the category of VPD, currently underserved online, can, with the availability of verification technology, open up new possibilities for applications serving individual needs. Collectively, these technologies support privacy and data minimisation by design and by default.

How would such a decentralised Web be more decent? The presumption of minimisation of data sharing, verifiability of processing and the ability to have separate and difficult-to-correlate identities with multiple services together make it possible to reduce, significantly, the ability of others to amass large volumes of data about an individual and to correlate behaviours across different services. These in turn reduce the risks of personal data being weaponised and used to manipulate individuals, groups or democratic processes. This includes at least the algorithmic component of the social bubble effect on misinformation, with unknown processes filtering what people see in terms of news and social media posts. It also opens opportunities for novel applications to combat misinformation, which users could apply to their own data – applications which would currently be hampered by the inaccessibility of user data under the centralised model. Identity is autonomous and less alienated, and VPD can be handled in a more granular and context-sensitive manner – allowing service providers to trust data which they need to (for, e.g., legal reasons) while still preserving individual sovereignty over it. Each of these affordances comes from a combination of the technologies we have described and cannot easily be done without them.

The gains are not solely for individuals. There are advantages for service providers too. Given the reliance many applications nowadays – particularly those based on machine learning – have on data for development and performance, there is a clear cost to innovation and to new entrants to the market of having user data concentrated in a small number of very large providers. In the decentralised model we advocate here, the barrier from existing commercial interests controlling the data disappears, making it easier for new entrants to access data and demonstrate innovative ideas. There is also a likely effect on competition, with more scope for providers to compete on greater differentiation: for example, it becomes easier to use, e.g., data privacy and trustworthiness as selling points when users can have choice and control without sacrificing functionality or connection to networks. Innovation is also encouraged by easier separation of concerns: where a centralised service may need to offer the entire user experience, functionality and infrastructure – frontend, authentication and authorisation, data hosting and management, among others – the decentralised model presented here allows providers to focus on their strengths and core offerings. Think of a high-quality user experience for, say, photographic filters, while facilities such as data management (e.g., Solid pod hosting) can be handled by someone else.

For all users, possibly the most important advantage gained is *resilience*. The lack of reliance on large and monolithic providers offers a greater ability to adapt behaviours, tools and infrastructure to changing needs and circumstances and to be flexible in how problems are approached and solved. It might seem that the idea of a personal data pod could go against this – that a user would still have all their eggs in one basket, but with the basket relocated from a tech giant to a space they control. In fact, however, while possible, this is not necessary: one can have multiple pods, perhaps segmented by different spheres of activity (work and home, for example), and have them connected, or not, to each other as desired. Controlling your own data also means you can back it up or transform, extend or adapt it also as circumstances demand, without losing control or the ability to prove its contents or provenance where needed. Providers can compete in this space too, with services to support managing how an individual expresses their digital identity online and manages the data underneath that. Improving resilience while maintaining trust is an important goal for the global communications infrastructures, as has been driven home forcefully by the significant changes to working, education and social practices required to handle the COVID-19 pandemic.

Barriers and Challenges

There are of course technical and social challenges with any new technology and its 'way of doing things': every technology has its scope of application. Some of the envisaged benefits of this type of approach are most clear when they are used on a large scale and network effects are realised. There is therefore a potential chicken-and-egg situation with regard to adoption – users may be reluctant to use a new technology if they experience only a burden of changing from an existing solution without an immediate benefit. As a general-purpose architecture, how-ever, there are many benefits which can be derived without mass adoption or which are already seeing some adoption – for instance, educational certificate verification, decentralised authoring, personal information management and so on. It is easier to adopt a new use of a piece of technology that one already uses than to adopt an entirely new one.

More critical for adoption is the support for an easy and familiar developer experience to spur the creation of new use cases and innovative applications. DLT development is in its infancy, although rapidly developing. Standards such as JSON-LD are specifically designed to fit into widespread JSON-based develop-ment practices, and emerging query tools such as LDflex turn querying remote Linked Data into something very similar to referencing a local in-memory data object. Barriers can also be anticipated from the different conceptual models of decentralised development, where the necessary application architectures can be quite different. The conceptual shift can be supported by technical standards such as those just mentioned, which put the developer experience first – other examples include a decentralised Solid application generator and the very recently announced (at the time of writing) ShapeRepo, which allows data 'shapes' to be drawn from a repository, to provide developers with existing used and tested data models for common applications or parts of applications, thereby both reducing development effort and promoting interoperability through shared Linked Data shapes.[16,17]

A more significant barrier to adoption is presented by the form of existing economic interests in centralised models. Technology giants derive massive value from serving as aggregation points for large volumes of personal data, and a large-scale migration away could affect their current business models and would no doubt be resisted or discouraged. It bears noting that discussions of the problems of data centralisation are a part of mainstream conversations beyond the technical sphere, and there have been calls for alternative models – including from com-panies such as Twitter.[18] It has been speculated that moves such as this follow from the realisation that corporations may be held accountable for, e.g., failure to deal with abuse properly, making decentralised governance seem more attractive.[19,20]

Beyond barriers to adoption, what problems might be anticipated as a result of this model? We foresee three high-level issues which may arise, all, in one sense or another, social. The first is that the personal data pod itself becomes a potential target – a privacy or security breach could be very dangerous if all of an individual's data are kept there (although this is perhaps not too different from the risks of a breach in a centralised account containing a similar volume of data). Architecturally, the use of SSI mitigates the risk of someone being *specifically* targeted due to the use of one-time DIDs and data minimisation approaches, although non-targeted attacks are unaffected. One could also conceive of a technically supported separation of data within a pod, via, e.g., a 'subpod' or separately encrypted areas. As noted previously, data portability and interoperability and separation of applications from data storage and management open up pod hosting as a potential competitive market in its own right, with scope for privacy and security to be more of a point of differentiation than it necessarily is in a model with storage tied more closely to services, where service functionalities could come to dominate in terms of distinguishing features.

On the user side, there is of course the difficulty that comes along with self-sovereignty, which is that managing one's own data may be a burden and, particularly given the complexity of digital privacy, quite confusing to manage. The user experience is key and requires active research to determine best practices, models and the necessary technological education, as well as technical means of supporting it and reducing the risks of users unintentionally exposing the wrong personal data due to the complexities of the task.

Finally, and particularly with regard to verifiable data, there are a range of issues which can arise if a system is trusted but it contains incorrect, out-of-date or insufficient data (particularly where such data originate from or need to be endorsed by a third party) or if the data are subject to misinterpretation. A verifier relying too much on software interpretations of data can be disempowering for individuals. These types of issue are not new factors coming with decentralisation, but they may take on a new aspect in the presence of, e.g., a blockchain integrity guarantee, which may be misunderstood as guaranteeing the truth of data rather than simply its tamperproof status. Because it is a known existing problem, there are already technical and legal frameworks for dealing with it which could be adapted. We would anyway argue that this risk remains greater in the situation where an individual does not control their own data, but that does not mean that it can be disregarded.

Conclusion

We have described some of the major issues with centralisation on the global Internet. After detailing DLTs and self-sovereign data and identities, we have described ways in which these technologies together have the potential to enable a fairer, more private and more innovative digital world, in which people are in control of their own digital lives. We have discussed the advantages of this approach, barriers to its adoption and some potential issues which it may bring with it.

There can be a tendency towards utopianism in visions of decentralisation. It is, of course, not a panacea. Social issues require, by and large, social solutions. But many of the issues attributed to today's Web seem to have arisen, at least in part, from the technical infrastructure of modern global communications; it is not beyond the realm of possibility that improvements to this infrastructure may alleviate some of them. We submit that a person-centred decent(ralised) Web, with self-sovereignty and trust, might be a step in that direction.

Notes

1. See https://www.theguardian.com/commentisfree/2018/mar/28/all-the-data-face book-google-has-on-you-privacy
2. See https://www.businessinsider.com/most-viewed-fake-news-stories-shared-on -facebook-2019-2019-11
3. See https://www.vice.com/en_us/article/xyd48w/this-dude-accidentally-convinced -the-internet-that-finland-doesnt-exist
4. See https://www.theguardian.com/news/series/cambridge-analytica-files
5. See https://www.w3.org/RDF/
6. See https://lod-cloud.net
7. See https://www.w3.org/TR/json-ld11/
8. See https://github.com/LDflex/LDflex
9. A cryptographic hash is a fixed length number produced by applying a specific function to a piece of data, with the properties that the same input data will always lead to the same hash – even a single bit of difference in the input data will produce a completely different hash – and the odds of two different data items having the same hash is astronomically small or zero. Because every hash is the same length, regardless of the input data, information is necessarily lost by the hashing function; this means it is not, in general, possible to recover the input data from a hash alone.
10. For example, by expert/automated analysis of the corresponding source code and verification that the deployed code has indeed been generated solely from the analysed code.
11. See https://w3c-ccg.github.io/did-primer/
12. See https://w3c.github.io/vc-data-model/
13. See https://chainpoint.org
14. Suppose that Bobble deletes accounts of anyone using a pseudonym, and its automated systems do not recognise her rare surname as a name, but as a dictionary word. One of the authors has encountered this precise issue 'in the wild'.
15. See https://ruben.verborgh.org/blog/2017/12/20/paradigm-shifts-for-the-decentralized -web/
16. See https://generator.inrupt.com
17. See https://shaperepo.com
18. See https://twitter.com/jack/status/1204766078468911106
19. See http://scripting.com/2019/12/12.html#a134957

20. See https://twitter.com/RubenVerborgh/status/1205513858389094401
21. See https://ruben.verborgh.org/blog/2017/12/20/paradigm-shifts-for-the-decentralized-web/, CC-BY 4.0, Ruben Verborgh.

References

Del Vicario, M., Zollo, F., Caldarelli, G., Scala, A., & Quattrociocchi, W. (2017). Mapping social dynamics on Facebook: The Brexit debate. *Social Networks, 50,* 6–16.

Farrell, T., Piccolo, L., Perfumi, S. C., Alani, H., & Mensio, M. (2019). Understanding the role of human values in the spread of misinformation. Conference for Truth and Trust Online.

Fernandez, M., & Alani, H. (2018, April). Online misinformation: Challenges and future directions. In P.-A. Champin, F. Gandon, & L. Médini (Eds.), *Companion proceedings of the Web Conference 2018* (pp. 595–602). New York, NY: ACM.

Goldreich, O., & Oren, Y. (1994). Definitions and properties of zero-knowledge proof systems. *Journal of Cryptology, 7*(1), 1–32.

Kochovski, P., Gec, S., Stankovski, V., Bajec, M., & Drobintsev, P. D. (2019). Trust management in a blockchain based fog computing platform with trustless smart oracles. *Future Generation Computer Systems, 101,* 747–759.

Koulolias, V., Jonathan, G. M., Fernandez, M., & Sotirchos, D. (2018). *Combating misinformation: An ecosystem in co-creation.* Paris: OECD Publishing.

MacDonald, N. E. (2015). Vaccine hesitancy: Definition, scope and determinants. *Vaccine, 33*(34), 4161–4164.

Mohammed, S. N. (2019). Conspiracy theories and flat-earth videos on YouTube. *The Journal of Social Media in Society, 8*(2), 84–102.

Nakamoto, S. (2008). *Bitcoin: A peer-to-peer electronic cash system.* Manubot. Retrieved from http://www.bitcoin.org/bitcoin.pdf

Reveley, J. (2013). Understanding social media use as alienation: A review and critique. *E-Learning and Digital Media, 10*(1), 83–94.

Saleh, F. (2020). Blockchain without waste: Proof-of-stake. Available at SSRN 3183935.

Sambra, A. V., Mansour, E., Hawke, S., Zereba, M., Greco, N., Ghanem, A., ... Berners-Lee, T. (2016). Solid: A platform for decentralized social applications based on Linked Data. Technical Report, MIT CSAIL & Qatar Computing Research Institute.

Tobin, A., & Reed, D. (2016). The inevitable rise of self-sovereign identity. *The Sovrin Foundation.* Retrieved from https://sovrin.org/wp-content/uploads/2018/03/The-Inevitable-Rise-of-Self-Sovereign-Identity.pdf

Wood, G. (2014). Ethereum: A secure decentralised generalised transaction ledger. *Ethereum project yellow paper, 151*(2014), 1–32.

Chapter 19

How Do We Know What Is True?

Natalie Smolenski

Abstract

What is truth and *what are the conditions* for its manifestation? We can induce from the evidence of the experience of all human subjects capable of communication and intersubjective behavior that we exist in a world that (1) we share and (2) is accessible to all of us. From this, we can infer that the experience of truth is not merely subjective, but depends upon objective referents to be meaningful. The interplay of subjectivity and objectivity in the meaning-making processes of human subjects is the condition of possibility for truth.

This essay proposes two ways of pursuing truth. One is a scientific project that requires generations of rigorous study and collective building. The other is a simple set of guidelines that can be used day to day by anyone. Both are important. Not everyone will be a professional scientist, but everyone can use simple scientific tools to bring their thinking and actions more in line with truth.

Keywords: Epistemology; science; subjectivity; objectivity; phenomenology; experience

Valletta, Malta, is the site of one of the world's most renowned pieces of Baroque art, Michelangelo Merisi da Caravaggio's "The Beheading of St. John." The piece is evocative not only on its own terms but also because it takes us back to a time when the production of art was an integral component of human ritual life. Worship and encounters with the sacred were central to the production and conception of what art meant.

Today, our approach to images is predicated upon a flat metaphysics, where religious understandings of the world have been superseded by a kind of secular collapsing of multiple orders of reality into one. Prior to this modern understanding of metaphysics, however, reality was seen as ontologically layered: each layer of reality corresponded to a different layer of truth. For example, medieval Christian

Media, Technology and Education in a Post-Truth Society, 271–276
doi:10.1108/978-1-80043-906-120211019

traditions, Eastern and Western, had the concept of a "true image," often called an *icon*: a representation that accesses an order of reality that is somehow *more true* than the ordinary, mundane reality in which we exist day to day. This is not because icons represent their subjects more accurately; they are highly caricatured and aestheticized depictions of a saint or holy person. Rather, they serve a ritual function as a kind of "bridge" between one order of reality and another.

These varied ways of understanding the worlds which give rise to true phenomena draw our attention to the ontological status of truth. In other words, *what* is truth and *what are the conditions* for its manifestation? I propose that we take an inductive approach to begin answering these questions: we can induce from the evidence of the experience of all human subjects capable of communication and intersubjective behavior that we exist in a world that (1) we share and (2) is accessible to all of us. From this, we can infer that the experience of truth is not merely subjective, but depends upon objective referents to be meaningful.

For example, the historical question of "what happened" is not simply a question about my own perception or the perception of others – it invokes the objectivity of an order of reality that is inhabited and accessible by many different subjects. No pursuit of justice, morality, ethics, or law is comprehensible or even possible without some understanding of such an objective world. Likewise, we cannot hope to have any purchase on the world around us – the ability to build things that hold over time through the pursuits of science, engineering, and all manner of cultural and economic production – without a shared, objective world which we can each interpret and shape in line with our individual and collective capacities.

But if we do share an objective reality, if that is indeed the very condition for the possibility of truth, a logical next question becomes, "How do we know this reality? How do we know what is true?" That is the question of epistemology. And due to the unique history of the human species, most of how we learn about what is real and true is social – it relies on other people.

Authority and Personal Experience

The marvelous human development of culture – knowledge that is communicated, accrued, and revised between humans and human generations as a supplement to the genetic inheritance of DNA – has enabled us to build civilizations and consume resources at a level unmatched by any other species. This is not because every human is taught everything every other human knows or experiences everything every other human has experienced. Rather, we evolved social technologies to divide the labor of knowing things between ourselves so that we could all collectively benefit from everyone's knowledge without everyone having to know it. This means that there may be a limited area of knowledge where I am the expert – where I am learning things through direct experience and then reasoning about them to a buildable and verifiable conclusion – but most things I learn socially. Traditionally, this has meant relying upon authorities – whether those authorities are individual people or "the culture" at large – to teach me about things I don't directly know or help me understand things I don't know how to interpret.

But the reliance on authority also has significant limitations. When authorities are exposed as ignorant, self-interested, morally compromised, and even fraudulent, people lose trust in their knowledge and judgment. Today, as a result of the rapid acceleration of information technologies, it is easy to expose virtually any authority as compromised in some areas of their lives. And because we are more educated and interconnected than ever before, it's easy to instantly find exceptions and alternatives to whatever claims local authorities are making.

When people lose trust in authorities, they may retreat into their own personal experience of the world as a kind of antidote. Personal experience may seem "more true," in many ways, than what an authority says. But ultimately, it does not provide much additional clarity on what exactly is true, because the very same person – not to mention two or more different people – can create different interpretations from the same "experience." In other words, "experience" is not *direct* evidence of anything; it is simply data from which people still have to make meaning. And they do so very differently, using different interpretive frameworks.

Historian Joan Scott wrote about this limitation of using personal experience as a direct lens on truth in a well-known essay, "The Evidence of Experience." Scott writes, "When experience is taken as the origin of knowledge, the vision of the individual subject (the person who had the experience or the historian who recounts it) becomes the bedrock of evidence on which explanation is built. Questions about the constructed nature of experience, about how subjects are constituted as different in the first place, about how one's vision is structured – about language (or discourse) and history – are left aside. The evidence of experience then becomes evidence for the fact of difference, rather than a way of exploring how difference is established, how it operates, how and in what ways it constitutes subjects who see and act in the world."[1]

In other words, people may *experience* other people as "different" from them and then use that (limited) experience as the justification for thinking less of them or treating them poorly. But as Scott points out, this "experience" is so limited that it does not leave room to ask questions like, "How has this difference come about? What does this difference actually mean? To what extent does this difference actually matter?" In other words, if I don't have an historical account of how differences came to be and what they mean or don't mean, personal experience can be used as a tool for violence and oppression.

Personal experience is morally neutral; it can be used to justify kind, charitable actions toward others as well as violent, cruel actions. It can even turn into authoritarianism when people insist on imposing it on others. Think of how many charismatic religious leaders and dictators have justified their power by elevating their own "personal experience" with some kind of revelation (i.e., from a deity, ancestor, or transcendental intelligence) as absolute truth. If we are to actually find truth, we need a better way than relying on either authority discourses or personal experiences.

This essay proposes two ways of pursuing truth. One is a scientific project that requires generations of rigorous study and collective building. The other is a simple set of guidelines that can be used day to day by anyone. Both are important. Not everyone will be a professional scientist, but everyone can use simple scientific tools to bring their thinking and actions more in line with truth.

The Science of the Subject

The first path toward truth is, unsurprisingly, a scientific one: the science of the subject. This means the science of the being for whom truth is a meaningful reality. In other words, in order to answer the question, "What is truth?" we have to know who is asking the question and why. Truth is not something that objects pursue or find meaningful; it is rather something that subjects – thinking, feeling beings – find meaningful. These beings could be human or nonhuman; there are many different kinds of subjects. The important thing is that they seek truth because they are always in the process of building out models of the world around them based on limited data. The primary way they do this is by negotiating what is and is not real with other subjects, with whom they inhabit a world that is both shared and accessible. This is what the term "intersubjective" means: a shared reality that is constituted in a social field composed of multiple subjects.

Truth, then, is a kind of provisional agreement or a set of working assumptions that exist between subjects so they can effectively coordinate action and build knowledge and projects that hold over time. But this agreement can only exist if people really believe that their provisional understanding of truth is "the way things are" – that it expresses real knowledge about the nature of the world and reality. This is why some philosophers use the term "truth in motion" instead of "truth": because it is always evolving; it is a living thing.

The science of the subject has been percolating in Western philosophy since at least the Renaissance period, when the discovery of perspective in art could have been said to usher in a new ability to take a perspective on human subjectivity itself. We see this breakthrough paralleled in the work of Descartes, with his insight that thoughts are reflections on a reality that is separate from those thoughts themselves. Descartes is often misinterpreted as saying that mind and matter are completely separate phenomena. What he was in fact doing was making an analytical distinction that allowed humans to take a perspective on our own thoughts. The literary theorist Mikhail Bakhtin has traced this capacity to interrogate subjectivity in the evolution of Western literary genres, from ancient heroic stories until the modern novel.[2] Ancient storytellers did not reliably differentiate between narrative and truth and rarely described the interiority of characters. Bakhtin attributes the growing importance of interiority and psychological character development in the Western literary tradition to the influence of contemplative traditions, including forms of Eastern mysticism.

During the nineteenth century, the nascent science of subjectivity became a science of hermeneutics. Many thinkers contributed to its development, but here I will invoke Wilhelm Dilthey, perhaps the most well-known proponent of this school of thought. He posited that "the scientific explanation of nature (*erklären*) must be completed with a theory of how the world is given to human beings through symbolically-mediated practices. To provide such a theory is the aim of the philosophy of the humanities."[3] Following Dilthey, if the humanities are aiming for a science of understanding, then we cannot take any particular evidence – an image, text, artifact – without also understanding the world in which that evidence was produced and made meaningful. By whom? For whom? For what purpose? The answers to those questions form a "hermeneutic circle" that we can then use to get at what Hans-Georg Gadamer called "the ontological event of truth."[4]

A science of the subject enables us to use subjective phenomena to answer objective questions. These include not only "What happened?" but also "What happens?" which is the question asked by social sciences to better understand the regularities and patterns in human behavior. Answering these questions gives us the insight that allows us to modify human behavior over time and potentially achieve progress – a better world with better possibilities for all. For this reason, a science of the subject is socially and politically a critical discipline.

Everyday Science

Truth is based on trust, which is a social phenomenon. It is only the possibility of shared truth that makes human cooperation possible. Without shared truth, humans fritter away energy and resources on conflicts that could have been avoided or quickly resolved. This results in the destruction of life and things that have already been built while precluding the building of new things and the improvement of human life. The lack of shared truths also makes everyday life more difficult and stressful.

But how do we arrive at shared truths? – By having a shared method for drawing conclusions from evidence. In other words, we can bring the same methods used by scientists to understand the world into our own everyday lives. This enables us to both agree and disagree with each other more skillfully and less violently.

Using scientific methods means collecting, describing, and evaluating evidence and then reasoning from that evidence in a way that other people can access, critique, and improve over time. Scientists, after all, do not claim to have "the absolute truth" – they have greater or lower confidence in whether something is true based on evidence and the quality of their reasoning from it.

What does this mean in practice? To take a topical example, let us say you want to determine whether the claims in a media article are true. That means you would go through several steps, which map nicely onto the methodology used by historians to evaluate historical texts:

- *Source criticism*: What is the source of the claim? The author and the publication both have histories of past claims. How often have they made erroneous claims in the past? What can you trust them to reliably do well?
- *Context of publication*: What larger debate or conversation is the article responding to? Is there an implicit or explicit social objective the author is trying to achieve?
- *Thesis*: What is the point the author is trying to make?
- *Supporting evidence*: What evidence does the author use to back up their point? What is the quality of this evidence?
- *Reasoning*: How does the author get from evidence to argument? Is her reasoning sound, or are there problems with it?

Using the above method will give you a pretty good general sense of the degree to which the claims being made in the article are true. You will have greater or lesser confidence in your analysis based on your methodological reasoning. Others may disagree with you, and as long as they are using the method above, you have a basis for engaging them productively in conversation.

People are socialized to want to have all the answers now. This is certainly how authority discourses operate. But if we want to progress as a species, we will need to become comfortable with not having final answers or absolute knowledge, all the while having the courage to act in light of knowledge we *are* confident in today. Scientific methods are not a way of hedging and hiding from responsibility or the need to take action. They are forms of honesty about what we know and what we do not, and they enable us to make informed decisions in light of that.

In other words, to prevent human life from becoming a social and political catastrophe – a war of powerful factions trying to pass off their own authority structures and interpretive frameworks as absolute truth through violence – we need to all begin thinking like scientists in our everyday lives. This does not mean getting rid of authorities or personal experience; these are part of how evolution has conditioned us to navigate the world, and we cannot simply change our programming. Nor do we even need to.

We can innovate using the tools we have. We can channel our inherited tendencies into something better: for example, placing trust in the authority of method rather than the authority of particular people or their social position. We can teach people from the youngest age that authority and experience are important and very old technologies, but they are not the sources of absolute truth. Instead, we can move toward truth much more effectively using a much newer technology – the scientific method – which anyone can use either professionally or as part of their everyday lives. This pedagogy, and this method, is how we arrive at truth and change the world for the better.

Note

1. Scott (1991).
2. Bakhtin (1981).
3. https://en.wikipedia.org/wiki/Wilhelm_Dilthey.
4. Gadamer (1989).

References

Bakhtin, M. M. (1981). *The Dialogic Imagination: Four Essays by M. M. Bakhtin*. (Ed. M. Holquist, Trans. C. Emerson & M. Holquist). Austin, TX: University of Texas Press.

Gadamer, H. G. (1989). *Truth and method*, 2nd rev. edn. (1st English edn, 1975, trans. by W, Glen-Doepel, Ed. J. Cumming & G. Barden), revised translation by J. Weinsheimer and D. G. Marshall, New York, NY: Crossroad.

Scott, J. (1991). The evidence of experience. *Critical Inquiry*, *17*(4), 773–797. (Summer).

Chapter 20

Social Technologies and Their Unplanned Obsolescence

Daniel Hughes

Abstract

Social Technologies and their Unplanned Obsolescence seeks to sidestep the various contents of the post-truth debate to consider the manner in which any body of knowledge and practice gets taken up and extended at all. This bottom-up consideration of the material conditions of bodies of knowledge and practice is presented polemically, as a critical homily of sorts, and is concluded with a forward-looking call to action.

Keywords: Society; knowledge; logic; computation; civilization

This is a moment of authorities in crisis. The institutions underpinning our era are fraying. From the family and neighborhood to governance and money, from systems of education to market construction – our social technologies are being found wanting. Most of us do not regularly think about our kin networks, democracies, universities, or capital markets as technologies. It is only under the pressure of an ineffective or collapsing organizing norm that these things that we have mistaken for stable reality are made, through their unplanned obsolescence, to display the contingency at their core (that is, the particularity of their *having been built*) and, in this, indirectly signaling something of the invariant scaffolding that affords the operation of their set of actual and possible variants in the first place.[1] This last part is the interesting part from the vantage point of truth.[2]

During the proceedings of the 3CL's "Understanding the Post-Truth Society," Mike Casey proposed from the stage that "all truth is consensus."[3] I agreed with him at the time and still do in the broadest possible sense, but it is also accurate and important to point out the obvious corollary: not all consensus is true. In taking these phrases together, one begins to take up the question of truth as such. There is something important about the difference between the working assumptions of a group consensus, on the one hand, and the establishment of

Media, Technology and Education in a Post-Truth Society, 277–284
doi:10.1108/978-1-80043-906-120211020

something that holds, on the other.[4] We use working consensus in the ongoing task of trending toward an absolute elaboration – something philosophers call an ideal pole, and this directly relates to the possibility of an ongoing, provisional realization of cross-world objectivity with regard to anything whatsoever.[5] Along this vector of elaboration, we encounter varieties of consensus as an unfolding series of inputs and outputs that become leading prompts toward next arrangements of knowledges and practices up to the high bar of refactoring our form of life (the ways of comportment that habituate and characterize belonging) and their social technologies (specific knowledges that are used through prostheses).

The most powerful form that group consensus of this sort takes is social technology. A social technology is the embedding of a knowledge that holds, in whatever sense we might mean from useful to lawful, into the fabric of the world in a manner that allows populations without direct knowledge of the genesis of the consensus to use it as a knowledge prosthesis. This is what we have done as a species with our dietary norms, etiquettes of hospitality, market systems, advanced locomotion, real-time presence projection, and the like. Knowledge is built into a technology so that it can outlive the expert communities that came to the various consensuses that layer into the complexity enabling the social technology.

The base unit of group consensus is the pack. The pack, a primal but largely undertheorized mode of being together, is at root a purpose-driven social unit that sets for itself a concrete objective: the hunt. The hunt is an umbrella term for a certain solving-for, which tends to involve the search for and utilization of resources. These may be anything from skills to nutrition to property to ideas. A hunt is only possible if the pack is closely aligned in their outlook and actions.[6] The ongoing recalibration of packs to one another and the surrounding world, in light of what they are solving for, is the foundation of their adaptive success. A pack is often the first nonfamilial social configuration that an individual aligns with (a hunting party, sports team, neighborhood gang, vocational apprenticeship, religious mission, scientific lab, or other such purposeful group arrangement).[7] When the thinking and doing of a pack coalesces around a social technology that is generalizable – that "holds" – we can speak of "breakthrough": a truth-prosthesis that opens up the ability of wider populations to exercise the leverage afforded by general theories at scale.[8]

One example of this process that we are accustomed to talking about in the University setting is tech transfer or commercialization, which moves something valuable from lab to market. This work of translation is undertaken when results are well-formed, repeatable, and valuable enough to justify the refining focus that enables a wider population to begin to utilize a breakthrough at the bench. Pure and experimental research (a hunt for insight, causal explanation, repeatable results) becomes a viable offering taken up by a general public because what holds during R&D (the truth of something: the accurate characterization of its core properties and patterns of interaction with other somethings) is usefully embodied as an idea in a controlled arrangement (a prosthesis of any sort – habitual, pneumonic, analog, digital, biochemical, etc.) that focuses action and intent when used in a way that brings about ampliated outcomes for a non-specialist user without an expert's direct capacity.

In this sense, a truth-prosthesis is a special case of a knowledge-prosthesis in that it consistently channels an indirect capacity that could, in principle, enable any population capable of utilizing its affordances – its user interface – to wield capacities that harness general theories (the speed of light, barometric pressure at sea level, the tensile strength of a solid, etc.) as opposed to practices that primarily carry forward the particular adaptations of historic people groups (not boiling a young goat in its mother's milk, eating food with a specific hand or fingers, hospitality obligations under various circumstances, etc.). Both represent deeply layered knowledge and practice that can be taken up by non-specialists at scale, but only the truth-prosthesis deals directly in world-spanning, generalizable knowledge and, as such, has replaced an identity prerequisite for a user interface prerequisite.

In practice, worlds are filled with an admixture of both identity-driven and interface-driven prostheses and the various expertise of their populations. This ensemble of prostheses enables novel automations that illustrate the old Clarke adage that "any sufficiently advanced technology is indistinguishable from magic."[9] This technomagic is made possible by the sedimentation of the complexity of the precise knowledges that together enable a simple set of common uses (combustion engines, petroleum engineering, city planning, and actuarial science layering together into a civilization of mass itinerancy, for example). As these truth automations layer one on top of the other they compound and open up the possibilities of the newly ampliated world resting in the fixed forms of memory and action that represent the storage and compute capabilities of a vector of social achievements that moved from a breakthrough "at the bench" (wherever said innovations occurred) to an enabling platform presumption in a society (however widely it is taken up). The material familiarity of the modern world is the direct result, not simply of a homogenization of culture but of sedimented social technologies that generally platform otherwise extremely heterogenous people groups because the ratio of knowledge-prostheses to truth-prostheses begins to rise exponentially in favor of the latter due to its animating universality.

What distinguishes the complexity of an ensemble of truth-prostheses from a complicated bureaucracy, cargo cult, or another social arrangement that may in part function like or resemble the complexity of a society on a universal vector is exactly this strange inoperativity of the unplanned obsolesce at the heart of the knowledge-prostheses that never make the generalizable jump to truth-prostheses. Over time, the accelerating centripetal force of what holds gets baked into a society to such a degree that the identity-driven social technologies begin to be reimplemented on the new platform. This relativizes the old ways as such and creates an inevitable impasse that must be managed until an alternative can be gestated.[10] Our modern fundamentalisms, nostalgias, and exotic imports of other people's traditions are all means that we employ to address this impasse. It is a way to manage a gap where the materials at hand make it difficult to move the identitarian knowledge-prostheses through to the development of more general theories and then the various packs using them to make breakthroughs to things beginning to approximate a novel series of truth-prostheses and from these social technologies the future politics, communal identities, and spiritual purposes that are no longer simply the uprooted authority discourses of a prior time.

The catalyst of truth as such is thinking. One can only imagine the knotty tendrils of inherited achievements that must afford any given next step in any genuinely complex arrangement, and it is only as one surveys this imagined genetic history through the discipline of coming into a field's knowledge and practice that one can begin to realize in themselves the possibilities inherent in the continuation and extension of the field through one's own work. What this looks like concretely is idiosyncratic to the person, domain, and period. Nevertheless, it is only through the disciplined entrance into the real and imagined communities of the *something* being elaborated that one becomes the thinker thinking the thought that affords the next possibility. This is the necessary and sufficient base condition for any truth: the living discipline of its thinkers, or as I prefer to call it, the pack who can fully utilize and extend its priors.

The pack is the site of truth's possibility. At its zenith, a pack becomes one of the expert communities that carry forward the traditions of knowledge and practice that are the annals of buildable knowledge for a given domain: what we call the arts and sciences. The various undertakings that make up these broad categories are not simply fields. They are practiced disciplines. It is required of one that they come into the skills and knowledge of these communities of builders at work within their fields. Because they are active sites of research and practice with genetic timelines and deep, narrow bodies of knowledge, one must build up the intuition for the problems and the tools. Even should the knowledge of the discipline be published widely, it is only by directly inhabiting these living traditions that one accesses facts whose origin and properties can be genetically accounted for. It is in and from these communities of research and practice that we inherit a useful, durable consensus that is the material through which we fashion our next instruments and hypotheses that propel us into the new worlds still in seed within the old. This is the case in whatever disciplinary context you are able to join, whether that is midwifing a generation, hunting bison, compounding medicine, or constructing a Dyson sphere. The only qualitative difference among them will be the manner in which the outputs hold as social technologies.

The question then, before any generation, is really just that of intent. To what will we train our attention with enough focus and duration as to generate new buildable knowledge and practice? What goals will we track? This is a fundamental question for every era of humanity on this side of our species' capacity to utilize collectivity as a knowledge practice. It takes on added urgency for those of us after both the natural philosophy and industrial revolutions, as we have levered the stakes through the scope and scale of our institutional and ecological interventions (collapse and transformation being too close in kind to distinguish at times).[11] Add to this the practical proliferation of the possible areas of focus after the informational turn spurred on by our social technologies that utilize the theory of general computation, and one sees the ways in which even the sciences can fall into a static morass through losing the productive wedge of inquiry's focus. The solutions to these problems are not trivial, but they are addressable. In my view, these solutions can be summarized as the advance of a critical awareness of purpose (goal tracking over long time durations) as the organizing principle of one's vocation and avocations, the rebirth of education as problem-organized lifelong learning, and the development of computational intelligences up to the high bar of co-investigators. We have only covered the first in this introduction to a theory of the pack.

So, at the risk of being condemned both for solutioning and for being philo-sophical (and not doing nearly well enough at either), I must say clearly that the path through this time of authorities in crisis is dwelling with our grandest uni-versal aspirations in the narrowest ways possible. This is how we achieve things: purposefully thinking and doing together. We must find our people, and we must do the things with them that push forward our practices and knowledges such that we are ready to not merely terraform Mars, but to seed noetic purpose with eidetic insight across the peoples of Earth – to not simply object to the surveillance of state capitalism, but to architecturally preclude it in advance; to not content ourselves with the narrow benefits of privately owned, automated intelligences, but to build machines that help all of us do hard things over the long haul. The list is long, and our time is short.

The advancement of purpose under the conditions of scarce time requires a fight a violence that carves out the protected spaces that can incubate thinking-doing in community. Not only have we left the allocation of human focus to happenstance; but we have created Rube Goldberg machines to capture lifetimes of attention as an alternative to purpose. This is why we need each other. We need to be able to put our shields up with our pack to form the protective perimeter that affords the form of life necessary for our work to be achieved – whatever that is. This is not utopian. This is the most concrete, practical, fundamental precondition to not leaving the use of our most scarce resource (purposeful focus) to chance. This is the solution to both societal collapse and personal malaise, as it addresses the energy needed to construct and maintain valuable complexity at both personal and societal scales. We must find our purposes worth pursuing with wholeheartedness that are nevertheless the civilizational projects for the worlds we would inhabit. This is the only path through which our better futures come.

This is how we achieve truth. We find or found our packs and, through the skills and practices of our forms of life, we do the things with them that push forward our knowledges such that the institutional forms that carry our working assumptions and universal projects out beyond our lifetimes become the tech-nological preconditions for the next societal upgrade cycle. Concerns about a collapse into positivism or fictions of progress are real but are largely dealt with by a fundamental acceptance of loss as such and the self-correcting nature of societies filled with competing, wholehearted packs. The theory of the pack is itself something that many of us must inquire after and become experts in if we are to assemble the truth-prostheses that platform the *bildung* that our collective futures inherit as political economy and collective purpose. How our forms of life accelerate and hamper the sorts of worlds that we must achieve to live out our highest aims of universal emancipation, liberty, justice, fraternity, knowledge, and exploration are open questions requiring more than surface engagement.

There are trade-off decisions to be made, and I believe that they need to be made in light of the *raison d'être* of our societies, communities, labs, and mon-asteries. This is a roll-up-our-sleeves moment. We cannot have everything. We must contend for the truth of our lives, and in so doing become the guarantors of the worlds to come.

Notes

1. There is a long history of debate as to the extent to which one should ascribe dependence or independence to structures and objects (Benacerraf, 1964; Husserl, 1906–1907, 1929). It is difficult to take up the topic of truth without discussing ontology. I will, nevertheless, do my best.
2. "Interesting" as it invokes all of the knotty challenges inherent in the problem of relativism and the possible "attitudes" and type systems that form a path through it (Husserl 1936a, 1936b).
3. Held in Malta on October 10–11, 2019. See https://connectedlearning.edu.mt/videos-post-truth-conference
4. Let us presume that we can use this notion of what holds as a placeholder for the definitions and debate surrounding the collection of interlaced, precise, and distinct concepts invoked when we say such things as valid, sound, consistent, distinct, clear, or complete.
5. An ideal limit pole is the abstraction that motivates the movement from the casual worldview language to the idea of causal determinism that is, in Husserlian analogy, a "cloak of ideas" that guides precision in the investigation of regularities summed up as "Nature" or "Culture" (Husserl, 1936a, pp. 48–53, 301–314; Husserl, 1936b).
6. That is, the members of the pack must have the baseline empathy and language that condition belonging to some form of containing community as such. This "community of empathy" (Husserl, 1929, p. 9; Husserl, 1936b, p. 360) and "linguistic understanding" (Husserl, 1936b, p. 360) with whatever heritable "grammatically established" meaning forms (Husserl, 1900–1901, Ch. 1; Husserl, 1913, pp. 49–50) they take part in and, ideally, can directly trace as established priors (Husserl, 1936b, p. 362) is a necessary social form for specific solving-for pack arrangements. It is the membrane of belonging, this form of life, that enables pack formation as a solving-for not only because of the direct capacities carried forward by the general language and intuition of the life world and the specific skills and specialist intuitions of the guild of the solving-for but also, in the midst of this necessary naiveté and desired specializations, the possibility of it affording the opportunity for a critical reflection (*Besinnung*) that provides the interface between the formal (validity in virtue of form) and the true (those "ultimate substrate objects [that] are *individuals... back to which all truth ultimately* relates" (italics in the original)) by virtue of one making "ultimate cores intuited" (Husserl, 1929, p. 203f) through *Besinnung* as a bridging logic differentiating kinds of intention in the concrete activities of a pack (ibid 140f). Interestingly, *Besinnung*, as a mode of judgment that interfaces the logic of noncontradiction and the logic of truth, is, on Husserl's account, that which ultimately enables formal ontology (Husserl, 1929, pp. 78, 120, 168f) and, provocatively, is a logical practice that can be mechanically carried out through a novel type checking, as judgments carry with them a syntax and are reducible to judgment forms which Husserl calls "ultimate cores" (Husserl, 1929, p. 202f). It

should be emphasized that this linkage is between all possible proof and theory forms (what Husserl called "supramathematics" – see Hill, 2018, p. 57 and Haddock, 2006, pp. 155–181) and any possibly existing substrate object. This sets up an interesting conversation about the computational theory of mind – first discovered by Husserl in the 1890s in "On the Logic of Signs (Semiotic)" (1994, pp. 20–46). For more on radical *Besinnung*, see Hartimo, 2018. For more on Husserl's logical grammar, see Klev, 2017. For more on the computational theory of mind see Husserl, 1891; 1900–1901; 1913; 1929.

7. Note that, on this account, form of life (the ways of comportment that characterize) and pack (the alignment toward a solving-for) are not simply synonyms for more colloquial notions such as political identity, communities of practice, communities of purpose, and the like which get carved in various relative ways – despite any overlap that exists.

8. This is why there is the universal experience of *adoption* across all societies when a people encounter an innovation that is adjacent to their form of life such that its benefits are evident vis-à-vis whatever is placeholding or lacking in their current arrangement of knowledges and practices. It is this, above all else, that deprecates traditional knowledges as the people who once inhabited them encounter a social technology that has become an adoptable truth-prosthetic.

9. In his 1962 book *"Profiles of the Future: An Inquiry into the Limits of the Possible,"* science fiction writer Arthur C. Clarke formulated his famous Three Laws, of which the third law is the best-known and most widely cited: "Any sufficiently advanced technology is indistinguishable from magic."

10. During the past several centuries, this impasse has sometimes been examined by cultural historians under the rubric of "secularization"; however, this account is insufficiently precise and, more often than not, neither leaves room for the many expressions of identity-driven social technologies that continue to flourish on a new platform or for the scientific possibilities inherent in the gaps themselves.

11. The potential catastrophic effects of any social technology are orders of magnitudes greater for layered truth-prostheses versus local and lossy knowledge-prostheses. It is, perhaps, even more problematic than this simplistic comparison would suggest, for every modern society is beset by a composite of truth- and knowledge-prostheses. This creates, at times, an inner tension between the clumsiness of remedial priors and the effectiveness of a forgotten truth.

12. Some of these inheritable traits (in performances, phrases, grammars, protocols, etc.) that are taken up in a social fabric as technology or sedimented priors and decay become so pivotal as to be taken for nature itself. Phenomenologically, these are the substructive attachments that function at a near invisible level of effectiveness and that require the most effort to trace.

References

Benacerraf, P. (1964). What numbers could not be. In B. Paul & H. Putnum (Eds.), *Philosophy of mathematics: Selected readings* (pp. 272–294). Englewood Cliffs: NJ: Prentice-Hall.

Clarke, A. C. (1962). *Profiles of the future: An inquiry into the limits of the possible.* New York, NY: Harper & Row.

Hartimo, M. (2018). Radical *Besinnung* in *Formale und transzendentale Logik* (1929). *Husserl Stud, 34*, 247–266. doi:10.1007/s10743-018-9228-5

Hill, C. O. (2018). On limning the true and ultimate structure of reality. In P. M. W. Hackett (Ed.), *Mereologies, ontologies, and facets: The categorial structure of reality*. Lanham, MD: Lexington Books.

Husserl, E. (1891[1994]). On the logic of signs (Semiotic). In *Early writings in the philosophy of logic and mathematics*, Translated by Dallas Willard. Boston: Kluwer.

Husserl, E. (1900–1901). *Logical investigations Volumes 1–2*, Translated by J. N. Findlay, London: Routledge. 1970.

Husserl, E. (1906–1907). *Introduction to logic and theory of knowledge*, Translated by Claire Ortiz Hill, Dordrecht: Springer. 2008.

Husserl, E. (1913). A draft of a *preface* to the *logic investigations*, 1913. Translated by Philip J. Bossert and Curtis H. Peters, *Introduction to the logical investigations* (pp. 11–52). The Hague: Martinus Nijhoff. 1975.

Husserl, E. (1929). *Formal and transcendental logic*, Translated by Dorion Cairns, The Haag: Martinus Nijhoff. 1969.

Husserl, E. (1936a). *Crisis of the European sciences and transcendental phenomenology: An introduction*, Translated by David Carr, Evanston: Northwestern University Press. 1970.

Husserl, E. (1936b). On the origin of geometry. In P. McCormick & F. A. Elliston (Eds.), *Husserl: Shorter works* (pp. 255–270). Notre Dame: University of Notre Dame Press. 1981.

Klev, A. (2017). Husserl's logical grammar. *In History and Philosophy of Logic, 39*(3), 232–269. doi:10.1080/01445340.2017.1399782

Rosado Haddock, G. E. (2006[2012]). Husserl's philosophy of mathematics: Its origin and relevance. In Roberto Poli (Ed.), *Against the current: Selected philosophical papers. Vol. 4: Categories* (pp. 145–181). Berlin: De Gruyter.

Tainter, J. A. (1988). *The collapse of complex societies*. Cambridge: Cambridge University Press.

Index